The Problematics of
Moral and Legal Theory

THE PROBLEMATICS
OF MORAL AND
LEGAL THEORY

Richard A. Posner

The Belknap Press of
Harvard University Press
Cambridge, Massachusetts
London, England
1999

Library of Congress Cataloging-in-Publication Data

Posner, Richard A.
The problematics of moral and legal theory / Richard A. Posner.
p. cm.
Includes bibliographical references and index.
ISBN 0-674-70771-0 (alk. paper)
1. Law and ethics. 2. Sociological jurisprudence. I. Title.
BJ55.P67   1997
170—DC21
98-29596

CONTENTS

PREFACE

This book grew out of a series of lectures given in 1997—two Holmes Lectures at Harvard, the James Madison Lecture at New York University, and the J. Byron McCormick Lecture at the University of Arizona. That year, as it happens, was the one hundredth anniversary of the publication of Holmes's greatest essay, "The Path of the Law,"[1] and one way to understand the present book is as an extended homage to Holmes's ideas about morality and law. I am far from agreeing with everything that Holmes wrote, and shall point out in Chapter 3 serious oversights in his essay. But he was on the right track, and one aim of my lectures was to push the engine a bit farther along.

I have rewritten, reorganized, and reresearched the lectures for this book, and have rounded out the reworked lectures with material from other pertinent recent writings of mine, including a reply to five distinguished critics of my Holmes Lectures. The result is a whole that I immodestly dare to hope is more than the sum of its previously published parts. The theme—which, stated most compendiously, is the demystification of law and in particular the freeing of it from moral theory, a great mystifier—is not a new one for me. It figures prominently in two of my previous books, *The Problems of Jurisprudence* (1990) and *Overcoming Law* (1995). I have tried to develop the theme further here, but with as little repetition of my previous writings as possible, so that the book can be seen as completing a trilogy on the major normative issues that beset the modern judge, moralist, and policymaker.

My primary interest is the law; but it is now recognized both within and without the legal profession that lawyers, judges, and law professors

---

1. Oliver Wendell Holmes, "The Path of the Law," 10 *Harvard Law Review* 457 (1897).

cannot "do" law without help from other disciplines. They don't know enough about the activities that the law regulates and the effects of legal regulation. The profession needs help, but there is disagreement about where it should turn for help. Moral philosophy and pragmatism offer the starkest choice. The philosophically inclined tend to believe that methods of or akin to those of moral philosophy should be used to decide the difficult questions in law. Pragmatists—at any rate my type of pragmatist, for the word covers a multitude of sins—believe that those methods don't work in any domain. They believe that the judge or other legal decision-maker thrust into the open area, the area where the conventional sources of guidance run out (such sources as previously decided cases and clear statutory or constitutional texts), can do no better than to rely on notions of policy, common sense, personal and professional values, and intuition and opinion, including informed or crystallized public opinion.[2] Pragmatists also believe, however, that intuition and opinion and the rest can sometimes be educated by immersion in "the facts." I have put this term between quotation marks to signal that it is to bear a wider meaning than in the law of evidence. It is a sense that takes in the analytic methods, empirical techniques, and findings of the social sciences (including history). In broadest terms, then, and with some exaggeration as we shall see, this book asks whether, when the methods of legal positivism fail to yield a satisfactory resolution of a legal issue, the law should take its bearings from philosophy or from science. And it answers, "from science."

But this is not a book just for lawyers and others who are interested in law. I argue not only that moral philosophy has nothing to offer judges or legal scholars so far as either adjudication or the formulation of jurisprudential or legal doctrines is concerned, but also that it has very little to offer anyone engaged in a normative enterprise, quite without regard to law. Only it is *particularly* clear that legal issues should not be analyzed with the aid of moral philosophy, but should instead be approached pragmatically. The proper methods of inquiry are therefore those that facilitate pragmatic decision making—the methods of social science and common sense.

The book is in two parts, each containing two chapters. The first part is primarily critical, the second primarily constructive. Chapter 1 tackles

2. As Holmes put it, "The felt necessities of the time, the prevalent moral and political theories, intuitions of public policy, avowed or unconscious, even the prejudices which judges share with their fellow-men, have had a good deal more to do than the syllogism in determining the rules by which men should be governed." Oliver Wendell Holmes, Jr., *The Common Law* 1 (1881).

normative moral theory on its own terms, arguing that people who make philosophical arguments for why we should alter our moral beliefs or behavior are wasting their time if what they want to do is to alter those beliefs and the behavior the beliefs might influence. Moral intuitions neither do nor should yield to the weak arguments that are all that philosophers can bring to bear on moral issues.[3]

I call this position "pragmatic moral skepticism." It must not be confused with philosophically more radical isms. I am not a moral nihilist, nor an epistemological skeptic or relativist, but merely a limited skeptic, as an example will show. That the Nazis killed millions of defenseless civilians is a fact; its truth is independent of what anyone believes. That the Nazis' actions were morally wrong is a value judgment: it depends on beliefs that cannot be proved true or false. I thus reject moral realism, at least in its strong sense as the doctrine that there are universal moral laws ontologically akin to scientific laws. I am a kind of moral relativist. But my metaethical views are not essential to pragmatic moral skepticism, the doctrine that moral theory is useless, although they help to explain why it is useless. The doctrine is supported by bodies of thought as various as the psychology of action, the character of academic professions in general and of the profession of academic philosophy in particular, and the undesirability of moral uniformity; and above all by the fact that the casuistic and deliberative techniques that moral theorists deploy are too feeble, both epistemologically and rhetorically, to shake moral intuitions. The analogy (of a pregnant woman forced to carry her fetus to term to a person forcibly attached by tubes to a famous violinist for nine months in order to save the violinist from dying of kidney disease) with which Judith Jarvis Thomson defends a right of abortion, and at the other end of the spectrum of abstraction the elaborate contractarian and natural-law arguments that John Rawls, Ronald Dworkin, John Finnis, and others make on behalf of their preferred resolutions of issues in applied ethics, are convincing only to readers predisposed to agree with the philosophers' conclusions. The class of innovators whom I call "moral entrepreneurs" do have the power to change our moral intuitions. But moral entrepreneurs are not the same as academic moralists, such as Thomson and the others I have named. Moral entrepreneurs persuade, but not with rational arguments. Academic moralists use rational arguments; but in part because of the sheer feebleness of such arguments, they do not persuade.

3. By moral "issues" I mean *contested* moral questions. When there is no contest, when everyone agrees on what's right, there is no issue and the need for theory does not arise.

Chapter 2 carries the discussion explicitly into the realm of law. I examine issues in jurisprudence, constitutional law, and (to a limited extent) common law and statutory law. I try to show with reference both to individual theorists—Dworkin again, Jürgen Habermas, and others—and to particular cases that moral theory, and such cousins of it as jurisprudence and constitutional theory, are useless in the resolution of concrete legal issues. This is true even when those issues concern such morally charged subjects as abortion, affirmative action, racial and sexual discrimination, and homosexual rights. Consider the constitutionality of laws forbidding physician-assisted suicide, the issue that impelled a group of distinguished moral philosophers led by Dworkin to submit an amicus curiae brief in the Supreme Court that the Court ignored in its decisions upholding those laws. Judges are properly wary about using moral or constitutional theory to decide cases.

At the same time, as I illustrate with the Supreme Court's decisions invalidating sex segregation in military academies and a state constitutional provision forbidding local governments to prohibit discrimination against homosexuals, judges are insensitive to the limitations of their own knowledge of the social realities out of which cases arise. They are right to distrust theory that academics press upon them, but they have as yet nothing to put in its place—unless it is an attitude of caution. That is the right attitude in the circumstances. Until judges acquire a better knowledge base, the limitations of moral and constitutional theory provide a compelling argument for judicial self-restraint, although to accept it would be to renounce the dream of many constitutional theorists that the Supreme Court might make over American society in the name of the Constitution but in the reality of radical egalitarianism, Catholic natural law, laissez-faire economics, or reactionary populism, depending on the theorist. Constitutional scholars would be more helpful to the courts and to society as a whole if they examined constitutional cases and doctrines in relation not to what passes as theory in jurisprudential circles but rather to the social context of constitutional issues, their causes, their costs, and their consequences. This is a neglected perspective, which I illustrate in Chapter 2 by reference to the "real world" effects of constitutional criminal procedure.

The first two chapters emphasize the *localness* of moral and jurisprudential conceptions, which are put forth as being universal primarily for rhetorical effect. The chapters also emphasize the frequent confusion of *moral* with *normative* as a result of which the fact that judges have to decide which party "should" win a case is erroneously taken to mean that judges are necessarily engaged in moral reasoning.

But if Supreme Court Justices, and the rest of the practical legal profession for that matter, are not paying any attention to moral and constitutional theory, why am I bothering to flay the theorists? The answer is that they are influential in the law schools and that their influence is pernicious; it is deflecting academic lawyers from their vital role (the focus of the second part of the book) of generating the knowledge that the judges and other practical professionals require if they are to maximize the social utility of law. But this answer merely pushes the inquiry back a stage, where two further questions loom: Why do moral theory and cognate approaches to the challenges posed by difficult legal cases have as strong a grip as they do on the academic legal mind? And how exactly, once those dubious approaches are rejected, can the legal system be improved? Part Two of the book addresses these questions. The answers require, I argue in Chapter 3, an understanding of the changing nature of professionalism in relation to law. Throughout Western society a traditional professionalism that emphasized guildlike restrictions and the cultivation of professional mystique is being challenged by a new, more functional, more empirical and scientific, in a word more *rational* (in a Weberian sense) professionalism foreseen long ago by Holmes. Moral theory is a methodologically conservative response to the challenge. But it is not conservative enough to satisfy judges, and it is intellectually inadequate for the reasons explained in the first two chapters. Thus it is doubly useless. At the end of Chapter 3 I give an example of how social science can help answer important questions about the legal system that leave traditional legal thinkers, as well as those influenced by moral philosophy, baffled. The example is that of the steep differences among the states in the amount of tort litigation, differences explicable by a combination of economic and sociological variables.

From the standpoint of the legal profession's official self-understanding, which continues to be formalistic, pragmatism is, in contrast to moral philosophy, a radical response to the challenges that modernity, with its rationalizing trend, poses to law. Yet not only does it strike a chord of recognition among judges and lawyers, as among other Americans; it also derives support from the new, the more rational, professionalism. But pragmatism must be distinguished from postmodernism, a dead end for law, as I argue using as exemplars of postmodern legal critique Duncan Kennedy and Stanley Fish. Or perhaps I should say *extreme* postmodernism, or a *frequent* dead end for law. For there is an affinity between my position and that of such postmodernists as Richard Rorty—as Fish, even, at times[4]—and of some postmodernist law professors, such as Pierre Schlag.[5] Schlag, like most postmodernist legal thinkers, is a greater skeptic than I, however, and perhaps as a result has no suggestions for improving the operation of the legal system; I have a number. Still, I commend his criticisms, and those of his colleague Paul Campos, of the American legal establishment and orthodox legal thought. Only I would never say, as Campos does, that we have a "sick legal system" in a "sick culture."[6] I recoil from such pessimistic generalities.

Explaining the pragmatic approach to law and distinguishing it from the postmodern approach are the tasks of Chapter 4. I point to the progress that academic law has made in developing a pragmatic scholarship of administrative law—one of a number of examples that could be given. (The existence of such examples is part of the explanation for why I am not a pessimist.) I then argue for pragmatic adjudication as a station on the road to the mature science of law sketched in Chapter 3, and I give a number of examples of how the pragmatist resolves difficult cases. If the end of that road is ever reached, it will mean that traditional conceptions of law have been overcome or superseded, as Holmes foresaw in "The Path of the Law," and that the law is drawing abreast of the rapidly professionalizing fields, not all of them conventional professions. The last section of Chapter 4 sketches a few of the institutional reforms that would help us to keep moving along this road, of which the most controversial is to make the third year of law school optional.

Pragmatism is a method, approach, or attitude, not a moral, legal, or political algorithm, so it will not resolve any moral or legal disagreement. Yet the reader will sense from time to time that I have pretty definite views about how a number of these disagreements should be resolved. So let me confess here that when I make recommendations about policy, including legal policy, I am guided mainly by the kind of vague utilitarianism, or "soft core" classical liberalism, that one associates with John Stuart Mill, especially the Mill of *On Liberty.* As is well known, Mill was not a strict or

4. See, in particular, Stanley Fish, "Mission Impossible: Settling the Just Bounds between Church and State," 97 *Columbia Law Review* 2255 (1997).

5. See, for example, Pierre Schlag, *Laying Down the Law: Mysticism, Fetishism, and the American Legal Mind* (1996); Schlag, "The Empty Circles of Liberal Justification," 96 *Michigan Law Review* 1 (1997).

6. Paul F. Campos, *Jurismania: The Madness of American Law* ix (1998).

consistent utilitarian[7] or an orthodox proponent of laissez-faire. And as I argue in the section of Chapter 1 entitled "Even Mill," Mill's moral or political philosophy cannot be shown to be correct any more than any other moral or political philosophy can be. Yet it sketches a form of life that when properly understood is attractive to many people in the United States and similar wealthy modern societies, and not just to me. That is ground enough for me to indicate how I would resolve particular issues. But it is a secondary aspect of the book.

Not all my readers will want to go down the road that the book maps out. But those who do not may still find some value in the book's criticisms of moral and legal theories and theorists, in its analyses of such important social phenomena as moral entrepreneurship and professionalism, and in the evaluation that I offer of some famously controversial legal decisions. I shall be reasonably content if I do no more than persuade some readers that there is a misallocation of the intellectual resources that are invested in law. Too large a fraction is going to the articulation and elaboration of abstract normative theories and too small a one to the development and application of social scientific theories and to the collection of data about how the legal system actually operates and with what costs and other consequences.

There is a name for the scholarly niche that this book occupies, and the name—some readers will be surprised to hear *me* say this—is sociology. This is a book about a profession—or rather professions, not only the law at large but also academic law and academic moral philosophy as their own professions. It employs Weberian insights concerning professionalization and its alternatives, including charismatic moral entrepreneurship. It expresses skepticism about the knowledge claims advanced by certain academic disciplines, in particular moral philosophy and constitutional theory, and such skepticism is another leitmotif of sociology. Sociologists are skeptical about professions as well as academic disciplines. They insist that what is "professed" may mask the pursuit of self-interest—which is an assumption of this book as well. The spirit of the book is Weberian in the further sense that it questions moral progress and affirms the existence of deep political conflicts unlikely to be dissolved by moral or political theory. The opposite of "Weberian" in this sense is "[Woodrow] Wilsonian."

But if I did not point out the sociological cast of my analysis, few readers would tumble to it. The sociology of law is barely visible in the

---

7. See C. L. Ten, *Mill on Liberty* (1980).

American university scene. It has been eclipsed by economic analysis of law, philosophy of law, feminist jurisprudence, and critical legal studies. Its remnants have largely been absorbed into the amorphous "law and society" movement, an agglomeration of the social sciences that has in common only that none of them is economics. Much of my recent academic writing has dealt with traditional topics in sociology, ranging from professionalism and expert-knowledge claims—the sociological topics of this book—to social norms, privacy, aging, sex, litigiousness, reputation, equality, and economic development; yet no one thinks of my work as sociological. The occlusion of sociology of law is an interesting development that bears on this book and, more broadly, on the relation between law and the social sciences. But I have discussed the matter at some length elsewhere[8] and shall content myself in this book with indicating in Chapter 3 some of the contributions that sociology of law has made and can make to placing the law on a scientific footing—which is where the law belongs.

I have had a lot of help with this book, which it is a pleasure as well as a duty to acknowledge. I thank Héctor Acevedo-Polanco, Sorin Feiner, Anup Malani, Christopher Ottele, Rebecca Rapp, Edward Siskel, Andrew Trask, and Mark Woolway for very helpful research assistance. For comments on the whole or major parts of the manuscript, or of the lectures on which it is partially based, I am greatly indebted to the five critics of my Holmes Lectures (Ronald Dworkin, Charles Fried, Anthony Kronman, John Noonan, and Martha Nussbaum); to members of the lecture audiences, including Lucian Bebchuk and Robert Nozick; to participants in workshops at Harvard and the University of Chicago; to anonymous readers for two university presses; and to Michael Aronson, Stephen Breyer, Richard Craswell, Neil Duxbury, Thomas Eisele, Ward Farnsworth, Robert Ferguson, Alan Gewirth, Ruth Bader Ginsburg, Amy Gutmann, Russell Hardin, Frances Kamm, John Langbein, Brian Leiter, Lawrence Lessig, Frank Michelman, Charlene Posner, Eric Posner, Richard Rorty, Stephen Schulhofer, David Strauss, Cass Sunstein, Dennis Thompson, and John Tryneski.

8. See my article "The Sociology of the Sociology of Law: A View from Economics," 2 *European Journal of Law and Economics* 265 (1995).

Part I

The Wrong Turn

Chapter 1

MORAL THEORY

Introduction: From Moral Realism to Pragmatic Moral Skepticism

The idea that there is a moral order accessible to human intelligence and neither time-bound nor local, an order that furnishes objective criteria for praising or condemning the beliefs and behavior of individuals and the design and operation of legal institutions, echoes down the corridors of Western intellectual history. The outpouring of scholarly reflection from the time of Aristotle to the present that it has inspired has in turn inspired a host of theories in part derivative and in part parallel concerning the form and content of legal norms. Unfortunately the generative idea itself, and the literatures in philosophy and law that elaborate and apply it, are spurious—or so I shall argue in this chapter with regard to moral theory and in the next with regard to legal theory.

The argument has both a strong and a weak form. The strong is that moral theorizing does not provide a usable basis for moral judgments (such as "abortion is bad" or "redistributing wealth from rich to poor is good") and cannot make us morally better people in either our private or our public roles. The weak form is that even if moral theorizing can provide a usable basis for some moral judgments, it should not be used for making *legal* judgments. It is not something judges are or can be made comfortable with or good at; it is socially divisive; and it does not mesh with the issues in legal cases.[1]

1. In the course of my argument I shall try to answer the principal criticisms made of an earlier version by Ronald Dworkin, Charles Fried, Anthony Kronman, John Noonan, and Martha Nussbaum in the May 1998 issue of the *Harvard Law Review.* I reply in the same issue under the title "Reply to Critics of 'The Problematics of Moral and Legal Theory,'" 111 *Harvard Law Review* 1796 (1998). A

Morality is the set of duties to others (not necessarily just other people—the duties could run to animals as well, or, importantly, to God) that are supposed to check our merely self-interested, emotional, or sentimental reactions to serious questions of human conduct. It is concerned with what we owe, rather than what we are owed, except insofar as a sense of entitlement (to happiness, self-fulfillment, an interesting life, an opportunity to exercise our talents, to realize ourselves, and so on) might impose a duty on others to help us get what we are entitled to. Although morality operates as a check on our impulses, this doesn't necessarily make it a form of reason. A dog is constrained by a leash without having to engage in a process of reasoning. Similarly, a check on an emotional reaction can be another emotion (pity might check anger) rather than an argument. When swerving to avoid hitting a pedestrian, or when helping an elderly person across the street, one is not enacting the conclusion of a process of moral reflection.

The genuineness of morality as a system of social control is not in question, although I shall argue that morality has less effect on behavior than moralists believe. The propriety of making morality a subject of inquiry is not in question either, whether the inquirers are sociologists, anthropologists, historians, or others concerned with identifying and explaining the moral code of a particular society or epoch; or economists or game theorists (often the same people) who relate morality to rational choice; or philosophers interested in exploring the ontology or epistemology of moral inquiry, as opposed to prescribing our moral duties.

Nor is the significance of *normative* reasoning in question. So when "moral theory" is used as a synonym for normative reasoning, or when "moral" is used as an impressive synonym for "political,"[2] my only criticism is that these usages create confusion. Another confusing equation is of "moral" with "ethical." It is better to reserve the latter term for the set of attempts to answer the question "How shall I live?" and the former term

number of the criticisms are too picayune to interest many readers of this book, so anyone interested in them and in my responses to them should read the debate in the *Harvard Law Review*. See id. at 1718–1823.

2. Ronald Dworkin's conflation of moral and political terms has been remarked. See, for example, Thomas D. Eisele, "Taking Our Actual Constitution Seriously," 95 *Michigan Law Review* 1799, 1818–1819 (1997). Dworkin proposes, as we shall see in the next chapter, that judges should engage in moral reasoning. His proposal would fall completely flat if he substituted "political" for "moral." Dworkin, as a moral theorist who wants judges to apply moral theory, figures prominently in this book as a target of my criticisms.

for the subset that consists of answers that stress duty to others. Nietzsche gives ethical advice, but (on some construals, anyway) is not a moralist.

My particular target is the branch of moral theory I shall call "academic moralism." Academic moralism is applied ethics as formulated by present-day university professors such as Elizabeth Anderson, Ronald Dworkin, John Finnis, Alan Gewirth, Frances Kamm, Thomas Nagel, Martha Nussbaum, John Rawls, Joseph Raz, Thomas Scanlon, Roger Scruton, and Judith Jarvis Thomson. This is a diverse list (and the list is only partial), but there is at least a family resemblance among the persons listed; and the family is what I am calling academic moralism. The members of the family think that the kind of moral theorizing nowadays considered rigorous in university circles has an important role to play in improving the moral judgments and moral behavior of people—themselves, their students, judges, Americans, foreigners. Some of these moralists are primarily legal philosophers (Dworkin, Finnis, and Raz) or political philosophers (Rawls) rather than moral philosophers. Some defend a complete moral system, such as utilitarianism or the ethics of Kant, and others specific applications of moral theory, for example to the moral and legal debates over abortion, euthanasia, and surrogate motherhood. All of them want the law to follow the teachings of moral theory, though not always at a close distance.

In contrast, Annette Baier, Gilbert Harman, Richard Rorty, and Bernard Williams are examples of philosophers of morality who, like Nietzsche, are either not at all or not primarily moralists. Some philosophers of this school are skeptical of normative moral theory.[3] More are skeptical about normative moral theory as it is practiced in universities today (I shall explain the significance of this qualification in a moment), and thus of academic moralism. Others are interested in studying morality as a phenomenon or as a set of concepts, rather than in preaching. A further complication is that the same person may do academic moralism part of the time and another type of philosophical or legal thinking the rest of the time. An example is Dworkin, who in addition to being a moralist is, as we shall see in the next chapter, an analyst of jurisprudential theories. One can accept much of his jurisprudence, in particular his rejection of legal positivism as either description of or guide to decision

---

3. See generally *Anti-Theory in Ethics and Moral Conservatism* (Stanley G. Clarke and Evan Simpson eds. 1989); also Richard Rorty, "Human Rights, Rationality, and Sentimentality," in Rorty, *Philosophical Papers*, vol. 3: *Truth and Progress* 167 (1998).

making by American judges, while rejecting his moralism. Indeed, that is essentially my position.

I shall be arguing first of all that morality is local, that there are no *interesting* moral universals. There are tautological ones, such as "murder is wrong," where "murder" means wrongful killing, or "bribery is wrong," where "bribery" means wrongful paying. But what counts as murder, or as bribery, varies enormously from society to society. There are a handful of rudimentary principles of social cooperation—such as don't lie *all* the time or break promises without *any* reason or kill your relatives or neighbors indiscriminately—that may be common to all human societies,[4] and if one wants to call these rudimentary principles the universal moral law, that is fine with me. But they are too abstract to be criterial. Meaningful moral realism is therefore out, and a form (not every form) of moral relativism is in. Relativism in turn invites an *adaptationist* conception of morality, in which morality is judged—nonmorally, in the way that a hammer might be judged well or poorly adapted to its goal of hammering nails into wood or plaster—by its contribution to the survival, or other ultimate goals, of a society or some group within it. Moral relativism implies that the expression "moral progress" must be used with great caution, because it is perspectival rather than objective; moral progress is in the eye of the beholder.

Many so-called moral phenomena can be explained without reference to moral categories. The moral vocabulary is to a great extent epiphenomenal or polemical, and indeed hypocritical. Moral principles that claim universality can usually be better understood as just the fancy dress of workaday social norms that vary from society to society. What is universal are the moral *sentiments*, that is, moral emotions. They include guilt and indignation, and certain forms of disgust,[5] though not altruism, which, as we shall see, is not primarily a *moral* sentiment. The identification of the moral sentiments, for example by David Hume and Adam Smith, illustrates the kind of moral philosophy that I do *not* criticize in this book. But the moral sentiments are object neutral, and hence not really moral. "Moralistic" would be a better word for them. Pity and hatred, for example, are universal, but the objects of pity and hatred are not.

4. See Donald E. Brown, *Human Universals* 138–139 (1991); Steven Pinker, *The Language Instinct: How the Mind Creates Language,* ch. 13 (1994). There may be prudential universals, such as "Know thyself," but they are not moral as I defined the term earlier—they belong to the broader ethical domain.

5. See the interesting discussion in William Ian Miller, *The Anatomy of Disgust,* ch. 8 (1997) ("The Moral Life of Disgust").

And however all this may be, academic moralism has no prospect of improving human behavior. Knowing the moral thing to do furnishes no motive, and creates no motivation, for doing it; motive and motivation have to come from outside morality. Even if this is wrong, the analytical tools employed in academic moralism—whether moral casuistry, or reasoning from the canonical texts of moral philosophy, or careful analysis, or reflective equilibrium, or some combination of these tools—are too feeble to override either narrow self-interest or moral intuitions. And academic moralists have neither the rhetorical skills nor the factual knowledge that might enable them to persuade without having good methods of inquiry and analysis. As a result of its analytical, rhetorical, and factual deficiencies, academic moralism is helpless when intuitions clash or self-interest opposes, and otiose when they line up. It is fortunate, moreover, that academic moralists have no prospects for achieving their implied aim of imposing a uniform morality on society. Not that they agree on what that morality should be; but each moral theory is implicitly uniformitarian, while what a society like ours needs is moral variety—which is *not* the same thing as tolerance merely of different moral *beliefs*.

What is more, a modern academic career in philosophy is not conducive to moral innovation or insight. And even if it were, there is so much disagreement among academic moralists that their readers (who are in any event few outside the universities) can easily find a persuasive rationalization for whatever their preferred course of conduct happens to be. Indeed, moral debate entrenches, rather than bridges, disagreement. Exposure to moral philosophy may lead educated people to behave *less* morally than untutored persons by making them more adept at rationalization. There is, as we shall see, evidence that moral reflection does in fact undermine the capacity for moral action.

If academic moralism thus is ineffectual in changing people's behavior, one may wonder how moral change comes about. My answer will emphasize both material conditions and "moral enterpreneurs," and will show why the modern university professor is not equipped to play the role of moral entrepreneur, with the result that the fruitful moral debates take place outside the precincts of academic moralism. So why hasn't academic moralism withered and died? The answer is to be found partly in the spiritual yearnings of people who are attracted to a career in moral philosophy, partly in the rhetorical needs of people who want the courts or other agencies of government to play an aggressive role in the formation of social policy, partly in the career incentives of humanities professors, and partly in other factors—none related to the truth value of academic moralism.

It is because of the importance of distinguishing the moral entrepreneur from other moralists that I define my main target in this chapter as *academic* moralism. Moral entrepreneurs play a role in the evolution of morality; other moralists do not; and the modern university professor is prevented by the character of a modern academic career from being a moral entrepreneur, with rare and largely irrelevant exceptions. Earlier moralists—the authors of the classic works of moral philosophy, such as Plato, Hume, Bentham, Kant, and Mill—were for the most part not professors (though Kant was) and in any event lived in times when knowledge was less specialized and esoteric and the line between theory and practice much less distinct. The modern moral philosopher is firmly imprisoned in an ivory tower.

I call my metaethical stance, as sketched above, "pragmatic moral skepticism." Let me indicate how it differs from more familiar positions with which it might be confused.

Moral relativism. I believe that the criteria for pronouncing a moral claim valid are given by the culture in which the claim is advanced rather than by some transcultural ("universal") source of moral values, so that we cannot, except for polemical effect, call another culture immoral unless we add "by our lights." But I reject the "vulgar relativism" that teaches that we have a *duty* to tolerate cultures that have moral views different from ours.[6] Vulgar relativism is just another school of academic moralism, like Kantianism or Aristotelianism. I am also not a moral relativist in the "anything goes" sense more accurately described as moral subjectivism or moral skepticism.[7] And I shall be at pains later to distinguish moral relativism from cognitive or epistemological relativism, which is dogged by the problem of self-reference.

Moral pluralism. The idea that moral values are irreducibly plural, so that justice and loyalty, for example, cannot be commensurated and thus weighed against each other to resolve a moral issue,[8] is related to and

6. See Bernard Williams, *Morality: An Introduction to Ethics* 20–26 (1972). What my type of moral relativism does do, however, is spike one of the arguments against tolerance.

7. Ronald Dworkin, in his article "In Praise of Theory," 29 *Arizona State Law Journal* 353, 361–363 (1997), runs moral relativism and moral subjectivism together, while in another and philosophically more ambitious article he runs together moral relativism, moral subjectivism, and moral skepticism. Dworkin, "Objectivity and Truth: You'd Better Believe It," 25 *Philosophy and Public Affairs* 87 (1996).

8. See, for example, Isaiah Berlin, *The Crooked Timber of Humanity,* ch. 1 (1991); George Crowder, "Pluralism and Liberalism," 42 *Political Studies* 293 (1994).

supports moral relativism but is not identical to it, since many pluralists believe that reason enables us to choose between incommensurables.[9]

Moral subjectivism. The view that moral statements are purely subjective, so that (at best) morality is relative to the beliefs of each individual—an individual acts immorally only when he acts contrary to whatever morality he has adopted for himself—is moral subjectivism. I am sympathetic to this position but do not accept it fully. Moral terms have definitions, and the definition will often fit the circumstances unequivocally; the faithless spouse is—faithless. But the morality that condemns the traitor, the adulterer, etc., cannot itself be evaluated in moral terms. That would be possible only if there were precise, and hence operational, transcultural moral truths. If a person decides to opt out of the morality of his society, the way an Achilles or an Edmund (in *King Lear*) or a Meursault or a Gauguin or an Anthony Blunt did, or for that matter as the conspirators against Hitler did, there is no way of showing that he is morally wrong, provided that he is being consistent with himself *and* that such consistency is a tenet of his personal moral code (more on this later). The most that can be said about such a person, though it is not nothing, is that he is acting contrary to the moral views held by most of the people in his society.

A watered-down version of moral subjectivism is consistent with moral relativism when what is emphasized in the latter doctrine is the rejection of transcultural moral truths. There is no inconsistency in saying that all moral truths are local but adding that one's own morality is hyperlocal, being limited to oneself. A new morality—that of Christianity, for example—may start with a single person.

Moral skepticism. The merely pragmatic moral skeptic is not a moral skeptic in the strict sense of one who believes that moral truth is unknowable. It is a fact about our society and societies like ours that infanticide is immoral unless, perhaps, the infant is acephalic or otherwise profoundly defective. This is an important qualification, but for the moment let me confine the term "infanticide" to the killing of normal babies. Anyone in our society who practiced infanticide so defined would be confidently adjudged immoral by almost anyone else one might ask, and if he claimed that infanticide was permitted by his private morality, emphasis would fall on the word "private." To that extent, I might even consider myself a moral realist, believing that there is a fact of the matter about some moral claims, though except for those rudimentary principles of social coopera-

9. See, for example, Isaiah Berlin and Bernard Williams, "Pluralism and Liberalism: A Reply," 42 *Political Studies* 306 (1994).

tion that are useless for resolving any actual moral issue only a *local* fact, in the same way that the sentence "It is 35 degrees Fahrenheit in Chicago today" asserts a local fact.

In between metaphysical moral realism (Catholic natural law doctrine, for example, although there are secular versions as well) and the weak local realism that I accept is the "right answers" moral realism of Dworkin, Nagel, and many, probably most, other contemporary academic moralists. Utilitarian and neo-Kantian ethics, the most influential modern schools of academic moralism in the West, both illustrate "right answers" moral realism. It could also be called natural-law theory without metaphysics— in other words, without nature.[10] It is summarized in Nagel's remark that "[moral] realism need not (and . . . should not) have any metaphysical content whatever. It need only hold that there are answers to moral questions and that they are not reducible to anything else."[11] But I claim that there are no *convincing* answers to *contested* moral questions unless the questions are reducible to ones of fact. This view marks me as a moral skeptic in the loose sense of one who doubts the possibility of making objective judgments about the claims moral theorists want to make. The nondogmatic moral skeptic and the weak moral realist converge.

Belief that moral theory cannot resolve controversies enables me to reconcile a qualified acceptance of moral subjectivism with a rejection of strict moral skepticism. A person who murders an infant is acting immorally in our society; a person who sincerely claimed, with or without supporting arguments, that it is right to kill infants would be asserting a private moral position. I might consider him a lunatic, a monster, or a fool, as well as a violator of the locally prevailing moral code. But I would hesitate to call him immoral, just as I would hesitate to call Jesus Christ immoral for having violated settled norms of Judaism and Roman law or Pontius Pilate immoral for enforcing that law. Had I been a British colonial official (but with my present values) in nineteenth-century India, I would have outlawed suttee. This is an example of the rejection of vulgar relativism; the fact that suttee (the immolation—nominally, at least, voluntary—of the widow on her husband's bier) was an accepted practice of Hindu society did not make it morally binding on anyone outside that society. But I would have suppressed the practice because I found it

10. See Lloyd L. Weinreb, *Natural Law and Justice*, ch. 4 (1987).

11. Thomas Nagel, "Universality and the Reflective Self," in Christine M. Korsgaard et al., *The Sources of Normativity* 200, 205 (Onora O'Neill ed. 1996). For amplification of this view, see Nagel, *The Last Word*, ch. 6 (1997).

disgusting, not because I found it immoral. We tend to find deviations from our own morality disgusting. Our reactions prove nothing about the wrongness of the "disgusting" morality. No doubt Hindu men thought widows who resisted their fate disgusting.

It was right to put the Nazi leaders on trial rather than to shoot them out of hand in a paroxysm of disgust. But it was *politically* right. It created a trustworthy public record of what the Nazis had done, and it exhibited "rule of law" virtues to the German people that made it less likely that Germany would again embrace totalitarianism, which for obvious reasons the Allied nations didn't want it to do. But the trial was right not because it could produce proof that the Nazis *really* were immoralists; they were, but according to our lights, not theirs. That they tried to conceal their genocidal activities might appear to show that they recognized a universal moral law. But alternative explanations abound. Publicity would have warned the intended victims and stimulated flight, concealment, or resistance. And Germans who had been socialized before Hitler came to power were apt to have qualms about genocide. Had Hitler won the war and Germany prospered, those qualms might well have died with the older generation.

Noncognitivism. The noncognitivist (or expressivist) believes that moral claims are expressive rather than referential, and what they express is an attitude or emotion that has no cognitive content. For example, the subset of noncognitivists known as emotivists believe that a statement such as "You are unjust!" is an expression of anger no different (from a cognitive standpoint) from slapping the person in the face. I have the same reaction to noncognitivism as I have to moral skepticism; strictly, I think it is false, because insofar as a moral claim, or for that matter a slap in the face, embodies an evaluation of conduct, it has a cognitive content; we can say it is wrong to be angry at the person you slapped, because he was not acting contrary to the moral code, as you believed he was. But I agree with the spirit as it were of noncognitivism, because many moral claims are just the gift wrapping of theoretically ungrounded and ungroundable preferences and aversions.

Moral particularism. The moral particularist believes either that there are no general moral principles, just particular moral intuitions—in which event I am a moral particularist—or, more interestingly, that there are universal moral truths but they must be applied to particular moral issues with greater sensitivity to social context than exhibited by Kant and his avatars. Not believing that there are universal moral truths that have any bite, I reject this sense of moral particularism, which in practice, moreover, like moral pluralism, tends to be undisciplined and ad hoc—a game played without rules. The analogy in law is the ruling that is confided to the uncabined discretion of the trial judge, such as a decision involving the scheduling of a case or when to terminate the cross-examination of a witness because it has gone on too long. The lack of criteria for such a ruling, or, if there are criteria, the lack of any method of weighting them, places the ruling, in all but the most extreme cases, beyond the possibility of rational evaluation.

To summarize, I embrace a version of moral relativism, reject ambitious moral particularism, accept the descriptive accuracy (but not the normative authority) of moral pluralism, and accept diluted versions of moral subjectivism, moral skepticism, and noncognitivism. I have not exhausted the isms that have attracted moral theorists, my purpose being merely to distinguish the approaches with which my own is likely to be confused. My approach is similar to that of Oliver Wendell Holmes, Jr., as reconstructed from his scattered and fragmentary writings on morality. It is opposed to metaphysical and "right answers" moral realism and so to natural-law theory whether metaphysical or nonmetaphysical, but it overlaps weak moral realism.

But readers need not accept Holmes's or my (or anyone's) metaethics in order to accept the argument of this chapter, which, crudely put, is that there is nothing to academic moralism. For example, even if I am wrong in thinking that there are no interesting moral universals, they would be unusable in moral argument unless we could determine what they are, and so it would be as if they did not exist. It is a question of fact—it has an answer and one independent of what anyone thinks—whether Alexander the Great had an odd or an even number of hairs on his head when he was twelve years old. Only it is a question impossible to answer with our present methods of inquiry—as are difficult moral questions.

Though my objections to academic moralism do not depend on each other, they support each other. For example, the (sociological) objection that it is ineffectual supports the (metaethical) objection that it is epistemically feeble. When there is nothing materially or psychologically at stake in a debate, the observer is likely to side with the debater who makes the better arguments. Some readers of this chapter, being young or otherwise uncommitted to any position on the merit or utility of academic moralism, will be persuaded by me if they conclude that I have better arguments than the moralists. But in the case of moral controversy, the audience for academic debate is likely to be either uninterested or, because of self-interest or moral intuition, already committed. The committed cannot be swayed by, or the uninterested persuaded to take an interest in, arguments about where one's moral duty lies. So there is a *futility* to academic moralism.

Understand, however, that my criticisms of *moral* theory are not criticisms of *theory.* Economic theory, and the parts of the natural sciences with which I have at least a nodding acquaintance, such as evolutionary biology, seem to me both beautiful and useful. I also find attractive and useful, and indeed employ throughout this book, the very different style of theorizing from the scientific that is associated with Nietzsche and Weber; so let me not be accused of "scientism," the belief that the only worthwhile knowledge is scientific knowledge in a narrow sense and hence that the only theories that lead to the acquisition of knowledge are scientific theories. Dworkin's demonstration that legal positivism is not a workable approach for American judges is a genuine contribution to knowledge, although not to "scientific" knowledge in the most common sense of the word; it is best described as a contribution to philosophical sociology.

Yet it is significant that the most successful theories are found in science and particularly in those areas of natural science in which a theory, because it is about observable phenomena and "real" (physically existing) entities, can be tested by comparing the predictions generated by the theory with the results of observation. Two things are required: that the theory yield empirically refutable predictions (otherwise it cannot be tested—the fate of the theory that there is life after death) and that the data that would refute it empirically can be observed. Theories in the natural sciences tend to satisfy the first requirement but sometimes stumble over the second. Evolution, for example, cannot be observed because most of it occurred before there were any observers who left records. Various forms of indirect evidence for the theory of evolution can be adduced, however; they include fossil records, the study of genes, experience with the breeding of animals, and the structure and behavior of plants and animals. These pieces of evidence, together with the absence of an alternative theory for which there is scientific evidence, cumulatively provide strong support for the theory of evolution. Such indirect verification is widespread in science and often highly reliable. Consider how we know—and we do know, with all but metaphysical certainty, which is unattainable—that no human being has ever eaten an adult hippopotamus in one sitting, that no cats grow on trees, and that the earth is more than 10,000 years old and used to be a habitat of dinosaurs.

Economic theory is closely related to the theory of evolution; concepts of maximization, competition, unconscious rationality, cost, investment, self-interest, survival, and equilibrium play parallel roles in both theories. Evolution deals with unconscious maximizers, the genes; economics with conscious maximizers, persons. The empirical difference is that unlike the theory of evolution, economic theory deals with observable social behaviors, such as price movements, the number and size of firms, input costs, shortages, wages, methods of compensation of employees and other agents, capital investment, savings and interest, taxes, population growth, and industrial output. But because experiments that would isolate the effect of a particular economic variable on observable behavior are difficult to construct, the economist usually has to fall back on the methods of statistical inference to correct for other possible causes of observed behavior. These methods, given the data, are sometimes unsatisfactory. But not always; and in addition there have been a fair number of "natural" experiments in economics—such as the adoption and abandonment of price controls in different places and different times, tariff reduction, the deregulation of transportation, and the fall of communism—that provide evidence in support of the central predictions of economics. Among these predictions are that price ceilings give rise to shortages, queuing, and black markets; that output under competition is higher than output under monopoly; that price discrimination leads to arbitrage; that workers in dangerous or disagreeable jobs receive wage premia; that free trade increases prosperity; and that increases in excise tax rates lead to higher prices and lower output. Lately there have also been some controlled experiments in economics.

I do not claim that economic and biological theories are successful because they are true, or even that they are true. They are successful because they help us to predict, understand, and to a limited extent control our physical and social environment; they yield knowledge that makes a difference (the pragmatic criterion of knowledge). Since morality is a feature of the social environment, it is a legitimate subject of theoretical reflection too. But as I have already suggested, theories about morality are not the same thing as moral theories. This chapter presents a theory about morality. A moral theory, in contrast, is a theory of how we *should* behave. It tries to get at the truth about our moral obligations. It addresses such questions as the following: Is it always wrong to lie or to break a promise? Is infanticide immoral? Sex discrimination? Prostitution? Euthanasia? Affirmative action? Enforceable contracts of surrogate motherhood? Should a person put loyalty to country above loyalty to friends? Is it proper to kill one innocent person to save ten innocent persons? Should a rich person be permitted to buy medical care that a poor person could not afford? Is eating meat immoral? Does fairness require compensation for injuries inflicted without fault? Is it wrong to limit immigration? Should people be forced to donate inessential organs (one's second kidney, for example) to the necessitous? These are questions not about whether moral beliefs are widespread, where they come from, and how likely they are to influence behavior—the sort of question that an anthropologist, a historian, a sociologist, a psychologist, or an economist might study. They are not even questions about the use of moral terms, the sort of thing an analytic philospher might study. They are questions about whether we ought to act in particular ways.

Academic moral theory should be distinguished from moral preachment outside the academy. The Jesus Christ of the Gospels is a moralist, but, unlike Plato or Aquinas, he is not a theorist and does not make academic-style arguments. My concern is with the type of moralizing that is or at least pretends to be free from controversial metaphysical commitments, such as those of a believing Christian, and so might conceivably appeal to the judges of our secular courts.

The critical and the constructive employment of moral theory should also be distinguished. If a moralist, academic or otherwise, makes a fallacious philosophical argument for a particular moral position, it is a proper office of the moral theorist to expose the fallacy. Just as the most worthwhile function of general philosophy may be to dispel philosophical errors, so the most worthwhile function of moral theory may be to dispel errors in moral reasoning. Whether it is an *important* function is another matter. If moral views and behavior are impervious to moral argument, they should be impervious to bad arguments as well as good. The argument that God must exist because He is by definition perfect, which implies that He possesses all "good" attributes, including existence, is easily shown to rest on the fallacy of supposing existence an attribute. But how many people ever based their belief in God on that or any other argument and so would have been shaken by its refutation?

A good deal of modern moral theorizing has been aimed at showing that utilitarianism is an unsatisfactory moral theory. The primary method of attack has not been to challenge the actual policies advocated by utilitarians, but to argue that utilitarianism implies other, unacceptable policies, which most utilitarians hadn't even thought of, such as taxing ascetics for the benefit of hedonists, permitting rape if the pleasure that the rapist derives from the coercive character of the act exceeds the victim's pain, permitting the punishment of innocent people and the torture of suspects, increasing the sum of human happiness by subsidizing procreation, and placing sentient animals on a moral plane with human beings (which might require subsidizing animal procreation at the expense of human). This method of refutation is called *reductio ad absurdum,* and is a form of logical argument. It cannot actually *refute* utilitarianism, because the utilitarian may be willing to follow wherever his theory logically leads. But if he is not, if he rejects the policies logically entailed (he didn't realize) by his theory, then the elaboration of that logic may alter moral beliefs. More realistically, it may cause utilitarians either to deny that the hypothetical policies are actually utility maximizing (we shall see an example in the next chapter) or to reground their favorite policies in pragmatic considerations.

Still another important distinction is between proposing and arguing for a position, which is to say between discovery and justification. One function of moral philosophy is the articulation of possible moral systems with or without accompanying arguments. In a mutable or pluralistic moral culture, moral philosophy offers people choices of how to live, or how to think about how to live. In this it resembles, indeed might be thought a form of, art, religion, or therapy. But it is not a matter of offering reasoned answers to moral questions. And it is also—this innovative, imaginative, or inspirational role of moral theory—not the sort of role that modern academics are well suited to play or that judges are comfortable in playing.

A distinction that I shall *not* make is between moral *theory* and moral *reasoning.* Not that they can't be distinguished; but the distinction would have no bearing on my argument. One thinks of "moral theory" as something big, the sort of thing found in Kant or Sidgwick or Rawls, and "moral reasoning" as the process of reasoning to the resolution of a specific moral issue but without getting entangled in facts—for then it would cease to be purely moral reasoning. Moral reasoning is different from pointing out either logical or factual mistakes in moral argument, the former being a legitimate therapeutic task of philosophy and the latter a task for the social sciences. Only when a moral claim is logically and empirically unassailable does it belong to moral reasoning as I am using the term.

With terms defined and other groundwork laid, we are ready to proceed to the exploration of the thesis of this chapter: that academic moralism is a useless endeavor.

Understanding Morality

The Relativity of Morals

REALISM VERSUS RELATIVISM

Both strong (that is, metaphysical) moral realists and some intermediate ("right answers") ones seek to identify a phenomenon that exists independently of theory: the "moral law," perhaps, or a "moral faculty." The suggestion is of a conceptual, psychological, juridical, or even material entity, respectively parallel to the number system, to the psychology of self-interest that generates many economic phenomena, to positive law, or to the stars. A universal moral law might enable us, at least if we are scientific realists, to conceive of moral theory on the analogy of scientific theory and thus to reject moral relativism, the bane of normative moral philosophy.

Not much needs to be said about the kind of metaphysical moral realism that one encounters in Plato and in canon law. The only warrant for believing that there is a moral law that is "out there" in the very strong sense claimed by a Plato or an Aquinas—a moral law that has been promulgated by a process analogous to the promulgation of positive law or that has a tangible reality akin to that of the stars—is faith in a Supreme Lawgiver and in a spiritual reality as real as a material reality; and explicit religious arguments are not a part of academic moralism. Even deeply religious academic moralists, who in our society are mainly Catholic and Jewish, appeal not to Judaism or Catholicism as such (that is, to belief in a divinity who authors or underwrites the moral law) but to the Catholic natural-law tradition or the Jewish ethical tradition, as the source of their moral arguments.

Not all metaphysical moral realism, however, has even an indirectly religious cast. Charles Larmore acknowledges as metaphysical his view that "reality also contains a normative dimension, constituted by reasons for belief and action," a dimension that we gain access to through "reflection" conceived of as an "organ of knowledge."[12] But in practice this organ of knowledge operates, rather, as an organ of assertion, as when Larmore states:

> Can we not in good conscience consider our own moral universalism as superior to earlier and very different tribal moralities, while acknowledging that thereby we have also lost the possibilities of good they embodied? The weighing of heterogeneous goods is not likely to yield a cardinal ranking. But surely we can have reason to believe that some such goods are more important than others, in the given circumstances or overall, and even a lot more important. (p. 162)

Larmore acknowledges that this may strike the reader as "just so much assertion" (the usual office of "surely") and admits that he has no "fully satisfactory" reply to the charge (id.).

He does try, as do a number of other contemporary moral realists, such as David Brink, John McDowell, and Peter Railton, to justify the claim that moral principles are as objective as scientific principles. The way this generally is done, however, is to "level down" science to moral inquiry by emphasizing the degree to which even physical objects are actually mental constructs—consequences of our categorizing sense data in particular ways. This approach may succeed in equating scientific to moral inquiry at the semantic level, but it leaves untouched the vast practical difference in the success of these enterprises. The difference stems from the fact that science, dealing as it does with phenomena that are "mind independent" to a much greater degree than the principles of morality are, can utilize methods of precise observation that enable disagreements to be resolved with confidence, rather than dragging on interminably.

This is an important point, and one to which I'll return later in this chapter. It is not, however, conclusive against moral realism, because, like realism generally, moral realism need not depend on either a metaphysical grounding or a robust empirical methodology. It is possible to be realistic about purely symbolic realms—to state, with great and warranted confidence in the truth of the statement, that a mathematical computation, or a move in chess, or the construction of a sentence, is erroneous. There could be a universal moral law in the sense of a set of principles that

12. Charles Larmore, *The Morals of Modernity* 8 (1996); see also id. at 9. He defends his position in id., ch. 5.

all competent adults always and everywhere recognize as duties, perhaps duties from which solutions to specific moral issues could be deduced or otherwise convincingly derived. Could be; but there doesn't appear to be a universal moral law that is neither a tautology (such as "don't murder") nor an abstraction (such as "don't lie all the time") too lofty ever to touch ground and resolve a moral *issue,* that is, a moral question on which there is disagreement.

Every society, every subculture within a society, past or present, has had a moral code, but a code shaped by the exigencies of life in that society or that subculture rather than by a glimpse of some overarching source of moral obligations. To the extent it is adaptive to those exigencies, the code cannot be criticized convincingly by outsiders. Infanticide is abhorred in our society but routine in ones that cannot feed all the children that are born.[13] Slavery was routine when the victors in war could not afford to feed or free their captives, so that the alternative to enslaving them was killing them. Are infanticide and slavery "wrong" in these circumstances? It is provincial to say that "we are right about slavery, for example, and the Greeks wrong,"[14] so different was slavery in the ancient world from racial enslavement as practiced, for example, in the United States until the end of the Civil War and so different were the material conditions that nurtured these different forms of slavery.[15] To call infanticide or slavery presumptively bad would be almost as provincial as unqualified condemnation. The inhabitants of an infanticidal or slave society would say with equal plausibility that infanticide or slavery was presumptively good, though they might allow that the presumption could be rebutted in peaceable, wealthy, technologically complex societies.

I have given explanations for infanticide and slavery that are consistent with modern beliefs concerning cruelty and inequality. This may prime the reader to argue that I have conceded the universality of those beliefs, merely insisting that they be applied with a sensitive regard to circumstances. But in the first place, our modern beliefs concerning cruelty and inequality are contingent, rather than being the emanations of a universal

13. See James Q. Wilson, *The Moral Sense* 20–23 (1993); *Infanticide: Comparative and Evolutionary Perspectives,* pt. 4 (Glenn Hausfater and Sarah Blaffer Hrdy eds. 1984); Sarah Blaffer Hrdy, "Fitness Tradeoffs in the History and Evolution of Delegated Mothering with Special Reference to Wet-Nursing, Abandonment, and Infanticide," 13 *Ethology and Sociobiology* 409 (1992).

14. Dworkin, "Objectivity and Truth: You'd Better Believe It," note 7 above, at 121.

15. Dworkin appears to confuse slavery in ancient Greece with American Negro slavery. See id. at 121 (reference to "the biological humanity of races they enslaved"). Greek slavery was not racial.

law. One reading of Nietzsche is that he is against morality.[16] But another is that he simply preferred, on aesthetic grounds impossible to refute, the moral code of a warrior society, a code both cruel and inegalitarian, to that of bourgeois society. (He must have liked the aphorism that ends Blake's *The Marriage of Heaven and Hell,* if he knew of it: "One Law for the Lion & Ox is Oppression.")

Nietzscheans are not encountered often in our society, and maybe everyone else agrees that slavery and infanticide are immoral unless justified by the sort of exigent social circumstances that I noted. This will not console a thoughtful moral realist. The immorality of slavery and the immorality of infanticide are for many moralists prime candidates for universal moral principles,[17] yet now we see that they are contingent on local circumstances. The same is true of gruesome forms of punishment,[18] though one need not go as far as Foucault, who seems to have preferred them to modern punishments as being less insidious and therefore less effective in extinguishing rebellious impulses.[19] The only plausible candidates to be universal moral principles are too abstract to guide the resolution of an actual moral dispute. What is more, these moral horrors that we like to denounce, like infanticide and slavery, slip out of focus the more we look at them. What *is* infanticide, exactly? Is it killing a one-week-old fetus? How about an eight-month-old fetus? Is it letting a severely deformed or retarded infant die? And what is slavery exactly? Is it inability to change employers? So were baseball players slaves of the owners before the reserve clause was abolished? Are prison inmates slaves? Children in a regime of compulsory education? Military draftees? Jurors? People who "slave away" at bad jobs and cannot get anything better? All these questions have answers, but not answers that owe anything to a universal moral law.

The constant resort to the rhetoric of objectivity and realism in debating moral issues has been cited as evidence for moral realism.[20] This

16. See Brian Leiter, "Nietzsche and the Morality Critics," 107 *Ethics* 250 (1997). In *On the Genealogy of Morals,* for example, Nietzsche seems to reject morality in favor of health.

17. As Lincoln put it, "If slavery is not wrong, nothing is wrong." Letter of Abraham Lincoln to Albert G. Hodges, April 4, 1864, in *The Collected Works of Abraham Lincoln,* vol. 7, p. 281 (Roy P. Basler ed. 1953). For other examples, see Renford Bambrough, *Moral Scepticism and Moral Knowledge* 19–21 (1979). Bambrough's book is a powerful criticism of moral skepticism but fails to show how any moral issue can actually be resolved unless the contestants' disagreement is at root one of fact.

18. See Richard A. Posner, *Economic Analysis of Law* § 7.2, p. 249 (5th ed. 1998).

19. See Michel Foucault, *Discipline and Punish: The Birth of the Prison* (1977).

20. David O. Brink, *Moral Realism and the Foundations of Ethics* 29 (1989). For criticism of Brink's

mistakes rhetoric for reality. It is the equivalent of treating as evidence for the existence of God the fact that believers talk about God as existing. We dress up our preferences and intuitions in universalistic language to give a patina of objectivity to a subjective belief or emotion.

To say that a moral principle can be judged only by reference to its social setting, or more narrowly still to the common beliefs of its adherents and of its opponents, is not, however, to say that it can never be judged. Some moral principles, like unenforced laws, lag behind social change, and for the same reason: they don't have much practical impact, so the benefits of "repeal" are small; and they require collective action to change, so the costs of repeal are large. The existence of obsolete, or otherwise dysfunctional, moral principles provides a broad field for functional criticism. One reason for the widespread condemnation of the Nazi and Cambodian exterminations, though they were "innovative" rather than inertial, is that we can see in retrospect that they were not adaptive to any plausible or widely accepted need or goal of the societies in question. The genocidal policies that the United States pursued toward the American Indians were adaptive and so receive less criticism, especially as Americans who are not Indian (which is to say, the vast majority of Americans) are the beneficiaries of those policies. Stalin's cruel policies, including purges, induced famine, and forced industrialization, were widely defended when it was thought that they had somehow helped the Soviet Union to prevail in the war against Nazi Germany or prepared the ground for a Utopian society; now that they are known to have been flops, we deride them.

We deplore human sacrifice in part because we are more squeamish than premodern people (a point I'll return to), in part because we instinctively judge other cultures by our own standards, but in part because we know that human sacrifice does not avert drought, flooding, famine, earthquakes, or other disasters and is thus a poor means to a society's ends.[21] When moral claims are founded on testable hypotheses—when, in other words, they are defended as functional—a space is created for moral criticism based on empirical investigation. We can then employ the moral premises of the culture whose morality is at issue, and reasoning from

---

brand of moral realism, see Michele M. Moody-Adams, *Fieldwork in Familiar Places: Morality, Culture, and Philosophy* 137, 174–175 (1997).

21. I emphasize this kind of *instrumental* criticism of moral codes, specifically codes of sexual morality, in Richard A. Posner, *Sex and Reason*, ch. 8 (1992). It seems to me the only defensible way of criticizing a moral code apart from pointing out logical contradictions that are internal to the code.

common premises reach a conclusion that our local interlocutor may be forced as a matter of logic to accept (if he is logical). If the only reason that virgins are hurled into volcanoes is to make crops grow, empirical inquiry should dislodge the practice. But when human sacrificers do not make falsifiable claims for the efficacy of the practice, so that the issue becomes a choice of ends rather than a choice of means to an agreed end (making the crops grow), our critical voice is stilled. Or rather, it becomes a voice expressing disgust—a reaction to difference—rather than a voice uttering reasoned criticisms.

Human sacrifice is passé; a contemporary example of a practice that outrages most Americans is female genital mutilation, which is common among African (including Egyptian) Muslims. Defenders of the practice claim that it is indispensable to maintaining the family in the circumstances in which the practice is followed. The claim is arguable.[22] If it is correct, the moral critic is disarmed; for there is no lever for exalting individual choice or sexual pleasure over family values; the dispute is again over ends rather than over means. For the same reason, it is vacuous to complain that the mutilated girls are often too young to be able to make a responsible choice (assuming they are even given a choice) of whether to undergo the procedure. The moral code of these societies is not founded on principles of freedom, autonomy, or equality, and there is no privileged standpoint from which to argue that it should be. It is equally beside the point to argue that some people in these societies are opposed to female genital mutilation. This is true, and is part of the larger truth that societies are never moral monoliths.[23] There are competing moralities within these societies, as there are within our society. The hope of philosophers who stress the moral diversity within every society is that members of the same society will be reasoning from the same moral premises, so that if they disagree on some moral question this must mean that one of them has made a logical or an empirical mistake, in which event there may be a demonstrably correct answer to the question, at least for that society. The hope is forlorn. Moral contestants, even when they are members of the same society, typically do not agree on all the premises from which they argue. And so moral pluralism provides no leverage for moral critique, but if anything reinforces the lesson of moral relativism.

22. See id. at 256–257.

23. A point stressed by Moody-Adams, note 20 above. With specific reference to female genital mutilation, see id. at 207–211.

Here are two more examples. Abortion is moral in cultures that have liberal attitudes toward sex or that have adopted a feminist ideology, but is immoral in ones that want to limit sexual freedom, promote population growth, or advance religious beliefs in the sanctity of human life. These cultures coexist in the United States, and their respective adherents do not share enough moral common ground to reason to agreement. They can denounce each other, and if they want call each other's moralities immoral. But this is name-calling, rather than appealing to a common set of premises from which persuasive arguments could be derived by logical or empirical means.

Sexual intercourse with animals ("bestiality") was a capital offense in Colonial America, the severity of the punishment reflecting fear that such intercourse could produce dangerous monsters.[24] The fear is now known to have been unfounded, yet many states continue to impose criminal penalties for such intercourse, although not the death penalty.[25] The contemporary statutes are based on a revulsion against "unnatural" sexual acts. Such revulsion is impervious to proof, so the advance of knowledge that dispelled the fear of monstrous progeny does not undermine these statutes as they did the earlier, more severe ones. This example shows that factual inquiry, not moral reasoning, can sometimes have an impact on moral issues, though it failed to reduce the entire issue of punishing bestiality to one of fact.

MORAL PROGRESS

The relativity of morals implies that there is no moral progress in any sense flattering to the residents of wealthy modern nations—that we cannot think of ourselves as being morally more advanced than head shrinkers and cannibals and mutilators of female genitalia. The qualification ("in any sense flattering") is important, however. If someone proposed reintroducing slavery, we would be entitled to regard the proposal as retrogressive. This would imply moral progress since 1860. But we would not be entitled to say that we are morally better than Americans in 1860 either because we all know that slavery is evil and many of them did not or simply because the institution is no more. For in saying that reintroducing slavery would be morally retrogressive we would be describing our own moral feelings rather than appealing to an objective order of morality that

24. John D'Emilio and Estelle B. Freedman, *Intimate Matters: A History of Sexuality in America* 17 (1988).

25. See Richard A. Posner and Katharine B. Silbaugh, *A Guide to America's Sex Laws*, ch. 14 (1996).

might enable moral comparisons to be drawn between us and our predecessors.

A curious aspect of the belief in "objective" moral progress is that we tend to think that the "right" side prevails in most major wars (for example, the Napoleonic Wars, our Civil War, the two world wars, and now the cold war). The causation may run the other way: The winners impose their morality, or their victory demonstrates the flawed factual premises of the losers' moral principles—for example, Hitler's belief that the United States was weak because of its sizable black and Jewish minorities, or Khrushchev's belief that the Soviet Union would surpass the United States in economic productivity.

Educated citizens of wealthy modern nations do know more about the material world than their predecessors and some of their contemporaries; they also have a longer perspective. Armed with their greater knowledge they can show that certain vanished moral codes were not effective instruments for achieving social goals (in some cases that is why these moral codes vanished), and perhaps that some current ones are maladaptive in this sense as well. If a moral code does not further the interests of the dominant groups in a society, or if it weakens the society to the point of making it vulnerable to conquest (even if only by arousing the fear or hatred of a stronger nation), or if it engenders unbearable internal tensions, then either the code or the society will become extinct. The moral code of the antebellum South, the moral code of the Nazis, and the moral code of the Soviet Union are all examples. As we have a different moral code, which naturally we prefer (it is ours), we like to describe the disappearance of the bad old codes as tokens of moral progress.[26] And so we call their adherents "immoral." That is just an epithet. What we should be saying is that the codes of these societies were not adaptive. If a foreign moral code is adaptive, our criticisms of it will not be grounded in premises that the foreign society would accept; the criticisms will just be a

---

26. "Anyone who is convinced that slavery is wrong, *and knows that his view is now shared by almost everyone else,* will think that general moral sensibility has improved, at least in that respect, since slavery was widely practiced and defended." Dworkin, "Objectivity and Truth: You'd Better Believe It," note 7 above, at 120 (emphasis added). Note the uncharacteristic (for Dworkin) conflation of public opinion with moral opinion. And note how this style of argument could have been used in the 1950s to demonstrate the following form of moral "progress" in the domain of sexuality: "Anyone who is convinced that homosexuality is wrong, and knows that his view is now shared by almost everyone else, will think that general moral sensibility has improved, at least in that respect, since homosexuality was widely practiced and defended [for example in ancient Greece]."

statement of our values. If Hitler or Stalin had succeeded in their projects, and if their moral codes had played a role in that success (by promoting discipline or solidarity, perhaps), our moral beliefs would probably be different. We would go around saying things like "You can't make an omelette without breaking eggs." In the end, Hitler and Stalin failed not because their projects were immoral but because their projects were unsound and their system of governance was excessively centralized and hence brittle despite the illusion of strength that centralization conveys.

The case of Stalin, and of communism more generally, casts doubt on the claim that utilitarian and Kantian thought, each in its own way "inclusive" rather than ethnocentric, has "had a revolutionary impact on Western moral thought, despite the fierce resistance it has encountered, and the staggering violence and brutality that have been perpetrated by those committed to reversing it."[27] It is plain from the sentence as a whole, as well as from the discussion that precedes and follows it, that the author considers the "revolutionary impact" of Kantian and utilitarian inclusiveness or universality a sign of moral progress. Yet the staggering violence and brutality inflicted in the name of communism from the days of Lenin and Stalin to those of Mao and Pol Pot were not part of any resistance to inclusiveness. Marxism and communism are internationalist and universalist ideologies, rather than, as Nazism was, racist, nationalist, and sexist. Their violence and brutality were inflicted in the name of a universalist vision (albeit not a Kantian or utilitarian one), though the actual motivation may have had more to do with the perpetrators' personality and political situation than with any body of systematic thought. Even the Nazis, in their own way, were inclusive, having taken the first measures for the protection of endangered animal species.[28] Inclusiveness has no moral valence (if it did, where would the abortion rights movement, which seeks to expel the fetus from the moral community, be?), so its (irregular)

27. Samuel Scheffler, *Human Morality* 10 (1992). This is typical of the claims—and of their ungroundedness—that many philosophers make for the influence of moral philosophy. Compare Schneewind: "That form of life [the Western liberal vision of the proper relations between individual and society] could not have developed without the work of moral philosophers." J. B. Schneewind, *The Invention of Autonomy: A History of Modern Moral Philosophy* 5 (1998). He offers no evidence for this claim.

28. Luc Ferry, *The New Ecological Order,* ch. 5 (1995). The founding statement of the Nazi movement for the protection of animals was by Hitler: "In the Reich cruelty toward animals should no longer exist." Id. at 91. Ferry remarks "the disturbing nature of this alliance between an utterly sincere zoophilia (it was not limited to words but was borne out in law) and the most ruthless hatred of men history has ever known." Id. at 93.

growth in the last two centuries cannot be considered a sign of moral progress. Philosophers' claims of moral progress illustrate the fallacy of teleological history.

The reality of moral progress is questioned, surprisingly, by the anti-relativist Moody-Adams.[29] Pushing hard on the point, for which I cited her earlier, that societies are not moral monoliths, she argues that people have always known that slavery was wrong but have "affected ignorance" of the fact.[30] That is, they have for reasons of self-interest refused to acknowledge the immorality of slavery. There is thus no progress in moral thought; we have always known what is right. Implicitly Moody-Adams is arguing for the universality of moral concepts (such as the evil of slavery) that are far more specific than the rudimentary principles of social cooperation that can claim universality. But her argument is unconvincing. Have there never been, as she implies, *any* sincere believers in slavery? How can she be sure that Aristotle was in bad faith in defending slavery? Or Aquinas? Or Locke? It is not as if people as intelligent as they could not have believed that slavery was moral under some conditions. Religious, prudential, biological, even humane reasons (slavery as the only feasible alternative in early times to killing prisoners of war) were long available in defense of the practice. Some of these reasons were sound given the circumstances in which they were put forward. Others were unsound but represented the best thinking of the period; many premodern biological beliefs are of this character.

Moody-Adams does not examine the reasons that were given for slavery in the past or attempt to weigh them against the arguments for prohibiting slavery. She assumes an implausible plasticity of social arrangements, as if it had really been open to the Greeks to adopt egalitarian policies, or medieval Europeans to become vegetarians or tolerate atheists. In arguing that the history of human misery is a function of insufficient energy in moral inquiry, rather than of material circumstances, she falls prey to the fallacy of believing that because something can be imagined, it must be feasible. The institutions of liberal democracy that make slavery unthinkable, such as universal suffrage and freedom of political speech, depend on material conditions involving income, modes of work, systems of communication, technologies of reproduction, and the extent of literacy and education that did not exist hundreds or thousands of years ago. Even

29. See, for example, Moody-Adams, note 20 above, at 98, 103–106.

30. Id. at 92; see also id. at 101–103. "Affected ignorance" is what the law calls "willful ignorance," what the laity calls acting like an ostrich, and what Sartre called bad faith.

today, such desiderata as equal treatment of men and women may not be feasible for all nations. A nation that lacks the resources necessary to educate its entire population will have to make painful choices that may involve what in a wealthy country would be invidious discrimination. It would be fatuous to think such a nation morally as well as economically backward and to suppose that its situation could be improved by preaching to it.

REALISM AGAIN

Moody-Adams is implicitly positing a mind-independent moral reality, always and everywhere existent, accessible to human intelligence. Most academic moralists today, even if they describe themselves as moral realists, do not assume that there is such a reality; instead, as I noted earlier, they point out that it is not indispensable to objective reasoning. Mathematics is a rigorous discipline, but the ontology of numbers is deeply mysterious. Unicorns do not exist, but it is possible to make true and false assertions about them; for example, the assertion that a unicorn has two horns is false. And in like vein Dworkin, who is not a metaphysical moral realist, claims that "the wrongness of abortion," if it is wrong (which is not his view), "does not depend on anyone's thinking it wrong."[31] Even if, as I believe, Dworkin is incorrect and morality is always a matter of local beliefs (that is, of someone's "thinking it wrong"), within each locale it may be possible to evaluate behavior by its conformity to a moral system, although judgment about the morality of the system itself must be withheld. It is indeed "startlingly counterintuitive to think there is nothing wrong with genocide or slavery or torturing a baby for fun"[32]—in our culture. That's the rub. The moral dictionary is local. Number theory is the same in every language; and unicorns I suppose have one horn regardless of the language. If "unicorn" were defined, in defiance of its etymology, as having anywhere from 1 to n horns, depending on the local language group, it would lose its universality; it would be like a moral term.

The most serious problem for moral theory in today's America is not the absence of a mind-independent or otherwise universal or objective

31. Dworkin, "Objectivity and Truth: You'd Better Believe It," note 7 above, at 99. See also id. at 109. For a powerful criticism of Dworkin's theory of moral objectivity, and of moral realism generally, see Brian Leiter, "Objectivity, Morality, and Adjudication," in *Objectivity in Law and Morals* (Brian Leiter ed., forthcoming).

32. Dworkin, "Objectivity and Truth: You'd Better Believe It," note 7 above, at 118.

moral reality. It is not even international moral pluralism, as dramatized by the case of female genital mutilation. It is moral pluralism *within* the United States. A left-liberal secular humanist from New York or Cambridge does not inhabit the same moral universe as a Mormon elder, an evangelical preacher, a Miami businessman of Cuban extraction, an Orthodox Jew, an Air Force commander, or an Idaho rancher. These universes intersect at various points, but not at the points that interest many academic moralists. The reason that moral pluralism is a problem for moral theory is that without a mind-independent reality *or* a tight logical or linguistic system it is difficult to say, if "the wrongness of abortion does not depend on anyone's thinking it wrong," what its wrongness (or rightness) *does* depend on. The secular humanist, the Mormon elder, and the others do agree that genocide, slavery, and baby torture are wrong. But their agreement is irrelevant because it cannot be stretched to cover any *contested* moral questions, as we would quickly discover by asking a Serb whether the Serbs have committed genocide in Bosnia and a pro-choice feminist whether abortion is a form of baby torture. The acceptability of a moral principle is inverse to its capacity to resolve an actual issue. Facts matter; the Serb may be mistaken about history, about the intentions of Bosnian Muslims, about the motives and beliefs of his own leaders, or about the conduct of other Serbs, and he may change his answers to moral questions if persuaded of the falsity of his factual assumptions. But dispelling factual error is not a task for moral theory or one that moral theorists are equipped by their training or experience to perform.

Michael Perry, a liberal Catholic law professor, argues that objective morality dictates his liberal Catholic position on abortion.[33] Joan Williams, a feminist law professor, shoots his position full of holes.[34] But then, refreshingly, rather than offer her own moral argument, Williams acknowledges that her conviction that the Constitution confers a much broader right of abortion than Perry will acknowledge reflects her "social position as a class-privileged woman in a highly secular society where a key luxury of the ruling class is satisfying work, where work roles are virtually the only avenue to economic independence and social influence, and where attention is typically focused on social rather than spiritual accomplishments" (p. 257). Having confessed the perspectival character

33. Michael J. Perry, *Morality, Politics and Law: A Bicentennial Essay* (1988).
34. Joan Williams, "Religion, Morality, and Other Unmentionables: The Revival of Moral Discourse in the Law," in *In Face of the Facts: Moral Inquiry in American Scholarship* 251, 254–257 (Richard Wightman Fox and Robert B. Westbrook eds. 1998).

of her belief, she properly acknowledges the impossibility of ever reaching agreement on the issue of abortion with people who do not occupy her social position.

SELF-REFERENCE PROBLEMS

The most common philosophical objection to relativism is that it is self-refuting. This would be a compelling objection to my position if I were arguing for *epistemological* relativism or making a *moral* argument for moral relativism. I am doing neither. Consider beauty. A powerful argument can be made that it is relative. Most of us think warthogs ugly, but if warthogs could speak they would tell us that warthogs are beautiful and human beings ugly, and there is no fact to which we and the warthogs could appeal in order to resolve the disagreement. The argument that standards of beauty are relative in this way may be wrong, but it is not self-refuting. If warthogs could speak, they might agree that standards of beauty are relative.

I cannot avoid the paradox of self-reference completely. If moral theory does not convince because it lacks the cogency of scientific reasoning, how likely is this chapter to convince? Why then have I written it, especially if I am right that the academic moralists, against whom the chapter is written, have no impact on either personal behavior or public policy? May it not be that I fear their impact, that it is this fear which has motivated me? I am enough of a Freudian not to consider myself an expert on my own motivations, so I shall say only that fear is not the only possible motivation for writing a book of this kind, that there are degrees of cogency of nonscientific theoretical work, and that I gave a reason earlier for thinking that this chapter might be more persuasive than an argument for a change in moral beliefs or behavior. But can't it be argued that the chapter is covertly moral—is in fact commending a kind of existential morality (antimorality as morality) in which people take responsibility for their actions without the comfort of supposing that they are acting in accordance with universal moral norms? It is like the argument that when Nietzsche opposes health to morality, he is really just opposing one moral theory to another.

These are not trivial or easily answered questions. They recur in the next chapter, where I criticize the very idea of constitutional theory yet might be thought merely to be offering a theory of my own in substitution for the existing theories. But none of the questions undermines my effort to show not that moral philosophy as a whole, let alone morality, is bunk, which is not what I believe, but that the subset of moral philosophy that I call academic moralism is incapable of contributing significantly to the resolution of moral or legal issues or to the improvement of personal behavior.

Reconceiving Morality Functionally

A good deal of moral and immoral behavior is explicable without regard to moral categories.[35] This suggests that moral theory may not have a large domain and that moral discourse may be largely a mystification rooted in a desire to feel good about ourselves—to feel that we are more than just monkeys with big brains, that we are special enough for God to want to be our friend.[36]

Why is it, for example, that the more bystanders there are at the scene of an accident the *less* likely the victim is to be helped?[37] It is not because of deficiencies in moral training or insight; it is because the expected benefit to each bystander of stepping forward—the altruistic benefit of helping a person in distress, discounted (multiplied) by the probability that the victim will not be helped by someone else if you hang back—is less the more bystanders there are. Someone, you think to yourself, will surely step forward, someone better at this sort of thing than you are. The cost to each bystander of intervening is no less, however, so the benefit to each is less likely to equal or exceed the cost.[38]

35. An economist, for example, would explain the intuition behind Judith Jarvis Thomson's suggested solution to the "trolley" hypothetical in two words: ex ante. See "The Trolley Problem," in Thomson, *The Realm of Rights* 176 (1990). A trolley is hurtling down the track, about to kill five people, but it can be switched to a spur where it will kill only one person. This is contrasted with a case in which a surgeon is asked to kill one person and harvest his organs to save five others. It is apparent that people would agree in advance to a regime in which the operator of a dangerous machine tries to minimize the harm caused by it, but it is equally apparent that they would not agree to be subject to being conscripted to be an organ donor with fatal results, though they might well agree to be subject to being conscripted for dangerous military service if necessary to save the nation from a disastrous defeat.

36. Primates, it seems, especially chimpanzees, which are closest to us genetically, behave in accordance with implicit moral codes that are much like those of human beings. See Frans de Waal, *Good Natured: The Origins of Right and Wrong in Humans and Other Animals* (1996).

37. For the evidence, see Bibb Latané, Steve A. Nida, and David W. Wilson, "The Effects of Group Size on Helping Behavior," in *Altruism and Helping Behavior: Social, Personality, and Developmental Perspectives* 287 (J. Philippe Rushton and Richard M. Sorrentino eds. 1981); also Robert B. Cialdini, *Influence: How and Why People Agree to Things* 133–136 (1984).

38. Suppose the benefit of a rescue to a rescuer is 100 and the cost 80. If there is only one potential rescuer, he will rescue, since 100 > 80. But suppose there are ten potential rescuers and each thinks that there is a 30 percent chance that if he doesn't perform the rescue one of the other nine will. Then

The example assumes that there is such a thing as altruism; and indeed there is. But even when directed toward strangers rather than, as is more common, toward members of one's family, altruism need have nothing to do with any moral law or even with morality, though this is in part a matter of how "altruism" is defined. Defined broadly, as helping behavior not motivated by the promise of a reward or the threat of a punishment, it is something that can be and often is motivated by love or by some dilute form of it such as compassion or sympathy. And love and its cognates are not moral sentiments. The injunction to love thy neighbor is an appeal to duty, not to emotion.

The broad definition of altruism leaves open the question whether a particular altruistic act is motivated by love or sympathy or some other positive feeling toward the person helped, by a sense of moral obligation (as academic moralists are predisposed to believe), or by the essentially aesthetic or prideful desire to act in accordance with a heroic conception of oneself.[39] The last of these motivations is underemphasized, even though it identifies a genuine role for moral philosophy, that of self-discovery. Through reading the classics of moral philosophy you might discover that you were an Aristotelian, a Stoic, a Humean, a Rousseauan, a Benthamite, a Millian, a Nietzschean, or even a follower of G. E. Moore. A moralist cannot persuade you by the methods of reason to one morality or another, but he can *offer* you a morality that you can accept or reject for reasons of pride, comfort, convenience, or advantage, though not because it is "right" or "wrong."[40] If you accept it, you can then try to spell out its implications in the hope that so many other people accept it too that your demonstration of those implications will alter people's views on specific issues.[41] Alternatively, you may acquire from the moralist a vocabulary in

each will reckon the net expected value of the rescuing at 70 (.7 × 100). Since the cost (80) now exceeds the (expected) benefit, he will not rescue.

39. See Nancy Eisenberg, *Altruistic Emotion, Cognition, and Behavior,* ch. 3 (1986). Other motivations are possible as well; those motivations are self-interested. See Eric A. Posner, "Altruism, Status, and Trust in the Law of Gifts and Gratuitous Promises," 1997 *Wisconsin Law Review* 567. The infrequency of anonymous donations is evidence that one motive for altruism is a desire to be admired. See id. at 574 n. 17; Amihai Glazer and Kai A. Konrad, "A Signaling Explanation for Charity," 86 *American Economic Review* 1019, 1021 (1996); William M. Landes and Richard A. Posner, "Altruism in Law and Economics," 68 *American Economic Review Papers and Proceedings* 417 (May 1978).

40. A contemporary work in this vein is Richard Rorty, *Achieving Our Country: Leftist Thought in Twentieth-Century America* (1998).

41. Thus in my book *Sex and Reason,* note 21 above, I tried to spell out the implications for the regulation of sex of adopting Mill's political and moral philosophy but disclaimed the possibility of convincing anyone to adopt his philosophy. See id., ch. 8.

which to articulate and refine your preexisting moral views. You may have been a latent Millian who, until reading about self-regarding acts in *On Liberty*, could not have articulated your unease at certain forms of government intervention or social censure.

But the shock of recognition that induces acceptance of a moralist's system need have nothing to do with truth or reasoned argument—or even with altruism. Much of the appeal of the Sermon on the Mount, as of religious rigorism generally, is precisely its impracticability; it provides a guide for action that will set the actor apart from the herd; it appeals to a sense of pride, of feeling oneself to be exceptional.

Thus, rather than poets and novelists being moral philosophers manqué, moral philosophers are poets and novelists manqué. They can do no more for our moral development than poets and novelists, who give us different worldviews, different perspectives or vocabularies, to try on for size.[42] This is not nothing, but it is different from changing the reader's moral views through reasoned argument. Plato's paean to homosexual love in the *Symposium* was passed over in embarrassed silence by his admirers for many centuries until a change in sexual mores made it available as a prestigious citation in support of the change. Until then it fell flat because not enough people were sympathetic to homosexuals for his message to fructify. When Plato wrote, philosophy had not yet become academified, and the line between it and literature was indistinct. The *Symposium* is a moving work, but it contains no arguments or evidence that would trouble those who believe that homosexuality should be discouraged. It moves us as literature moves us. At its best, moral philosophy, like literature, enriches; it neither proves nor edifies.

Evaluative literary criticism bears the same relation to literature as the exegetical works of modern moral philosophy bear to its canonical works. A literary critic cannot give the reader convincing reasons why one work of literature is finer than another unless the reader happens to agree on what the criterion of literary quality should be. But the critic can point to

42. See Richard A. Posner, *Law and Literature* 326–332 (enlarged and rev. ed. 1998). Cf. Rorty: "It would be better [for Western moral philosophers] to say: Here is what we in the West look like as a result of ceasing to hold slaves, beginning to educate women, separating church and state, and so on. Here is what happened after we started treating certain distinctions between people as arbitrary rather than fraught with moral significance. If you would try treating them that way, you might like the results." Richard Rorty, "Justice as a Larger Loyalty," in *Justice and Democracy: Cross-Cultural Perspectives* 9, 19–20 (Ron Bontekoe and Marietta Stepaniants eds. 1997). See also Rorty, "Philosophy as a Kind of Writing: An Essay on Derrida," in *Pragmatism: A Reader* 304 (Louis Menand ed. 1997); James M. Jasper, *The Art of Moral Protest: Culture, Biography, and Creativity in Social Movements* 370 (1997) ("like artists, they [protest organizers] are offering us visions to 'try on' so we can see what fits").

features of the work that the reader may have missed and that, when understood, may move the reader to enthusiasm for the work. Evaluative literary criticism is more apt to sway people than moral theory is because people's aesthetic commitments are usually weaker than their moral commitments.

This is not to deny that the classic moral philosophers had insight into human personality and aspirations and the requisites of human cooperation. To the extent that the social conditions that molded their views persist in our society, these philosophers have something to say to us that is not just poetry, although why it has to be said in their original voice rather than restated in a modern idiom unconcerned with maintaining continuity with the classics is mysterious. Consider Benthamism. Its details are anachronistic, and sometimes absurd even by the standards of Bentham's time; and we saw that utilitarianism as a philosophy can be made to seem absurd just by pressing it to its logical conclusion. But in the conditions of modernity, any viable society is going to have to concern itself with the happiness of the population. There is nothing in theory to refute a Nietzschean project of maximizing the power of an elite;[43] it just is not in the cards in an age in which the increase and diffusion of wealth have made the average person, not just the exceptional one, self-confident and assertive. Utilitarianism epitomizes this inevitability and so cannot be completely refuted.

But I have strayed from the topic, which is altruism. Evolutionary biology hypothesizes that altruism derives from the evolutionary imperative of inclusive fitness—the drive to maximize the number of copies of one's genes by maximizing the number of creatures carrying them weighted by the closeness of the relation.[44] The inclusive fitness of a social animal like man is greatly increased by his having a proclivity to help his relatives, so it is plausible that this proclivity evolved as an adaptive mechanism.[45] In the prehistoric era in which our instinctual preferences were formed, people probably lived in small, isolated bands, so most of

43. See Leiter, note 31 above, at 36–39; Felix E. Oppenheim, "Justification in Ethics: Its Limitations," in *Justification (Nomos XXVIII)* 28 (J. Roland Pennock and John W. Chapman eds. 1986).

44. See, for example, Matt Ridley and Richard Dawkins, "The Natural Selection of Altruism," in *Altruism and Helping Behavior,* note 38 above, at 19; Elliott Sober and David Sloan Wilson, *Unto Others: The Evolution and Psychology of Unselfish Behavior* (1998); Robert Trivers, *Social Evolution,* chs. 3, 6, 15 (1985). So, other things being equal, having three nephews (each a 25 percent genetic copy of you) will contribute more to your inclusive fitness than having one child (a 50 percent genetic copy).

45. See, for example, Susan M. Essock-Vitale and Michael T. McGuire, "Predictions Derived from the Theories of Kin Selection and Reciprocation Assessed by Anthropological Data," 1 *Ethology and Sociobiology* 233 (1980).

the people with whom they dealt were people with whom they had *continuous* dealings. It may not have been essential, therefore, to be able to discriminate between intimates, with whom one had relations based on trust as a result of blood ties or reciprocal dealings, and those others—call them "strangers"—with whom one did not have repeated face-to-face interactions.[46] Conditions today are different. We interact a great deal with strangers. But the genes are easily fooled when confronted with conditions to which man did not have a chance to adapt biologically because they did not exist in prehistoric times. That is why a pornographic photograph can arouse a person sexually or a violent movie frighten the audience, why people are more frightened of spiders than of cars, and why men do not clamor to be allowed to donate to sperm banks. Voting, giving to charities, and refraining from littering, in circumstances in which there is neither visible reward for these cooperative behaviors nor visible sanctions for defection, may illustrate an instinctual, and as it were biologically mistaken, generalization of cooperation from small-group interactions, in which altruism is rewarded (and thus reciprocal) and failures to reciprocate punished, to large-group interactions in which the prospects of reward and punishment are so slight that cooperation ceases to be rational.[47] Charities know that the way to get people to give money for the feeding of starving children is to publish a picture of a starving child, seeking thereby to trigger feelings of sympathy, rather than to talk about a moral duty. (Probably most Americans would be offended to be told, other than by their own religious advisors, that it was their *duty* to support the needy.)

We react to such appeals, and approve of others who react that way, not because there is a moral law but because we are a social animal. A cat is not. If it sees another cat (unless its own kitten) in distress, it reacts with indifference. This is not because cats are stupid, but because the fewer cats

46. Paul H. Rubin, "Evolved Ethics and Efficient Ethics," 3 *Journal of Economic Behavior and Organization* 161, 165–167 (1982); Rubin, "The State of Nature and the Origin of Legal Institutions" 5, 12 (Emory University Department of Economics, unpublished, 1998); Charles J. Morgan, "Natural Selection for Altruism in Structured Populations," 6 *Ethology and Sociobiology* 211 (1985); Morgan, "Eskimo Hunting Groups, Social Kinship, and the Possibility of Kin Selection in Humans," 1 *Ethology and Sociobiology* 83 (1979).

47. See Cristina Bicchieri, "Learning to Cooperate," in *The Dynamics of Norms* 17, 39 (Cristina Bicchieri, Richard Jeffrey, and Brian Skyrms eds. 1997); Oded Stark, *Altruism and Beyond: An Economic Analysis of Transfers and Exchanges within Families and Groups* 132 (1995). Generalization (less grandly, pattern recognition) seems an innate, and very valuable but of course fallible, capacity of the human animal. Rubin, "The State of Nature and the Origin of Legal Institutions," note 46 above, at 11–14, points out the flexible definition of the "in group" whose members are bound together by altruism would have been valuable for survival even under prehistoric conditions, and so may be an evolved capacity.

there are, the better it is for cats—the hunting is easier. Cats grow up solitary; children grow up in groups. A moral code will develop in children from their interactions with each other and with adults.[48]

Some feminists admire bonobos, a species of primate in which the female is dominant. It would make as much sense to admire sharks, vultures, or leeches. These creatures are adapted each to its particular environment, which is neither our environment when we evolved to our present state (the "ancestral environment," as evolutionary biologists call it) nor our present environment.[49] To admire bonobos or deplore sharks is like calling a warthog ugly. A shark that had a moral lexicon would pronounce the eating of human swimmers moral, just as a warthog with an aesthetic vocabulary would snort derisively at the Venus de Milo.

Evolutionary biology has a further bearing on moral reasoning: it suggests a reason why we may not be very good at it. If human beings evolved to their present biological state when they were living in tiny, isolated bands, they didn't need morality in its modern sense of a set of duties toward unknown persons as well. So there is no reason to believe that the human brain evolved a capacity for reasoning intelligently about moral questions. Of course we can reason on many matters that were of no concern to our remote ancestors; the brain is to a considerable extent a general-purpose reasoning machine. Yet we find it difficult to reason about such questions as whether we have free will, what there was before the universe (or before time), and how causality operates (if it does operate) at the subatomic level—questions that lack close counterparts in those that confronted early man. The question of what duties we have to complete strangers may be baffling because it likewise is remote from the questions that troubled our very distant ancestors.

The Moral Sentiments

Altruism as I have discussed it thus far fits comfortably into the picture of man as "economic man," motivated by self-interest; you help a stranger because you "like" him or her, even if only momentarily. But not all acts of

---

48. See Jean Piaget, *The Moral Judgment of the Child* (1948). See generally *Psychological Foundations of Moral Education and Character Development* (Richard T. Knowles and George F. McLean eds. 1992).

49. "Bonobo society offers females a more relaxed existence [than chimpanzee society] . . . The rich forest habitat of the bonobo evidently permits such an organization. Our ancestors . . . adapted to a much harsher environment [the savanna]. It is dubious that a bonobolike primate could have made it in a savanna habitat while keeping its social system intact." Frans de Waal, *Bonobo: The Forgotten Ape* 135 (1997). But it is legitimate for feminists to invoke bonobos against anyone who claims that the behavior of primates shows that human males are inherently patriarchal.

helping are directed toward people we like or feel sympathy for. Some of us will make a sacrifice to help people we actually dislike; this is not uncommon in the dealings people have with their aged parents. This kind of altruism, when it is not just showing off, is the product of a genuine moral sentiment. Call it dutiful or disinterested altruism. The converse is the indignation we direct at people who misbehave even if their misbehavior imposes no cost on us. These emotions, and the behaviors they impel, reflect the influence of rules that are obeyed (though not by everyone) even when there is no legal or other tangible sanction for disobedience or reward for obedience.

The efficacy of such rules might seem to imply the existence of a moral faculty—a faculty that moral theories might move—alongside the faculty of rational calculation of advantage and disadvantage. But all that the moral emotions really imply is that we are a social animal with a large brain. The sociality makes desirable, and the large brain makes feasible, the development and enforcement of rules of social cooperation and differentiation as an alternative to the kind of hard-wired role differentiation found in ants. The most important rules of cooperation in a human society are embodied in its moral code. To be effective, the rules must be obeyed. Many of them are self-enforcing; if you don't cooperate with other people, they won't cooperate with you, and so you'll lose the benefits of cooperation. Some rules are enforced by law. Some become internalized as duties whose violation engenders the disagreeable feeling that we call guilt. Where there are no sanctions at all, not even guilt (and not all people feel guilt if they violate a particular provision of their society's moral code), it is difficult to understand why a person would obey such a rule unless it were consistent with self-interest; that is, the *motivational* effect of an unenforced rule is obscure.[50] I shall return to that point; for the present I wish only to point out that the capacity to feel guilt, and the moral emotions more broadly, imply the existence not of a distinctive moral faculty but merely of internalized rules of conduct. Such rules often are morally indifferent. We feel guilty if we forget to brush our teeth. Lady Macbeth felt guilty about being unable to stab Duncan while he slept. She is an unusual "person," who like many Shakespearean villains (Iago is the clearest example) seems particularly villainous because her viciousness is not adequately motivated, is gratuitous. But guilt about "yielding" to pity is not unusual and is not always misplaced.

50. See John Deigh, *The Sources of Moral Agency: Essays in Moral Psychology and Freudian Theory* (1996), esp. ch. 7.

Other moralistic reactions, such as indignation, also bear no steady relation to morality. We are more indignant at the driver who runs down a child carelessly than at the more careless driver who through sheer luck misses the child.[51] The difference between our reactions is difficult to refer to morality; it is more easily referred to altruism, which comes into play only in the first incident. We are hurt by the loss of the child even though it is not our own child. Altruism typically is nonmoral—like love—so the example shows that the moral emotions are independent of morality, or at least of any consistent body of moral rules. Members of a criminal gang are indignant about informers; the *quality* of their emotion is the same as that of the good citizen who is indignant about traitors; the only difference is who is included in the primary circle of altruistic feeling.

There may be *more* moral sentiment in the average gang member than in the average law-abiding citizen. Law, a substitute for moral sentiment, is unavailable to gang members. They are forced back on the oldest system for enforcing human cooperation. Even before there was a state with coercive powers, there must have been rules of conduct, explicit or implicit but more or less enforced; a human society could not survive without such rules. Obtaining compliance with them must have depended on the moral emotions as well as on supernatural beliefs, force and the threat of force, and love and reciprocal altruism. The universality of these emotions, their inarticulateness, their beginnings in very early childhood,[52] their survival value under the conditions in which early man lived, and their animal parallels all suggest that they are instinctual,[53] just as altruism is. Because they are instinctual, they continue to be an important element of human psychology, and they are evidence that this psychology is indeed more complex than assumed in the simplest economic models of self-

---

51. See Bernard Williams, "Moral Luck," in his book *Moral Luck: Philosophical Papers 1973–1980* 20 (1981); also Williams, "Moral Luck: A Postscript," in his book *Making Sense of Humanity, and Other Philosophical Papers 1982–1993* 241 (1995). This point is overlooked in James Griffin's discussion of the "fat tourist" moral dilemma. See Griffin, *Value Judgement: Improving Our Ethical Beliefs* 102–103, 110 (1996). The fat tourist is blocking, albeit innocently, the way to safety of a group of thin tourists; killing him to remove the block is not the same atrocity (as Griffin believes) as killing an innocent person who does not have any causal relation to the peril of others in order to save the others. Why sheer causality, shorn of any triggering effect on altruism, should affect our moral sentiments is a big puzzle for moralists.

52. See generally *The Emergence of Morality in Young Children* (Jerome Kagan and Sharon Lamb eds. 1987).

53. See Robert L. Trivers, "The Evolution of Reciprocal Altruism," 46 *Quarterly Review of Biology* 35, 49 (1971); J. Hirshleifer, "Natural Economy versus Political Economy," 1 *Journal of Social and Biological Structures* 319, 332, 334 (1978).

interested behavior.[54] Originally the moral emotions would have operated primarily within the family. But their potential scope was broader, for the reason discussed earlier.

Emotions have a cognitive element, not only in the sense of often being triggered by information, but also in the sense of expressing an evaluation.[55] To be indignant about some act of which one has learned is to disapprove of it. But as the example of the criminal gang suggests, the moralistic emotions have no fixed objects. They are morally neutral in the same way that a schedule of criminal punishments (one year's probation, six months in jail, ten years in the penitentiary, a $5,000 fine) is neutral with respect to the substantive content of the criminal law; different societies attach the same punishments to different conduct. The universality of the moral emotions no more proves the existence of a universal moral law than the universality of criminal punishment proves the existence of a universal criminal law. The moral emotions are enforcers, generally of norms important to cooperation. But the content of those norms is relative to the needs, circumstances, and history of particular cultures. A culture might have a norm of genocide, in which case the focus of indignation would be resistance by the victims.

It is thus misleading to cite indignation as an example of an emotion that "presuppose[s] moral beliefs" and so together with like emotions demonstrates "the ramification of moral concerns throughout our mental and social lives."[56] All that indignation demonstrates, even when it is disinterested in the sense of not being triggered by an infringement of the indignant person's own rights or interests, is that groups have norms the violation of which can trigger emotional reactions. The norms can be as ugly as one pleases.

The Academic Moralist and the Moral Entrepreneur

The Problem of Motivation

The ambition of the academic moralist is to change people's moral beliefs to the end of changing their behavior (why try to change their beliefs otherwise?). The ambition is unrealistic. It is not even clear why a change

54. For a comprehensive discussion, see Matthew Rabin, "Psychology and Economics," 36 *Journal of Economic Literature* 11 (1998).

55. See, for example, Robert C. Solomon, *The Passions* (1976); Ronald de Sousa, *The Rationality of Emotion* (1987); Martha C. Nussbaum, *Upheavals of Thought: A Theory of the Emotions* (University of Chicago Law School, 1997, unpublished).

56. Scheffler, note 27 above, at 68.

in moral beliefs should be expected to lead to a change in behavior. Academic moralists believe that if one is persuaded that one ought to do something because it is the moral thing to do, this recognition, this acceptance, will furnish a motive to do it; Kantians believe that it is irrational to act otherwise.[57] Yet not only is there no logical contradiction in saying "I know I should donate a kidney to my sick brother, but I'm not going to do so"; there is no direct causal relation between perception, moral or otherwise, and action. Merely *seeing* a train bearing down on you will not make you want to get out of its way, though we talk as if it would. The perception does not contain a desire to avoid pain or death. Being persuaded that a proposed course of action would be morally wrong might lead to your changing course because you are the kind of person who obtains satisfaction from doing what you think is the right thing, but the satisfaction would have to come from somewhere else than the moral code. You would have to *want* to obey the code. Criminals, if we set to one side their "exaggerated" group loyalties, generally have the same moral beliefs as the law-abiding.[58] They just don't want to act on those beliefs.

The problem of motivation might seem as acute in science as in morality, but is not. Why should a scientist seek truth rather than (when they conflict) happiness?[59] Because the institutions of science have been designed to reward scientists for true discoveries and punish them for false ones. Moral codes also come with machinery for aligning individual self-interest with the social interest embodied in the code. The part of a moral code that overlaps with the law is enforced by legal sanctions. Other parts are self-enforcing, that is, are enforced by the threat of retaliation or of withdrawal of cooperation by other participants in the system of morality. But most academic moralists, though not those who hope to get the ear of judges or legislators, believe that enforcement is beside the point, that all the moralist has to do is convince people of what is right and compliance will follow.

Sometimes it does follow. Some people take pride in being "good,"

57. See, for example, Christine M. Korsgaard, "Kant's Formula of Universal Law," 66 *Pacific Philosophical Quarterly* 24 (1985).

58. Wilson, note 13 above, at 11. Most people are not criminals, but I am unaware of evidence that would permit an estimate of how many of the law-abiding refrain from crime for reasons of morality as distinct from fear of punishment, lack of motive, altruism (natural rather than dutiful), or other considerations of self-interest narrowly or broadly defined.

59. Cf. David Bloor, *Knowledge and Social Imagery* 10–11 (2d ed. 1991); Brian Z. Tamanaha, *Realistic Socio-Legal Theory: Pragmatism and a Social Theory of Law* 163–167 (1997); Dick Pels, "Karl Mannheim and the Sociology of Scientific Knowledge: Toward a New Agenda," 14 *Sociological Theory* 30 (1996).

which is to say better than most other people. But that is pride rather than morality. It is related to the striving for status, a striving that need not require either publicity or the prospect of material gain.[60] A person can derive satisfaction from knowing that he is better dressed than anyone around him, though only he knows this, and likewise from knowing that he does not yield to the temptations of petty cheating or other minor vices that most of his fellows do.

Moral pride is not a dependable spur to moral behavior. It is object neutral and therefore consistent with romantic outlawry and other dangerous forms of egoism. A different kind of person from that envisaged by academic moralists—a Promethean or a Nietzschean rather than a Swedish socialist or a scrupulously observant Christian—might take pride in flouting the norms of those who, in Nietzsche's phrase, are tame because they have no claws. Such a person might agree with Nietzsche that moral preening is a form of self-aggrandizement psychologically no different from the antisocial forms.[61] This person might consider nature normative and therefore rebel against trying to make people more sociable than they were before the rise of organized societies.

Conceivably a person might want to do the conventionally right thing because he was innately good (so Augustine was wrong), or perhaps innately nothing but made good by education. It would be perilous to put much weight on either possibility. So academic moralists who want to alter behavior, as they must want to do in order to feel good about their profession unless they are just dilettantes or careerists, ought to worry a lot about how to motivate people to do what they persuade them is the "right" thing to do, just as legal scholars ought to worry about how to motivate life-tenured federal judges to behave in accordance with the best conception of the judicial function.[62]

The problem of motivation does not vitiate the academic moralists' project completely. As I said earlier, there is a machinery for enforcing the

60. See Robert H. Frank, *Choosing the Right Pond: Human Behavior and the Quest for Status* 23–38 (1985); Elias L. Khalil, "Symbolic Products: Prestige, Pride and Identity Goods" (Ohio State University–Mansfield, Department of Economics, 1997, unpublished).

61. The egotism of altruism is illustrated by the opening sentence of Bertrand Russell's autobiography: "Three passions, simple but overwhelmingly strong, have governed my life: the longing for love, the search for knowledge, and *unbearable pity for the suffering of mankind.*" *The Autobiography of Bertrand Russell, 1872–1914* 3 (1951) (emphasis added). For some tart words on the altruistic personality, see James Fitzjames Stephen, "Philanthropy," in Stephen, *Liberty, Equality, Fraternity—and Three Brief Essays* 292 (1990 [essay first published in 1859]).

62. On the problem of judicial motivation, see Richard A. Posner, *Overcoming Law*, ch. 3 (1995).

moral code. If an academic moralist can persuade enough people to change their views, the moral code will change, and the enforcement machinery will click in and many people will obey the new norms, especially if the norms are embodied in law, as many moral precepts are. But the first "if" is a big one. Remember that morality is a domain of duty. People resist the piling on them of additional duties. Even if human beings are innately good or are made good by education or are proud to be good, the vast majority of them—of us—are unwilling to pay a high price in selfish joys and comforts forgone to be good. In fact we are reluctant to pay *any* price to be good. We can avoid having to pay, without suffering the pangs of conscience, by denying that morality requires us to act otherwise than as we are acting.

Academic moralists strive to prevent that denial but lack the requisite tools. They have a lot to overcome, compared say to literary critics; that's why the moralists need *cogent* arguments, not just plausible ones. Also, unlike literary critics, to have any effect they have to convince a large number of people to change their ways. For until that happens, people who refuse to change will not bear any social sanctions for their refusal; they will remain the moral majority.

A person's moral code is not a balloon that the philosopher's pinprick will burst; it is a self-sealing tire. For every argument on one side of a moral issue there is an equally good one on the other side. Even if it is not "really" equally good (that is, even if some nontrivial version of moral realism is correct), the lack of any agreed means of measuring ("weighing") moral arguments will make a pair of opposing arguments equal enough to create a standoff. It is ironic that so many moral theorists attack "commodification" (that is, commercialization) on the ground of incommensurability—for example, of money and health—when moral debate offers so many better examples of incommensurability, of the lack of a common metric of comparison. Incommensurables can be compared; we compare them whenever we choose between them, and that is often. They can even be rationally compared, in the sense that rational arguments can be made on both sides of a face-off between incommensurables.[63] But the volleying back and forth of these rational arguments does not result in victory for one side; the ball is too easy (or too hard—it makes no difference) to return. In a debate between a conservative Catholic natural lawyer and a radical feminist, for example, the premises from which each of the debat-

63. See generally *Incommensurability, Incomparability, and Practical Reason* (Ruth Chang ed. 1997).

ers starts are so different that the arguments of the two sides cannot be put in the same scale and weighed. We saw that this was true even when the debate was between a *liberal* Catholic natural lawyer (Michael Perry) and a *liberal*, not radical, feminist (Joan Williams).

Debate either will be interminable or will be resolved by a change in social conditions or by force (politics in one form or another), or sometimes by a charismatic moral innovator. For think: when was the last time a moral code was changed by rational persuasion, intoning or refining the arguments of Aristotle, Aquinas, Kant, Hegel, or Mill? Rational debate often *entrenches* moral disagreement, by forcing the debaters to take a stand, to recognize their differences, to commit themselves.[64] Think how we acquire our moral views. We acquire them mostly in childhood, when moral instruction based on theory takes a back seat to parental example, to peer pressure, to other experience, and to religion.[65] Once ingrained in us, a morality is difficult to change. Sometimes it is changed, but either by material circumstances (or factual information) or by a very different type of moral advocate from the academic moralist—a "moral entrepreneur."

Moral entrepreneurs typically try to change the boundaries of altruism, whether by broadening them, as in the case of Jesus Christ and Jeremy Bentham, or by narrowing them, as in the case of Hitler (putting to one side his "zoophilia"). They don't do this with arguments, or at least good ones. Rather, they mix appeals to self-interest with emotional appeals that bypass our rational calculating faculty and stir inarticulable feelings of oneness with or separateness from the people (or it could be land, or animals) that are to constitute, or be ejected from, the community that the moral entrepreneur is trying to create. They teach us to love or hate whom they love or hate. The techniques of nonrational persuasion, which prominently include the example of their own way of life, that moral entrepreneurs employ are not part of the normal equipment of scholars.[66]

64. Once having taken a position, a person will tend to interpret subsequent evidence as supporting it ("confirmation bias"); therefore argument may, simply by eliciting evidence on both sides of the controversy, have a polarizing effect. Rabin, note 54 above, at 26–28.

65. See Robert Coles, *The Moral Intelligence of Children* (1997), esp. pp. 179–182.

66. Martha Nussbaum acknowledges the tension between moral philosophers and moral entrepreneurs (whom she calls "prophets"). Nussbaum, "Rage and Reason," *New Republic*, Aug. 11 and 18, 1997, p. 36. She notes that "Mill's *The Subjection of Women* didn't have much influence with its calm, rational arguments." Id. at 37. Yet Mill, who was not a professor, was less academic than modern philosophers. And it is noteworthy that Bentham, an extremely influential moral entrepreneur, published very little of what he wrote, devoting most of his time to formulating and trying to "sell" practical schemes (ranging from universal suffrage to the Panopticon prison) that embodied his philosophical ideas, rather than to academic-style writing. The abolitionist movement was powered

More precisely, these techniques are not used by the vast majority of scholars; for there are examples of moral entrepreneurship in the modern academy,[67] even the modern legal academy, the outstanding example there being Catharine MacKinnon. Her influential version of radical feminism is not offered without supporting arguments. But her influence is not due to the quality of those arguments. It is due to her polemical skills, her singlemindedness, her passion, and what passes for martyrdom in the academy today: her inability, until well into her career, indeed until long after she had become one of the most influential legal thinkers in the nation, to obtain tenure—a setback that was due to her defiance of the conventional norms of academic law. An example of failed moral entrepreneurship in the legal academy is Duncan Kennedy, a more proficient scholar than MacKinnon but a less impressive personality and one handicapped in the moral entrepreneurship sweepstakes by his early receipt of tenure from the Harvard Law School. This gave him a status that makes his rebellious stance faintly ridiculous. He personifies that oxymoron the "tenured radical."

Religions know that to motivate people to act against or outside their normal conception of self-interest requires carrots and sticks, rituals to build a sense of community, habituation, and either pageantry or an ostentatious simplicity. The military knows, and early Christianity knew, that motivating people to sacrifice or to risk their lives requires psychology to forge group loyalties and often the promise of posthumous rewards, whether salvation or glory.[68] You won't get far by trying to persuade people that your cause is, upon reflection, morally best.

The Christian martyrs and the Japanese *shimpu* (kamikaze) pilots are impressive examples of the ability to transcend a quotidian sense of self-

---

much more by religious enthusiasm than by Enlightenment rationality, which diluted its universalistic moral principles with "scientific" racism. See David Brion Davis, *Slavery and Human Progress*, pt. 2 (1984), esp. pp. 108, 131–135.

67. The clearest example in philosophy is Peter Singer, whose book *Animal Liberation*, first published in 1975 (a revised edition was published in 1990), played a significant role in the growth of the animal rights movement. See, for example, Gary L. Francione, *Rain without Thunder: The Ideology of the Animal Rights Movement* 51–53 (1996). Singer's book is written for a general audience. It contains little technical philosophy, makes little effort to respond to philosophical criticisms, and relies heavily on vivid descriptions of animal suffering (including photographs) for its effectiveness. Jasper, note 42 above, at 167, calls Singer's book "a gold mine of gruesome photos," but points out that the idea of animal *rights*, which has been extremely influential (remember the name of the movement), owes nothing to Singer's book (Singer is a utilitarian) and is philosophically dubious. Id. at 167–168.

68. See, for example, Rodney Stark, *The Rise of Christianity: A Sociologist Reconsiders History* 179–194 (1996).

interest, the kind of ability that moral philosophers want to develop in us in at least a diluted form.[69] In neither case was the motivation founded on moral theory; and it is possible to regard the martyrs as fools and the kamikazes as murderers. This suggests that it's not even certain that we want people to be *really* "good." It might make them dangerously docile— one recalls Churchill's description of German soldiers in World War II as "lethal sheep." A society that has lots of rather selfish, rather shallow, and even rather cowardly people may be best, though this may depend on whether the society's goal is glory or happiness. Which goal it should be the moral philosopher cannot say, though a military expert might say that the goal of glory, if defined in terms of military success, is or is not attainable in a particular society, and a psychologist or a sociologist might say that the goal of happiness is or is not attainable in another society.

The existence of moral entrepreneurship may seem inconsistent with an adaptationist theory of morality. If morality reflects the material needs of a society, how can it be changed unless those needs change? The answer lies in the fact noted earlier that because moral norms are usually created by a decentralized process rather than imposed by a legislature or a supreme court, there is often a lag between a change in material conditions and the adaptation of the moral code to the new conditions. American Negro slavery became anachronistic in the eighteenth or early nineteenth century, and its successor, the Jim Crow laws, during World War II. The anachronistic character of these moral systems created fertile ground for moral entrepreneurs, such as Lincoln in the earlier period and Martin Luther King, Jr., in the later. Successful moral entrepreneurs are like arbitrageurs in the securities markets. (The unsuccessful are apt to be dismissed as cranks.) They spot the discrepancy between the existing code and the changing environment and persuade the society to adopt a new, more adaptive code. That is why we usually find successful examples of moral entrepreneurship in periods or places of crisis, flux, or transition.

69. During and for years after World War II, most Americans believed that the kamikaze pilots had been drunk, chained into their cockpits, or otherwise coerced or bamboozled into undertaking suicide attacks. We now know that the pilots were genuine volunteers and that most of them were motivated by altruism, honor, duty, and patriotism. See, for example, Edwin P. Hoyt, *The Kamikazes* (1983); Rikihei Inoguchi and Tadashi Nakajima, *The Divine Wind: Japan's Kamikaze Force in World War II*, ch. 21 (1958); Bernard Millot, *Divine Thunder: The Life and Death of the Kamikazes* (1971); Richard O'Neill, *Suicide Squads: Axis and Allied Special Attack Weapons of World War II: Their Development and Their Missions*, chs. 1, 4, 5 (1981).

The Scholarship of Morality

MORAL VERSUS FUNCTIONAL ANALYSIS

Social scientists can criticize moral codes by showing a lack of functionality, of instrumental efficiency or rationality. They might point out that norms against polygamy and homosexuality are functional in societies that place a high value (for practical reasons, be it added) on companionate marriage, but are anachronisms when the social importance of marriage declines, so that people who are unmarried by choice become less anomalous (as may be happening in wealthy nations today). (I touch on this issue in the next chapter, in discussing Martha Nussbaum's testimony in the *Romer* case.) Or they might point out that while the kind of vengeance-promoting code of "honor" found in the Homeric and other primitive societies, and in the American South and West in the nineteenth century, is functional when the state is very weak, its survival in parts of the modern-day American South is dysfunctional, causing more violence than it deters.[70]

Benjamin Franklin said that honesty is the best policy; and one way to interpret this precept is that for people who have a better prospect than to be members of the criminal class a steady policy of honesty is a more dependable formula for maximizing one's self-interest than the cleverer-seeming policy of choosing between honesty and dishonesty on a case-by-case basis. Even criminals, especially when they operate in gangs, might, as I suggested earlier, be better off if they behaved honestly toward their associates. Because the requisites for survival in the conditions in which humankind evolved have made us innately skillful at "reading" people for signs of sincerity and insincerity, the best way to show oneself as trustworthy is to be trustworthy, rather than to employ trustworthiness as an occasional tactic—as a mask that might slip at a critical time. Altruistic parents may wish to instill a norm, enforced by guilt or shame, in their children for the sake of the children's own advancement rather than because the parents have been persuaded by moral philosophers that honesty is right for everyone. It is right for them and for their children, but for instrumental reasons. The benefits of habitual, hence sincere, unstrategic, compliance with the norm may exceed the costs of occasionally forgoing a

70. See Richard E. Nisbett and Dov Cohen, *Culture of Honor: The Psychology of Violence in the South* (1996), esp. pp. 88–91; David Hackett Fischer, *Albion's Seed: Four British Folkways in America* 892 (1989).

dishonest advantage. And the cost of guilt will never be incurred if the norm is so well and deeply planted that it is never violated.

It may be objected that functionality or survival is just another moral norm, so that to commend it as a guide to the study of morality is to do what academic moralists do—defend a controversial moral stance. But this objection confuses instrumental reasoning with reasoning about ends, and value clarification with value argument. To advise a person or, for that matter, an entire society about the consequences of alternative paths to the goal that the person or society has chosen is not to commit oneself to a moral view. If a person wants not to live but to die, the expert can advise that person about the different methods of bringing about death—their cost, legality, associated pain, length of time required, and so forth. If a society wants to die—if it has a Masada complex—the expert can likewise advise it on the means. Most societies want to survive, so the usual social functionalist analysis, the sort of thing that economists do all the time, is oriented in a more positive direction. The point is that the expert, the scholar, does not choose the goal, but is confined to studying the paths to the goal and so avoids moral issues. If, as is sometimes the case, the goals of the society are contested—some people want prosperity while others would sacrifice prosperity to equality—then all the expert can do is show how particular policies advance or retard each goal. He cannot arbitrate between the goals unless they are intermediate goals—way stations to a goal that commands a consensus.

Economists ranging from Stanley Jevons and Francis Edgeworth to Oscar Lange and Abba Lerner and thence to Friedrich Hayek, Milton Friedman, John Harsanyi, Murray Rothbard, and David Friedman have tried to make of economics a source of moral guidance by proposing, often under the influence of utilitarianism, that the goal of a society should be to maximize average utility, or total utility, or wealth, or freedom, or equality (not for its own sake but as a means toward maximizing utility), or some combination of these things. These are doomed efforts. What economists can say, which is a lot but not everything, is that *if* a society values prosperity (or freedom, or equality), here are policies that will conduce to the goal and here are the costs associated with each. They cannot take the final step and say that society ought to aim at growth, equality, happiness, survival, conquest, stasis, social justice, or anything else. Economists discussing a "hot" topic, such as whether human cloning should be permitted, might estimate the private benefits and social costs (as these terms are understood in economics) of human cloning, and even advise on the consequences of ignoring costs and benefits in fashioning public policy. But they could not tell policymakers how much weight to give costs and benefits as a matter of social justice.

HIGH MORAL THEORY

Functional analysis, which can dissolve some moral issues (as we have just seen), is not philosophical analysis. This is not just a matter of definition. People who major in philosophy in college, or who get advanced degrees in philosophy, do not acquire from their studies the tools required for the analysis of social and policy issues. They do not learn law or medicine, psychology or economics, business or public policy, statistics, biology, political science, sociology, anthropology, social work, or history.[71] Yet right away they find themselves back in school, using their academic training to teach and write. People who specialize in moral philosophy as students and later as professors spend their working time reading and discussing and annotating and elucidating the great texts of the philosophical tradition, from Plato to Rawls, and mastering the analytic techniques that the authors of these texts employed to deal with the issues that interested them. The texts are products of widely different societies over a period of almost two and a half millennia. When viewed together as constituting a canon or tradition of insight and analysis, they lose all reference to the particulars of the society in which each was written. Moral philosophers don't read them as would historians or anthropologists seeking to identify dysfunctional rules of conduct in the societies in which the texts were written. They read them as having something to say about a society that is not the text writers' own, namely our society. To be read so, they have to be read as statements of general truths. "The philosopher's self-indulgence is over-generalization."[72]

It is inevitable that they be so read, for the canonical philosophers are difficult to understand. Many wrote obscurely, or in foreign languages, some of them "dead" languages that cannot be fully understood even by

71. This is not true of all philosophers. Some acquire an impressive competence in a second field, such as political science, literary criticism, cognitive psychology, mathematics, history of science, classics, evolutionary biology—even law. As yet, however, these interdisciplinarians have had little success in bringing philosophical insights to bear on social, political, and economic controversies.

72. Griffin, note 51 above, at 104.

scholars. They wrote in social contexts vastly different from modern-day America (Rawls is the major exception),[73] and because meaning is contextual the interpretation of their writings may require immersion in history, as well as linguistic mastery in a narrower sense. Even after being carefully combed by the philologists, the classic texts bristle with ambiguities. The mastery of these texts and of the methods of analysis employed in them is the work of a lifetime, or perhaps of all time, since many of the questions of interpretation that they raise may be unanswerable. Little time is left in a scholarly career for investigating the particulars of any concrete moral issue. As a result, moral philosophers are tempted to mine the canonical texts for a few overarching concepts, such as duty or human flourishing, that they can use to *deduce* the answers to contemporary moral questions without having to investigate contemporary social conditions ("What Plato would allow").[74] They say such things as "the first step towards a substantive account of justice must be to establish some inclusive principles of justice."[75] Other moral philosophers, those who think like canon lawyers or common law lawyers, hope to use the method of casuistry or analogy to move from our settled moral intuitions to cases in which our intuitions give out.

The hope of the textmongers, whether they are moral universalists or moral particularists—that is, whether they think that little or much local context must be added to the general principles from which they start—is the more forlorn. To those not overly impressed by the prestige of the classics, the idea that Plato, Aristotle, Kant, Hegel, or even Mill holds the key to solving any modern social problem is as implausible as thinking that the Bible does, and reflects a similar mindset. Religious, philosophical, and literary texts have value as consolation and inspiration, as stimuli

73. Or is he? *A Theory of Justice* (1971), with its emphasis on the redistribution of income and wealth from the better off to the worse off, is beginning to seem extremely dated. Since 1971 the inequality in the distribution of income and wealth has grown, but public interest in the issue has diminished to nearly the vanishing point. The focus of egalitarians has shifted to inequalities within groups of more or less homogeneous incomes: middle-class women versus middle-class men, middle-class homosexuals versus middle-class heterosexuals, middle-class blacks and Hispanics (the two groups that, along with middle-class women, are the principal beneficiaries of affirmative action) versus middle-class whites, middle-class disabled versus middle-class able-bodied, middle-class workers over 40 (the earliest age at which the protections of the Age Discrimination in Employment Act kick in) versus middle-class workers under 40. *A Theory of Justice* has nothing to say about those issues.

74. The quotation is the title of a paper by Jeremy Waldron in *Theory and Practice (NOMOS XXXVII)* 138 (Ian Shapiro and Judith Wagner DeCew eds. 1995).

75. Onora O'Neill, *Towards Justice and Virtue: A Constructive Account of Practical Reasoning* 157 (1996).

to reflection, and as sources of wonder and pleasure. The modern academic philosopher, more properly the historian or philologist of philosophy, has therefore a useful role to play in explaining what the classical philosophers were trying to say, a role akin to translation and to literary and artistic criticism and scholarship. What the classics don't have are the answers to, or the methods for answering, contemporary moral questions. For one thing, all but the most recent (and "recent classic" is almost an oxymoron) were created in morally very different social climates from ours, so that before they can be made to do moral work for us they have to be "cleaned up,"[76] just as the Old Testament notoriously does. The essential and the accidental must be separated; Aristotle's defense of slavery, for example, or Kant's misogyny, prudery, and enthusiasm for capital punishment and for the governmental system of Frederick the Great must be categorized as accidental. This is an even more ambitious and uncertain interpretive task than figuring out what the classic philosophical texts say; indeed, it may be impossible, and "interpretation" in this setting just a polite word for picking and choosing. Whenever Aristotle or Aquinas or Kant is trundled out to do battle in modern moral debate, one wonders whether the "real" Aristotle or Aquinas or Kant is being brought into the fray or whether these big names are merely the stalking-horses for the modern moralist who has invoked them.

The grand moral theories also founder on the recalcitrance of moral intuitions—their imperviousness to argument. A moral theory might begin plausibly enough with the claim that human beings owe special duties to each other by virtue of the power of reason that most human beings possess but animals do not. Yet it would be monstrous in our culture to deduce that severely retarded human beings are entitled to no more consideration than animals or even that they are entitled to less consideration than the smartest animals, who are smarter than the dumbest people; just to refer to people as "dumb" grates on our sensibilities. We have, most of us, a passionate loyalty, rooted in the genes, to our own species, which moral philosophy cannot dislodge, so that it sounds like a joke to ask why computers should be our slaves merely because their intelligence is silicon-based rather than carbon-based. Collisions between principles and intuitions can be avoided by keeping the principles vague, as when Onora O'Neill says that the objective of justice "is to establish institutions and

76. For an interesting discussion of efforts to clean up Aristotle, see Larmore, note 12 above, at 164–167.

practices which (as far as possible) prevent and limit systematic or gratuitous injury."[77] But the price is banality.

Not everyone has a strong intuition about every issue of morality. Those who do not may seem fair game for the academic moralist. But we have to distinguish here among three types of person. The first is one who is not interested in a particular moral issue. That is the situation of many people with regard to the issue of abortion; they do not think of it as touching their own lives. They might therefore be swayed by academic moralists—except that they have no incentive to attend to what moralists have to say about the issue. The second type of person has a certain moral queasiness about something he does. Maybe he eats meat, yet knows there's a philosophical argument for vegetarianism. This type of person is likely to avoid investigating the moral issue further, and so steers clear of academic moralism. (This is the "affected ignorance" that Moody-Adams complains of.) The third type of person considers some moral issue to be very important but cannot decide how to resolve it, because of conflicting intuitions. Maybe he feels strongly both that fetuses are human beings and that a law criminalizing abortion subjects women to a kind of slavery. He faces a moral dilemma, and moral theory no more can resolve moral dilemmas than mathematics can square the circle. "Moral dilemma" is the term we use to describe a moral issue that moral theory *cannot* resolve.[78] When was the last time a moral dilemma was resolved? Moral theory is like a system of mathematics that has never gotten beyond addition.

REFLECTIVE EQUILIBRIUM

The method of reflective equilibrium tries to weave our embedded principles and intuitions into a coherent structure.[79] When used modestly in specialized fields of applied moral theory, such as bioethics, it can produce a commonsensical type of policy analysis, illustrated by a book by James Childress on bioethics.[80] His approach has been criticized as insufficiently theoretical.[81] That is its strength. Philosophically ambitious reflections on

77. O'Neill, note 75 above, at 173.

78. It's not much of a consolation to be told that the existence of a moral dilemma presupposes moral values. Bambrough, note 17 above, at 95–96. Otherwise there would not be a dilemma, or at least a moral one. But remember that I am not denying the existence of moral values—only the cogency of moral theory. (No matter how many times I say this, I am going to be accused of disparaging morality.)

79. See, for example, T. M. Scanlon, "The Aims and Authority of Moral Theory," 12 *Oxford Journal of Legal Studies* 1 (1992).

80. James F. Childress, *Practical Reasoning in Bioethics* (1997).

81. As he complains in id. at 32.

bioethical issues produce such unappetizing novelties as a "view of person-hood [that] implies that infanticide need not wrong a newborn infant and that infants lack any serious moral right not to be killed."[82] Bioethics in the style of Childress is a field broken off from philosophy.

No one has to surrender his moral intuitions to moral theory. You may feel, contra Rawls, that your natural endowment—your intelligence and appearance and so forth—is, despite its fortuitous character, a proper source of moral entitlements, in the same way that the infliction of a fortuitous, even an unavoidable, injury may be a proper source of moral condemnation. Since we're blamed for the bad things that we do for reasons beyond our control (the residue of the ancient Greek view of nature as normative), maybe we should be praised for the good things that we do for reasons beyond our control. If you feel this way, reading Rawls, who regards "the distribution of natural abilities as a collective asset,"[83] will not change you. And it should not. He offers no argument that will appeal to people not already predisposed in favor of the welfare liberalism that he appears to be advocating. He offers a form of life that you may not cotton to.

> Rawlsian man in the original position is finally a strikingly lugubri-ous creature: unwilling to enter a situation that promises success because it also promises failure, unwilling to risk winning because he feels doomed to losing, ready for the worst because he cannot imag-ine the best, content with security and the knowledge he will be no worse off than anyone else because he dares not risk freedom and the possibility that he will be better off.[84]

If you don't like this lugubrious creature, or don't feel that your genes are something you rented from a common pool, you're not going to be persuaded otherwise by Rawls.

Because the academic mind prizes consistency, academic moralists be-lieve that pointing out that a person's moral beliefs or behaviors are incon-sistent can be a powerful agent for moral change. They believe that if you

---

82. Dan W. Brock, *Life and Death: Philosophical Essays in Biomedical Ethics* 385 n. 14 (1993).

83. Rawls, note 73 above, at 179.

84. Benjamin R. Barber, "Justifying Justice: Problems of Psychology, Politics and Measurement in Rawls," in *Reading Rawls: Critical Studies on Rawls'* A Theory of Justice 292, 299 (Norman Daniels ed. 1989). Rawls does not justify his principle (to which Barber alludes) of maximizing the welfare of the worst off ("maximin") in terms of risk aversion in the technical economic sense; but he comes close to it in discussing the "strains of commitment." Rawls, note 73 above, at 176–178. See also id. at 153–154.

point out to a meat eater that because he considers suffering a bad thing and animals suffer as a result of his diet he is being inconsistent, you may persuade him to become a vegetarian. But behavioral consistency is a weaker ordering principle than logical consistency. To defend a proposition and its negation is a lot more difficult than to tell a story that will make a unity of "inconsistent" behavior or reconcile one's behavior with an inconsistent belief about how one *should* behave. The meat eater can distinguish between human and animal suffering; can deny that animals have to suffer in being killed for food (they can be killed painlessly, and since they do not know what is going to be done to them, they do not suffer psychologically in anticipation); can point out that his own consumption of meat is too slight to affect the number of animals killed; can even argue that to put animals on a par, as it were, with human beings could make us less sensitive to *human* suffering (could, for example, put the annual slaughter of tens of millions of turkeys for Thanksgiving on a level with the Holocaust); can point out that Genesis explicitly invites us to eat meat; or can equivocate, by confining his meat eating to the meat of animals raised and killed humanely, or to road kill, or by adopting the position that the moral philosopher R. M. Hare calls "demi-vegetarianism."[85] If you want to turn a meat eater, especially a nonacademic one, into a vegetarian, you must get him to love the animals that we raise for food; and you cannot argue a person into love. If you want to make a person disapprove of torturing babies, show him a picture of a baby being tortured; don't read him an essay on moral theory. An academic moral argument is unlikely to stir the conscience, incite a sense of indignation, or engender feelings of love or guilt. And if it does, one has only to attend to the opposing moral arguments to be returned to one's starting point.

Dworkin claims that many people who are not philosophers or even intellectuals nevertheless have "a yearning for ethical and moral integrity" or "want a vision of how to live" and thus "might well ask themselves, for example, whether their views about abortion presuppose some more general position about the connection between sentience and interests or rights."[86] The picture is of people standing around waiting to connect

85. R. M. Hare, *Essays on Bioethics,* ch. 15 (1993). Hare means only that he doesn't eat *much* meat. This makes demi-vegetarianism a bit like demi-pregnancy. He admits that he doesn't *enjoy* eating a lot of meat; so his moral theory coincides happily with his dietary preferences. It is a triumph of casuistry in the pejorative sense of that word.

86. Ronald Dworkin, "Darwin's New Bulldog," 111 *Harvard Law Review* 1718, 1722, 1726 (1998).

with professors. Few people are like that; few outside the academy talk or listen in the highfalutin style of academic moralism. But even if many people could understand and be moved by Dworkin's arguments about abortion and other issues of law or public policy, as soon as these people were exposed to the counterarguments they would be moved back to wherever they had been before they heard him. Every move in normative moral argument can be checked by a countermove. The discourse of moral theory is interminable because it is indeterminate.

Even among intellectuals, few are committed to consistency between moral beliefs and actual behavior. The skilled and conscientious geriatric physician who treats his aged patients with the utmost care and solicitude may be a child molester, and if confronted with the tension between his professional and his personal behavior might reply that he can't help being a child molester or that while he feels guilty about molesting children he is consoled by the fact that he does much good in his professional life or that the molestation reflects unbearable tension created by the devotion and scruples of his professional life. This is an extreme example; how much easier it is for ordinary high-minded people to rationalize their common-place cruelties, prejudices, meanness, and cowardice. We are rational in the sense that we fit means to ends more or less intelligently given the information we have, but the ends don't have to fit together; indeed, if they did, people would be awfully dull (this is one reason that so much academic moralism is dull). One of the questionable assumptions of Rawls's theory of justice is that a rational person is a single self, with consistent preferences, over his adult lifetime.[87] Few people experience their lives in this way. There is nothing irrational about having a sequence of selves (young, middle-aged, old, healthy, sick, and so on) with inconsistent preferences—the young self, for example, refusing to save money or take care of his health for the sake of his old self to be—or about playing a variety of roles at the same time (mother, investment banker, pill-popper, adulteress) that are not well integrated, at least in the sense of "integration" that appeals to academic moralists.[88]

MORAL CASUISTRY

The analogical or casuistic approach is no more trenchant than the deductive. Analogies stimulate inquiry; they do not justify conclusions. Con-

---

87. Rawls, note 73 above, at 295.

88. See Richard A. Posner, "Are We One Self or Multiple Selves? Implications for Law and Public Policy," 3 *Legal Theory* 23 (1997).

sider Judith Jarvis Thomson's comparison of a woman forced to carry her fetus to term with a person forced to spend nine months in bed connected by tubes to a stranger (a famous violinist) in order to prevent his dying from kidney disease.[89] The comparison is offered to show that abortion should not be forbidden, at least on the ground that it is always wrong to take innocent life. The stranger has no right to force a person to spend nine months connected to him by tubes, even though the stranger's life is at stake. No more should a pregnant woman be forced to spend nine months connected to her fetus, even though the fetus's life is at stake.

I find it difficult, despite the fame of Thomson's analogy in moral-philosophy circles, to take this "reasoning" seriously. To begin with, we can have no settled or reliable intuitions concerning her hypothetical case, because it is far outside our experience; it belongs to science fiction. In the second place, a woman normally is not immobilized by being pregnant. Third, the fetus is not a "stranger" to its mother in the ordinary sense of the word, which is the sense it bears in the analogy. The law punishes the neglect of a child by its parents, even if the child was the result of a rape; and Thomson does not suggest that she disapproves of such punishment or thinks it anomalous that the parents do not have the same legal duties to other people's children as they do to their own. Fourth, it is by no means obvious that the law should *not* impose a general duty to rescue strangers when the rescue can be effected without mortal peril to the rescuer. The laws of many European countries and now of several U.S. states do impose such duties;[90] the objections to them are of a practical character unrelated to the morality of refusing to be a Good Samaritan.

Perhaps most important, a doctor performing an abortion does not merely "pull the plug" on the fetus.[91] In a first-trimester abortion he uses either surgical instruments or a suction pump to remove the fetus from the uterus ("curettage"). In a second-trimester abortion he either uses surgical instruments to the same end or he injects a chemical that either kills the fetus and by doing so induces premature labor or just induces premature labor. Whatever the method, he is employing force for the purpose and with the effect of killing the fetus, and though the killing is a

89. Judith Jarvis Thomson, "A Defense of Abortion," 1 *Philosophy and Public Affairs* 47 (1971).

90. See John P. Dawson, "*Negotiorum Gestio:* The Altruistic Intermeddler," 74 *Harvard Law Review* 1073 (1961); Alberto Cadoppi, "Failure to Rescue and the Continental Criminal Law," in *The Duty to Rescue: The Jurisprudence of Aid* 93 (Michael A. Menlowe and Alexander McCall Smith eds. 1993).

91. See Alan F. Guttmacher and Irwin H. Kaiser, "The Genesis of Liberalized Abortion in New York: A Personal Insight," in *Abortion, Medicine, and the Law* 546, 557–564 (4th ed., J. Douglas Butler and David F. Walbert eds. 1992), for a lucid clinical description of abortion techniques.

by-product rather than the sole end, the same is true when a child kills his parents in order to inherit their money. The surgical procedure used in second-trimester abortion routinely includes the crushing of the fetus's cranium, and even in first-trimester abortion the fetus is sometimes removed piecemeal, for we are told that "if a fetus beyond 10 weeks age is recognized, the fragments should be reassembled to see if the fetus is essentially complete"[92] (because any fetal tissue remaining in the uterus could cause infection). In the rare third-trimester abortion, the doctor kills the fetus either by injecting a chemical into its heart or by drilling a hole in its cranium and removing its spinal fluid through the hole.

The precise technique is unimportant, although it is a commentary on the low quality of the abortion debate that the supporters of abortion rights never talk about what abortion actually involves while the opponents never talk about the compelling reasons that women and girls frequently have for deciding to have an abortion. What is important for the present discussion is that abortion is killing rather than letting die. So because opponents of abortion consider the fetus a full-fledged human being—and Thomson grants them their premise for the sake of argument—they consider doctors who perform abortions and the women who hire them to be murderers. This is consistent with not deeming the failure to rescue a true stranger a crime at all even if such failure could be thought a "taking" of innocent life; action and inaction often carry a different moral valence even when the consequences are similar.

So Thomson's famous analogy is no good. But that is almost beside the point, because you couldn't argue the opponents of abortion out of their position even with a good analogy. Analogies are at most suggestive. And most opposition to abortion is founded on religious conviction, which is a show stopper; one of the strongest norms of debate in our society is that you don't question a person's religious convictions.

You couldn't argue the opponents of abortion out of their position even if it were founded on simple altruism—on thinking of fetuses as babies. The more that fetuses are seen as babies (with the help of ultrasound),[93] the greater will be the opposition to abortion, holding religious conviction

92. Michael S. Burnhill, "Reducing the Risks of Pregnancy Termination," in *Prevention and Treatment of Contraceptive Failure: In Honor of Christopher Tietze* 141, 145 (Uta Landy and S. S. Ratnam eds. 1986). See also Guttmacher and Kaiser, note 91 above, at 558–560; David A. Grimes and Kenneth F. Schulz, "Morbidity and Mortality from Second-Trimester Abortions," 30 *Journal of Reproductive Medicine* 505 (1985).

93. See Cynthia R. Daniels, *At Women's Expense: State Power and the Politics of Fetal Rights* 15–21 (1993); John C. Fletcher and Mark I. Evans, "Maternal Bonding in Early Fetal Ultrasound Examina-

constant. Indeed, it seems that because of ultrasound, which enables even a very early fetus to be seen as a kind of human baby, more and more people are coming to think that abortion is morally wrong, whether or not they think it should be prohibited—a separate question. The pendulum may soon swing the other way, however, as techniques are perfected for detecting and terminating pregnancy within days, rather than weeks or months, of conception.[94]

If familiarity can alter moral opinion, so can unfamiliarity. "The hand of little employment hath the daintier sense."[95] Squeamishness is a big factor in morality. In poor societies most people have seen human corpses and have participated in killing, at least of animals. They are inured to blood and gore, and so they do not recoil from sports that involve the torture of animals. If it is a social project to make people peaceable or tame—the sort of project Nietzsche so hated and that Foucault discerned in the transition from cruel to "carceral" punishment[96]—one way to advance it is to shield people from the sight of blood and death. So despite our devotion to the free market we prohibit voluntary contracts to engage in public gladiatorial combat to the death. And despite our fear of crime we abhor the Islamic system of criminal punishments, with its floggings, amputations, stonings, and beheadings. But whether taming is the right project for a society is relative to circumstances. Squeamishness could spell extinction for a society in which the absence of professional police and of a professional military placed the burden of internal security and external defense on a large fraction of the adult male population. We congratulate ourselves on being morally more refined than our predecessors; actually we just have a different technology of security and defense, enabling us to kill from afar. Science has diminished the social value of brawn and of the brutal or brutish values that facilitate its effective employment. Science—not moral insight—has made us more civilized (by our lights). Being inarticulate, the brawny do not contribute directly to philosophical de-

tions," 308 *New England Journal of Medicine* 392 (1983); Sheryl Gay Stolberg, "Shifting Certainties in the Abortion War," *New York Times*, Jan. 11, 1998, § 4, p. 1. The other side of this coin is Robin West's report that she became "fervently prochoice" as a result of seeing a photograph of a woman who had died during an illegal abortion. West, "The Constitution of Reasons," 92 *Michigan Law Review* 1409, 1435 (1994). West notes, very much in the spirit of this chapter, "that moral convictions are changed experientially or empathically, not through argument." Id. at 1436.

94. See Tamar Lewin, "A New Technique Makes Abortions Possible Earlier," *New York Times*, Dec. 21, 1997, p. 1.

95. *Hamlet*, Act V, scene 1, lines 69–70.

96. See Foucault, note 19 above.

bate; being an increasingly marginal component of the society, they don't attract spokesmen from among the intellectuals, either; so the debate is biased in favor of the values of the educated middle and upper classes. As Nietzsche might put it, the regnant moral values are the expression of the will to power of the dominant groups in the society.

Amy Gutmann and Dennis Thompson, in an ambitious effort to make moral reasoning the core of what Rawls and they call deliberative democracy, take for granted that Judith Thomson's abortion analogy "should convince even people who perceive the fetus to be a full-fledged person that to permit abortion is not obviously wrong in the case of a woman who becomes pregnant through no fault of her own (for example, by rape)."[97] The word "obviously" signifies an equivocation characteristic of Gutmann and Thompson's book, a tacit admission that moral reasoning can at best refute only the most extreme moral contentions. It's like saying that legal reasoning can at best decide only the easiest cases—an assertion that will not satisfy people who consider it a powerful instrument for resolving disputes. But Gutmann and Thompson are wrong to think that Thomson's analogy carries even the little weight that they think it does; this is part of their larger wrongness of believing that moral reasoning can refute even extreme positions. Suppose the only way to release the involuntary rescuer from the stranger would be to put the latter through a meat grinder. I doubt that Thomson would consider this a morally justifiable expression of the rescuer's desire to be free, just because it is wrong (if it is wrong) to force a person to be a rescuer in the first place.[98]

What is so revealing about the treatment that Gutmann and Thompson accord to Thomson's analogy is that they appear not to *see* the distinction—though it is not a subtle one—between letting die and killing. The reason they do not see this is, I suspect, that they cannot really imagine

97. Amy Gutmann and Dennis Thompson, *Democracy and Disagreement* 85 (1996). The qualification "through no fault of her own" is not a part of Thomson's own analysis. See Thomson, note 89 above, at 49.

98. Actually, it is unclear from her article how she would treat this case, see id. at 66, though in her trolley paper she had said "How we die also matters to us. And I think it worse to die in consequence of being cut up, one's parts then being distributed to others, than to die in consequence of being hit by a trolley." Thomson, note 35 above, at 178. Martha C. Nussbaum, in her paper "Still Worthy of Praise," 111 *Harvard Law Review* 1776, 1779 (1998), says one could "argue that even 'chopping up' is a permissible response to a pregnancy resulting from such violent aggression" (i.e., a rape). I find this suggestion of a merger of the rapist and the fetus—so that killing the latter is somehow an appropriate response to being raped by the former—bizarre. It amounts to saying that if A shoves B, an innocent bystander, into C, C should be allowed to retaliate against B. If that's where moral philosophy leads, we can do without moral philosophy.

wanting to prohibit a woman who has been raped from having an abortion. The desire is too outré to register as a real possibility for them. Yet an appreciable number of people, not certifiably insane, feel differently, and moral philosophy has no resources for resolving the disagreement.

One can imagine the counterparts of Rawls, Guttman, and Thompson sitting around in Rome in 200 A.D. chewing over the moral issues presented by gladiatorial combat, concubinage, public nudity, divorce at the whim of the husband, and infanticide, all settled practices at the time but ones that Christianity opposed. These philosophers, being comfortable members of the Establishment (whatever corresponded in Imperial Rome to being a tenured professor at Harvard or Princeton), would probably have wanted to show, and would have had no difficulty in showing, that the Christians' ethical claims should receive no consideration, being based on the metaphysical assertions of an upstart foreign religion. "What the relativists, so-called, want us to worry about is provincialism—the danger that our perceptions will be dulled, our intellects constricted, and our sympathies narrowed by the overlearned and overvalued acceptances of our own society."[99] Philosophers are never so provincial as when they are placing beyond the pale of the "reasonable" the moral claims of people who do not belong to their narrow community.

The problem of what, if anything, government should do about abortion crosses the wavering line that separates moral from political and legal philosophy. It is entirely possible to think abortion immoral yet not want to prohibit it. As I shall note in the next chapter, much immoral conduct is not prohibited and much morally indifferent conduct is. This shows that there is more to policy than moral concerns. Thus when moral philosophers pursue a moral issue into the policy arena, they are in danger of jumping their traces. When Rawls, for example, descends from the abstractions of political philosophy to concrete issues of law and public policy, he becomes a superficial dispenser of the current "liberal" dogmas concerning abortion, campaign financing, income distribution, the regulation of advertising, socialized medicine, and the rights of women in divorce.[100] He also indulges in irresponsible historical speculation, as when he argues that there has *never* been a time in American history when a restriction on political speech could be justified.[101] That may be true ex

---

99. Clifford Geertz, "Anti Anti-Relativism," 86 *American Anthropologist* 263, 265 (1984).

100. See, for example, John Rawls, *Political Liberalism* 243 n. 32, 407 (paperback ed. 1996); Rawls, "The Idea of Public Reason Revisited," 64 *University of Chicago Law Review* 765, 772–773, 793 (1997).

101. Rawls, *Political Liberalism,* note 100 above, at 355.

post; yet it would not show that it would have been responsible ex ante to risk national disaster in order to maintain political liberty at its normal level. Considering the importance of the ex ante perspective in Rawls's political philosophy, one is surprised that he should ignore it when assessing the reasonableness of restrictions on political liberty in wartime before the outcome of the war can be known—the early days of the Civil War or of World War II, for example.

In criticizing Rawls's descents to the policy level, I do not wish to be understood as commending the abstract plane on which he normally dwells—that of "liberal theory," a discourse increasingly hermetic and esoteric.[102] This discourse, a form of academic moral theory as I am using the term, addresses the nonproblem of finding theoretical foundations for liberal democracy. The "problem" exists only as an academic teaser. No one of any consequence outside the academy worries about the foundations of liberal democracy, or whether it has any. Why *should* anyone worry? A successful practice does not require foundations. Liberal democracy is not under attack from people who have any political heft. And successful attacks on liberal democracy in other times and places (the Weimar Republic, for example) have not been powered by political theorists. (Or perhaps it would be more accurate to say that when there is widespread dissatisfaction with democracy, theorists can be found to attack it.) The only worriers are academics, and they worry at a level of abstraction that has no political significance.

Is Science So Different?

Moral philosophy is not unique in running aground on strong moral intuitions or emotional or political commitments. If science ever proves that there are systematic racial differences in the heritable component of intelligence, there will be outrage, just as the theory of evolution continues to provoke outrage in some quarters. The difference between scientific and moral theory is that the former can overcome opposing intuitions, in most societies anyway, because most people accept the authority of science. They do so because science is such a successful practice, compared to magic and ideology and wishful thinking, from the standpoint of societal survival and flourishing. Nazi hostility to "Jewish" physics, and Soviet belief during the period of Lysenko's ascendancy in the inheritance of acquired characteristics, illustrate the folly of pitting ideology against science.

102. For an example of its flavor, see Patrick Neal, *Liberalism and Its Discontents* (1997).

Science has power to convince skeptics because ordinarily it deals with what can be perceived, though often just with the aid of instruments. Although most of these instruments cannot actually be used by a lay person to verify an observation, we trust the scientific community not to jigger the instruments. We have reasons for this trust, the main one being the track record of science in delivering on its promises. The scientists said that an atomic bomb could be built; it was built; it exploded. Given the successes of science in predicting and altering the visible parts of the physical world, we believe that scientific instruments augment and correct rather than deform our perceptions. And we have confidence in perceptions, because they are public.

Our intuitions, however, are private.[103] When we perceive, we are seeing (hearing, feeling, etc.) something outside us, and to the extent that we have similar perceptual apparatus, whether natural or artificial, our perceptions will agree when we are looking at (listening to, etc.) the same thing. If your intuition about a moral question differs from mine, you cannot tell me to look harder, or to look through a microscope or a telescope, or to consult a reputable scientist or reputable anyone. You cannot show me that my intuition is an illusion, like the apparent movement of the sun or the bent appearance of a straight stick in water. There are no "crucial experiments," and no statistical regularities, by which to validate a moral argument. Nor are there useful "inventions" embodying moral theory, which is another way of saying that there has been no moral counterpart to scientific progress. It is true that we have abolished slavery, but we no longer have an economy in which slavery would be productive; the world is just emerging from an era in which more than a billion people lived in something rather akin to slavery unremarked by a large number of moral philosophers; we live in an era of unprecedented criminal violence and, some would say, of unprecedented selfishness as well; and the academic moralists who denounce their predecessors for indifference to the fate of the Jews in Nazi Germany or the blacks in South Africa during apartheid have been for the most part very quiet about the genocides in contemporary Bosnia and Rwanda.[104]

Not that the only progress of the human race has been scientific and technical. Obviously there has been material progress, though it is owed largely to scientific and technical progress. Average incomes in real (that is,

103. This contrast is stressed in Griffin, note 51 above, at 14.

104. Catharine MacKinnon has been a conspicuous exception with respect to Bosnia—but she is a moral entrepreneur.

inflation-adjusted) terms are vastly higher today than they were one thousand, one hundred, or even just fifty years ago. There has been political progress, particularly marked since the fall of communism, as a result of the spread of liberal democracy, a method of government that solves some perennial problems of governance, including the problems of orderly succession and of lethal religious strife, and does a better job than alternative systems of aligning the interests of rulers and ruled. It also provides a better framework for economic growth, which in turn promotes national security as well as material comfort, longevity, and other widely shared values. If the values fostered by liberal democracy are deemed moral values and the values promoted by alternative regimes (such values as military glory, ethnic or religious solidarity, respect for elders, a picturesque traditionalism, asceticism, closeness to nature, the aesthetization of politics, a code of honor, patriarchy, radical egalitarianism, social stasis, or artistic splendor) dismissed or demoted, the political progress that I have described can be equated to moral progress. But it is an equation that results from stipulation, not argument.

It might seem that the existence of inconsistent moral intuitions would make all of us more tentative about our own intuitions, more ready therefore to listen to the philosopher who wants us to change. But that is not how the formation of moral beliefs works. Moral intuitions are strongly felt even by people who know both that they are impossible to verify and that many other people have opposite intuitions. (How many "pro-life" or "pro-choice" people are *tentative* about their views, in recognition of the fact that many other people disagree with them?) That is one reason why, contrary to the fears of academic moralists, belief in moral relativism is unlikely to affect a person's moral attitudes or behavior.[105] What is strongly felt will yield to proof, but not to an opposing intuition.

Against the arguments for distinguishing scientific from moral theory can be urged the undoubted fact of diversity of scientific belief and the impossibility of bringing all doubters into line. This is the sort of thing one hears from scientific relativists, and it is paradoxical to find moral realists using the arguments of relativists to bolster moral realism. Still, it

---

105. "The world has produced the rattlesnake as well as me; but I kill it if I get a chance, as also mosquitos, cockroaches, murderers, and flies. My only judgment is that they are incongruous with the world I want; the kind of world we all try to make according to our power." Letter from Oliver Wendell Holmes to Lewis Einstein, May 21, 1914, in *The Essential Holmes: Selections from the Letters, Speeches, Judicial Opinions, and Other Writings of Oliver Wendell Holmes, Jr.* 114 (Richard A. Posner ed. 1992).

is striking how many people in this land and era of science and technology believe in astrology, UFOs, reincarnation, fortune-telling, diabolism, faith healing, and other scientifically specious theories, phenomena, and practices; the best example may be the tenacious rejection by a substantial minority of Americans of the theory of evolution. But what is notable about these antiscientific beliefs is that they either concern matters as to which nothing, or very little, of a practical nature turns on one's beliefs (the theory of evolution is an example) or are not held tenaciously enough to affect behavior. Virtually no one rejects scientific theory in those areas in which science impinges on everyday life. We fly in airplanes, consult doctors and follow their advice, vote for legislators who want to control acid rain or global warming, take vitamins, have vasectomies and CAT scans, vaccinate ourselves and our children, use computers, talk over the telephone, undergo in vitro fertilization, accept the "big bang" theory of the creation of the universe, and give up cigarette smoking, in all these ways demonstrating a deep faith in scientific theory.

There is no corresponding faith in moral theory. We don't say things like "Kantians taught us how to be X [the moral equivalent of being able to fly or generate heat from nuclear fuel cells or cure syphilis], so we'll accept their current teaching that Y [for example, we shouldn't eat animals]." Moralists like to say such things as, "The objectivity of ethics does not insure that we can answer every question. Neither does the objectivity of science."[106] This is true. But it is misleading because it insinuates a parity between ethics and science that, as a practical matter, does not exist. As Moody-Adams explains in rejecting the parity thesis, "there is no consensus among philosophical practitioners of normative inquiry about the kinds of considerations that might even qualify as confirmational constraints on the claims of moral theory." And it is not clear "how any such constraint might function in a process of testing and rejecting 'rival' or 'competing' theories in order to select one of those rivals as the best theory (up to now)."[107]

Thus, even if scientific realism is rejected in favor of the view that science yields "objective" results only because scientists happen to form a cohesive, like-minded community—even if, that is, we accept the view that consensus is the only basis on which truth claims can or should be accepted because consensus makes "truth" rather than truth forcing con-

106. Catherine Z. Elgin, "The Relativity of Fact and the Objectivity of Value," in *Relativism: Interpretation and Confrontation* 86, 97 (Michael Krausz ed. 1989).

107. Moody-Adams, note 20 above, at 132–133.

sensus—moral theorists are up against the brute fact that there is no consensus with regard to moral principles from which answers to contested moral questions might actually be derived. And even if (to come at the issue from the opposite direction) moral realism is correct, the lack of an agreed procedure for determining which version of it is correct (Catholic natural-law doctrine? Utilitarianism? Kantianism?) makes it impossible to forge consensus on the correct solution to particular moral problems. "Really existing" moral universals are useless if they are unknowable.[108] If at some level moral theory is like scientific theory, as moral realists believe, it is like failed scientific theory.

That is why there are so many unsolved *old* moral dilemmas.[109] Because there are no techniques for forging consensus on the premises of moral inquiry and the means of deriving and testing specific moral propositions, moral dilemmas are disputes about ends, whereas fruitful deliberation, the sort of reasoning that moves the ball down the field, is deliberation over means. When Dworkin says he thinks it clear that Picasso is a greater painter than Balthus,[110] he implicitly appeals to an agreed sense of what "greatness" in painting means. If agreement lapses, his argument collapses. The force of his example lies in the fact that artistic "greatness" has factual as well as purely aesthetic connotations; it includes criteria of scope, influence, and quantity of output, and the fulfillment of these criteria can be viewed as the means to the end of greatness. On those dimensions, Picasso does clearly outclass Balthus. If we asked instead who is the *better* painter, I would vote for Balthus and would be happy to argue my preference to Dworkin in an effort to improve his eye for art, by pointing out features of Balthus's art that he may have overlooked. But if I could not persuade him, I would not conclude that he was "mistaken" to persist in preferring Picasso.

What one would not expect is that our discussion would push us even further apart than we are now. But it is what one would expect if the issue were moral rather than aesthetic. Larmore, though himself a moral realist, observes that "the more we talk about such things" as "certain deep aspects of morality," "the more we disagree."[111] This puts moral theory at the

---

108. See Jeremy Waldron, "The Irrelevance of Moral Objectivity," in *Natural Law Theory: Contemporary Essays* 158 (Robert P. George ed. 1992).

109. See generally *Moral Dilemmas and Moral Theory* (H. E. Mason ed. 1996).

110. Dworkin, "Objectivity and Truth: You'd Better Believe It," note 7 above, at 133.

111. Larmore, note 12 above, at 168. See also id. at 169–174.

opposite end of the spectrum of fruitful inquiry from science. Scientific discourse tends toward convergence, moral toward divergence.

In support of his observation Larmore makes a point that Bayesian statisticians will recognize: our belief concerning a question (say, the morality of abortion) is a function not only of the arguments that are made to us but also of our prior beliefs. The more divergent those prior beliefs, the less likely the arguments are to make us converge.[112] Suppose I am 95 percent confident that abortion is morally wrong and you are 95 percent confident that it is morally okay, and you produce a highly convincing argument for your position. Even if the argument doubles my doubts and erases yours, so that I am only 90 percent confident that abortion is wrong and you are 100 percent confident that it is okay, we still disagree. What is more, if as is likely your argument incites me to find additional arguments for the wrongness of abortion, and those arguments, when I make them to you, in turn incite you to find more arguments for the opposite position, our disagreement may well be entrenched rather than reduced. Arguing for a position, as compared to holding it in silence, has a congealing effect because people don't like to admit that they're wrong. The taking of a strong public position operates as a commitment.[113]

Even Mill

I said that among the high theorists of moral philosophy, "even Mill" could not help us with any modern social problem. I qualified him in this way because of all the classic moral philosophers he seems closest to us, or at least to me. Mill's concept of individualism appeals to me. His harm principle, with its distinction between self-regarding and other-regarding activities, seems a good though rough guide to the proper scope of government. I also find his pragmatic conception of free speech attractive. And his defense of tolerance, nonconformity, and experimentation (including "experiments in living"), and his dislike of paternalism and moral busybodies, resonate with me. I consider myself a pragmatist, and Mill the first pragmatist. In short, I find the form of life described and commended in On Liberty highly congenial.

What I do not find in the work is either arguments that would have weight with doubters or a theoretical apparatus that could be brought usefully to bear on modern problems. Let me explain by reference to the

112. See id. at 173.
113. See also note 63 above.

harm principle, the heart of Mill's theory of limited government. The principle, as Mill articulates it, places even deeply offensive self-regarding acts out of bounds to moral censure as well as to legal prohibition. It does this primarily, however, by limiting the domain of morality to what we owe other people, so that *by definition* "self-regarding faults . . . are only a subject of moral reprobation when they involve a breach of duty to others."[114] Someone who believes that God condemns a number of self-regarding acts will think that Mill has missed the point entirely. There is no way to refute such a person; he and Mill do not reason from common premises.

The distinction between self-regarding and other-regarding acts, moreover, which is at the heart of the harm principle, can be thrown into the gravest doubt just by pointing out that people may be more connected than Mill, without evidence, assumes.[115] Promiscuity, alcoholism, drug addiction, gambling, suicide, hate speech, polygamy, and the manufacture, sale, and consumption of pornography are all, when there is no physical coercion involved at any stage, self-regarding acts as Mill defines the term. So on his analysis they should be protected not only from legal prohibition but also from "the moral coercion of public opinion" (p. 10). And while he believes it proper to prevent reprobated self-regarding acts from being conducted in public, this qualification is inconsistent with his criticism of the Puritans for closing down public amusements of all sorts. Public or private, the acts I have listed might make life in a community a misery for most people—not just prudes and busybodies—and might conduce to the commission of antisocial acts that Mill would deem other-regarding, as many feminists claim to be the case with pornography. How far society should go in shielding self-regarding acts from regulation by law or public opinion is a prudential or empirical question that should be answered on the basis of actual conditions in a particular society rather than by defining morality to exclude any concern for such acts.

Further evidence that Mill's moral theory does not hold water is his argument against self-enslavement: "it is not freedom to be allowed to alienate [one's] freedom" (p. 95). Any time we sign a contract we alienate our freedom, whether it is a contract for the sale of goods or an employment contract, and if the latter whether its duration is one year, ten years, or life. Suppose an altruist were offered $10 million up front in exchange

---

114. John Stuart Mill, *On Liberty* 73 (David Spitz ed. 1975 [1859]).

115. As pointed out long ago by James Fitzjames Stephen in *Liberty, Equality, Fraternity,* note 61 above, at 145–146.

for his becoming the offeror's slave. And suppose that knowing he had only a short time to live anyway, the altruist decided that he would prefer to give $10 million to charity than to be free. I don't see how such an exchange could be thought inconsistent with the idea of freedom, or could be considered anything other than a self-regarding act within Mill's framework. But my point is not that self-enslavement should be permitted. It is as contrary to our moral code as to that of Mill's time. The embarrassment for Mill is that it is *not* contrary to the moral code found in *On Liberty.*

Likewise inconsistent with the harm principle is Mill's treatment of polygamy. He claims that it is a "direct infraction" of "the principle of liberty" (p. 85) and makes clear that England, though obligated in his view to leave the Mormons of Utah to their own devices, is not required to permit polygamy or even to recognize polygamous marriages made by Mormons in Utah as valid in England. But why is not permitting polygamy in England or anywhere else required by the principle that the state and public opinion are not to interfere with self-regarding acts, which include consensual transactions between competent adults? Mill himself says that polygamous marriage "is as much voluntary on the part of the women concerned in it, and who may be deemed the sufferers by it, as is the case with any other form of the marriage institution" (pp. 85–86). And he does not propose to outlaw marriage. So once again we see him, just like a conventional utilitarian, flinching from pushing his moral philosophy to its logical extreme, where it would run up against deep moral intuitions.

Mill requires creative interpretation not only to make sense but also to avoid anachronism. *On Liberty* endorses a degree of laissez-faire in economic affairs that is inconsistent with most modern views of the appropriate scope of economic regulation and also, as we shall see in the next chapter, furnishes a basis for arguing against *Brown v. Board of Education* and for permitting racial segregation on a local or regional basis. Since interpretation is a game played without rules, *On Liberty* can be patched and pounded and dusted and touched up, and, thus "restored" ("cleaned up," as I put it earlier), can be repositioned on its pedestal as an icon of modern liberalism. But the point of such a project could only be a polemical one. It could have nothing to do with solving modern problems.

However, this cannot be the last word on *On Liberty.* I said earlier that moral claims can be profitably discussed if they depend on factual claims. My only examples were cases in which exploding a factual claim undermined the moral claim. Equally important is the factual claim that is offered to bolster a moral claim and that is *not* exploded. One of Mill's arguments in *On Liberty* for freedom of speech is that even a true opinion benefits from criticism, because unless the holders of the opinion have to defend it from time to time they will cease to understand it, and it will lose all its vitality. This is a testable hypothesis; it can be refuted or confirmed. If it is confirmed (it is supported by the tendency of moral debate toward divergence rather than convergence), this would not establish a moral duty to recognize a right of free speech but it would be a telling argument in favor of such a right for anyone for whom intellectual progress is a value. It would not be like arguing that to deny freedom of speech to a person is to deny his dignity as a human being;[116] *that* would be a moral rather than a factual argument.

The Perils of Moral Uniformity

Every academic moralist believes implicitly that his is the right approach and everyone should follow it. Everyone should agree with him that abortion is wrong or that capital punishment is wrong; should be pacifist or belligerent, hedonistic or ascetic; should defend or attack pornography. But given the variety of necessary roles in a complex society, it is not a safe idea to have a morally uniform population. On the one hand, we need soldiers, police, jailers, judges, spies, and other operators of society's security apparatus; also politicians, entrepreneurs, managers of huge enterprises, and administrators of lunatic asylums. On the other hand we need mothers, nurses, forest rangers, kindergarten teachers, zookeepers, and ministers of religion. We need gentle, kind, and sensitive people, but we also need people who are willing to employ force, to lie, to posture, to break rules, to enforce rules, to fire people, to rank people. (Pro-choicers think we also need people who will kill fetuses, and supporters of capital punishment that we need executioners.) We need people who are empathetic and sympathetic but also people who are brave, tough, callous, and obedient—and others who are brave, tough, callous, and defiant. One can *imagine* everyone being brought up to be such a finely calibrated moral being that he could adjust his suite of moral feelings to meet the exigencies of every social role, or so perfectly socialized that society would have no need for discipline or defense. But that would not be a realistic expectation. Failing it, we are better off with moral variety, and this places the entire project of moral education in question.

It is true that many academic moralists believe in tolerance for Mill's

---

116. As in Thomas Scanlon, "A Theory of Freedom of Expression," 1 *Philosophy and Public Affairs* 204 (1972).

"self-regarding acts." But tolerance is not approval. The moralists want everyone to have the same moral values. They don't think it's good that some people are selfish, cruel, vengeful, madly ambitious, manipulative, elitist, monomaniacal, irresponsible. A related point, one that can be tied back to moralists' inability to resolve moral dilemmas in a convincing fashion, is that they disvalue conflict and hence tragedy. Much literature dramatizes moral dilemmas, "no-win" situations well illustrated by that of Hamlet caught between a duty to avenge his father's murder and a duty to leave vengeance to God. Abortion may be thought tragic in the "no-win" sense, so the moralist who claims that abortion is morally "right" or morally "wrong" may be thought to be denying the tragic element in life.[117] The law has to deal with these tragic situations somehow, but it does not have to yield to the moralist who believes that no moral dilemma is beyond the power of moral reasoning to resolve. It is better for the law to adapt to the elements of ineradicable conflict in modern social life than to submerge them under a factitious intellectual harmony.

Discussions of judicial behavior similarly tend to deny the existence of ineradicable conflict by assuming, usually tacitly, that every judge should be the same kind of judge—empathetic or legalistic, activist or restrained, liberal or conservative, depending on the analyst's taste—when what we really need is (within limits) a variety of types of judge, if we are to have confidence in the robustness of judge-made law.[118] A uniform judiciary would not be a national disaster, however; moral uniformity would be. A society of goody-goodies, the sort of society implicitly envisioned by academic moralists, not only would be boring but would lack resilience, adaptability, and innovation. A society of Jewish or Islamic fundamentalists, Nietzschean *Übermenschen,* or Japanese samurai would not be dull, but it would be brittle, frightening, and perilous. Moral inbreeding may be as dangerous as biological inbreeding.

Professionalism's Cold Grip

The Motivational Impotence of Academic Moral Inquiry

I have offered reasons for doubting that academic writing and university teaching about morality are likely to influence, directly or indirectly, peo-

---

117. See Christopher W. Gowans, *Innocence Lost: An Examination of Inescapable Moral Wrongdoing,* chs. 1, 9 (1994), on the tension between tragedy and moral theories that deny the necessity of choosing among courses of action each of which involves moral wrongdoing.

118. See Richard A. Posner, *The Problems of Jurisprudence* 448 (1990).

ple's behavior for the good. I now examine the evidence bearing on this issue. One bit of evidence is that the moralists and their students appear not to behave more morally than other educated people—scientists, for example, or even lawyers and economists. As one moral philosopher puts it: "Evidence of moral expertise is displayed in reliably living a moral life, and there is absolutely no evidence that moral philosophers do this better than—or even as well as—non-philosophers."[119] Maybe we shouldn't expect even the best moral philosophers to be moral; maybe only people who are troubled by the discrepancy between the moral code and their own behavior would be attracted to a career in moral philosophy. But this point would not apply to most undergraduates enrolled in courses in moral philosophy. And so one would like evidence that such a course of study is a genuinely edifying experience for at least some of them, and hence that the morality of scientists, lawyers, and so forth is owed even in small part to an undergraduate education in moral philosophy. The fact that few moral philosophers (Moody-Adams is a notable exception) are even interested in the evidentiary issue is a clue that academic moralism is afflicted by professional isolation.

Another bit of evidence for the ineffectuality of academic moral instruction is that moral philosophers are so eager to minimize their teaching loads. They would much rather write articles read only by each other than improve the morality of the next generation. Either they are careerists, or they secretly disbelieve in the efficacy of moral philosophy in improving morality—or both. "For every article and book written, hundreds of students are not taught."[120] This was said with reference to classics professors, but applies equally to philosophers, and of course the two groups overlap. The authors whom I have just quoted remark sarcastically on "the Plato lecturer [who] ditches forty students to fly 2,000 miles to pontificate to twenty on ethics, in preparation of writing for forty, only to haggle on return over travel compensation."[121]

Systematic evidence concerning the edifying effects of moral philosophy is hard to come by, but there is some. From the Oliners' comprehensive statistical study of German and Polish rescuers of the Jews from the Holocaust,[122] it is possible to cull all the variables that they found to be

119. Moody-Adams, note 20 above, at 175.

120. Victor Davis Hanson and John Heath, *Who Killed Homer? The Demise of Classical Education and the Recovery of Greek Wisdom* 155 (1998).

121. Id. at 220.

122. Samuel P. Oliner and Pearl M. Oliner, *The Altruistic Personality: Rescuers of Jews in Nazi Europe* 261–366 (1988).

statistically significant in explaining the propensity to rescue.[123] Although most of the ethical variables are positively related to the propensity to rescue, one of them, "obedience," is negatively related to it. And the only educational variable that has a statistically significant effect on the propensity to rescue is being a student, and it is *negatively* related to that propensity. The religious variables are significant but difficult to interpret, since both "being very religious today" and "being irreligious today" have a positive effect, but being in between has a negative effect, while religiosity during the war has no effect.

So education and religion, conventionally believed to be important sources of moral values, have no consistent or demonstrable effect on what can fairly be described as moral heroism (from our standpoint—not the Nazis'). But being a caring person, or having had Jewish friends (but not Jewish coworkers), or living in the country (where the sense of community is greater than it is in a city, and probably the Nazi presence was less pervasive), or being hostile to Nazism or authoritarian politics, or having had a good relationship with one's parents, or having a cellar (which would reduce the riskiness of being a rescuer), or having links to the Resistance but not being active oneself in it (which would increase the risk of detection) predisposed people to rescue Jews. All this is pretty much as one would expect. But it does suggest—along with the behavior of German moral philosophers during the Nazi period[124]—that moral theory has little to do with moral practice.

Michael Gross, reinterpreting the data compiled by the Oliners and other students of rescuers of the Jews, concludes that morally reflective people were *less* likely to be rescuers than morally unreflective people.[125] Effective rescue required collective rather than merely individual action, and the "morally competent" tend to be "politically incompetent" because political competence requires (as Gross explains with reference not only to Jewish rescue but also to peace activism and abortion activism) parochial

---

123. See Richard A. Posner, "1997 Oliver Wendell Holmes Lectures: The Problematics of Moral and Legal Theory," 111 *Harvard Law Review* 1637, 1710–1717 (1998).

124. See George Leaman, *Heidegger im Kontext: Gesamtüberblick zum N.S.-Engagement der Universitätsphilosophen*, pt. 2 (1993), esp. pp. 25–27. Professors were notable by their absence from the cells of resistance to Hitler that developed during his rule. Alice Gallin, *Midwives to Nazism: University Professors in Weimar Germany 1925–1933* 4–5, 100–105 (1986).

125. Michael L. Gross, *Ethics and Activism: The Theory and Practice of Political Morality* 150 (1997). There is also evidence that aggressive gun-toters are more likely than more "civilized" people to play the Good Samaritan role. See Ted L. Huston et al., "Bystander Intervention into Crime: A Study Based on Naturally-Occurring Episodes," 44 *Social Psychology Quarterly* 14 (1981).

motivations. Those who rescued the Jews were motivated by material self-interest, civic and patriotic norms often unrelated to the Jews' fate, and small-group solidarity—motivations that are actually undermined by universalistic moral reflection.[126]

Martha Nussbaum, however, claims that another study of rescuers and other altruists, this a smaller-scale one by Kristen Monroe,[127]

> shows that the most salient common feature [of rescuers and other altruists] is a particular outlook on the relatedness of human beings, an outlook that holds that all human beings are interconnected, interdependent, and equal in worth. This outlook could, of course, be imparted in many ways, and philosophy is only one way through which it came to the rescuers. But it is a universal moral-theoretical view.[128]

The summary is inaccurate. Monroe does find that altruists tend to have "a particular way of seeing the world, and especially themselves in relation to others. All the altruists I interviewed saw themselves as individuals strongly linked to others through a shared humanity" (p. 213).[129] But the notion of people's being "equal in worth" is Nussbaum's addition; the rescuers in Monroe's study tended to value life in *all* its forms, nonhuman as well as human, rather than being egalitarian or socialistic (see pp. 206–207).[130] And there is no hint in her study that any of the rescuers or other altruists became such through philosophy.[131] Although one of them, an ethnic German who lived in Prague during the Nazi era, described himself "as some combination of agnostic, Kantian, and pantheist," he was emphatic that he "never made a moral decision to rescue Jews" (p. xi).

Monroe's book contains no index references to philosophy or education, instead emphasizing the spontaneous, unreflective, nontheorized,

126. See Gross, note 125 above, pt. 3.

127. Kristen Renwick Monroe, *The Heart of Altruism: Perceptions of a Common Humanity* (1996).

128. Nussbaum, note 98 above, at 1783 n. 33 (citation omitted).

129. It should be noted, however, that her interview sample was very small. It consisted of only twenty altruists, of whom five were philanthropists, five were "heroes" (ordinary people who risked their lives to save people in danger), and ten were rescuers of Jews. Monroe, note 127 above, at 16–17.

130. But don't think that the love of animals is a dependable route to love of man. See note 28 above.

131. For corroboration, see Jasper, note 42 above, discussing protest movements. His book contains no index references to philosophy or moral philosophy. It does ascribe some influence to philosophers with regard to the animal-rights movement, see id. at 167–169, but with the important qualification that I noted in note 67 above.

even non-Western character of altruistic behavior, whether episodic or, as in the case of much of the rescue activity during World War II, stretched out over a long enough period to give rescuers plenty of time to engage in reflection if they want to; they don't want to. Monroe *denies* that altruistic behavior emanates from "the conscious adoption of and adherence to certain moral values" (p. 231). Even "the ethical messages transmitted by critical role models," such as parents (no teachers or ministers were mentioned by the altruists in her sample), are not predictive of altruism (pp. 181–185). She finds to her surprise that "it was the rescuers, the individuals who came closest to pure altruism on my conceptual continuum, who deviated most from the universal moral principles of ethics and morality. Furthermore, this deviance was necessary in order to act altruistically" (p. 185)—here she anticipates Gross's study.

Less dramatic evidence of the futility (for Gross and perhaps Monroe the perversity) of instruction in moral theory, but evidence that may resonate more deeply with members of the legal profession, is the transformation of law students over the course of an elite legal education. Many of these students come to law school full of idealism and determined to resist the lures of large-firm practice. They receive an idealistic education by law professors many of whom believe that law and morals interpenetrate. Yet upon graduation almost all the students go to work for large law firms, chastened by the realization that their ideals, far from being strengthened by the idealistic teaching of their professors, have been shattered by material constraints and inducements trivial in comparison to those that any moral exemplar ever faced. This phenomenon, termed "public interest drift," is well documented[132] and is illustrated by the finding that while as many as 70 percent of first-year students at the Harvard Law School expressed a desire to practice public-interest law, by the third year the figure had fallen to 2 percent.[133] A few do find employment in the public-interest sector, at considerably lower wages than in private firms—an indication of altruistic motivation.[134] Many of these, however, stick it out for only a few years; some are compensated by forgiveness of law-school loans; and some find the work more interesting, and the hours shorter,

---

132. See Howard S. Erlanger et al., "Law Student Idealism and Job Choice: Some New Data on an Old Question," 30 *Law and Society Review* 851 (1996), and studies cited there.

133. Id. at 851–852, citing Robert Granfield, *Making Elite Lawyers: Visions of Law at Harvard and Beyond* 48 (1992).

134. Robert H. Frank, "What Price the Moral High Ground?" 63 *Southern Economic Journal* 1 (1996).

than at a private law firm. The fraction of true, practicing idealists among recent graduates of our leading law schools must be very tiny, despite the penetration of the curriculum by academic moralism.

A few psychological studies find gains in "moral judgment" from college education, including college courses that have a significant component of moral education.[135] But the authors acknowledge that the link between moral judgment and moral behavior is weak because of insensitivity, weakness of will, and lack of motivation.[136] Gross notes empirical data that "there are relatively few principled moral thinkers in any given population, and efforts to cultivate extensive moral development have proved disappointing."[137]

Academic moralists are apt to reply not that instruction in moral philosophy has a *direct* effect on moral behavior or even moral beliefs but that it increases students' moral sensitivity and thus enables them to think through any moral dilemmas they encounter after graduation. The implication, however, *must* be that the graduates will behave more morally as a result of having been sensitized to, and made more skillful in resolving, moral issues. For if they behave no better than the uninstructed, this means either that the instruction has failed even to get them to think more, or more clearly, about moral issues, or—the problem of motivation—that knowing what's right has had no effect on their propensity to do what's right.

If anything, instruction in moral philosophy is likely to engender moral skepticism by exposing students to the variety of moral philosophies (some monstrous by contemporary standards) and to the methods of analysis by which to criticize, undermine, modify, and upend any given moral philosophy. More important (for, as I said earlier, being a moral skeptic is unlikely to affect one's behavior), instruction in moral philosophy equips students both to craft a personal philosophy that places the fewest restrictions on their own preferred behavior and to rationalize their violation of conventional morality. This is true in spades for their professors. Academic moralists pick from an à la carte menu the moral principles that coincide with the preferences of their social set. They have the intel-

135. See, for example, James Rest and Darcia Narváez, "The College Experience and Moral Development," in *Handbook of Moral Behavior and Development,* vol. 2: *Research* 229 (William M. Kurtines and Jacob L. Gewirtz eds. 1991).

136. Id. at 243–244. See also Steven Thoma, "Moral Judgments and Moral Action," in *Moral Development in the Professions: Psychology and Applied Ethics* 199, 201 (James R. Rest and Darcia Narváez eds. 1994).

137. Gross, note 125 above, at 85.

lectual agility to weave an inconsistent heap of policies into a superficially coherent unity and the psychological agility to honor their chosen principles only to the extent compatible with their personal happiness and professional advancement.

If some moral principle that you read about in a book and that may have appealed to your cognitive faculty collides with your preferred, your self-advantaging, way of life, you have only to adopt an alternative morality or, if you're bold enough, an antimorality (like that of Nietzsche, who famously attributed the morality of "good" people to their will to power) that does not contain the principle; and then you will be free from any burden of guilt. Do you find Kantian strictures against lying irksome? Then read Nyberg.[138] Better yet, identify with one of the great liars of history, Odysseus for example. The better read you are in philosophy or literature, and the more imaginative and analytically supple you are, the easier you will find it to reweave your tapestry of moral beliefs so that your principles allow you to do what your id tells you to do. Not knowledge, but ignorance, is the ally of morality. The medieval Roman Catholic Church recognized this when it told its priests not to ask parishioners at confession about specific sexually deviant practices, lest the priests give them ideas.[139] To be confident that instruction in moral reasoning improves people's behavior you would have to agree with Socrates that people are naturally good and do bad things only out of ignorance.[140] Who believes that, and on what evidence?

There is a deeper point hidden here: that morality may be losing its grip on modern people (Americans, for example, despite their ostentatious religiosity), owing to currents that moral education cannot stanch. Increasingly, it seems, we are constrained in our personal behavior by law and reciprocity rather than by social norms. Privacy, wealth, urbanization, occupational and geographical mobility, and education and information however acquired—all of which have become abundant in modern times—foster individualism. They do this by emancipating people from familial and other small local groups, which undermines the coercive

138. David Nyberg, *The Varnished Truth: Truth Telling and Deceiving in Ordinary Life* (1993).

139. See, for example, Thomas N. Tentler, "The Summa for Confessors as an Instrument of Social Control," in *The Pursuit of Holiness in Late Medieval and Renaissance Religion* 103, 114–115 (Charles Trinkaus and Heiko A. Oberman eds. 1974).

140. As Nussbaum puts it, "in order to believe that a logical argument can produce a result in calling the soul to an acknowledgement of its own deficiencies," moral philosophers have to believe "that at least a good part of evil is based on error . . . [and] that people have many good beliefs and good intentions." Nussbaum, note 66 above, at 36.

power of norms because norms are more effective when people are under the observation of their peers and cannot easily leave the peer group. Although there is no dearth of norms today, including new ones of anti-smoking, political correctness, antibigotry, even picking up after your dog, the new norms are to a considerable extent optional and the old ones are becoming so. (They are also, these new norms, rather peripheral to people's lives, and widely flouted.) Nowadays you can choose the norms you like by choosing the activity, the occupation, the church, the social set that has a system of norms compatible with your character and preferences. You *might* be enticed into a community, an activity, an occupation, a church, and so on by features unrelated to its norms and find yourself willy-nilly bound by its norms—but one way in which activities compete for new adherents is by relaxing normative constraints. With some exceptions, such as Mormonism and ultra-Orthodox Judaism, modern religions in America and the other wealthy countries keep up the number of their members by reducing the cost of membership, which they do by minimizing the number of hedonistic and other self-interested pursuits forgone.

Moral pluralism—which, remember, undermines as a practical matter the authority of morality—is due in part to moral philosophy itself. Higher education encourages feelings of superiority. Moral philosophers, who invariably today hold a doctoral degree, are not immune from such feelings, which are exacerbated by their knowing that their work is neither highly valued by society nor highly remunerated. They may reciprocate society's contempt. They may come to feel that its moral code should not bind them, that instead society should adopt, or at least condone, the moral philosopher's moral code. Normally this code will be the code of the philosopher's immediate social milieu, or "set," rather than either an "objective" order of goodness (for there is none) or the expression of profound individual insight.

The moral codes of academic philosophers tend in fact to be at once nonstandard and hackneyed, predictable, and seemingly unexamined. The liberals favor abortion rights à outrance, women's rights, greater equality of incomes, and a mild socialism. They disapproved of Soviet-style communism, but very quietly, with maybe a soft spot for East Germany, or Cuba, or Yugoslavia—or even Mao's China. They are internationalists, multiculturalists, environmentalists, sometimes vegetarians. They are against capital punishment, and so it might be said of them unkindly that they pity murderers (and penguins, and sea otters, and harp seals) more than fetuses. They support the theory of evolution when the question is whether creationism should be taught, but reject it when the question is whether there is a biological basis for any of the differences in attitude or behavior between men and women. They want to regulate cigarette smoking out of existence but to permit the smoking of marijuana. They argue for abortion by analogizing mother and fetus to strangers (Thomson's analogy) but against surrogate motherhood by emphasizing the bond between mother and newborn. They are for the strongest possible public measures of safety and health but against requiring people who are infected by the AIDS virus to disclose the condition to people whom they might infect. They believe that people are prone to wishful thinking, cognitive dissonance, rationalization, hyperbolic discounting (shortsightedness), false consciousness, and all sorts of other cognitive disabilities that make market choices and folk beliefs lack authenticity; but they do not consider the effect these disabilities are likely to have on the power of academically directed moral deliberation to engender moral improvement. They are secular (or deist) and therefore consider sexual practices morally indifferent and fear the Religious Right. They are politically correct, and they vote Democratic.[141]

Other moral philosophers hold the opposite of each of these positions. They pity fetuses but not the animal victims of environmental torts or of cruel methods of hunting and trapping. They are against multiculturalism—unless it is religious. They object strenuously to governmental efforts to discourage cigarette smoking and alcohol imbibing but are vigorous supporters of the "war against drugs." They fear the multicultural Left, and vote Republican. Some of them expound an orthodox Catholic view in a manner incomprehensible to the secular mind. John Finnis's criticisms of homosexuality come packaged in such sentences as "The union

---

141. Duncan Kennedy has a pertinent observation on this theme, anent the policy preferences of Ronald Dworkin: "Hercules"—Dworkin's model judge, who Dworkin claims decides cases on the basis of principle, not policy—"is not just a liberal; he is a systematic defender of liberal judicial activism from Brown [v. Board of Education] to the present. He is actually a left liberal, as close as you can get in terms of outcomes to a radical." Kennedy, *A Critique of Adjudication* [*Fin de Siècle*] 128 (1997). "Over the course of his career, Dworkin has endorsed as the legally 'right answer' not just Brown without delay and racial quotas, but civil disobedience, nonprosecution of draft card burners, the explicit consideration of distributive consequences rather than reliance on efficiency, judicial review of apportionment decisions, extensive constitutional protection of criminals' rights, the constitutional protection of the right of homosexuals to engage in legislatively prohibited practices, the right to produce and consume pornography, and abortion rights." Id. at 127–128 (footnotes omitted). Dworkin contends that Kennedy's summary is inaccurate. Ronald Dworkin, note 86 above, at 1721 n. 12. He's wrong. Posner, note 1 above, at 1797–1798.

of the reproductive organs of husband and wife really unites them biologically."[142] It is unclear what this means, why it is morally relevant, or how it distinguishes sterile marriage, at least when the couple *knows* that it is incapable of reproducing, from homosexual coupling (the distinction Finnis is particularly interested in drawing), or whom he hopes to persuade. It may seem unfair of me to quote Finnis out of context. But the context is dominated by even stranger sentences, which read as if they had been translated from medieval Latin[143] and makes one wonder whether Finnis agrees with Aquinas that masturbation is a worse immorality than rape.[144] Still, with difficulty one can dig arguments out of Finnis, as Paul Weithman has done,[145] as one can out of Aquinas. They are not arguments that will appeal to anyone who does not already agree with Finnis, however, or even to everyone who shares his theological and metaphysical premises, as Weithman does.[146]

Finnis's stance is dictated by his religion, not by "reason." But this is no less true of his secular opponents, provided that "religion" is understood

142. John Finnis, "Is Natural Law Theory Compatible with Limited Government?" in *Natural Law, Liberalism, and Morality: Contemporary Essays* 1 (Robert P. George ed. 1996).

143. "The union of the reproductive organs of husband and wife really unites them biologically (and their biological reality is part of, not merely an instrument of, their *personal* reality). Reproduction is one function and so, in respect of that function, the spouses are indeed one reality, and their sexual union therefore can *actualize* and allow them to *experience* their *real common good—their marriage* with the two goods, parenthood and friendship, which are the parts of its wholeness as an intelligible common good even if, independently of what the spouses will, their capacity for biological parenthood will not be fulfilled in consequence of that act of genital union." Id. at 15. Robert George makes the same point in a more modern idiom, but I still can't make any sense out of it: "The mated pair may, of course, happen to be sterile, but their intercourse, insofar as it is the reproductive behavior characteristic of the species, unites the copulating male and female as a single organism." Robert P. George, "Public Reason and Political Conflict: Abortion and Homosexuality," 106 *Yale Law Journal* 2475, 2499 n. 112 (1997). Intercourse known by the participants to be sterile is not "reproductive behavior," and even reproductive intercourse does not unite the participants "as a single organism." But I agree with George's criticism (the theme of the article from which I have just quoted) of John Rawls for trying to rule out of political bounds moral arguments based on religious belief even when the believers offer rational grounds, threadbare as they may seem to nonbelievers, for their beliefs.

144. Thomas Aquinas, *Summa Theologiae*, pt. II-II, qu. 154, art. 12.

145. Paul J. Weithman, "Natural Law, Morality, and Sexual Complementarity," in *Sex, Preference, and Family: Essays on Law and Nature* 227 (David M. Estlund and Martha C. Nussbaum eds. 1997).

146. For an attack on the *religious* legitimacy of a distinctively Christian ethics, see Max Charlesworth, *Religious Inventions: Four Essays*, ch. 4 (1997). Charlesworth remarks pertinently: "Christian[s] are now known more by their attitudes on issues such as abortion, euthanasia, artificial contraception and so on, than they are by their following of the precepts of the Sermon on the Mount." Id. at 136. The "Christian" position on these issues, as Charlesworth points out, has no roots or even seeds in the Gospels.

broadly enough to include any unshakable commitment that determines where one stands on fundamental issues of value. Secular humanism is a religion in this sense. Thomas Nagel is a self-proclaimed atheist,[147] yet he thinks that no one could *really* believe that "we each have value only to ourselves and to those who care about us."[148] Well, to whom then? Who confers value on us without caring for us in the way that we care for friends, family, and sometimes members of larger human communities? Who else but the God whom Nagel does not believe in? Nagel is a Christian rigorist manqué, who wants people to feel bad about not being supermoral—about not always telling the truth, about not giving away their money to the undeserving poor, and about not making other sacrifices that don't come naturally to people.

Finnis and the other moralists who derive their moral codes from religious orthodoxy make a tactical mistake when they try to use reason to defend their beliefs. They play into the hands of their secular opponents, who want to make reason the only legitimate basis for making moral claims. Rather than playing on the opponents' turf, religious moralists should point out that secular moralists' views are founded as much as their own are on faith, and that argument, understood as a form of rhetoric or theater, occupies the same position in secular moral theory that liturgy does in religion.

The most important thing to understand about modern moral philosophers, whether one is interested in the truth or the persuasiveness of their arguments, is that they are professionals rather than seers, prophets, saints, rebels, or even nonconformists. Their moral values are those of their set (their "reference group," sociologists would say),[149] humanities professors. This group has two main subsets, the liberal-secular and the conservative-religious. The social pressures that play upon these professionals create a form of life against which the wings of moral theory beat feebly. It is a form of life that in many cases is morally chaotic on the level of theory, to say nothing of practice, both personal and professional.[150] The same aca-

147. Nagel, *The Last Word*, note 11 above, at 130.

148. Id. at 121; and see id. at 122, where he declares this belief "highly unreasonable and difficult to honestly accept."

149. "In choosing specific people one chooses a specific world to live in." Peter L. Berger, *Invitation to Sociology: A Humanistic Perspective* 120 (1963).

150. About the latter, Hanson and Heath remark pointedly: "Part-time teachers, T.A.'s, and poorly paid graders are the most embarrassing of all of the university's cons. Elite, very liberal-thinking men and women hire those below at a tenth of their own pay to teach their classes and grade their papers." Hanson and Heath, note 120 above, at 236. See also id. at 149, 151–152, 250.

demic moralist is apt to be hard in defense of the right to have an abortion[151] or to engage in unsafe sex regardless of the risk to an unsuspecting sexual partner while being soft over the death of sea otters in oil spills and proclaiming what Holmes called the "slapdash universals. (Never tell a lie. Sell all thou hast and give to the poor etc.)"[152] An academic moralist of a different stripe might be full of pity for a one-minute old fetus but pitiless toward homosexuals, foreigners, and victims of racial or sexual discrimination in any form other than affirmative action.

The age of professionalism—in moral philosophy as in medicine—is also, and in consequence, the age of what Weber memorably called the disenchantment of the world.[153] It was not always thus in moral philosophy, or in medicine for that matter. Socrates was not a tenured professor; and he gave his life for his principles. Cicero was proscribed. Seneca was murdered on the authority of Nero. Hobbes was an exile, as were Locke and Rousseau. Bentham was a lawyer, an economist, and a practical reformer, but not a professor; and, with a fine sense of theater, he directed that his corpse be preserved and exhibited in perpetuity as an inspiration to his followers. Mill was not a professor either; he was a civil servant, an economist, and a member of Parliament. Nietzsche gave up a safe berth as a professor of philology and became an impoverished outcast.[154] Wittgenstein was a soldier in World War I and a medical orderly in World War II, a mechanical engineer, an architect, a secondary-school teacher, a flouter of academic conventions, a nonpublisher, an exile; he gave away all his money (a fortune), and he abandoned his professorship. Bertrand Russell spent time in prison for his beliefs. All that is history. Philosophy has

151. As when Frances Kamm, in a pro-choice book, tiptoes up to the question whether abortion is a form of infanticide: "we must be careful as we assume the fetus to be not only a person but an infant. We should be on guard that we are then not more resistant to killing it from merely biological or sentimental motives, if there are insufficient reasons from a moral point of view for not killing." F. M. Kamm, *Creation and Abortion: A Study in Moral and Legal Philosophy* 6 (1992).

152. Letter to Lewis Einstein, July 23, 1906, in *The Essential Holmes: Selections from the Letters, Speeches, Judicial Opinions, and Other Writings of Oliver Wendell Holmes, Jr.*, note 105 above, at 58.

153. For references and discussion, see Anthony T. Kronman, *Max Weber*, ch. 8 (1983). Dean Kronman, an expert both on Weber and on the application of moral theory, recognizes and deplores this fact; he believes that professionalization is fatal to the enterprise of moral philosophy. Anthony T. Kronman, "The Value of Moral Philosophy," 111 *Harvard Law Review* 1751, 1764–1767 (1998).

154. The resignation of his professorship in May 1879 was precipitated by poor health, but he had already decided that "in the long run an academic existence is impossible for me." Letter to Franz Overbeck, August 1877, quoted in R. J. Hollingdale, *Nietzsche: The Man and His Philosophy* 133 (1965). See also David Breazeale, "Introduction," in Friedrich Nietzsche, *Untimely Meditations* vii, xxix–xxx (1997); Ronald Hayman, *Nietzsche: A Critical Life* 190 (1980). As early as 1874 he was thinking of giving up his professorship. See id. at 171.

become as thoroughly professionalized as accounting. This has implications for both method and knowledge. Professionals tend to adopt a complex and esoteric mode of analysis and expression (see Chapter 3). Modern moral philosophers are no exception. Their fine-spun arguments are gossamer that cannot budge the rock of moral intuition.

A profession's tendency to build a wall around itself is held in check when it is a service profession, with customers to please, or when it makes falsifiable claims, whether the predictive claims of a science or the claim of the armed forces to be able to defeat an enemy. Academic moral philosophy, with limited exceptions—Childress's bioethics, for example—has no customers outside its own ranks for its scholarship (as distinct from its teaching, where it has students to please—the fewer the better) and makes no falsifiable claims. Unhindered by external checks and balances, the academic moralist has no incentive to be useful to anybody, and so is free to pursue academic prestige by encouraging brilliance. Moral philosophers compete with one another for academic fame and fortune by demonstrating how carefully they have read the canonical texts, how cleverly they can develop an analogy or spot an inconsistency, how consistently they can reason from premises to conclusions, how many fine distinctions they can draw, and how deftly they can skewer an opponent. But like high IQ in general, the intellectual gifts moral philosophers exhibit need not, and in their normative work usually do not, generate a positive social product.

It is, however, on the score of life experience, rather than that of method, that modern moral philosophers fall farthest short of their predecessors. Lifetime academics, they never leave school. They take no professional risks until they get tenure. After that they take few professional risks, and never any personal risks. They live a comfortable bourgeois life, with maybe a touch of the bohemian. They either think Left and live Right, or think Right and live Right. I do not mean to criticize. I like academic people. I consider myself basically one of them; I am as unheroic as they; I am the same kind of comfortable bourgeois. I just don't think that they—that we—are a likely source of moral entrepreneurship.[155] Academic moralists are as remote from life as mathematicians, and some

155. For similar arguments from within philosophy, see Annette Baier, "Doing without Moral Theory?" in Baier, *Postures of the Mind: Essays on Mind and Morals*, ch. 12 (1985), reprinted in *Anti-Theory in Ethics and Moral Conservatism*, note 3 above, at 29. Let me make clear, however, that although I admire science, I do not delude myself that scientists are morally superior human beings. For some pertinent remarks on this score, see Gordon Tullock, "Are Scientists Different?" *Journal of Economic Studies*, no. 4/5, 1993, p. 90.

of them are proud of it.[156] They are not moral innovators, let alone moral heroes or the makers of such heroes. And this by conviction as well as temperament. Being teachers and intellectuals, moral philosophers exaggerate the importance to moral change of instruction, analysis, culture, debate, and intelligence, and so are deflected from attempting moral entrepreneurship. Not that such an attempt would succeed. The academic cocoon is not a nurturing environment for moral courage and imagination. Liberal democracy makes it difficult for *anyone* to be a moral entrepreneur because by tolerating dissenters it makes it difficult for them to prove their courage and thus cut an inspiring figure. Had Ralph Nader not been harassed by General Motors, he might never have become a social prophet; and even with the "advantage" of being persecuted (though only mildly), he adopted an ostentatiously modest style of living in order to further signal his moral distinction.

There isn't even evidence or reason to believe that academic moralists have superior moral insight when compared with other people. In saying that they are not moral entrepreneurs I was emphasizing the problem of "selling" a new morality; but academic moralists are not even closet inventors. They dress up in academic language the moral opinions of their set, the opinions that are "in the air," the opinions held by powerful senior colleagues or in some cases by passionately opinionated students. And so in complaining that academic moralists lack the charisma necessary to change the moral code of their society, I am not denying the division of labor by criticizing innovators for not also being marketers.

One can, it is true, *imagine* the academic moralist thinking up moral innovations and the charismatic leader picking them up and imparting them to the masses. In this spirit Peter Unger, acknowledging that his book urging Americans to give away all their money above subsistence needs to poor children in the Third World will have only a handful of readers, expresses the hope that someone will write a bestseller advocating his position.[157] The division of labor that he envisages is similar to that between the production manager and the sales manager of a business firm. Something like this is indeed discernible in the history of morality. Chris-

---

156. "In both morality and mathematics it seems to be possible to discover the truth simply by thinking or reasoning about it." T. M. Scanlon, "Contractualism and Utilitarianism," in *Utilitarianism and Beyond* 103, 104 (Amartya Sen and Bernard Williams eds. 1982).

157. Peter Unger, *Living High and Letting Die: Our Illusion of Innocence* 156 (1996). To spur his tiny anticipated readership to open their pockets, Unger considerately lists the toll-free phone numbers of three charities. Id. at 175.

tianity was influenced by the thought of Plato and the Stoics, and later by Aristotle; modern notions of gender equality owe a debt to Mill; Rousseau influenced the Jacobins; Hegel influenced Lenin and Stalin via Marx, and pragmatism via John Dewey. Could our modern academic self-proclaimed successors to the giants of moral philosophy be turning out moral innovations that in the fullness of time will be absorbed into our moral code through the efforts of moral or religious middlemen? One doubts it. The modern academic career is not conducive to moral innovation. Modern academic moralists, even those who have had the profound *academic* impact of a Rawls,[158] are narrow specialists, professionals. They tidy up after the moral innovators, who are (or were) not other modern-style academics, but instead the classic figures of the past; or practical people, such as politicians; or preachers and visionaries; or, yes, at times rebellious youth.

Not all academic moralists are content with intellectual monasticism. The "public intellectual" hopes to communicate directly with, and so to influence, an audience not limited to other academics. It is a forlorn hope, at least for a moral or political philosopher in a society, such as that of the United States, in which the public has no interest in philosophy. The American public wants pragmatic solutions to practical problems rather than philosophical debate.

The desire of the academic moralist to "go public" is significant, however, in its revelation of ambivalence about the philosopher's calling. That ambivalence pervades Moody-Adams's book *Fieldwork in Familiar Places.*[159] Although she "seeks to provide a plausible conception of moral objectivity and to defend a cautious optimism that moral philosophy can be an aid in serious, everyday moral inquiry" (p. 1), and to this end vigorously attacks moral relativism, we have seen that she also attacks moral realism and the idea that moral theory can be thought the problem-solving equal of science. And that is just the beginning. She criticizes moral philosophers for "attempt[ing] to turn moral problems into philosophical puzzles" and warns that "the results may make good or even great philosophy, but they will prove unsatisfactory as a form of moral inquiry" (p. 136). She finds "no reason to think that the process of moral inquiry

158. Even Frank Michelman, Rawls's biggest fan among law professors, is agnostic on the question whether Rawls has actually had any impact on American law. Frank I. Michelman, "The Subject of Liberalism," 46 *Stanford Law Review* 1807, 1808 (1994).

159. Note 20 above. It can also be found, among many other places, in Kronman, "The Value of Moral Philosophy," note 153 above.

might eventually result in 'convergence' on some one theory" (p. 143). "Philosophy is not authoritative in moral argument; nor is it even *primus inter pares*" (p. 176). She rejects "the notion that the proper task of moral philosophy is to validate systematic moral conceptions" (p. 184) and regards the sort of disagreement that Rawls and Nozick have over the nature of political justice as simply irresolvable.[160] While she finds value in the "tendency [of moral theory] to encourage self-scrutiny" (p. 170), she quickly qualifies this encomium by acknowledging that "moral theories do not, indeed cannot, solve moral problems" (p. 173). Her intermittent declarations of continued faith in moral inquiry by philosophers are not backed up by argument or persuasive examples. The only examples she gives are of nonacademic moral entrepreneurship, such as civil rights demonstrations in the early 1960s. It's almost as if she thought that moral inquiry as it should be conducted by philosophers *had not yet begun,* that the discipline was still in the ground-clearing stage, where fallacies are uprooted and wrong turns signposted. Twenty-five hundred years is a long time to be standing at the starting gate, waiting for the race to start.

Martha Nussbaum has expressed a similar though more muted ambivalence about academic moralism. She is known for wanting to treat Greek tragedies, the novels of Henry James, and other works of imaginative literature as works of moral philosophy, and one of her motives for doing so is her opposition to "the academicization and professionalization of philosophy."[161] But faced with a challenge by an outsider (me), she closes ranks with the other moral philosophers and endeavors to catalogue the successes of moral philosophy in the world of action.[162] To make the catalogue at all impressive, however, she is forced to cast far afield—not only to Rousseau, Cicero, Locke, Montesquieu, Marx, and Burke, none of whom was an academic, and to Amartya Sen, who is an economist as well as a philosopher (indeed primarily the former), but also to John Dewey qua philosopher of education. She says that if Cicero and the other nonacademics on her list were living today they *would* be tenured academics, but in saying this she misses the distinction between moral entrepreneurs and academic moralists. These are different vocations. The conditions of

160. It leads to the standoff that Hilary Putnam calls "respectful contempt." Putnam, *Reason, Truth and History* 165–166 (1981). See also Weinreb, note 10 above, at 240.

161. Martha C. Nussbaum, *Love's Knowledge: Essays on Philosophy and Literature* 20 (1990). See also Nussbaum, note 66 above; Martha C. Nussbaum, *The Fragility of Goodness: Luck and Ethics in Greek Tragedy and Philosophy* 15–16 (1986).

162. Nussbaum, note 98 above, at 1780–1782, 1792–1793. Further page references to her paper are in the text.

the modern academy (tenure, specialization, and so forth) prevent its inhabitants from acquiring the vision and influence of the long-dead philosophers whom she cites.

Nussbaum gives only two examples of the influence of academic moralism on thought or action in the United States: Peter Singer's advocacy of animal rights and the philosophical literature on bioethics. They are bad examples—that of Singer because, as I have pointed out, he does not write like an academic philosopher or (more to the point) offer much in the way of philosophical argument; that of bioethics because, as I have also pointed out, the best philosophical bioethics, illustrated by Childress's work, is the least philosophical.

Nussbaum says that "there are many different routes to influence" and adds that "sometimes ethical theorists are also influential politicians"— but the most recent of her examples, Marcus Aurelius, died 1,800 years ago (p. 1792). She notes that some other ethical theorists have been "practical entrepreneurs" (id.), but her only examples are Dewey (as founder of progressive education) and Sen, the economist (in getting the United Nations Development Program to adopt his measure of welfare).[163] Most ethical theorists were and are neither politicians nor entrepreneurs but writers and teachers. Nussbaum acknowledges the narrowness of the life experience of academic moralists, implies that they should try not to spend their whole lives in the university, concedes that, "too often, our insularity is evident in the way we write" (p. 1794), acknowledges the difficulty that philosophers encounter in trying to address a broader audience than their fellow academics and that "the journals in which one must publish to get tenure discourage a more flexible use of style . . . The jargon-laden non-writing of the philosophical journals is a good style for persuading no human being" (p. 1795). Good philosophers who influence people's beliefs "employ the resources of the imagination" to draw people "into philosophical argument in the way that Plato does, or Cicero, or Hume, or Rousseau, or William James" (pp. 1794–1795). All her exemplars are long dead. And that is not adventitious. For in her references to jargon and insularity and tenure imperatives and never leaving school Nussbaum has identified just those features of modern moral philosophy that show it to be a profession in the Weberian ("disenchanted") sense. It is a sense incompatible with moral entrepreneurship and hence with a reasonable expectation of altering people's moral beliefs

---

163. The all-time greatest entrepreneur among moral philosophers, Bentham, was also an economist and lawyer.

or practices. Normative moral philosophy today is indeed "academicized and professionalized."

The Persistence of Moral Debate and Academic Moralism

To summarize the discussion to this point, a society's moral code changes when changes in material conditions (such as the recession of close combat, the advent of ultrasound images of early pregnancy, the supersession of magic by science, and the technological changes—improved methods of birth control, household labor-saving devices, and the substitution of machinery for brawn in many jobs and of services for manufacturing— that have enabled the vastly increased participation of women in the labor force) challenge factual assertions entangled in the moral code; or when a charismatic moral leader, perceiving a mismatch between existing morality and a changing society, uses nonrational methods of persuasion to alter moral feeling. Academic moralism, however, is not an agent of moral change. The persistence of moral debate does not undermine this conclusion. Interminable moral disagreement and debate may not prove that there is nothing to academic moralism, but assuredly do not prove that there is something to it. Given morality, moral pluralism, moral change, and the moral emotions, we can expect moral discussion that will generate competing moral claims, whether or not it generates rational backing for those claims and whether or not philosophers participate in the discussion.

The puzzle is the persistence not of moral discussion but of academic moralism. The increasing scope and sophistication of the natural and social sciences have compressed the space within which a generalist can say anything interesting about a specific issue. Philosophy is the field of residual speculation, and it is continually losing subjects to specialized fields. (It is losing bioethics and jurisprudence and moral sociology, to take examples germane to this book.) It is more and more difficult for a philosopher to talk intelligently about social behavior. Philosophical critiques of economic policy are a case in point. An economist or sociologist would find comical the claim by a distinguished moral philosopher that private philanthropy has a built-in tendency to "encourag[e] a 'culture of dependency'" and that this shows we need a welfare state.[164] By creating legal rights to welfare, a welfare state is more likely to encourage depend-

---

164. Onora O'Neill, *Construction of Reason: Explorations of Kant's Practical Philosophy* 231–232 (1989).

ency than private citizens would be, since they would be free to reduce or withdraw their largesse at the first sign of dependency. Another moral philosopher advocates workers' cooperatives on the ground that "environmental protection tends to harmonize more with the interests as well as the ideals of worker-managed firms than with the interest of capitalist firms," because "workers, unlike capitalists, have to live in the communities where they work and so must live with the pollution they create."[165] But since workers include office workers as well as factory workers, since not all the firm's factories may pollute, and since the effects of the pollution caused by a factory may be felt far away, the majority of a cooperative's worker-owners may not be affected by the firm's pollution. Even if they are, they have more to lose from pollution-control measures than shareholders would: they could lose their jobs. Elsewhere in the same book workers are said to undervalue workplace dangers,[166] but it is not explained why this should be less true of worker-owners who must choose between fewer jobs and less pollution. The plywood cooperatives of the Pacific Northwest, the principal "success story" of worker-owned industrial firms in the United States, have, according to an admirer of worker-owned firms whom the philosopher cites, the same dirty, noisy, and dangerous working conditions as capitalist sawmills.[167]

This philosopher (Elizabeth Anderson) is, as it happens, both a feminist and a critic of the free market and rampant commodification; and this pairing, while common (an example from legal philosophy is Margaret Jane Radin),[168] is awkward. Feminists want women to get out of the home and the taxpayer to subsidize day care to enable them to do so. What is envisaged is the commodification of child care—formerly performed outside the market, by housewives, now to be performed inside the market, by hired workers in day-care centers. The ubiquity of the "working woman" signifies a massive expansion of the use of the market to direct the allocation of resources. Feminists also find irksome the rigidities of the

165. Elizabeth Anderson, *Value in Ethics and Economics* 213 (1993).

166. Id. at 195–203.

167. Christopher Eaton Gunn, *Workers' Self-Management in the United States* 130 (1984). For economic criticisms of worker-controlled firms, see, for example, Michael C. Jensen and William H. Meckling, "Rights and Production Functions: An Application to Labor-Managed Firms and Codetermination," 52 *Journal of Business* 469 (1979); Jan Winiecki, "Theoretical Underpinnings of the Privatisation of State-Owned Enterprises in Post-Soviet-Type Economies," 3 *Communist Economies and Economic Transformation* 397 (1991).

168. See Margaret Jane Radin, *Contested Commodities* (1996).

traditional concept of marriage; they want in effect to commodify marriage by making it more of a contractual and less of a status relationship.

Michael Sandel, another philosophical critic of commodification, surprisingly conjoins approval of baby selling with condemnation of contracts of surrogate motherhood.[169] He reports that a doctor named Hicks, practicing medicine in the rural South during the 1950s and 1960s, "had a secret business selling babies on the side." Hicks was also an abortionist, and "sometimes he persuaded young women seeking abortions to carry their babies to term, thus creating the supply that met the demand of his childless customers."[170] Sandel believes that the doctor's "black market in babies" had morally redeeming features but that surrogate motherhood has none. He points out that compared to Dr. Hicks's "homespun enterprise, commercial surrogacy, a $40 million industry, is big business." But he is comparing one seller in a market to an entire market, and moreover one seller in an illegal market, where sellers conceal themselves, to an entire legal market. With more than a million abortions a year, the potential for "baby selling," if legalized, to eclipse commercial surrogacy is manifest.

Sandel's principal ground of distinction is that commercial surrogacy, unlike what Dr. Hicks did, encourages commodification. "Dr. Hicks's black market in babies responded to a problem that arose independent of market considerations. He did not encourage the unwed mothers whose babies he sold to become pregnant in the first place." He did not have to. Demand evokes supply. Women who knew there was a market for their baby if they did not want to keep it would tend to use less care to avoid becoming pregnant. No doubt fewer women knew there was a market than would have known it had the market been a legal market rather than a black market. But Sandel does not suggest that Dr. Hicks's practice is morally redeemed by its illegality!

Anderson, Radin, and Sandel are well-regarded moral theorists, as is Michael Walzer, who advocates a form of "industrial democracy" that would (it seems, because he leaves the concept vague) substantially curtail the normal economic rights of owners of business firms, with adverse

169. See Michael Sandel, "The Baby Bazaar," *New Republic,* Oct. 20, 1997, p. 25. A similar but more elaborate moral argument against surrogate motherhood is made in Anderson, note 165 above, ch. 8.

170. Cf. Elisabeth M. Landes and Richard A. Posner, "The Economics of the Baby Shortage," 7 *Journal of Legal Studies* 323 (1978).

economic consequences that Walzer does not discuss.[171] I am not picking on lightweights. But the time is past when even the ablest moral theorists were interchangeable with economists as analysts of markets. Today, informed criticism of markets comes primarily from within economics, from economists such as John Donohue, James Heckman, Albert Hirschman, John Roemer, and Amartya Sen,[172] although, consistent with what I said earlier, when an economist ventures a moral claim, it is the proper business of the moral philosopher to challenge that claim.[173]

The persistence of weak academic fields is neither unusual nor surprising. Competition among and within universities has only limited efficacy in aligning the incentives of university faculty and administrators with the social interest in the production of valuable knowledge and an educated citizenry.[174] This is in part because of universities' nonprofit governance structure, in part because of tenure, and in part because of the absence of external constraints on low-cost (that is, nonscientific) university research; philosophy professors do not depend on peer-reviewed research grants. But above all it is because of the high cost of information—to students, their parents, and prospective employers of students—about the quality and value of particular universities and departments. The consequence is inertia in adjusting the supply of a particular academic "product," such as books and articles by academic moralists, to the social demand.

Yet such adjustments do occur. Recent years have seen the closing of a number of library, education, and dental schools, and of departments of linguistics, sociology, and classics. There aren't separate departments of moral philosophy, so it is difficult to determine how this field is doing. My impression is that it is holding its own, though only barely and for reasons that owe nothing to the intellectual or social value of academic moralism. One reason is moral pluralism, which multiplies not only the number of moral issues for academic rumination but also the number of perspectives,

171. Michael Walzer, *Spheres of Justice: A Defense of Pluralism and Equality* 291–303 (1983).

172. The weasel word in this sentence—"primarily"—is an acknowledgment that there is some highly competent philosophical critique of economics (apart from Sen's). It is well illustrated by Jean Hampton, "The Failure of Expected-Utility Theory as a Theory of Reason," 10 *Economics and Philosophy* 195 (1994). Despite her rather ominous title, however, this is not an article likely to cause many economists or policymakers sleepless nights; it is pitched at too high a level of abstraction to engage with their interests. This is typical of the critique of economics by philosophers who, unlike Sen, are not also economists.

173. See, for example, Jules L. Coleman, *Markets, Morals, and the Law* (1988); Ronald Dworkin, "Is Wealth a Value?" in Dworkin, *A Matter of Principle* 237 (1985).

174. For some pertinent observations, see Arthur Levine, "How the Academic Profession Is Changing," *Daedalus*, Fall 1997, pp. 1, 4–5—as well as Hanson and Heath, note 120 above, *passim*.

and on both accounts stimulates academic inquiry and debate. Another is a certain exhaustion in traditional philosophical inquiry, which has incited a search for new topics. Another is that people drawn to texts bristling with interpretive problems will find plenty of such texts in the canon of moral philosophy. And of course moral philosophy may attract people who believe, however mistakenly, that teaching and research in moral philosophy *can* make the world a better place, as well as people who have a strongly religious (whether or not theistic) temperament but no religious vocation.

Two other reasons for the persistence of academic moralism may be even more important. First, the revulsion against Nazism, although understandable without reference to morality, being based on altruism for the victims and fear of the perpetrators, created a demand for a powerful vocabulary of condemnation. To write of Nazism as a failed experiment in social organization by limited, violent, and dangerous people who didn't share our values seems inadequate to our anger. I have no objection to the employment of moral terminology to denote degrees of indignation. Expressing indignation is one of the functions of a moral vocabulary, as emotivists overemphasize. But the existence of a universalistic terminology of condemnation—the use of generalization and even exaggeration as rhetorical devices or to vent anger—does not show that there are universals denoted by our terms. Appealing to universal moral values (the "brotherhood of man," for example) may have political value as a rhetorical counter to the kind of aggressive ethnocentrism epitomized by Carl Schmitt's slogan "all right is the right of a particular *Volk*,"[175] but political value is not moral truth.

Moralists warn us that we may not be able to repress dangerous tendencies in ourselves or others unless we believe that when we say that particular conduct or its perpetrators are immoral, we are saying something that is true, rather than expressing fear and revulsion or at most uttering a local truth (true for us, not necessarily for those we hate). This *may* be psychologically astute, but it is no answer to the skeptic; the fact that a belief is socially valuable is no evidence of its truth, unless the society would be endangered if the belief were false. But the warning is not even psychologically astute. Most people obey the moral code of their society without thinking. You swerve to avoid the child in the middle of the road without thinking about whether children have moral rights greater than those of

---

175. Quoted without indication of source in Mark Lilla, "The Enemy of Liberalism," *New York Review of Books*, May 15, 1997, p. 38.

squirrels; you do this whether you are a moral skeptic or a metaphysical moral realist or something in between. A person who somehow managed to become perfectly reflective about his behavior would be a kind of monster. One is better off surrounded by ordinary, morally unreflective people: the implication of Gross's study.

But the main reason for the persistence of academic moralism despite its manifold shortcomings may have nothing to do with revulsion against Nazism or any of the other points I have made. It may be that academic moralism promotes a certain kind of solidarity. We saw Professor Finnis attacking homosexuality in a style of argument unlikely to be intelligible, let alone persuasive, to people who do not share his religious beliefs. This leads me to conjecture that his principal *intended* audience consists of his coreligionists, people already convinced of the immorality of homosexuality. (His unintended audience consists of his secular critics.) The same is true of the people on the other side, such as Thomson, Gutmann, and Thompson. They too are preaching to the converted.

Most preaching *is* to the converted. It serves the important function of convincing people who think like you that they are not alone in their beliefs; that they have the backing of someone who is confident, competent, articulate, and thoughtful; and that there is a language in which to express and, by expressing, solidify and vivify these beliefs. It forges a community of believers, and by doing so brings people out of their intellectual isolation and stiffens their backbone, because few people have the courage of their convictions unless they think that many other people share those convictions. Academic moralism is not really about making us better. It is about manning the ramparts, and rallying the troops, that defend the groups into which we are divided.

In making this observation I am not contradicting my earlier claim that academic moralism does not change people's beliefs. There is a difference between changing and solidifying beliefs. The tendency of moral debate to generate moral divergence suggests that moral argument doesn't always just bounce off the skulls of the people to whom it is addressed. It serves also to remind them of, and to confirm them in their intuitive (and perhaps only vaguely apprehended) moral beliefs. This is an important rhetorical function. But it should not be confused with either inspiring people to change their beliefs or way of life or giving them rationally persuasive grounds for doing so.

Chapter 2

LEGAL THEORY, MORAL THEMES

The term "legal theory" is not as familiar as it should be. It is distinct both from legal philosophy (or jurisprudence), which however it subsumes, and doctrinal analysis. Legal philosophy analyzes high-level abstractions related to law, such as legal positivism, natural law, legal hermeneutics, legal formalism, and legal realism. Doctrinal analysis is the analysis of legal rules, standards, and principles by lawyers (including judges and law professors) who bring to such analysis no more than their legal training plus the linguistic and cultural knowledge, techniques, and presuppositions that they share with the rest of their social community. Legal theory includes legal philosophy but is broader, because it also includes the use of nonlegal methods of inquiry to illuminate specific issues of law; it excludes only doctrinal analysis.

Some legal theorists consider moral principles part of law and want to apply moral theory directly to legal issues. Others, constitutional theorists in particular, have proposed legal theories that either are based on moral (or cognate political) theory or have a form similar to, and the methodological difficulties characteristic of, moral theory. And many of the schools of jurisprudence, the most abstract branch of legal theory, are likewise either based on or formally similar to moral theory. This chapter is about the infection of legal theory by moral theory and about the profession's efforts to resist the infection.

Jurisprudence and Moral Theory

We can study the entanglement of jurisprudence with moral theory by tracing the evolution of jurisprudential thinking from H. L. A. Hart to

Ronald Dworkin and thence to Jürgen Habermas. The feature of these jurisprudential theories that I want to emphasize is their pretensions to universality. Each theorist announces principles he thinks applicable to any legal system, yet each is actually best understood as describing a national legal system—English in the case of Hart, American in the case of Dworkin, German in the case of Habermas. Once this is seen, any tincture of moral theory in their jurisprudential systems can be recharacterized in political or pragmatic terms and the moral theory discarded.

Hart versus Dworkin

The concept of law that Hart set forth in his book of that title—a classic of legal positivism—is law as a system of rules.[1] A rule of recognition enables people to spot when a particular rule of conduct is part of the system of *legal* rules of conduct, which are applied by judges, who correspond to umpires in games, another rule-based activity. Just as games would fall apart if umpires had discretion whether or not to enforce the rules, the legal system would fall apart if "scorer's discretion" were allowed to judges. But because many legal rules are less precise than rules of games, judges often cannot decide cases by applying an existing rule of law. When faced with cases that are thus "legally unregulated" (p. 252), judges exercise discretion. In fact, they are legislators in such cases—makers of rules. Being *unelected* legislators, they are bound to proceed modestly if they conceive their "creative" decisions to be legislative. If, instead, judges are doing, not making, law when they decide those cases, they are acting within the scope of their authorized function and professional competence and so need not be timid. This is Ronald Dworkin's view. The law comprises not merely the rules laid down by legislatures and other promulgators of formal legal rules, but also the principles, notably including moral principles, that legislators or judges might draw upon in creating new rules. Judges have a duty to be moral philosophers.[2]

It is revealing that while Dworkin rarely discusses legal doctrines other

1. H. L. A. Hart, *The Concept of Law* (1st ed. 1961, 2d ed. 1994). My page references will be to the second edition, which is unchanged from the first except for a substantial Postscript, in which Hart discusses his differences with Dworkin.

2. See, for example, Ronald Dworkin, "Introduction," in Dworkin, *Freedom's Law: The Moral Reading of the American Constitution* 1 (1996); Dworkin, "In Praise of Theory," 29 *Arizona State Law Journal* 353 (1997); Dworkin, "Reply," 29 *Arizona State Law Journal* 431 (1997). For criticism, see Michael W. McConnell, "The Importance of Humility in Judicial Review: A Comment on Ronald Dworkin's 'Moral Reading' of the Constitution," 65 *Fordham Law Review* 1269 (1997).

than common law doctrines or, more frequently, doctrines that the Supreme Court has conjured from the vaguest provisions of the U.S. Constitution—provisions that judges have treated as essentially directives to the courts to create constitutional doctrine by the common law method—Hart's book does not even contain an index reference to "common law." The common law is an embarrassment to his account.[3] While acknowledging that "in some systems of law, as in the United States, the ultimate criteria of legal validity might explicitly incorporate[,] besides pedigree, principles of justice or substantive moral values, and these may form the content of legal *constitutional* restraints" (p. 247, emphasis added), Hart does not extend this dispensation to the common law. The common law cannot be fitted to the idea of a rule of recognition. Because the materials out of which judges make common law are not limited to enactments of positive law, there is no place to look for the rules—nothing for the rule of recognition to base recognition on. And unlike constitutional law, common law cannot be dismissed as a foreign innovation; much of English law *is* common law.

It is no answer to the positivist's quandary, as Holmes (who had a broad positivist streak) thought, to deem the common law a body of legislation promulgated by judges as the delegates of legislatures. It would deprive the rule of recognition of any "ruledness"; anything the judges did would be lawful, just because they were doing it. And this approach would imply (an implication that Holmes made explicit in calling judges "interstitial" legislators)[4] that whenever in deciding a common law case the judges modified, extended, or even just refined a rule of the common law—the sorts of thing that judges in common law countries do all the time, even in a system such as the English that lays great emphasis on judges' standing by previous decisions—they would not be judging; they would be legislating. This characterization of the judicial role not only overlooks important differences between common law courts on the one hand and legislatures on the other; it also entails the startling proposition that *most* of what American appellate judges do, except when deciding appeals that involve purely factual issues or are so open and shut—so plainly controlled by some rule—that they can be decided without an opinion or other statement of reasons, is legislation. A further objection to the positivist concep-

3. A. W. B. Simpson, "The Common Law and Legal Theory," in *Oxford Essays in Jurisprudence: Second Series* 77, 80–84 (A. W. B. Simpson ed. 1973).

4. Southern Pacific Co. v. Jensen, 244 U.S. 205, 221 (1917) (dissenting opinion). See also Benjamin N. Cardozo, *The Nature of the Judicial Process* 113–115 (1921).

tion is that judges and lawyers are not aware of a division between the judge as applier and as maker of law. There is no point in the process of argument or decision at which the judges or lawyers say, "We've exhausted the law; it's time to legislate."

Hart's view is, not surprisingly, more plausible when applied to England than when applied to the United States. Parliament has taken upon itself more responsibility vis-à-vis the courts for making the rules of law than American legislatures have done vis-à-vis American courts.[5] If some doctrine of English law needs patching up, English judges can decide, with a better conscience than their American counterparts in the same situation, to leave the matter to the legislature to correct.[6] Since English judges have this option, if they reject it and create rules they may be thought to be legislating. But a more basic point is that judges are not just legislators in robes even when they are making rules. They differ from real legislators in what they can properly base rules on. Dworkin argues that judges in their rulemaking role may base them only on principles, whereas legislators may base them on policies as well.[7] In making this distinction he swings to the opposite extreme from Hart and exaggerates the difference between legislative and judicial rulemakers. It is true that judges are supposed to be, and the conditions of their employment as well as the methods and procedures they use encourage them to be, more principled than legislatures, less swayed by the importunings of narrow interest groups and by ignorant public opinion. But what Dworkin calls "policies" can be principled, while some of his principles strike many observers as highly debatable policies suspiciously convergent with the program of the left wing of the Democratic Party. This is a detail. The important point is that if a big part of judging consists not of "legislating" in Hart's sense of an essentially uncanalized exercise of discretion but instead of the methodical application of principles and policies drawn from a world of thought and feeling

5. See Patrick S. Atiyah, "Judicial-Legislative Relations in England," in *Judges and Legislators: Toward Institutional Comity* 129 (Robert A. Katzmann ed. 1988); William S. Jordan III, "Legislative History and Statutory Interpretation: The Relevance of English Practice," 29 *University of San Francisco Law Review* 1 (1994).

6. A better conscience but not a perfect one. If the doctrine affects only a small number of people, Parliament may not get around to reforming it, because of the competing demands on its time. Christopher Staughton, "The Role of the Law Commission: Parliamentary and Public Perceptions of Statute Law," 16 *Statute Law Review* 7, 9 (1995).

7. For a compact statement of his position, see Ronald Dworkin, "Political Judges and the Rule of Law," 64 *Proceedings of the British Academy* 259, 261 (1978).

not circumscribed by lawyers' knowledge, the idea of law as a system of rules is undermined.

Hart's reply that principles are a kind of rule—a weak or vague rule, like a presumption (a weak rule) or a standard such as negligence (a vague or multifactored rule), or a "latent" rule (p. 268)—misses Dworkin's point. Principles and rules are related hierarchically rather than coordinately. Rules mediate between principles and action. They translate principles into directives for action. They are subtended by principles. In Joseph Raz's reformulation of legal positivism, principles are not law because their source (the common morality, the teaching of the great philosophers, or whatever) is not a source of law.[8]

Hart acknowledges that when judges act as legislators they are subject to limitations from which legislators are free. Apart from limitations of a purely *Realpolitik* character, the judge must "act as a conscientious legislator would by deciding according to his own beliefs and values" (p. 273).[9] This is not much of a concession. To decide according to one's "own beliefs and values" is not to decide in accordance with, or to be disciplined by, principle or policy. One is not surprised to find Hart implying on the preceding page of his book that whenever the judge decides a case in which "no decision either way is dictated by the law," he is "step[ping] outside the law" (p. 272).[10] Hart really does think that law is a system of rules.

Patrick Devlin, a fellow positivist, is even more emphatic. He acknowledges that judges sometimes "stretch the law" to do substantive justice, and he does not disapprove—provided the judges don't *acknowledge* that they are stretching the law.[11] Devlin cannot admit a place in the concept of law for the moral feelings that shape our response to the "equities" of a legal dispute. When judges act on those feelings they are behaving lawlessly, but not badly, so they must conceal what they are doing, rather than cease doing it.

In "strong" versions of positivism, including Hart's, a necessary condition of making a rule of primary obligation a rule of law is that the rule be

8. See, for example, Joseph Raz, "The Problem about the Nature of Law," in Raz, *Ethics in the Public Domain: Essays in the Morality of Law and Politics* 179 (1994).

9. One might have thought that a legislator would have a representative function and therefore could not properly decide *only* according to his own beliefs and values.

10. Raz is explicit about this, as we have seen. See also his paper "Authority, Law, and Morality," in Raz, note 8 above, at 194, 213.

11. Patrick Devlin, *The Judge* 90–93 (1979).

picked out by a legal system's rule of recognition. In "weak" versions, it is a sufficient condition. For the first type of positivist all the Nazi laws were indeed law, but the "law" applied by the Nuremberg Tribunal was not; while for the second type of positivist, the "weak," the Nazi laws were law, but the law applied by the tribunal also may have been law. A "strong" natural lawyer insists that law is law only if it conforms to natural law. A "weak" natural lawyer, however, is indistinguishable from a "weak" positivist. This is Dworkin's position. He does not deny that the Nazi laws were law in a permissible sense of the word.[12] But he thinks that the freewheeling decisions of the Supreme Court during Earl Warren's tenure were also law. Although Dworkin is not a natural lawyer in the traditional sense of a believer that legal obligations can be derived from religious or other metaphysical principles, any more than he is a metaphysical moral theorist, he does not resist the labeling of his theory of adjudication as a natural-law theory.[13]

I think that Hart is descriptively, though not semantically, more accurate in his account of judicial activity in the open area, the area where the rules run out. The cases in that area are frequently indeterminate, rather than merely difficult. In deciding such cases the judge is bound to be making a value choice based on intuition and personal experience—albeit a choice less likely than a legislator's to reflect the pressure of special-interest groups or the passions of the moment—rather than engaging solely in analysis, reflection, or some special mode of inquiry called "legal reasoning." But I disagree with Hart's blanket statement that when judges do these things they are stepping outside the law. It depends on what is expected of judges, and this differs among different legal systems. Likewise I think that Dworkin exaggerates the determinateness of legal reasoning and that it is no accident that the controversial decisions of the Supreme Court that he declares to be principled conform to his political preferences. What he should be saying is that when judges render political decisions they are still doing law, because law is interpenetrated with politics. One thing law is is simply the *activity* of judges, and that activity frequently has a political dimension. Not that "lawless judge" is an oxymoron. It means that the judge is being *too* political to conform to the

---

12. Ronald Dworkin, *Law's Empire* 103 (1986).

13. See Ronald A. Dworkin, "'Natural Law' Revisited," 34 *University of Florida Law Review* 165 (1982). For discussion and critique of Dworkin and two other modern legal theorists, John Finnis and David Richards, as natural lawyers, see Lloyd L. Weinreb, *Natural Law and Justice*, ch. 4 (1987).

reigning conception in the judge's society of the outer bounds of a judge's decisional freedom. But that is all it means.

Issues of candor to one side, where Dworkin's concept of law as embracing principles as well as rules falters is in its corollary: that judges who conceive of their function more narrowly than Dworkin thinks they should and so decline to appeal to a broad range of principles in deciding new cases, or who appeal to what Dworkin considers mere policies rather than principles, are lawless.[14] This would be plausible only if his definition of law as including principles and excluding policies were orthodox, which it is not; it is merely his view and that of some other scholars but of very few judges. To call judges lawless because they do not accept Dworkin's jurisprudence would be absurd.

By moving to a high enough level of abstraction, we can find an area of agreement between Hart and Dworkin. For Hart, most of what supreme courts do is to legislate; for Dworkin, it is to practice applied moral philosophy. These sound very different; but Raz explains that whenever conscientious judges go beyond the application of rules, they perforce engage in moral reasoning, for they are making normative decisions that do not originate in the law.[15] With this acknowledgment Raz joins Dworkin in bringing moral theory into the courtroom. The only difference besides nomenclature (the moral theorizing of the judge is for Dworkin a part of law but for Raz an addition to law—a second hat for judges) is that Raz thinks the open or legally uncharted area, where judges have to fall back on moral theory, is small, and Dworkin thinks it's large. They are both right, for they are describing different systems; in one of which, the English (Raz's, as Hart's), it is small, and in the other of which, the American (Dworkin's), it is large. But the difference in nomenclature is important too, though only atmospherically. Raz's judges, when they are in the open area, are doing nothing but moral philosophy—there is no law for them to apply. That should make them timid. Dworkin's judges, when they are in the open area, are doing law, because moral philosophy *is* law, for Dworkin.

Where Raz and Dworkin err most pertinently to this book is in dividing the judicial function into applying rules and doing moral theory. The

14. See, for example, Ronald Dworkin, "Bork: The Senate's Responsibility," in Dworkin, *Freedom's Law,* note 2 above, at 265.

15. See Joseph Raz, "The Inner Logic of the Law," in Raz, note 8 above, at 222, 232.

proper divisions are applying rules and making rules. Of all the aids to making rules, moral theory is one of the least promising. Raz and Dworkin have made the mistake of equating normative reasoning with moral reasoning.

Habermas

The preface to Hart's book says that the reader is free to take the book as "an essay in descriptive sociology" (p. v), and so taken it is illuminating as a stylized description of the English legal system by a knowledgeable insider, just as Dworkin's jurisprudence is illuminating as a stylized description of the methods of liberal Supreme Court Justices, and just as the discussion of corrective justice in the *Nicomachean Ethics* is illuminating as a stylized description of the Athenian legal system of Aristotle's day,[16] though in the case of both Dworkin and Aristotle, "idealized" might be more accurate than "stylized." What is striking about Hart's book when it is regarded as description (or self-description) rather than as philosophy is that it is almost as descriptive of the Continental as of the English legal system. Hart's emphasis on law as a body of rules, his lack of interest in the common law, his conception of the judge as primarily an applier of rules laid down by legislatures, and his desire to demarcate a realm that is law and not politics add up to a mindset characteristic of Continental legal systems since the French Revolution but not of the English legal system before this century or of the American legal system ever.[17]

This observation about the Continental flavor of Hart's jurisprudence provides background for understanding the contemporary German philosopher and sociologist Jürgen Habermas, author of a major book on jurisprudence.[18] Another helpful bit of background is Habermas's personal history (for Hart and Dworkin it is enough to know that they are English and American, respectively). Habermas was a month short of his sixteenth

16. Cf. S. C. Todd, *The Shape of Athenian Law* 264–268 (1993).

17. Hart acknowledges (pp. 292–295) the similarity of his concept of law to that of the Austrian legal positivist Hans Kelsen, while noting a number of differences. And there is an evident similarity between the influential views of the late-nineteenth-century English lawyer A. V. Dicey and the concept of the *Rechtsstaat* that, as we are about to see, is a prominent feature of Continental, especially German, legal thinking. Compare A. V. Dicey, *Introduction to the Study of the Law of the Constitution*, ch. 4 (4th ed. 1893), esp. pp. 191–192, with William Ewald, "Comparative Jurisprudence (I): What Was It Like to Try a Rat?" 143 *University of Pennsylvania Law Review* 1889, 2053–2055 (1995).

18. Jürgen Habermas, *Between Facts and Norms: Contributions to a Discourse Theory of Law and Democracy* (1996). Page references to his book appear in the text of this chapter.

birthday when Hitler's Reich collapsed. Shocked to learn of the Nazi atrocities, he proceeded through the West German university system appalled by its unapologetic continuity with the past. Its philosophy departments were staffed almost entirely by professors who had served uncomplainingly during the Nazi period and who looked up to Heidegger (whom Habermas sarcastically calls the "felicitously de-Nazified Heidegger")[19] as the lodestar of German philosophy. From these early experiences Habermas acquired a lifelong un-German distaste for the idea of German nationhood, for the German philosophical tradition insofar as it nourishes nationalism and political extremism whether of the Right or of the Left (Habermas is a social democrat), and for totalizing theories of a religious or other metaphysical cast. He derides "the longing of many intellectuals for a lost German identity" as "kitsch," and says, much in the spirit of my first chapter, that "philosophers are not teachers of the nation. They can sometimes—if only rarely—be useful people."[20] For inspiration he reaches back to Kant, who preceded the creation of the German nation and built his moral and political philosophy on universalistic rather than ethnic foundations.

Kant's building materials, however, were metaphysical ideas that Habermas rightly considers unavailable in the predominantly secular, morally heterogeneous, socially complex and differentiated, relativist, and historicist era in which we live, where "normative orders must be maintained without metasocial guarantees" (p. 26). In place of the idea that each of us can use our God-given reason to construct a pipeline to ultimate scientific and moral truths, Habermas has borrowed from Charles Sanders Peirce and greatly elaborated the pragmatic creed that truth, whether of a scientific, a moral, or a political character, is most usefully regarded as what a community of rational, disinterested, undominated inquirers would arrive at if given all the time in the world. These communities do not have all the time in the world, so the agreements they arrive at are tentative and revisable. But they are the best that we can hope for and, in fact, are on the whole good enough.

Habermas thinks that his theory, the theory of "communicative action" or "discourse theory," is consistent with the rejection of totalizing visions because its aim is merely to secure the preconditions for rational inquiry, rather than to anticipate the end of that inquiry. It seeks, in the manner of

19. *Autonomy and Solidarity: Interviews with Jürgen Habermas* 156 (Peter Dews ed., rev. ed. 1992). See also id. at 192.
20. Id. at 179, 199.

Holmes's reworking of Peirce,[21] to identify and maintain workably competitive markets in ideas and opinions, and it places its faith in competitive outcomes in those markets. So it is interested in equality of incomes, say, not as a goal that might be deduced from utilitarianism or Marxism or some other moral or political theory but only insofar as some measure of equality may be necessary to protect the rationality of political debate against being impaired by imbalances in the amount of money donated to particular candidates or causes.

Almost as important to Habermas's jurisprudence as discourse theory is the German jurisprudential tradition—or rather the limitations of that tradition. German jurisprudence has historically been organized around the concepts of *Rechtsstaat* and *Sozialstaat* ("justice state" and "social state"). The first is the idea that government must operate exclusively through highly abstract laws uniformly enforced. These are laws that in their administration by judges and other officials, as well as in their formulation by legislatures, abstract from the unique situation of particular persons or classes of person; hence laws that, for example, enforce property rights regardless of consequence and without consideration of competing goals or interests; laws, in short, out of which every drop of equitable discretion has been wrung. (So plea bargaining is improper— still the official position of the German legal system.) Such a rigid conception of the rule of law eventually proved politically unrealistic. It was modified in the direction of the *Sozialstaat,* which seeks to make operational the merely formal rights created by the *Rechtsstaat* and (both to that end and, independently, for the sake of social justice) to reduce social and economic tensions by creating entitlements to public services, such as education.

Missing from both concepts, however, is any reference to democracy. The theory of the *Rechtsstaat* was formulated by Kant in eighteenth-century Prussia, an absolute monarchy (praised by Kant in his 1784 essay *Was ist Aufklärung?*) at a time when England was already a constitutional monarchy. It is a theory of limited rather than of popular government, a theory under which, as Habermas explains, the legitimation of "the constitutional state . . . is premised solely on aspects of the legal medium through which political power is exercised, namely, the abstract rule structure of legal statutes, the autonomy of the judiciary, as well as the fact that administration is bound by law and has a 'rational' construction" (p. 73). The *Sozialstaat,* which originated in Bismarck's Germany, was paternalis-

---

21. See Abrams v. United States, 250 U.S. 616, 630 (1919) (dissenting opinion).

tic rather than popular and has bred welfare dependency and other dysfunctions as well as being in tension with the abstract, formal, and nondiscretionary character of *Rechtsstaat* norms.

Habermas does not believe that it is possible to legitimate law by reference either to natural law (law as morality) or to legal positivism (law as authoritatively promulgated rules). The reason is given by his title: law resides *between* facts and norms. It is on the one hand a part of social reality and on the other a part of the normative (moral) order, but it is not fully the one or the other. In particular, it is not simply a subset of moral duties. It binds only the people who happen to be subject to a given legal system. It employs coercion, and thus secures the compliance even of people for whom law, or a particular law, is not morally obligating. It constrains only behavior, and thus "enforces norm-conformative behavior while leaving motives and attitudes open" (p. 116). Indeed it "complements morality by relieving the individual of the cognitive burdens of forming her own moral judgments" (p. 115). It even creates a space in which people can opt out of certain moral duties. Habermas is emphatic that "legally granted liberties entitle one to *drop out* of communicative action" (p. 120, emphasis in original) and thus to live the unexamined life or the thoroughly private life.

While unwilling to dissolve law into morality, Habermas believes that law is not effective unless most people obey it not because they are coerced or bribed to do so but because they accept the moral authority of the law. But how is its moral authority to be secured? Habermas believes that all but one of the possible ways are either disreputable (the tradition of the German *Volk,* for example) or, because we live in a "postmetaphysical" world, unavailable. Among the modern metaphysicians of the law, for Habermas, are Rawls and Dworkin. Neither considers himself to hold a metaphysical conception of justice or law; but both orient law toward concrete moral ends; and "in a pluralistic society, the theory of justice can expect to be accepted by citizens only if it limits itself to a conception that is postmetaphysical in the strict sense, that is, only if it avoids taking sides in the contest of competing forms of life and worldviews" (p. 60). At the other end of the spectrum from the metaphysicians are the positivists, like H. L. A. Hart, who give "priority to a narrowly conceived institutional history purged of any suprapositive validity basis" (p. 202); this cannot serve to confer legitimacy on the legal system either.

The only grounding for a legitimate legal system in the modern world that survives Habermas's criticisms is democracy. He recognizes the element of paradox in the suggestion. For he is strongly committed to the core ideas of the *Rechtsstaat* and the *Sozialstaat:* that law is supposed to protect the people from the government and the weak people from the strong people. In a democracy the people *are* the government, so how can the law protect the people *from* the government? And democracy means majority rule; another name for the majority is the stronger (though sometimes only by virtue of the voting rules); and majorities sometimes like to coerce minorities. Law and democracy—democracy in its populist form, at least—seem inconsistent.

The dilemma dissolves, according to Habermas, when democracy is approached from the direction of discourse theory. Epistemic or deliberative democracy, the democracy of inquirers, unlike populist or plebiscitary democracy, presupposes both the traditional negative liberties associated with the *Rechtsstaat* and the positive liberties associated with the *Sozialstaat.* People who, by virtue of the rights (including welfare rights) that the law confers on them, are neither intimidated nor desperate can participate rationally in political debate, and the laws that are enacted will be legitimate because supported by a consensus achieved through rational discourse. The laws secure the conditions for epistemic democracy by conferring essential rights, and epistemic democracy in turn secures the legitimacy of the laws.

Habermas is aware that modeling the political process as a system of fully rational, and in particular fully *disinterested,* inquiry may appear to be hopelessly unrealistic. Interest groups, the selective and distorting attentions of the media, public ignorance and apathy, and other interrelated social phenomena that neither the *Rechtsstaat* nor the *Sozialstaat* regulates—indeed, that the *Rechtsstaat* fosters by creating the preconditions of capitalist development—deflect the political process from the deliberative ideal. Habermas wants to regulate these things; indeed, borrowing a leaf from John Hart Ely,[22] he considers the central and virtually the only task of constitutional law to be to secure "equal opportunities for the political use of communicative freedoms" (p. 127). His only criticism is that Ely lacks a theory of democracy. His criticism of other American constitutional theorists is that they are antidemocratic and so do not provide a solid grounding for the legitimacy of constitutional law. They cast the Supreme Court in the role of "a pedagogical guardian or regent" of an incompetent "sovereign," the people (p. 278). "The addressees of law would not be able to understand themselves as its authors if the legislator

---

22. See John Hart Ely, *Democracy and Distrust: A Theory of Judicial Review* (1980).

[or judge] were to discover human rights as pregiven moral facts that merely need to be enacted as positive law" (p. 454).

Consistent with these criticisms, which fit Dworkin like a glove, Habermas believes that there is too much hand-wringing over the imperfections of political democracy. Political parties being coalitions of disparate interests, it is difficult for a politician to formulate an appeal for votes in terms limited to the narrow interests of the members of his coalition. The politician is constrained to speak in broader terms of principle, and this forces the voting public to think in terms of principle too. It may even commit the politician to a public-spirited position in order to maintain consistency: "concealing publicly indefensible interests behind pretended moral or ethical reasons necessitates self-bindings that . . . lead to the inclusion of others' interests" (p. 340). And people form their views about political questions not only by listening to politicians and media pundits but also by reflection on personal and social experiences acquired in the family, at work, in political or cultural movements, and in other voluntary nonpolitical associations. This competition in points of view enables people to form political opinions that are authentically their own. Although Habermas thus rejects the view that people are "'cultural dopes' who are manipulated by the [television] programs offered to them" (p. 377), he is not so naive as to suppose that self-interest can be eliminated from the political process. Quite the contrary, it is because of the "weak motivating force of good reasons" (pp. 113–114) (a highly apropos phrase) that law has its irreducible "factive" as well as normative component. "Bargaining processes are tailored for situations in which social power relations cannot be neutralized in the way rational discourses presuppose" (p. 166). Compromises arrived at through bargaining rather than consensus when the latter proves unattainable are legitimate so long as the bargaining interests have equal power and therefore "equal chances of prevailing" (p. 167). This is another basis for redistributive policies viewed not as ends in themselves but as procedural preconditions for legitimate law.

Habermas's jurisprudence is farther away from academic moralism than Dworkin or even than Hart, who, in allowing to judges an area of discretion, implicitly (and his disciple Raz explicitly) authorizes the use of moral theory in that area. Habermas, more committed to democracy than either Dworkin or Hart, appears not to envisage *any* role for judges in checking democratic decision making. Yet Habermas's concept of democracy is idealistic; and, as he recognizes, indeed emphasizes, at present the ideal is at best approximated rather than completely realized. The unanswered question is how much latitude should be permitted to judges when they deal with issues that have not been addressed in a manner that satisfies his criteria of deliberative democracy.

The answer is: maybe more than Habermas assumes. He exaggerates the extent to which legislative enactments or even judicial decisions can be regarded as the outcome of rational discourse in his exacting conception of it as speech oriented to understanding.[23] The subject matter of enactments and decisions is often, perhaps typically, too emotional or too freighted with uncertainty (or both) for the participants to be able to reach agreement. Peirce was a scientist as well as a philosopher. His notion of an ideal deliberating community was based on the model of the scientific community. In that community, the criteria of validity are both agreed upon and operational, enabling the community to reach the nirvana of observer independence—the condition in which people who have different values and perspectives are brought into uncoerced agreement. The political community is not like that, and we have seen that moral theory is not an apt tool for forging uncoerced agreement on moral issues—indeed it may drive people further apart. The outcomes of legislative "deliberations" usually reflect compromises between bargaining interests with unequal power (what Habermas means by equal bargaining power and how he proposes to create it are mysteries), or the power of opportunistic coalitions (as where religious fundamentalists and radical feminists agree to support a ban on pornography), or sheer ignorance and confusion. Or they may reflect divergent estimates of consequences, as where both liberals and conservatives agree to reduce sentencing discretion—the former in the hope that it will reduce unjust disparities and discriminations, the latter in the hope that it will lead to longer sentences. Unbridgeable gaps in values and perceptions are often visible in split judicial decisions as well.

When the stakes are high, emotion engaged, information sparse, criteria contested, and expertise untrustworthy—a pretty good description of the democratic process—people do not simply yield to the weight of argument, especially argument derived from the abstractions of moral or political theory. Habermas himself warns against "avant-gardism": the "consensually veiled domination of intellectual spokespersons" (p. 470). "Powerful in word, they grab for themselves the very power they profess to

23. Perhaps, as Rawls argues, Habermas asks too little of the law—only that it be legitimate, rather than that it also be just. John Rawls, *Political Liberalism* 427–431 (paperback ed. 1996). The fact that law issues from a freewheeling democratic process may make it legitimate without making it just.

dissolve in the medium of the word" (p. 489). These are pretty good descriptions of legal theory à la Dworkin. And elsewhere Habermas has distinguished between "discourse," where agreement is secured through the force of argument, and aesthetic evaluations, which are not expected to convince all doubters even if there is no time limit on deliberation.[24] Political and judicial disagreements are far more often of the latter kind than of the discourse kind, where disagreement would dissolve if only deliberation continued long enough.

It would be odd to base the prohibition of police torture, for example, on a consensus achieved by a weighing of the arguments pro and con. The reasons that are given for the prohibition—that it makes the police lazy or arrogant, or brutalizes them, or produces false information, or is likely to be used against political enemies and social outcasts, or makes the state too powerful and intimidating, or lowers the "tone" of the society, or incites disorder—cannot be shown to outweigh the fact that torture is a generally effective method of eliciting information about difficult-to-solve crimes.[25] And "rights" are on both sides of the issue, the rights of victims balancing the rights of suspects. The revulsion against torture (a *qualified* revulsion, since a fair amount of psychological coercion of criminal suspects is either authorized or winked at) lives largely below thought, just as our other moral intuitions do. Academia, however, selects for people who like to make and weigh arguments.

Torture is an easy case because there is consensus, though it owes little if anything to discourse in Habermas's sense. Many other issues on the legislative and judicial agenda today can be resolved neither by a convergence of intuitions (as in the case of torture) nor by discourse. They can be resolved only by power, or by the nonrational methods of persuasion that produce religious conversions and other Gestalt switches. Habermas disagrees, and to make the political climate more congenial to discourse theory urges "curbs on the power of the media" (p. 442). But he does not explain what those curbs might be or how they would be consistent with the preservation of freedom of expression—one of the liberties that under-

24. See Georgia Warnke, "Communicative Rationality and Cultural Values," in *The Cambridge Companion to Habermas* 120, 126–129 (Stephen K. White ed. 1995).

25. I do think, however, that the medieval and early modern system of criminal justice, which made confessions elicited by judicially administered torture the centerpiece of the criminal process, became dysfunctional once alternative methods of fact finding became feasible. See Michel Foucault, *Discipline and Punish: The Birth of the Prison*, pt. 2 (1977); David Garland, *Punishment and Modern Society: A Study in Social Theory*, ch. 8 (1990); John H. Langbein, *Torture and the Law of Proof: Europe and England in the Ancien Régime* 7–12 (1976).

gird the democratic legitimacy of the law—or why curbs are necessary given the competitiveness and diversity of the media and his own rejection of the view that people are "cultural dopes." He favors liberal immigration policies on the pragmatic ground of the value of multiplying perspectives. But he does not consider the effect on the likelihood of achieving rational consensus of admitting as citizens entitled to vote and otherwise participate in the political life of the nation large numbers of people whose values were shaped in societies that do not resolve conflict by deliberative means. So even if it would be good if political decision making were more deliberative, Habermas has no persuasive ideas for making it more deliberative.

Americans may wonder what exactly is the problem to which Habermas's theory of law is offered as the solution. He would say that it is the problem of law's legitimacy. It is not clear that there is such a problem in all countries—or, in particular, in the United States. He says that "law must do more than simply meet the functional requirements of a complex society; it must also satisfy the precarious conditions of a social integration that ultimately takes place through the achievements of mutual understanding on the part of communicatively acting subjects" (p. 83). Yet if law meets "the functional requirements of a complex society" by providing a reasonably predictable, adaptable, and just framework for peaceful social interactions, where "just" means nothing more pretentious than consistent with durable public opinion, who is going to raise an issue of legitimacy *about the framework,* that is, about the law itself? Particular laws, particular judicial decisions, particular enforcement decisions and institutional details will sometimes be challenged as illegitimate. An example would be a decision by a judge who had been bribed, or, more subtly, a judicial decision that rested on arguments that the legal culture ruled out of bounds for judges. These retail issues of legitimacy are not illuminated by discourse theory, and the wholesale issue does not arise. A successful practice does not require foundations.

Ironically given its universalistic outlook, Habermas's theory (like Hart's, like Dworkin's) speaks far more directly to his national, namely the German, situation than to the situation of other countries.[26] Americans do not need to be instructed in the values of diversity, the unavailability of

---

26. Habermas makes a similar point about Rawls: "As soon as he [Rawls] moves to his two principles, he is speaking as a citizen of the United States with a certain background . . . There is nothing universal about his particular design for a just society." *Autonomy and Solidarity,* note 19 above, at 200.

"metaphysical" groundings for political principles, the importance of democracy, or the preconditions for legitimate political institutions. These things are features of our form of life, the taken-for-granted background of discussion and debate. The Germany in which Habermas grew up did not have a secure, untroubled relation to diversity, democracy, reason, or law. On the contrary, it seemed dangerously susceptible to totalizing visions, stifling cultural conformity, ethnocentrism, irrationalism, political extremism, and, in law, to excessive formalism and paternalism. Against all these tendencies, which seem weak and harmless a half century after the fall of Hitler but may have received a boost from the unification of the two Germanies, discourse theory may be a powerful antidote. Habermas's Germany has a *local* need for a *universalist* jurisprudence to inoculate Germans against excesses of nationalism. Americans are fortunate in not needing such a polemic so badly.

But while much of Habermas's jurisprudence is not "for us," his emphasis on the robustness of democracy, which has no counterpart in Hart's or Dworkin's more familar jurisprudential approaches, and his criticism of a Platonic Guardians conception of judges, have as much application to the United States as to Germany. Our intelligentsia takes democracy for granted, chafes under it, is impatient for an elite of academically guided judges to short-circuit it. Germans know better.

Moral Theory Applied Directly to Law

Hart, Dworkin, and Habermas do not exhaust the universe of jurisprudence. But they are sufficiently representative to suggest that judges looking for help in deciding difficult cases are not going to get much from jurisprudence. It is too abstract yet at the same time, as I have emphasized, too culturally specific to have much utility. The residue of jurisprudential speculations that may have some practical significance is the proposition that legal positivism (Hart) is not an adequate descriptive or normative theory of American law (Dworkin). Much of that law is the product of judicial decisions that cannot be justified by reference to the standard sources yet are not usurpative or even unsound. Our judges must be, and can hardly avoid, going outside those sources. But to where? One possible answer is moral theory. It is the answer to which the name "natural law" was traditionally attached and is the answer given by Dworkin as a corollary to his jurisprudential theory. But as long as there are other places outside "law" in its narrow positivist sense in which to look for answers to legal questions—and we shall see that there are—the only reason to look for the answers in moral theory would be that it is a better place to look than the alternatives. If the argument in Chapter 1 is correct, it is unlikely to be better, though this depends on the alternatives.

Law and Morality

Moral theory might seem an inescapable concern of law because of the overlap between moral and legal obligations. There is overlap even in a predominantly positivistic legal system, such as the English. Tort law and criminal law deal with responsibility for harmful acts and also with responsibility, or more commonly lack of responsibility, for failure to prevent harmful acts, as when liability is sought to be fastened on someone who could have rescued a person in distress without danger to himself, yet stood by. Criminal law bases responsibility, most of the time anyway, on culpable mental states. Contract law deals with the binding character of promises. The law of inheritance confronts such issues as whether a person shall be disqualified from inheriting by having murdered his benefactor. Whether ownership includes the right to evict a starving tenant is a question of property law. And so on ad infinitum. The reason for the overlap between morality and law is that they are parallel methods, the first being the earlier, for bringing about the kind and degree of cooperation that a society needs in order to prosper.

This might tempt one to say that law *backs up* morality, adding temporal sanctions to the sanctions of conscience, though selectively, with due regard for the costs and benefits of the addition. It might seem to follow that judges, in a system such as the American in which they have a lot of power to shape the law, would from time to time have to decide contested issues of morality in order to determine what system of morality the law should be following. I don't think so. Habermas is right to emphasize the distinction between law and morality. What law does is not helpfully described as backing up morality, and even if it were, it would not follow that when the relevant moral principles are contested the judges should choose between the contestants.

Many moral principles have no backing from law. Lying is not a tort or a crime (unless under oath), or charity a legal duty. The law is indifferent to most promise breaking. Seduction is no longer a tort in most states, and adultery has in practice been almost entirely freed from legal sanctions. Ugly group libels are constitutionally privileged, and much official misconduct is placed beyond the reach of legal sanction by doctrines of immunity. In most states bystanders can with impunity turn their back on persons in distress even when rescue would cost the bystander nothing in expense or risk. On the one hand, then, the law does not in general enforce morality. On the other hand, much of the conduct to which the law does attach sanctions is morally indifferent, such as fixing prices, trading securities on inside information, hiring an illegal alien when no one else is available to do the work, driving with your seat belt unfastened, breaking a contract involuntarily, and inflicting unavoidable injury in the course of a hazardous but socially necessary activity. There are reasons for the laws that punish these things, but the reasons owe little or nothing to moral intuition.

It is doubtful even that the laws punishing the sale and consumption of "controlled substances" can be justified by reference to morality, given that such close substitutes for the illegal drugs as cigarettes, alcoholic beverages, tranquilizers, and antidepressants have similar effects yet are lawful. The difference in legal treatment seems mainly a result of the association of certain drugs in the public mind with members of minority groups, hippies, rock stars, "drop-outs" and other disorderly youth, and "bohemians."[27] Criminalizing a service, moreover, tends to immoralize it. This is not because most people take their moral cues from the criminal law; it is because criminalization has a selection effect. Law-abiding people (that is, people who have better opportunities in legal than illegal businesses) exit, and the criminal class becomes the provider of the service, lending an unsavory air to it. Just consider who distributed alcoholic beverages before and after Prohibition, and who during it.

The discrepancy between law and justice is an old story, but it is obscured by the law's frequent borrowing of moral terminology, of such terms as "fair" and "unjust" and "inequitable" and "unconscionable."[28] This borrowing, which reflects in part the ecclesiastical origins of the

27. Avram Goldstein and Harold Kalant, "Drug Policy: Striking the Right Balance," 249 *Science* 1513, 1516–1517 (1990); Jess W. Bromley, "Our Society's Response to the Addictions," 38 *Clinical Chemistry* 1530 (1992); Patricia G. Erickson, "The Law, Social Control, and Drug Policy: Models, Factors, and Processes," 28 *International Journal of the Addictions* 1155 (1993); Jim Horner, "The War on Drugs: A Legitimate Battle or Another Mode of Inequality?" in *Inequality: Radical Institutionalist Views on Race, Gender, Class, and Nation* 225 (William M. Dugger ed. 1996).

28. And frequent it is. See James A. Henderson, Jr., "Judicial Reliance on Public Policy: An Empirical Analysis of Products Liability Decisions," 59 *George Washington Law Review* 1570, 1575–1578 (1991).

equity jurisdiction, has misled Dworkin into thinking that law is suffused with moral theory.[29] Holmes warned long ago of the pitfalls of misunderstanding law by taking its moral vocabulary too seriously.[30] A big part of legal education consists of showing students how to skirt those pitfalls. The law uses moral terms in part because of its origins, in part to be impressive, in part to speak a language that the laity, to whom the commands of the law are addressed, is more likely to understand—and in part, I admit, because there *is* a considerable overlap between law and morality. The overlap, however, is too limited to justify trying to align these two systems of social control (the sort of project that Islamic nations such as Iran, Pakistan, and Afghanistan have been engaged in of late). It is not a scandal when the law fails to attach a sanction to immoral conduct or when it attaches a sanction to conduct that is not immoral. Indeed, it is not a criticism of law to pronounce it out of phase with current moral feeling. It often is, and for good practical reasons (in particular, the law is a flywheel, limiting the effects of wide swings in public opinion). When people make that criticism—as many do of the laws, still found on the statute books of many states, punishing homosexual relations—what they mean is that the law neither is supported by public opinion nor serves any temporal purpose, even that of stability, that it is merely a vestige, an empty symbol.

It may be thought unhistorical to try to divorce law and morals in this way. To take the most exciting possibility, suppose that the framers of the Constitution, imbued with the philosophical thinking of the Enlightenment, intended judges to shape the meaning of the Constitution in accordance with evolving conceptions of moral theory. Then, in the absence of principled objection to honoring the framers' intentions, any discrepancy between constitutional law and the best moral theory would be due to error or malevolence on the part of judges or to inescapable practical considerations having to do with feasibility, priorities, resources, and public opinion.

This argument opens up too large a vista of historical inquiry to be

29. See, for example, Dworkin, "Reply," note 2 above, at 435. There is a long history of efforts to use "fairness" as the organizing principle of tort law. For a recent example, using Kant to give content to the word, see Gregory C. Keating, "The Idea of Fairness in the Law of Enterprise Liability," 95 *Michigan Law Review* 1266 (1997). I do not consider these efforts promising. My reasons, which are connected with the general skepticism about moral reasoning that I expressed in Chapter 1 of this book, are spelled out in Posner, *The Problems of Jurisprudence* 323–329 (1990).

30. It is a major theme of "The Path of the Law," 10 *Harvard Law Review* 457 (1897), which I discuss in the next chapter.

explored here, so let me merely state dogmatically that there is no convincing evidence for it. No philosopher took a hand in the drafting of any of the founding documents, or such successor texts as section 1 of the Fourteenth Amendment or Title VII of the Civil Rights Act of 1964. No evidence of the thought of Plato, Aristotle, Aquinas, Smith (of *The Moral Sentiments*), Kant, or even of Beccaria, Helvetius, Hume, Priestley, Hutcheson, or Bentham (despite the reference in the Declaration of Independence to "the pursuit of happiness"), can be found in any of these documents.

They are, it is true, informed by such salient Enlightenment notions as liberty, religious toleration, limited government, and political equality, and these had received philosophical treatment, for example by Locke and Montesquieu, mediated for Americans by Blackstone. But that is a far cry from supposing that those who drafted and ratified the Constitution were doing philosophy, let alone philosophy congenial to a modern outlook,[31] let alone that they meant to appoint the judges as philosopher kings or philosophical acolytes or that, if they did, judges should accept the appointment. Notions such as toleration and equality can be given a philosophical or religious construal—or they can be treated as policies instrumental to various social goals such as peace, strength, prosperity, and the conciliation of the disaffected. It is open to question whether Locke was the inspiration or the rationalization for the thought of the American revolutionaries.

Moreover, before philosophy became a specialized academic discipline, the boundaries between it and the sciences, both natural and social, were indistinct and often crossed. Bentham was a lawyer, an economist, and a practical reformer as well as a philosopher, and his suggestions for the reform of criminal justice can be accepted by people who reject utilitarianism; the suggestions do not collapse when their philosophical scaffolding is removed. Locke's influential political theory can be detached from its metaphysical foundations in Christian theology and its moral foundations in the idea that productive labor creates entitlements. Such political innovations as republicanism, the separation of powers, the system of checks

31. Consider in this connection the discrepancy between the original and modern meaning of the phrase "all men are created equal" in the Declaration of Independence. Originally it referred to the situation of man in the state of nature, not in society; hence it had no reference to the position of slaves. See Pauline Maier, *American Scripture: Making the Declaration of Independence* 135–136 (1997). The right of "all men" (that is, of all citizens) to "the pursuit of happiness" apparently comprehended such interests as safety, security, the right to acquire property, and the ability to decide how to live one's life. Id. at 134, 167, 270–271 n. 79.

and balances, and the secularization of politics can be separated from their philosophical aegis and evaluated without regard to philosophical principles. Locke can be discussed by both political scientists and moral philosophers; the discussions by the political scientists are likely to be the more fruitful.

Similarly, we can decide to treat criminals with dignity not because we buy into Kant's idea that people are entitled to be treated as ends but because we think—perhaps knowing nothing about Kant—that cultivating a "we-they" or "enemy within" or even a "medical" or "therapeutic" mentality of criminal punishment can have untoward political consequences and even impair the deterrence and prevention of criminal behavior. You wouldn't have to be a utilitarian to make a judgment of this sort. The point would be not that the "enemy within" approach to crime reduces the sum of American (or human, or cosmic) happiness, but that it collides with specific political and criminological objectives of our society. A moral vocabulary would be adopted for pragmatic purposes. And "pragmatic" is not a synonym for "moral" or even for "utilitarian." Such pragmatic social objectives as reducing the crime rate or making government less intimidating and therefore less powerful do not have to be validated by any moral theory. Nor can they be. If you happen not to agree with these objectives, either because you think it presumptuous to posit goals for an entire society or because you think (let's assume correctly) that they can be attained only by degrading or subordinating people whom you value more than the bourgeois and would-be bourgeois who value peace and prosperity above honor, glory, and God, moral theory will not and should not convince you otherwise.

Adjudication is a normative activity, and any time a judge is doing more than just applying positive law—and that is often, as Dworkin has shown—the problem of getting from "is" to "ought" rears its troublesome head and it may seem that the judge is plunged into the domain of moral theory. But ethics and practical reason are not identical with moral theory unless the term is to be used unhelpfully to denote all normative reasoning on social questions. Judges are expected to give reasons for what they do, and the reasons cannot always be found neatly packaged in the orthodox sources of law. From the reasons a judge gives across a range of cases can be stitched, if the judge is consistent, a "theory" that he might be called upon to defend. It does not follow that the judge would be helped by reading and thinking about moral theory. Consider education. We have had educational theory as long as we have had moral theory. Yet where is the evidence that teachers or educational administrators who are saturated with theory are better at what they do than those who are not? Moral theory, starting at the same point, with Plato, has as long a history of false starts and inconclusive debate as educational theory. Why then should we think a course in moral theory good for judges? Dworkin claims that "we have no choice but to ask [judges] to confront issues that, from time to time, are philosophical. The alternative is not avoiding moral theory but keeping its use dark."[32] Substitute "teachers" for "judges," "pedagogical" for "philosophical," and "educational" for "moral," and the fatuity of Dworkin's claim becomes evident.

Moral issues are no more inescapable in the practice of adjudication than issues of educational theory are in teaching. Judges need not take sides on moral questions, whether because the rejection of legal positivism creates the need or because law and morality are continuous or because morality gives law its content or because judges have been directed to apply the moral law. Considerations drawn from moral theory are only a subset of the normative considerations that are potentially relevant to adjudication. Moral issues can be elided or recast as issues of interpretation, institutional competence, practical politics, the separation of powers, or stare decisis (decision according to precedent)—or treated as a compelling reason for judicial abstention.

Anthony Kronman is wrong to say that "the kind of moral quandary in which ordinary men and women find themselves from time to time, and which demands the exercise of reason, is for judges a routine predicament."[33] He is confusing moral with normative, and moral reasoning with reasoning. Judges routinely confront issues that cannot be resolved by the application of an algorithm, that require instead the application of practical reason—that ensemble of methods, including gut reaction, that people use to make decisions when the methods of science or logic are unavailable or unavailing. This doesn't mean that the judge is in a "moral quandary" and has to employ something called "moral reason" to get out. Editing a newspaper requires the constant use of practical reason, but only very occasionally the making of moral judgments. Likewise adjudication. Judges get into moral quandaries only when the law points to a result that

32. Dworkin, "In Praise of Theory," note 2 above, at 375.

33. Anthony T. Kronman, "The Value of Moral Philosophy," 111 *Harvard Law Review* 1751, 1762 (1998). I hate to disillusion Dean Kronman, but judges *are* "ordinary men and women."

violates their deeply held moral beliefs. That is not a routine predicament in this country.

Because moral theory is optional for judges rather than an indispensable weapon in their armory, they are unlikely to arm themselves with it unless they consider it an objective method for resolving disputes. Legal moralists concede this. Moore (M. S., not G. E.) says that "when judges decide what process is due a citizen, or what equality requires, or when a punishment is cruel, they judge a moral fact capable of being true or false."[34] If no moral claim is capable of being adjudged true or false, judges will not feel comfortable posing and answering legal questions as questions about the moral law. I acknowledged in the first chapter that some moral judgments are so widely accepted that they can lay claim to the title of moral truth. Killing a human being is in our society (the essential qualification) immoral behavior unless there is an accepted justification; killing a fly is not. These truths, which give moral realism what little plausibility it can claim, do not interest a Moore or a Dworkin. They are interested in the moral truths discoverable by a process of reasoning when there is disagreement over what they are. Is it a fact that killing a human being is immoral if the human being is still a fetus or, in the case of an adult, if the killer is a physician killing at the victim's request? *Is* the fetus, though undeniably human, a human being? Is it "killing" if you just refuse to help someone who will die without your help? Moral theory cannot answer such questions because it has no tools for bridging moral disagreements.

It may be possible to make the relation between law and morality a little clearer by drawing a threefold distinction among the ways in which a moral issue can get into a case at law. First, the legal issue may have moral significance to some part of the community; for example, the legal issue of abortion rights has moral significance to pro-life and pro-choice people. Second, judges might decide some cases on moral grounds. And third, they might decide some cases using the argumentative methods of academic moralism. I acknowledge the first relation between law and morality. And the second: some legal principles, notably those of the criminal law, are plainly informed by the moral opinions of the community. But

---

34. Michael S. Moore, "Moral Reality Revisited," 90 *Michigan Law Review* 2424, 2470 (1992). See also Ronald Dworkin, "Is There Really No Right Answer in Hard Cases?" in Dworkin, *A Matter of Principle* 119 (1985); Dworkin, note 12 above, at viii–ix; and for criticism, Posner, note 29 above, at 197–203.

applying a moral principle to a legal issue is not the same thing as taking sides on contested moral issues and using normative moral philosophy to resolve the contest. *That* is the problematic relation between morality and law, as we are about to see in greater detail. You don't find moral theory deployed in appeals from convictions for rape or murder, even though the criminalizing of rape and murder is based upon a moral principle; and its absence is not missed.

Abstract Theory versus Casuistry

In the first chapter, I contrasted the type of moral theory in which the theorist attempts to proceed from general principles to specific issues with the type in which the theorist attempts to proceed from the intuitively obvious resolution of one issue to the consideration of a second, "similar" issue. ("Reflective equilibrium" can be thought of as a combination of these approaches.) We can trace this distinction into legal theory by comparing the approaches of Ronald Dworkin and Leo Katz, the approaches of an abstract moral reasoner and of a moral casuist, respectively, to issues of law.

Dworkin wants judges to "justify legal claims by showing that principles that support those claims also offer the best justification of more general legal practice in the doctrinal area in which the case arises" (pp. 355–356).[35] The best (or better) justification is the one that "fits the legal practice better, and puts it in a better light" (p. 356). In determining fit and goodness, the judge may find himself swept up in a "justificatory ascent" (id.), that is, challenged to consider how the justification that he has seized upon for his ruling coheres with ever broader swatches of legal doctrine as questions are raised about its consistency with this or that legal—or moral—rule or principle.

The concept of justificatory ascent is Dworkin's acknowledgment that judges more often reason upward from particular cases and arguments than downward from an overarching principle—such as egalitarianism, or utilitarianism, or Mill's concept of liberty—that makes the whole body of the law consistent. But he insists that through justificatory ascent a judge may be lofted to a high level of generality. So Cardozo, he says, "felt that [justificatory ascent was] necessary in *MacPherson v. Buick Motor Co.,* and

---

35. Page references are to Dworkin, "In Praise of Theory," note 2 above.

he changed the character of our law" (p. 358).[36] "Legal reasoning presupposes a vast domain of justification, including very abstract principles of political morality," and a judge must always be prepared "to reexamine some part of the structure from time to time" (p. 360). So judges entrusted with interpreting a constitution must undertake "a very considerable 'excursion' into political morality" or, equivalently, a "deep expedition into theory" (pp. 360, 372). The judge who refuses to confront philosophical issues is an "ostrich" (p. 376).

What Dworkin claims to be describing is not one approach among many, but "theory." Anyone who does not subscribe to his conception of how judges should decide cases is a member of "the anti-theory army," along with "the post-modernists, the prestructuralists, the deconstructionists, the critical legal students, the critical race scholars, and a thousand other battalions" of that army (p. 361). Dworkin's polemic against the appointment of Robert Bork to the Supreme Court accused Bork, an influential constitutional theorist, of having "no constitutional philosophy at all . . . He believes he has no responsibility to treat the Constitution as an integrated structure of moral and political principles."[37] Dworkin equates theory to philosophy to treating the entire Constitution, and through justificatory ascent the entire body of American law, as "an integrated structure of moral and political principles."[38]

This is persuasive definition with a vengeance. Far from bearing only the meaning upon which Dworkin insists, "theory" is a word with no definite meaning, especially in normative discourse. Just think of "critical theory" or (what is closely related) "Marxist theory" or the use of "theory" in literary and cultural studies. The successes of science have tempted the practitioners of a wide variety of other disciplines to describe their own work as "theory," even though it bears little relation to scientific work. A typical legal theory is merely a generalization claimed to subsume the leading cases in a particular field or subfield of law. More ambitious legal

36. The reference is to MacPherson v. Buick Motor Co., 111 N.E. 1050 (N.Y. 1916). It is a poor example for Dworkin's point. Cardozo's opinion does not explain the overarching principle in light of which privity (a direct contractual relation between manufacturer and consumer) should not be required to make the manufacturer liable to the consumer for a harm resulting from a defect in the manufacturer's product. The opinion is notable for its ingenious (or disingenuous) manipulation of precedent rather than for frank confrontation of the issues of principle or policy that the case raised. Edward H. Levi, *An Introduction to Legal Reasoning* 9–25 (1949); Richard A. Posner, *Cardozo: A Study in Reputation* 107–109 (1990).

37. Dworkin, "Bork: The Senate's Responsibility," note 14 above, at 267, 272–273.

38. Id. at 273. Dworkin strangely instances Justice Lewis Powell, a notoriously ad hoc adjudicator, as one who treated the Constitution in this way. Id.

theories use principles drawn from other fields of social thought, such as economics or political or moral theory, as criteria for evaluating doctrines and decisions. Some degree of generality or abstraction, and a demand for consistency, are the bedrock requirements of "theory." Beyond this it does not seem possible to specify preconditions for what is to count as either a moral or a legal theory.

Were this all that Dworkin meant by "theory"—an effort to achieve consistency and generality—he could not accuse Bork of lacking a constitutional theory. By "theory" he means his own approach to law, which is in the line of descent from Herbert Wechsler's influential article on "neutral principles."[39] Wechsler's approach in turn has affinities to the "legal process" school and to natural law, to both of which Dworkin has direct links.[40] The common element is the imposition of a master theme, such as democratic legitimacy, federalism, institutional competence, or, in Dworkin's case, equality, on the particulars of the law. The professors propose, and the judges impose.[41] That is why justificatory ascent is so important; it is the only way the judge who does not start with an academic master theme can get to one.

Justificatory ascent should not be confused with induction. After the judge has completed the ascent and glimpsed the sunny fields where

39. See David A. Strauss, "Principle and Its Perils," 64 *University of Chicago Law Review* 373, 376–381 (1997) (review of Dworkin's book *Freedom's Law*, note 2 above); Herbert Wechsler, "Toward Neutral Principles of Constitutional Law," 73 *Harvard Law Review* 1 (1959). "In nearly every respect, Dworkin's 'moral reading' [of the Constitution] was anticipated by the scholars of the late 1950s and early 1960s." Strauss, above, at 376. This is not to deny the considerable originality of Dworkin's approach; filiation is not identity.

40. See Neil Duxbury, *Patterns of American Jurisprudence* 294–297 (1995); Weinreb, note 13 above, at 119–121; Vincent A. Wellman, "Dworkin and the Legal Process Tradition: The Legacy of Hart and Sacks," 29 *Arizona Law Review* 413 (1987); William N. Eskridge, Jr., and Philip P. Frickey, "An Historical and Critical Introduction to *The Legal Process*," in Henry M. Hart, Jr., and Albert M. Sacks, *The Legal Process: Basic Problems in the Making and Application of Law* li, cxvii, cxxxi (1958 tentative (i.e., mimeo.) edition published in 1994); see also Dworkin, note 12 above. Duxbury, however, warns against exaggerating the continuity between the legal-process school and Dworkin. Duxbury, above, at 295–296.

41. "The courts are the capitals of law's empire, and judges are its princes, but not its seers and prophets. It falls to philosophers, if they are willing, to work out law's ambitions for itself, the purer form of law within and beyond the law we have." Dworkin, note 12 above, at 407. Dworkin always writes very well when he is criticizing. But when he is advancing his own proposals, he sometimes shifts to a key of almost ecclesiastical pomposity, as in the passage I have just quoted. About another such passage—"[Law] aims, in the interpretive spirit, to lay principle over practice to show the best route to a better future, keeping the right faith with the past," id. at 413—Pierre Schlag pertinently remarks: "When confronted with something like this, one wants to ask: *Just what 'law' is it that you are talking about here?*" Schlag, *Laying Down the Law: Mysticism, Fetishism, and the American Legal Mind* 5 (1996) (emphasis in original).

theory dwells, he kicks away the ladder. He accepts, by being forced to climb the ladder, that he cannot decide the case without adopting a master principle; once adopted, it decides the case. The ethereal character of such principles is shown by their creators' lack of sustained interest in particulars. As illustrated by the "philosophers' brief" that, as we shall see, so strikingly failed to engage with the difficult institutional issues raised by its proposal of a constitutional right to physician-assisted suicide, there is little texture to Dworkin's analysis of legal issues, just as there was little texture to Hart and Sacks's, or to Wechsler's. Dworkin operates with ideal types (in Weber's sense) of affirmative action, pornography, and abortion, just as Hart and Sacks operated with ideal types of the court, the legislature, and the administrative agency and Wechsler with an ideal type of apartheid, in which the harm to blacks from being prevented from associating with whites is exactly balanced by the harm to whites from being forced to associate with blacks if apartheid is prohibited. Dworkin's principles are different but the approach is the same, except that Dworkin evinces even less interest than Hart and Sacks, or Wechsler, in how a legal system actually works, in the practical capacities and political constraints of judges,[42] in the text and history of particular enactments, in the difference between holdings and dicta (and hence in the scope of particular precedents), in the data or theories of the social sciences that relate to the issues in cases that interest him, and in the effects of legal rules.

Dworkin's is one possible way of doing law, but it is not the only way that can claim to be theoretical. More important, it is not the best way. Apart from the deficiencies that it shares with academic moralism—of which indeed it is the application to law—it is too abstract for a case-based legal system. It might do better in a regime of abstract review such as one finds in the constitutional courts of central Europe and occasionally in U.S. state supreme courts.[43] Courts do abstract review when they determine the constitutionality of statutes before the statutes are ap-

42. How strange of him to say, "I agree with the critics that not *all* judges are trained in philosophy." Dworkin, "In Praise of Theory," note 2 above, at 375 (emphasis added). Virtually none are, especially today, though I shall give a couple of contemporary examples later. It is true that Learned Hand had studied philosophy at Harvard, and Holmes had a decidedly philosophical bent. But these were judges who had been educated in the nineteenth century—and both were moral skeptics to boot. The term "trained in philosophy" would have to be given a very special meaning to be descriptive of such Dworkinian judicial heroes as Warren, Brennan, Blackmun, and Powell, though doubtless some of the law clerks who ghostwrote the opinions that Dworkin admires had studied moral philosophy.

43. See, for example, András Sajó, "Reading the Invisible Constitution: Judicial Review in Hungary," 15 *Oxford Journal of Legal Studies* 253 (1995); Sarah Wright Sheive, "Central and Eastern European Constitutional Courts and the Antimajoritarian Objection to Judicial Review," 26 *Law and*

plied—in other words, before there is a case. The strength of the case system is its sensitivity to the particulars of specific legal disputes. Attention to particulars at once educates the judges and deflects them from overgeneralization. The weakness of the case system is that the education is incomplete because the "facts" revealed by the record of a lawsuit are often inaccurate and rarely systematic. But the cure is not high theory. What judges need is a better understanding of the practical consequences of their decisions.[44]

Most American judges are pragmatists rather than ideologues. But to come up with good pragmatic solutions they have to understand the empirical dimensions of the legal disputes brought to them. The well-known differences between male and female judges in their assessment of cases of sexual harassment are not due to theoretical differences. Very few of these judges are either male chauvinists or radical feminists. Their differences stem primarily from different perceptions of the incidence, and the psychological and other effects, of such harassment. It is not beyond hope that the differences could be narrowed by empirical study.

It helps in doing law, moreover, to know a great deal of law rather than just a handful of exemplary cases. Law is like a language. It is as difficult to write well about law at the operating level without an intimate knowledge of it as it is to write well about China without knowing Chinese. Dworkin rarely ventures outside the highly politicized domain of constitutional rights, and when he does the results are unimpressive. I mentioned his off-key discussion of the *MacPherson* decision. His article in praise of legal theory returns again and again to the DES cases,[45] finally asking challengingly, "Should the judge try to decide whether the drug manufacturers

Policy in International Business 1201 (1995); William M. Landes and Richard A. Posner, "The Economics of Anticipatory Adjudication," 23 *Journal of Legal Studies* 683, 710–713 (1994).

44. This point is made with reference to the use of feminist theory in law in Stephen J. Schulhofer, "The Feminist Challenge in Criminal Law," 143 *University of Pennsylvania Law Review* 2151 (1995): "The problems confronting women in criminal justice run so deep and have such complex links to the goals and structures of law that [feminist] theory is inherently incapable of carrying us very far along the path toward effective solutions. The problems can be worked out only by paying close attention to particulars." Id. at 2153. Rorty has put the general point nicely: "Disengagement from practice produces theoretical hallucinations." Richard Rorty, *Achieving Our Country: Leftist Thought in Twentieth-Century America* 94 (1998).

45. DES was a drug administered to many pregnant women in the 1950s to prevent miscarriage. The drug turned out to injure the *adult* daughters of many of the women who had taken the drug. By the time the problem was discovered and suits brought, it was impossible in most cases to figure out which manufacturer of the drug had supplied the drug that had injured the particular plaintiff.

are jointly liable without asking whether it is fair, according to standards embedded in our tradition, to impose liability in the absence of any causal connection?" (p. 371). Any genuine legal insider would consider this a strange question, and not only because the issue was not joint liability in the technical legal sense of the term.[46] We regularly impose *criminal* liability—for example, for failed attempts that cause no harm, or conspiracies nipped in the bud, or schemes to defraud that don't defraud anybody, or "victimless" crimes (such as the sale of hard-core pornography) that cannot be shown to cause any harm, or drunk driving where no accident results—without worrying about the absence of a causal connection between the defendant's conduct and the harm that the law is trying to prevent. In the law of torts, liability is standardly imposed on negligent persons whose acts are merely sufficient and not necessary conditions of harm and so do not fit the usual definitions of cause; is usually imposed on employers of the persons who cause the harm of which the plaintiff is complaining (under the doctrine of respondeat superior); is sometimes imposed on persons who merely fail to avert a harm (as in "crashworthy" products liability cases and cases of attempted but failed rescue); is imposed on persons who conspire with injurers; in effect is imposed on the estates, that is, the heirs, of injurers; is sometimes imposed (as in "loss of a chance" cases) on an injurer despite the victim's inability to prove causation by a preponderance of the evidence. The question whether it is "fair" to impose liability on a manufacturer of DES who cannot be shown to be the actual "cause" of the plaintiff's injury is thus naive. It is also unhelpful. It won't move us an inch closer to the intelligent evaluation of these cases.

I do not deny that philosophy, in the form not of moral theory but of careful analysis of difficult concepts, can be helpful in clarifying certain legal issues, such as intent, responsibility, and, yes, causation.[47] But to think that philosophy can be helpful by telling us to reflect on the fairness of imposing liability without proof of causation is to reveal an ignorance of the relevant terrain and the thinness—the essentially rhetorical character—of Dworkin's invocation of "theory."

46. Joint liability would mean that all the drug companies that had manufactured and sold DES were fully liable for all DES injuries, although each plaintiff would only be permitted one recovery. The issue, resolved in favor of the plaintiffs, in Sindell v. Abbott Laboratories, 607 P.2d 924 (Cal. 1980), was whether the liability of each company that might have been the one whose drug injured the plaintiff should be proportioned to the company's market share at the time when and in the place where the plaintiff's mother bought the drug.

47. See Posner, note 29 above, at 168–184 (intent), 324–325 (causation); United States v. Beserra, 967 F.2d 254 (7th Cir. 1992) (responsibility); Stewart v. Gramley, 74 F.3d 132 (7th Cir. 1996) (free will).

When we turn from Dworkin to Leo Katz, we enter a different world, remote from the heady abstraction of universalizing moral and legal theory. It is the world of old-fashioned casuistry, in which one tries to move from a settled moral intuition (in moral casuistry) or unshakable precedent (legal casuistry) in one case to a new case. It is the method we saw misused by Judith Jarvis Thomson. Katz's approach, illustrated by his book *Ill-Gotten Gains*,[48] is moralistic because it uses moral intuitions to determine the appropriate as well as the actual scope of the law.

His particular concern is with what he calls "avoision." This neologism denotes cases in which it is unclear whether a person's conduct should be considered lawful *avoi*dance of the law's prohibitions or illegal eva*sion*. He gives the following example. Two actresses are vying for the same part. Mildred knows that Abigail has been unfaithful to her husband. If she threatens Abigail with revealing this knowledge to the husband unless Abigail forgoes the audition, this would be the crime of blackmail. So instead she tells Abigail that she is mailing a letter addressed to the husband that reveals Abigail's infidelity and that the letter has been timed to arrive the morning of the audition. Knowing that Abigail will stay home to intercept the letter, Mildred will have achieved the same end as she would have by committing blackmail, yet her conduct is not criminal. Katz argues from such examples that the law is not consequentialist, because it often treats acts having the same consequence differently, in the actresses' case because it was brought about in a different way from that contemplated by the law of blackmail.

He lays particular stress on the different legal treatment of acts and of omissions to act: it is murder to drown a person, but it is no crime at all to let him drown by refusing, however gratuitously or even maliciously, to throw him a lifeline. If you yank a person in front of you to serve as a human shield against someone trying to shoot you and the person dies, you are guilty of murder, but it is no crime at all to duck behind the person even if by doing so you induce the gunman to aim in his direction with results fatal to him. (This is Katz's most challenging example.) And the law frequently attaches different sanctions to the same injury depending on the injurer's state of mind, to Katz a nonconsequentialist consideration. But it is the distinction between act and omission that is fundamental to his analysis, since most "avoision" consists of trying to replace an act with an omission that will have the same consequences.

Katz reasons from cases, mostly hypothetical rather than real, and some

48. Leo Katz, *Ill-Gotten Gains: Evasion, Blackmail, Fraud, and Kindred Puzzles of the Law* (1996). My page references to this book appear in the text of this chapter.

fantastic—for example, the case of two twins one of whom robs a bank and the other commits a murder and the court cannot tell which twin committed which crime and therefore, Katz argues, has to let both go. The use of fantastic hypotheticals invites one of the criticisms that I made of Judith Jarvis Thomson: that we cannot have secure intuitions about unrealistic hypotheticals. And the parallel to the DES cases shows that Katz cannot be correct in arguing that the twins should go scot-free. If both are punished for robbery, neither can complain. The one who committed the robbery is being punished justly, and the murderer is being punished leniently. With this example we have our first hint of the flawed character of Katz's method.

The casuistic method has a long history in law and ethics; it dates back to Socrates, has adherents in contemporary philosophy (as we glimpsed in Chapter 1), undergirds the common law system of England and the United States, and is the cornerstone of American law teaching. But "casuistry" has another meaning besides reasoning from cases: logic-chopping, the drawing of phony distinctions, the use of the forms of logic to defend irrational results, literal-mindedness, deceit by half-truths. Casuistry in this bad sense is illustrated by the Catholic doctrine of equivocation, "guiltlessly getting a falsehood [a]cross," as by swearing "that one has not done something, though one really has done it, by inwardly understanding that one did not do it on a certain day, or before one was born" (p. 29).[49] Katz likes casuistry so much that he endorses the doctrine of equivocation along with the other forms of "bad" casuistry, as well as the good kind. He says that the doctrine illustrates the "right to mislead by silence" (p. 45), an aspect of the distinction between acts and omissions. The equivocator does not state explicit falsehoods; he just leaves out the things necessary to prevent the listener from misunderstanding what he does say. Katz the logic-chopper is further in evidence when he asks rhetorically, concerning Mildred's avoidance or evasion of the law against blackmail, "Why exactly should we disapprove of someone for doing something *only* because of the law?" (p. 12). The danger of asking a rhetorical question is that it may be answered: Mildred concocted her scheme not only to avoid being punished for blackmail but also and more fundamentally to prevent Abigail from competing with her for a job.

49. The second passage is a quotation from Blaise Pascal, *The Provincial Letters* 140 (A. J. Krailshaimer ed. 1967). The doctrine of equivocation refutes the claim (offered to refute moral relativism) that "all [religions] condemn deception." Ronald M. Green, *Religion and Moral Reason: A New Method for Comparative Study* 11 (1988). An atheist would place deception at the heart of religion.

Katz's fondness for the "bad" casuistry reflects a mentality fairly described as premodern and further reflected in his implicit endorsement of the medieval doctrine of correspondences, or taking analogies literally. God is to the king as the king is to his subjects as the man is to his family. The fetus is a homunculus. The four elements correspond to the four humors. Sublunar music is replicated in the music of the spheres. And, Katz adds, inverting the rules for blaming yields the rules for praising: We blame the criminal more if his crime was deliberate, and we praise the discoverer more if the discovery was deliberate than if it was accidental. We lighten the sentence of the remorseful criminal for the same reason that we accord less praise to the vain (conceited, self-congratulatory) inventor or discoverer than to the modest one. The vain discoverer has bestowed upon himself some fraction of the praise he deserves, thus drawing down the amount owed him by others; the remorseful criminal has bestowed upon himself some fraction of the punishment he owes, thus reducing the amount of public punishment necessary to give him his full measure of deserved punishment.

What unites the elements of the premodern (and also the postmodern, as we'll see in the last chapter) approach to reasoning is the effort to give rhetoric pride of place over science, reversing what has been the dominant trend in Western thinking since the eighteenth century. Arguing from cases rather than from theory or facts, putting words ahead of things and mental states ahead of consequences, giving legal effect to unexamined verbal distinctions (such as act versus omission), reifying analogies—these are procedures remote from the mathematically or logically rigorous, and rigorously fact-tested, theorizing that is the scientific ideal. They lead Katz to conclude, first, that "a central feature of our legal and moral thinking [is] its nonutilitarian character" (p. xii)—that law, and in particular the criminal law, from which most of his examples are drawn, is "formalistic" in the (bad) casuistic, or "form over substance," sense. And, second, "the formalism of the law is merely a reflection of the formalism of morality" (p. 52). These formalisms, Katz contends, show that the law is not utilitarian and that utilitarianism is an inadequate moral theory because it aims at maximizing preference satisfaction, which is a matter of consequence rather than of intention or of formalistic distinctions such as the distinction between act and omission. He gives the following bad example of the law's refusal to honor preferences: if a woman about to be raped tells her assailant that she would rather die, and he kills her instead of raping her, he will be punished as a murderer even though she herself would have thought his deed less heinous than rape and rape is punished less severely than murder. All the example shows is that the woman considered rape *even worse* than murder, not that she considered the punishment for murder too severe.

The wrongness of this example is part of a larger, tripartite wrongness: Formalism is not inconsistent with utilitarianism; it is not possible to read off the principles of morality from the rules of the criminal law; those rules are for the most part not formalistic. Katz's idea of a utilitarian is someone who believes that if executing an innocent person would save two or more lives, we should do it. No one believes that. As soon as one asks whom society would entrust with the responsibility for picking innocent people for execution, it becomes apparent that killing the occasional innocent for the greater good would not actually maximize happiness.[50] Rights and rules, limiting official discretion, are components of an intelligent utilitarian political science. By dichotomizing continuous phenomena, however, rules produce difficult borderline cases. Many of them are decided nonarbitrarily by such devices as defenses, presumptions, and burdens of proof, but some can be decided only arbitrarily, producing the formalisms prized by Katz. Those formalisms, being inherent in a system of rules, are consistent with an overarching commitment to utilitarianism.

Katz makes the goofy "act utilitarian," who wishes to conduct all public business without using rules, the spokesman for *all* nonformalistic moral theories. You don't have to be an act utilitarian, or any other type of utilitarian, to spot the flaw in the doctrine of equivocation, which is that of divorcing ethics from consequences. The Jesuits developed the doctrine to enable them to lie their way out of heresy examinations by their religious enemies without committing a mortal sin. A consequentialist would say that in the circumstances that confronted them, telling the truth would have had worse consequences than lying about their religious beliefs, so lying was the ethically correct course. The Jesuits could not take this approach, because they didn't think it proper to trade off the good of truth-telling against the good of saving Catholic lives.[51] Neither principle would yield. The only way out was to redefine lying. Hence the doctrine

---

50. See Russell Hardin, *Morality within the Limits of Reason* 101–105 (1988). Katz's criticism illustrates the point that utilitarianism is characteristically attacked by pushing its logic further than utilitarians do.

51. Catholic hostility to trade-offs is nicely shown by the Catholic view on obtaining semen to test

of equivocation. The doctrine is ingenious, as well as understandable in the historical circumstances in which it originated. But it is neither moral, in any common sense of the term, nor reasoning.

The criminal law—to move to the second point of my disagreement with Katz—is not the mirror of morality, any more than law in general is. James Fitzjames Stephen, the greatest nineteenth-century English scholar of the criminal law, and no softy, called the criminal justice system "the roughest engine which society can use for any purpose."[52] Cruel, costly, frightening, and dangerous, it does not try to enforce morality but merely to prevent serious temporal harms (not necessarily culpable harms in any deep moral sense) where this can be done within tolerable margins of error and no adequate alternative means of prevention are available. What Mildred did was immoral; it is also a textbook example of the tort of intentionally interfering with advantageous business relations. Abigail could sue Mildred and obtain a judgment for punitive as well as compensatory damages. Because the line between fair and unfair competition is hazy, it is better in this case to use the gentler sanctions of tort law, where, incidentally, the victim bears the expense of prosecution, rather than the public having to do so as in a criminal prosecution. Of course, Abigail might be deterred from suing, lest her husband discover her adultery. But she might equally be deterred from filing a criminal charge—or even more so, since she would not get any money by doing so.

The difference in legal treatment that Katz emphasizes between drowning a person and letting him drown brings to mind the gravediggers' scene in Act V of *Hamlet*. One of the gravediggers jokes that to be allowed to be buried in hallowed ground Ophelia must not have drowned herself; she must instead merely have allowed the water to drown her, for then she wouldn't have been the author of her death. Katz would regard this as an adequate explanation for not punishing the person who refuses to throw a lifeline to a drowning man. But that person is acting (or failing to act) in what most of us would consider a profoundly immoral way. It is true that

---

for male infertility. It is prohibited to obtain the semen for the test by intercourse (even with one's wife) with an unperforated condom, because *"It is never lawful, even for a laudable purpose, to use the generative faculty in an unnatural way."* Gerald Kelly, "Moral Aspects of Sterility Tests," in *Ethics* 262, 263 (Peter Singer ed. 1994) (emphasis in original). Kelly's suggested solution is to use a perforated condom and hope that it traps some of the semen despite the perforation.

52. James Fitzjames Stephen, *Liberty, Equality, Fraternity* 151 (R. J. White ed. 1967), first published in 1873.

he is not punished, but this merely illustrates the imperfect overlap between law and morality. He is not punished for a variety of practical reasons: Such cases are rare. Amateur rescuers often make things worse. Punishing for not rescuing would make people steer clear of situations in which they might be in a position to perform a rescue. It is difficult to identify cases in which the rescuer would not have been imperiling himself. And imposing a legal duty of rescue would discourage altruistic rescues by making it more difficult for a rescuer to be recognized as an altruist (people will think he rescued to avoid liability); such recognition, as I noted in Chapter 1, is an important motive for altruism. Good or bad, these reasons (which are among the reasons Judith Jarvis Thomson's abortion analogy fails) for not criminalizing failures to rescue do not touch the morality of the conduct.

Katz asks which is worse: "*A* steals your wallet. *B* (a perfect stranger) lets you drown in a lake when he could easily throw you a life vest" (pp. 131–132). *A*'s act is criminal, *B*'s not. Desperately trying to align the moral with the criminal law, Katz claims that *B*'s is a "far more benign kind of outrageousness" (p. 132). The opposite is true. But it is not a good reason to condone the lesser enormity that, for the reasons I have mentioned, the greater must go unpunished.

Not only does the criminal law leave much evil conduct unpunished for practical reasons; it punishes conduct that many people do not consider evil, such as fornication, the operation of a gambling den, sodomy between consenting adults, the sale of marijuana, minor violations of the copyright laws, and a variety of esoteric business practices. A search through the federal criminal code reveals many outright absurdities, such as the criminalizing of any commercial use of the legend "Give a Hoot, Don't Pollute" without the permission of the Department of Agriculture.[53] The Pharisees were wrong. The positive law is not the moral law.

Yet despite its manifest imperfections, the law is not nearly as formalistic as Katz believes. He argues that if we tried to punish the ingenious schemes of tax avoidance that make lawyers rich, on the theory that the schemes take away from the government money that rightfully belongs to it, this would commit us to taxing at his *former* income the neurosurgeon who by abandoning his profession to become a beach bum "cheats" the Internal Revenue Service, his "partner" (by virtue of the Internal Revenue

---

53. 18 U.S.C. § 711a.

Code) in the practice of neurosurgery. So we don't punish the tax avoiders, and this, Katz argues, attests to the power of logical formalism in shaping law. In fact, by taxing real estate at its market value, the tax code forces some people to give up their homes and even livelihood, as when farmland is taxed at its value for residential development. Some tax systems even tax the "imputed" rent of homeowners (the rent they would receive if they rented their homes to others rather than occupying the homes themselves). This sort of thing is not done in the case of wages because of the practical difficulty of determining a person's maximum income, because most people try to maximize their incomes, and because nonremunerative jobs may confer large social benefits.

There is even a "substance over form" doctrine in tax law.[54] And a stockbroker who resorts to equivocation to sell stocks is as guilty of fraud as the broker who lies outright. Katz says that if you burn down a building for the insurance, knowing that someone in it will be killed, and the person is killed, you are guilty of murder; but if by some miracle the person escapes you are not guilty of attempted murder unless your aim was not, or not only, the insurance but also the death of the person. This is true. But because arson is a serious crime, it makes little practical difference whether the arsonist is also deemed an attempted murderer; the federal sentencing guidelines decree that in such a case the arsonist shall be punished as heavily as if he were guilty of attempted murder.[55]

Suppose that wanting to kill your enemy you go armed to his neighborhood, hoping he'll attack you so that you can kill him in self-defense. Fine, says Katz; it's just like buying a painting in order to destroy it, as opposed to destroying it without buying it. In fact the doctrine of moral rights, in force in much of the world but not mentioned by Katz, gives the artist inalienable rights over the integrity of his work.[56] And Katz's example of self-defense is really an example of dueling—and because dueling is criminal, self-defense is not a defense to killing a person in a duel.

Katz thinks that willful ignorance (Moody-Adams's "affected ignorance"), as when a person who fears that he is buying stolen goods instructs the seller not to tell him their provenance, will get you a lighter

---

54. See, for example, Gregory v. Helvering, 293 U.S. 465 (1935); Yosha v. Commissioner, 861 F.2d 494 (7th Cir. 1988).

55. See United States v. Martinez, 16 F.3d 202 (7th Cir. 1994).

56. See Henry Hansmann and Marina Santilli, "Authors' and Artists' Moral Rights: A Comparative Legal and Economic Analysis," 26 *Journal of Legal Studies* 95 (1997).

sentence, as it should, he thinks, because it illustrates the casuistic principle that Jesuits call "directing the attention." It won't; the criminal law equates willful ignorance to knowledge.[57]

Law is not being formalistic when it bases distinctions on the state of mind of the defendant. Dead is dead whether you're killed by a careless driver or a driver who is trying to kill you. But the second driver is more dangerous to society as well as more likely to respond to the threat of criminal punishment. Where there is parity of intention, we tend to give too much weight to consequences rather than, as Katz believes, too little. It may be pure fortuity that the same careless act causes death in one case and no injury in another; the former act will be punished, the latter not. The difference in treatment illustrates "moral luck," the subject of a philosophical literature mentioned in Chapter 1.

Katz is fascinated by the law's allowing a dying patient to refuse treatment[58] but (as we shall see shortly) refusing to let the patient authorize his doctor to kill him. The omission is permitted, the act forbidden, the consequence—death—the same. But whether right or wrong, the distinction is not merely a formalist reflex. Opponents of physician-assisted suicide worry about adding killer to the physician's job description, about impatient physicians hurrying indigent patients to a premature death, about impatient relatives badgering the patient to go quietly. These dangers are not wholly absent in refusal-of-treatment situations but are offset by the sheer bizarreness of forcing a mentally competent patient to submit to what are often futile, painful, and humiliating end-of-life treatments. The debate has nothing to do with Scholastic distinctions.

Katz says that you can escape tort liability, even if you're a careless person (say an airline that employs inexperienced pilots) who engages in dangerous activities, by buying a robot (an automatic pilot, say) to conduct those activities for you. Even if the robot is just as "careless" as you, that is, just as likely to malfunction from time to time and when that happens to injure people, you're off the liability hook provided that the robot is state of the art. That is not correct. Whenever an accident results from the malfunction, the manufacturer of the robot will be liable to the persons injured, under the doctrine of products liability. The price of the robot will reflect this expected liability cost, so the buyer of the robot will

57. See, for example, United States v. Ramsey, 785 F.2d 184 (7th Cir. 1986); United States v. Giovannetti, 919 F.2d 1223 (7th Cir. 1990).

58. See Cruzan v. Director, Missouri Department of Health, 497 US. 261, 278–279 (1990).

bear indirectly the liability that he thought (if he read Katz) he had shifted to the robot.

Why is the theft of $100 from a millionaire punished as severely as the theft of $100 from a poor person, when the latter surely causes more unhappiness than the former? Well, it isn't punished as severely. The federal sentencing guidelines provide enhanced punishment for preying on particularly vulnerable victims.[59]

My conclusion is that Katz's bag of Jesuitical-Talmudic tricks can no more explain or improve the law than the top-down moral theories of which Katz is so critical.

Some Famous "Moral" Cases

The stubbornness of moral dilemmas owes something to their being underspecified. The reason is internal to moral philosophy and is why some moral philosophers consider realistic novels, with their dense texture, to be aids to philosophical reflection.[60] The underspecification of the moral dilemma reflects the underspecialization of moral philosophy when conceived of as a method of resolving issues of law or policy. You don't have to know anything about cannibalism on the high seas to ponder the question whether the starving occupants of a lifeboat should be entitled to kill and eat the weakest or the poorest of them. You don't have to know anything about the family and sexuality to ponder the morality of abortion. These issues can be stated as dilemmas and argued over from very general premises about autonomy, responsibility, cruelty, humanity, and the bounds of the community. When such an issue arises in a legal case, it can receive a similarly abstract treatment. But it need not. Cases in the Anglo-American system of adjudication arise out of concrete disputes framed by the principles and usages of law.[61] There is no rule against bringing to bear a wide range of empirical data drawn from historical, psychological, sociological,

59. See United States v. Lallemand, 989 F.2d 936 (7th Cir. 1993).

60. See, for example, Martha C. Nussbaum, *Love's Knowledge: Essays on Philosophy and Literature* (1990); Colin McGinn, *Ethics, Evil, and Fiction* (1997).

61. Dworkin acknowledges the possibility that an issue unresolvable in one normative domain might be resolvable in another, specifically the legal. He points out that while the question whether Picasso or Beethoven was the greater artist may be unanswerable, if Congress directed the erection of a statue to whoever was the greater it might be determinable from the text or history of the statute what concept of "greatness" was to be employed and how it might be operationalized. Ronald Dworkin, "Objectivity and Truth: You'd Better Believe It," 25 *Philosophy and Public Affairs* 87, 137–138 (1996).

and economic research, as well as considerations of feasibility, prudence, and institutional capacity. Often when this is done the moral issue disappears, as happened in the first euthanasia cases to be decided by the Supreme Court.[62] This is a reason to regard moral theory as useless for law[63] even if it has some socially valuable uses in its original domain.

Euthanasia and Abortion

The question whether a person should be allowed to hire a doctor to kill him is a favorite of moral philosophers, so much so as to have provoked a distinguished group of them to join Dworkin in submitting an amicus curiae brief urging the Supreme Court to recognize a constitutional right to physician-assisted suicide.[64] The Court refused to recognize (or, more realistically, to create) such a right.[65] Yet it did this without taking sides on the philosophical issue, which had been vigorously contested as part of a larger debate on the morality of suicide,[66] the "philosophers' brief" representing but one point of view.[67] The Justices did not explain why they

62. Consider, as a further example, how the issue in the famous English cannibal case, Regina v. Dudley and Stephens, 14 Q.B.D. 273 (1884), is transformed when the full context of nineteenth-century maritime cannibalism is restored, as in A. W. Brian Simpson, *Cannibalism and the Common Law* (1984).

63. See Richard Craswell, "Contract Law, Default Rules, and the Philosophy of Promising," 88 *Michigan Law Review* 489 (1989), making a similar point about the attempts of Charles Fried and Randy Barnett to use philosophical theories about promises to construct a theory of contract law. And it is noteworthy that Philip Bobbitt's well-known typology of constitutional arguments excludes moral arguments. Bobbitt, *Constitutional Fate: Theory of the Constitution* 94–95 (1982).

64. The brief is reprinted in Ronald Dworkin et al., "Assisted Suicide: The Philosophers' Brief," *New York Review of Books*, March 27, 1997, pp. 41, 43–47. The signers of the brief, besides Dworkin, were Thomas Nagel, Robert Nozick, John Rawls, Thomas Scanlon, and Judith Jarvis Thomson.

65. Washington v. Glucksberg, 117 S. Ct. 2258 (1997); Vacco v. Quill, 117 S. Ct. 2293 (1997). Dworkin tries to put a positive spin on this defeat, but is highly critical of the Justices' opinions nonetheless, as well as, of course, the outcome of the two cases. Ronald Dworkin, "Assisted Suicide: What the Court Really Said," *New York Review of Books*, Sept. 25, 1997, p. 40. What is most interesting about Dworkin's post mortem is his belated though welcome recognition that experience with euthanasia, notably in the Netherlands where it is quasi-legal and quite common, is relevant to the constitutional question. See id. at 41–43; see also "Assisted Suicide and Euthanasia: An Exchange [between Ronald Dworkin and Yale Kamisar]," *New York Review of Books*, Nov. 6, 1997, p. 68. Yet Dworkin continues to insist that cases in which facts or consequences matter to constitutional decision making are "rare." Dworkin, "Reply," note 2 above, at 433.

66. See, for example, *Suicide: Right or Wrong?* (John Donnelly ed. 1990).

67. The other side of the philosophical debate is illustrated by Daniel Callahan, "Self-Extinction: The Morality of the Helping Hand," in *Physician-Assisted Suicide* 69 (Robert F. Weir ed. 1997); Susan L. Lowe, "The Right to Refuse Treatment Is Not a Right to Be Killed," 23 *Journal of Medical Ethics* 154 (1997); "Comments of John Finnis," in Lawrence Solum, Ronald Dworkin, and John Finnis, "Euthanasia, Morality, and the Law," 30 *Loyola of Los Angeles Law Review* 1465, 1473 (1997).

ducked the philosophical issue, but they had several compelling practical reasons (which the philosophers' brief ignored) for doing so. The first is that given the balance between the opposing philosophical arguments as they would appear to most people both inside and outside philosophy, the Court could not have written a convincing endorsement of either position.[68] It would have been seen as taking sides on a disagreement not susceptible of anything remotely resembling an objective resolution.

This objection is independent of metaethical theory, that is, of whether one is a moral realist, an emotivist, or anything in between.[69] Even if there is an objectively correct answer to every moral question that might arise in a case, the answer will appear arbitrary because there is no reasoning process that a judge might follow that would strike a detached observer as furnishing objective justification for the answer. This is an example of how the thesis of this chapter, the uselessness of moral theory for law, is detachable from the thesis of the first chapter, the uselessness of moral theory for morality and politics.

Second, there was no obstacle to a *democratic* resolution of the issue of physician-assisted suicide. The issue was on the legislative front burner in a number of states, and the people favoring the status quo—the legal prohibition of all forms of euthanasia—had the strength of inertia and intense conviction behind them, while the people favoring change were by and large the wealthier and better educated, who usually get their way in the political process as elsewhere. The political struggle not being one-sided, the case for judicial intervention was attenuated.

In favoring resolution of the issue by the democratic process, I may seem to be smuggling into the analysis a moral theory about the goodness of self-government. I would be if moral theory equaled social theory, so that every claim about the political or judicial process was necessarily a moral claim. But such a confusing equation should be avoided. If it is, and "moral theory" is given a narrower meaning, the case for judicial intervention is seen to be *pragmatically* weakened whenever democracy can be expected to "work" in some crude but serviceable sense because the competing views are well represented and fully aired in the political process. Though it is a point that Habermas can be cited in support of, it is a

68. For criticism of the "philosophers' brief" by a philosopher colleague of Dworkin's who shares his general ideological bent, see F. M. Kamm, "Theory and Analogy in Law," 29 *Arizona State Law Journal* 405, 414–416 (1997).

69. Jeremy Waldron, "The Irrelevance of Moral Objectivity," in *Natural Law Theory: Contemporary Essays* 158, 176–184 (Robert P. George ed. 1992).

moral point only if morality is a synonym for sound policy or if democratic decision making is thought in need of philosophical definition and justification.

Third, formulating actual protocols and safeguards for physician-assisted suicide requires complex technical and practical judgments that resist reduction to legally enforceable rules. In this respect the issue differs critically from the parallel issue of physician-assisted abortion.[70] We can count forward from conception, and so regulate abortions trimester by trimester under progressively stricter standards. We cannot count backward from death and, knowing when someone is going to die, allow him to accelerate the date by some more or less exact period. Crafting a legally administrable right of physician-assisted suicide requires investing such vague concepts as "dying" and "unbearable pain" with precise, operational legal meanings and specifying tiers of review to protect the dying patient from impatient physicians and relatives. The judgments required are quintessentially legislative or administrative rather than judicial. They are also difficult; the Dutch experience with euthanasia has revealed abuses that might be repeated in this country.[71]

Fourth, Supreme Court Justices, like other judges, work under time pressures that make them reluctant to engage with esoteric arguments presented in amicus curiae briefs. And fifth, judges more than law professors want to preserve the autonomy of law, not make law the handmaiden of other disciplines, especially one as remote from the understanding and affections of the average American, including the average and indeed the above-average judge, as moral philosophy. Dworkin considers the concern "that judges as a group lack the competence to engage in sustained analysis of difficult issues of political morality" to be "surely much exaggerated." He claims that judges don't need "much if any background in general philosophy" in order to be able to "reflect on complex moral issues," as distinct from issues of biology and economics, which he considers more challenging to the judicial intellect.[72] It is a common mistake to think that

---

70. The parallel was exploited in Judge Reinhardt's opinion in the Ninth Circuit in one of the euthanasia cases that came to the U.S. Supreme Court. Compassion in Dying v. Washington, 79 F.3d 790, 813–814, 829–831 (9th Cir. 1996) (en banc), reversed under the name of Washington v. Glucksberg, note 65 above.

71. See, for example, Herbert Hendin, *Seduced by Death: Doctors, Patients, and the Dutch Cure* (1997). How widespread those abuses are is not clear, however, either from Hendin's book or from the other anti-euthanasia literature. See Richard A. Posner, *Aging and Old Age* 242–243, 252–253 (1995), for a generally positive assessment of the Dutch experience.

72. Dworkin, "Reply," note 2 above, at 451.

"technical" problems are the most difficult to solve. Most technical problems are readily solvable by people who have the right training. Philosophical issues are not solvable by even the best-trained philosophers. Judges know or sense this and steer clear of such issues.

Dworkin gives no examples of judges who have had either the competence or the inclination to engage in reflection on complex moral issues. Two of the philosophically most competent judges in our history, Holmes and Hand, lacked the inclination completely. I have not seen it in Charles Fried either—a noted academic moralist turned state supreme court justice—though it may be too soon to tell. He *asserts* that his judicial work is informed by his philosophical reading and writing,[73] but as evidence he cites only one opinion and it does not support the assertion. One searches the opinion—a concurrence in a case involving a notification requirement for convicted sex offenders[74]—in vain for anything recognizable as moral philosophy. The opinion says that for the state to justify "a continuing, intrusive, and humiliating regulation" of a convicted person who has served his sentence by reference to the urgency of the need to prevent him from inflicting further harm on the community, "the urgency must be shown by the severity of the harm and the likelihood of its occurrence."[75] This sounds like Learned Hand's cost-benefit formula for determining negligence,[76] rather than like philosophy. Fried makes no overt effort to derive it from a moral principle, unless the claim that "we do not have a general regime regulating adult competent persons as such. Persons are left to choose freely and if they make the wrong choices they are subject to retrospective condemnation and punishment"[77] counts as a moral principle; I would call it a liberal truism. I begin to suspect—and there is a further hint in a discussion by Fried of homosexual rights[78]—that he equates moral principle to principle, and morality to normativity.

73. Charles Fried, "Philosophy Matters," 111 *Harvard Law Review* 1739, 1743 (1998).
74. Doe v. Attorney General, 686 N.E.2d 1007, 1016 (Mass. 1997).
75. Id. at 1016.
76. See United States v. Carroll Towing Co., 159 F.2d 169, 173 (2d Cir. 1947); Richard A. Posner, *Economic Analysis of Law* § 6.1 (5th ed. 1998). Earlier in his opinion, and in like vein, Fried had said that a notification requirement for convicted sex offenders "may be imposed after a careful weighing of three factors: the kind and severity of the regulatory imposition, the kind and severity of the danger sought to be averted, and the aptness of the fit between the remedial measure and the danger to be averted." 686 N.E.2d at 1016.
77. 686 N.E.2d at 1015.
78. Fried, note 73 above, at 1745 n. 43, citing Charles Fried, *Order and Law: Arguing the Reagan Revolution—A Firsthand Account* 82–83 (1991). Those pages are faintly Millian, but his discussion of homosexual rights as a whole, see id. at 83–85, has no philosophical compass that I can discern.

Another noted academic moralist turned judge, John T. Noonan, Jr., of the Ninth Circuit, wrote the original panel opinion in one of the euthanasia cases.[79] It is the finest of the many opinions in those cases. But he carefully refrains from suggesting in the opinion—what he believes as a Catholic and as a philosopher—that euthanasia is immoral.

We should not be surprised that the moral issue dissolved in the judicial consideration of the euthanasia cases.[80] However the issue is to be resolved, the Supreme Court had compelling practical reasons not to recognize a constitutional right. The philosophers' brief was beside the point.

We tend to forget that the Court had ducked the moral issue in the abortion cases as well. The discussion of the history of public policy toward abortion that takes up so much space in the Court's opinion in *Roe v. Wade*[81] is designed to show that abortion has not always and everywhere been anathematized. From the fact that it has provoked divergent moral reactions in the Western tradition the Court seemed to infer that there is no moral fact of the matter about abortion. To argue from disagreement to indeterminacy is fallacious; I do not want to defend the Court's implicit assumption that there is no moral issue about abortion; a moral issue is not resolved by being ignored. My point is only that the Court was trying to neutralize rather than resolve the issue.

The Court went on to treat the question of the right to an abortion as one largely of professional autonomy: the judgment whether to perform an abortion should be that of the doctor; the state should not intrude (at

79. Compassion in Dying v. Washington, 49 F.3d 586 (9th Cir. 1995). The panel decision was set aside by Noonan's court sitting en banc. The en banc decision was the one reversed by the Supreme Court under the name of Washington v. Glucksberg, see note 65 above, vindicating Noonan.

80. As they also did in England's counterpart case, Airedale NSH Trust v. Bland, [1993] All E.R. 858 (H.L.), which involved the question whether removal of life support from a patient in a vegetative state was lawful (the courts' answer was "yes"). The queasiness of the judges about the moral aspects of the question was well expressed by Lord Browne-Wilkinson in the House of Lords, who pointed out that while the judges of the Court of Appeal (the intermediate appellate court) had attached importance to "impalpable factors such as personal dignity and the way Anthony Bland would wish to be remembered," they had not taken into account "spiritual values which, for example, a member of the Roman Catholic church would regard as relevant in assessing such benefit." Id. at 879. In other words, the moral debate was a standoff, leading Browne-Wilkinson to opine that "the moral, social and legal issues raised by this case should be considered by Parliament," id., and that he had reached his own conclusion about how to decide the case on "narrow, legalistic, grounds." Id. at 884. Dworkin calls *Airedale* a "parallel case" to the Supreme Court's euthanasia case, Ronald Dworkin, "Darwin's New Bulldog," 111 *Harvard Law Review* 1718, 1727–1728 n. 32 (1998), thus echoing the argument of the philosophers' brief that there is no morally significant difference between killing and failing to save. This is the same mistake that Judith Jarvis Thomson made in equating abortion by a rape victim to the failure to save a famous violinist.

81. 410 U.S. 113, 129–152 (1973).

least when the abortion is performed early in the pregnancy).[82] The issue of professional autonomy could have been cast as a moral issue but was not, and is in any event remote from "the" moral issue about abortion, which has to do with the rights of the fetus.

There was more that the Court could have said without bringing in moral philosophy. It could have said, much as it would later say in the euthanasia cases, that abortion was an issue that could be left, at least initially, to resolution by the states. At the time *Roe v. Wade* was decided, there was considerable ferment in state abortion law and a rapidly growing number of legal abortions. Or the Justices could have said, again as in the euthanasia cases, that abortion was such a focus of irresolvable moral and religious debate that the Court could only stir up a hornet's nest in taking sides, as it would inevitably be seen as doing even if, as it did, it sedulously avoided the moral issue. (Recall the earlier distinction between a decision based on moral grounds and a decision that may have moral significance.) The approach of the euthanasia decisions is inconsistent with that of the abortion decisions. It is no surprise that both in the lower courts and in the Supreme Court much of the analysis of the claimed right to physician-assisted suicide involved efforts to distinguish, or to show that it was impossible to distinguish, the abortion decisions as precedents.

The dissenting Justices in *Roe v. Wade* did not discuss the moral issue either.[83] For them the existence of such an issue was a compelling reason to keep hands off. This is consistent with a general, and it seems to me prudent, policy for judges of not taking sides on moral issues. Dworkin has criticized the prudential position for ignoring "the moral cost, in the case of abortion, of many thousands of young women's lives being ruined in the meantime."[84] This criticism not only is hyperbolic—for the bearing of an unwanted child does not usually ruin the mother's life—but also begs the question. There is a moral cost on the other side—the lives of millions of fetuses killed. Judges are no more capable than philosophers of balancing "moral costs."

Dworkin claims that when a court decides a case in which there is a moral issue, it cannot avoid making a moral judgment. We have seen that this is wrong. Suppose Congress amended the Constitution to abolish the constitutional right of abortion, and afterward a case came up to the Supreme Court challenging a law forbidding abortion. The court would

82. See id. at 165–166.
83. See id. at 171–178, 223 (Rehnquist, J., dissenting); id. at 221–223 (White, J., dissenting).
84. Dworkin, "Reply," note 2 above, at 437.

throw out the case, giving victory to the opponents of abortion, but it would not be resolving a moral issue. Obvious as this point seems, Dworkin may not agree with it. For about the balance of moral costs in abortion cases he says that once *Roe v. Wade* was decided, early-pregnancy abortions imposed no moral cost comparable to the cost to pregnant women of being prevented from having abortions, because the Court's decision diminished the moral entitlement of the fetus by depriving it of its rights.[85] It seems to me that *Roe v. Wade* left the *moral* issue exactly where it found it. To think otherwise is to suppose that the Dred Scott decision made a positive contribution to resolving the issue of the morality of slavery or that *Plessy v. Ferguson* made a positive contribution to resolving the issue of the morality of racial segregation. We can see in these examples where thinking of law as a branch of moral philosophy can lead.

Segregation, Affirmative Action, Murderous Heirs

Another famous case in which the Court ducked a conspicuous moral issue was *Brown v. Board of Education.*[86] The Court did not say that integration was a moral imperative or that public school segregation denies to blacks equal concern and respect with whites. It said that education is terribly important to people in the modern world and that psychologists had found that segregation impaired the self-esteem and likely educational success of blacks. To these nonmoral points could have been added the difficulty of assuring that segregated schools were really equal in quality, segregation's ill-concealed purpose of maintaining blacks in a subordinate position, the suffering that resulted from being publicly declared inferior (the well-understood message of the segregation of public facilities ranging from drinking fountains to buses and schools), the inconsistency between segregation and U.S. foreign-policy objectives and propaganda, and, more subtly, the fact that barriers to trade (not only business and employment relations but also the noncommercial "trade" that consists of social interactions) hurt a minority more than they do the majority because the majority is more likely to be self-sufficient, just as the United States is more self-sufficient than Switzerland and hence less dependent for its prosperity on foreign trade.[87] Most of these points are independent of

85. Dworkin, note 80 above, at 1729 n. 43.

86. 347 U.S. 483 (1954).

87. See Gary S. Becker, *The Economics of Discrimination* (2d ed. 1971); Posner, note 76 above, § 26.1.

considerations of physical equality or even of educational quality, as can be seen by imagining that the southern states had spent the same amount of money per pupil on black schools and that as a result those schools provided as good an education as the white schools (that is, suppose that integration as such confers no educational benefits on blacks). The element of quarantine, of stigmatization, of a caste system would have remained along with the impeding of mutually advantageous trades, furnishing compelling arguments against the constitutionality of segregation unless the southern states had good counterarguments, which they didn't.

So there is plenty to say about public school segregation without getting entangled in moral issues. But it may seem that implicit in all the "practical" points that I listed *is* a moral theory—that suffering, that insult, is entitled to consideration in formulating a rule of law in a difficult case. But I want to insist once again on the difference between a moral principle and a moral *issue*. Morality is a pervasive feature of social life and is in the background of many legal principles. But the shared morality that forms the backdrop to a case, and that in *Brown* included a belief that government should have a good reason for inflicting material or emotional harm on its citizens or for allocating benefits or burdens on the basis of race, is like the stipulated facts of a case, which are a given rather than a subject of contention. Moral theory of the casuistic variety comes in when one wants to build on the existing bedrock of moral intuitions. Only there are no building blocks.

In speaking of "bedrock" I may seem to be sliding into moral realism. Not so. A moral principle may be unshakable at present without being "right." The fact that no one in a society questions a taboo against racial intermarriage doesn't make that taboo morally right. To think it does would be to embrace vulgar relativism, the idea that a society's acceptance of a moral principle makes that principle morally right. All it does is make the moral principle—a moral principle.

What distinguishes the segregation case from the abortion case is that most, perhaps all, of the Justices (possibly excepting Reed), and almost all the people in the Justices' set, thought that racial segregation in public facilities was immoral.[88] Yet the Court did not pitch decision on moral grounds. This was partly no doubt for a political reason: to minimize the offense to southern whites, who had a different morality so far as race was concerned. (Here is an example of the potential divisiveness of casting

88. See Richard Kluger, *Simple Justice: The History of* Brown v. Board of Education *and Black America's Struggle for Equality*, ch. 23 (1976).

judicial decisions in moral terms.) But it was also for another reason: that moral arguments are weak arguments in a court. And I could leave out "in a court." Everyone agrees, and in 1954 agreed, that the government should not inflict suffering gratuitously. They disagreed over whether segregation inflicts suffering and, if it does, whether the suffering is gratuitous. Everyone agrees, and in 1954 agreed, that the state is required to treat similarly situated people the same way. The question was whether "separate but equal" education violates this principle; and if the answer to that question was yes the court would then have to ask whether and in what sense blacks really are equal to whites, a proposition that in 1954 would have been contested, with many southerners arguing that blacks should not be recognized as even the political equals of whites.

Even if everyone had agreed that the races should be considered equal, it would still have been possible to make a "moral" argument that they should be kept separate, that mixing the races in public schools would lead inevitably to intermarriage and to the resulting erasure of racial distinctions that God or nature may, in creating different races, have ordained for inscrutable reasons. This is a moral argument that would have carried a lot of weight in the nineteenth century, and for that matter in the American South as late as the 1950s and 1960s. And then there is Wechsler's well-known claim[89] that prohibiting segregation violates the freedom of association of the whites who do not want their children to attend school with blacks. This is a moral argument for which support can be found in John Stuart Mill's contention that the Mormons should have been left to their own devices in Utah, provided only that persons who didn't like their laws were free to leave.[90] By 1954, blacks who didn't want to live under the Jim Crow laws had long been able to move to northern states that did not have such laws. Many had done so.

An opinion in *Brown v. Board of Education* that was determined to go down the moral path would have lost its way in a maze of arguments, counterarguments, and factual claims. Better to say either what the Court said, though it was incomplete and indeed disingenuous (for the Court was shortly to strike down segregation in other public facilities on the basis of a bare citation to *Brown*,[91] a case ostensibly limited to education),

89. In the article of his cited in note 39 above.

90. John Stuart Mill, *On Liberty* 86 (David Spitz ed. 1975).

91. See, for example, Mayor and City Council v. Dawson, 350 U.S. 877 (1955) (per curiam); Holmes v. City of Atlanta, 350 U.S. 879 (1955) (per curiam); Gayle v. Browder, 352 U.S. 903 (1956) (per curiam).

or simply that "everyone knows" that segregation by law in schools and other public places was meant to keep black people "in their place," that it was an ugly practice, a component of a caste system—ugly, that is, to the Justices deciding the case and to like-thinking people, not ugly *sub specie aeternitatis*—and that the equal protection clause was in some sense intended, or should be used, to prevent it. An opinion so drafted would not have been an impressive specimen of "legal reasoning," but it would have been honest. The Court's opinion was less honest but politically adroit. An opinion that tried to use moral theory on the issue would have lacked either virtue.

That is equally true of the judicial response to today's hottest legal question involving race: the constitutionality of affirmative action by public universities and other public agencies. One can get nowhere discussing the morality of affirmative action. Here is my nonmoral take on the issue: Americans today are uncomfortable with racial classifications used to allocate public benefits and burdens, yet recognize that the disaffection of blacks poses a serious social problem.[92] Although the problem may actually have been aggravated by affirmative action, which undermines the claims of all blacks to be recognized as true equals of whites, its sudden and complete elimination today throughout the public sector (and private, if the civil rights statutes were reinterpreted as prohibiting affirmative action) could not be "sold" to blacks as the elimination of an unjust preference. It would instead be provocative, exacerbating racial tensions, which is something that, on pragmatic grounds, our society can ill afford. So neither complete acceptance nor complete rejection of affirmative action would be a practical course of action, and, fortunately, neither extreme is compelled by clear constitutional or statutory texts or precedents. When affirmative action imposes heavy costs on identified whites (as when blacks are given superseniority in firms that lay off surplus workers in reverse order of seniority), it will probably be rejected. When it is plainly necessary either as a remedy for unlawful discrimination or in order to maintain the legitimacy and hence efficacy of the government's security apparatus (as in the case of affirmative action in police forces and correctional staffs), it will probably be accepted. In between these ex-

---

92. The discomfort is clear from polling data. See, for example, Sam Howe Verhovek, "In Poll, Americans Reject Means But Not Ends of Racial Diversity," *New York Times,* Dec. 14, 1997, p. 1. The lumping in of other groups with blacks as objects of governmental favoritism is highly questionable. The other groups, primarily women, Asians, and persons of Hispanic ethnicity, have (women and Asians particularly) far less need or claim for favoritism and are not disaffected to a degree that could foreseeably endanger the social peace. But I shall not try to pursue that issue here.

tremes, decision will turn on the values of the decision-makers—will be, in other words, inescapably political. This leads to the paradox that the acceptability of the decision may depend on the political diversity of the judiciary, which means that a proper resolution of the issue of affirmative action may depend on an anterior decision to use affirmative action to constitute the decision-making body!

To acknowledge the inescapably political character of an important class of judicial decisions will scandalize many legal thinkers. But no better solution to the issue of affirmative action is available through moral reasoning, which would bog down in interminable debates over historical injustices, justice between generations, entitlements, reasonable expectations, rights, and equality.

We can keep going back in our quest for moral decisions, for example to the nineteenth century and *Riggs v. Palmer*,[93] the "murdering heir" case that Dworkin likes to discuss.[94] The court held that the New York wills statute did not entitle a man who had murdered his grandfather to take under the grandfather's will, even though the grandson was named as a legatee and the will conformed in every particular to the requirements for validity set forth in the statute. In support of this conclusion the majority opinion expressly invoked the moral tradition, going back to Aristotle. But it did not do so in order to resolve a moral issue. There was no moral *issue*. Everyone agreed that the grandson had acted immorally and as a matter of sound moral principle should not be rewarded. The question was whether his immorality was a *legal* defense to his claim under the wills statute, which made no mention of a murdering heir. The answer was that it was, because no inference could be drawn from the draftsmen's failure to write in such an exception. They hadn't foreseen such a case. To interpret the statute as entitling the murderer to inherit would have disserved the intentions of testators, the principal interest that the statute protects; it would have been a goofy interpretation.[95] Furthermore, it would have

93. 115 N.Y. 506, 22 N.E. 188 (1889).

94. See Dworkin, note 12 above, at 458–459 (index references to "Elmer's case").

95. The dissenting judges were concerned that taking away the murderer's legacy added to the punishment for his crime without legislative warrant. This concern was questionable, to say the least. Compare two murderers, one who kills a poor person and derives no monetary benefit from the crime, and the other who kills his grandfather and obtains a legacy as a result. If they are given the same criminal sentence, the second murderer is actually punished more lightly, the legacy being a partial (it could even be a complete) offset to the sentence. He could be given a longer sentence and allowed to keep the legacy, but what would be the point?

In endorsing the result in Riggs v. Palmer, I don't mean to slight the dangers, which Holmes warned against in "The Path of the Law," that are involved in judges' trying to use their moral beliefs, however unexceptionable, to decide technical legal issues. For a striking example, see the opinions in Mazzei v.

created a totally arbitrary distinction between testamentary and intestate succession, since the grandson had pitched his entire argument on the wills statute.

This analysis owes nothing to moral theory. The only issue in the case was whether a proper interpretation of the wills statute—proper in the nonmoral sense of conforming to some notion of draftsmen's actual or probable intentions—permitted the outcome that uncontroversial morality commended.

If Not Morality, What?

The careful reader will have noticed that I am making a claim that in one respect is broader than that in Chapter 1. The argument there was that there is "nothing to" a certain type of moral reasoning, but it was only one type, what I called academic moralism, associated with a subset of contemporary moral philosophers. The argument here is that moral theory has nothing *for law;* this argument is not limited to academic moralism. The idea that racial discrimination is immoral owes very little to academic moralists; it owes a lot to nonacademic moral entrepreneurs such as Abraham Lincoln, Harriet Beecher Stowe, and Martin Luther King, Jr. Yet as *Brown v. Board of Education* illustrates, courts do not rely on moral entrepreneurs either. I don't mean that they are never cited in judicial decisions; but they are cited as representatives of uncontested moral positions rather than as authorities for taking one side or another of a moral issue.

There are exceptions, but they confirm the wisdom of the rule. Consider *Commonwealth v. Wasson,*[96] which cites Mill's *On Liberty* as authority for invalidating a statute forbidding homosexual intercourse. Its ground for citing Mill was a much older Kentucky case that had, as it were, received *On Liberty* into the law of Kentucky by citing it as authority for invalidating a law forbidding the possession of liquor.[97] The old case had been suffused with the laissez-faire ideology of its day, an ideology that has now been discredited as a basis for constitutional decisions.[98] Or consider

---

Commissioner, 61 T.C. 497 (1974), dealing with the deductibility from federal income tax of a fraud loss incurred by the participant in a criminal conspiracy. But I do wish to emphasize the difference between basing a judicial decision on a moral consensus and basing it on moral theory viewed as a method of resolving contested moral issues.

96. 842 S.W.2d 487 (Ky. 1992).

97. Commonwealth v. Campbell, 117 S.W. 383 (Ky. 1909).

98. See, for example, State v. Eitel, 227 So. 2d 489 (Fla. 1969); State v. Darrah, 446 S.W.2d 745 (Mo. 1969); Picou v. Gillum, 874 F.2d 1519, 1522 (11th Cir. 1989), all cases that cite Mill respect-

Commonwealth v. Bonadio,[99] which invalidated a state statute forbidding voluntary deviate sexual intercourse. The opinion quotes extensively from *On Liberty*—on the ground that the Constitution enacts Mill's concept of liberty, as shown by an 1894 decision by the U.S. Supreme Court[100] that reflects the same discredited constitutional doctrine invoked in the old case cited in *Wasson*. Used consistently rather than opportunistically as a constitutional authority, Mill would bring about a legal revolution—a return to a nineteenth-century conception of laissez-faire as constitutional doctrine—that would horrify the modern liberals who want to use Mill's concept of liberty to invalidate laws restricting sexual freedom. This illustrates a point in Chapter 1, that present-day academic moralists (and here I add their allies in constitutional theory) have to clean up their idols before pressing them into the service of a modern moral or legal agenda.

But if moral theory is thus not a resource for law, what is? The answer is easy for those who believe that all constitutional issues can be resolved by reconstructing the intent of the framers. But Dworkin and others have exploded that myth. Practical considerations can be used to resolve many constitutional issues that do not turn on disagreement over moral or political ultimates. But what about the issues that cannot be resolved so? The judge has two choices. One is to say that if public opinion is divided on a moral issue, courts should leave its resolution to the political process. The other is to say, with Holmes, that while the political process is ordinarily the right way to go, every once in a while an issue on which public opinion is divided so excites the judge's moral emotions that he simply cannot stomach the political resolution that has been challenged on constitutional grounds. That is the position in which the first Justice Harlan found himself in *Plessy v. Ferguson*[101] and in which Holmes found himself from time to time[102]—showing that moral skeptics, moral relativists, have the same moral emotions as everyone else and differ only in not thinking that moral disagreements can be bridged by moral reasoning.

I prefer the second route (discussed more fully below and in the next

---

fully but make clear that his laissez-faire economic views are not a part of modern American constitutional law.

99. 415 A.2d 47 (Pa. 1980).

100. Lawton v. Steele, 152 U.S. 133 (1894). See also Mugler v. Kansas, 123 U.S. 623 (1887), a case that, like *Campbell*, note 97 above, cites *On Liberty*.

101. 163 U.S. 537, 552 (1896) (dissenting opinion).

102. For example, in the wiretapping case. See Olmstead v. United States, 277 U.S. 438, 469 (1928) (dissenting opinion).

chapter). It leaves a place for conscience. If judges are carefully selected, as is generally true of federal judges, a judge's civil disobedience—his refusal to enforce a law "as written" because it violates his deepest moral feelings—is a significant datum. It portends the potential disaffection of the elite, which is the sort of thing that ought to give the political authorities pause. True, it injects a destabilizing element into the governance of the nation, but no more so than a license for the judges to engage in moral reasoning, given the indeterminacy of such reasoning. And it may retard destabilizing innovations in public policy by the populist branches of government—so that on balance it may promote rather than undermine political stability.

Legal professionals, especially those who want to expand the power of the judiciary, resist the idea that there is an irreducibly discretionary, in the sense of an unruled, a "subjective," element in constitutional adjudication. They resist in part for reasons of professional pride and self-interest but also because one's moral intuitions or (in Holmes's phrase) "can't helps"[103] don't seem to be very heavy counterweights to democratic preference as reflected in the actions of elected officials and their appointees. Hence the potential appeal of moral philosophy, which may seem to arm judges to prove that those actions are "wrong" and have to be prevented. In a civilized society, official acts that are *demonstrably* wrong are relatively infrequent, so the pragmatic moral skepticism that I argued for in Chapter 1 does cast rather a pall over the liberal judicial activism that is in vogue in the legal profession today, particularly among law professors; Holmes was not an activist. The professionalism that I said has paradoxically weakened rather than strengthened moral philosophy by depriving it of the "enchantment" that might enable it to alter the moral code has increased the demand of the legal professoriat for the kind of analytical rigor irrelevantly associated with modern moral philosophy. I do not say falsely associated with it. Many academic moralists are intelligent people and careful analysts. But they lack the tools for resolving moral disagreement. They cannot help the lawyers, and specifically the judges. The latter will have to

103. See, for example, Letter of Oliver Wendell Holmes to Harold J. Laski, Feb. 6, 1925, in *Holmes-Laski Letters: The Correspondence of Mr. Justice Holmes and Harold J. Laski*, vol. 1, pp. 705, 706 (Mark DeWolfe Howe ed. 1953). "When I say that a thing is true, I mean that I cannot help believing it . . . I therefore define the truth as the system of my limitations, and leave absolute truth for those who are better equipped. With absolute truth I leave absolute ideals of conduct equally on one side." Oliver Wendell Holmes, "Ideals and Doubts," 10 *Illinois Law Review* 1, 2 (1915). See also Holmes, "Natural Law," 32 *Harvard Law Review* 40 (1918).

look elsewhere, or perhaps will have to scale down their ambitions to remake society.

Constitutional Theory

Its Nature, Varieties, and Shortcomings

In the preceding section I was concerned with efforts to apply moral reasoning directly to legal issues. The indirect application through constitutional theory flavored with moral theory is at least as important. Constitutional theory is distinct on the one hand from inquiries of a social scientific character into the nature, provenance, and consequences of constitutionalism—the sort of thing one associates mainly with historians and political scientists, such as Charles Beard, Jon Elster, and Stephen Holmes—and on the other hand from commentary on specific cases and doctrines, the sort of thing one associates with legal doctrinalists specializing in constitutional law, such as Kathleen Sullivan, Laurence Tribe, and William Van Alstyne. A number of scholars straddle this divide, including Bruce Ackerman, Ronald Dworkin, Richard Epstein, Andrew Koppelman, Lawrence Lessig, Michael McConnell, Frank Michelman, and Mark Tushnet; and although I mean to keep to one side of it the straddle is no accident. Constitutional theorists are normativists; their theories are meant to influence the way judges decide difficult constitutional cases. When the theorists are law-trained, as most of them are, they cannot resist telling their readers which cases they think were decided consistently with or contrary to their theory. Most constitutional theorists, indeed, believe in social reform through judicial action.

Constitutional theory has at best limited applicability to constitutional law. Nothing pretentious enough to warrant the name of theory is required to decide constitutional cases in which the text or history of the Constitution provide sure guidance; no theory is required to determine how many senators each state may have. More difficult interpretive issues, such as whether the self-incrimination clause should be interpreted as forbidding the prosecutor to comment on the defendant's failure to take the stand,[104] can often be resolved pretty straightforwardly by considering the consequences of rival interpretations. Were a prosecutor allowed to argue to the jury that the defendant's refusal to testify should be taken as

104. As held in Griffin v. California, 380 U.S. 609 (1965).

an admission of guilt, it would be extremely difficult for defense counsel to counter with some plausible explanation consistent with his client's being innocent. So allowing comment would pretty much destroy the privilege—at least as it is currently understood. That is an important qualification. It has been argued that the current understanding is incorrect, that the historical and sensible purpose of the privilege is merely to prevent torture and other improper methods of interrogation; if this is right, there is no basis for the rule of no comment.[105] Maybe, as this example suggests, when fully ventilated no issue of constitutional law not founded on one of the numerical provisions of the Constitution is beyond contestation. But an issue can be contestable without being resolvable by the application of a general theory. There are large areas of constitutional law that the debates over constitutional theory do not touch and that I shall therefore ignore.

Constitutional theory in the sense in which I am using the term is at least as old as the *Federalist Papers*. Yet after more than two centuries no signs of closure are visible, or even, as it seems to me, of progress. The reason is that constitutional theory has no power to command agreement from people not already predisposed to accept the theorist's policy prescriptions. This is because it is normative in the same way that moral theory is, being abstract, unempirical, and often at war with strongly held moral intuitions or political commitments; because it is interpretive and the accuracy of an interpretation of an old document is not verifiable or otherwise demonstrable; and because normativists, including law professors, do not like to be backed into a corner by committing themselves to a theory that might be falsified by data, any more than a practicing lawyer wants to take a position that might force him to concede that his client has no case.

Constitutional theory is unresponsive to, and indeed tends to obscure, the greatest need of constitutional adjudicators, which is for empirical knowledge, as I shall argue shortly using as illustrations the Supreme Court's recent decisions requiring the Virginia Military Institute to admit women[106] and forbidding Colorado to ban local ordinances that protect homosexuals from discrimination on the basis of their sexual orientation.[107] Of course, just getting the facts right can't decide a case; there has

---

105. Albert W. Alschuler, "A Peculiar Privilege in Historical Perspective," in R. H. Helmholz et al, *The Privilege against Self-Incrimination: Its Origins and Development* 181, 203 (1997).

106. United States v. Virginia, 116 S. Ct. 2264 (1996).

107. Romer v. Evans, 116 S. Ct. 1620 (1996).

to be an analytic framework to fit the facts into. But the design of the framework is not the biggest problem in constitutional law today. The biggest problem is a lack of the very knowledge that academic research, rather than the litigation process, is best designed to produce; only a different kind of academic research from what constitutional theorists do.

The leading theorists are able and articulate, and it is possible that their debates have a diffuse but cumulatively significant impact on the tone, the texture, and occasionally even the outcomes of constitutional cases, though whether it is a good impact is a different question and one that cannot be answered on the basis of existing knowledge. The theorists do not have a large audience among judges, but they have a large audience among their own students and hence among the judges' law clerks, whose influence on constitutional law, though small, is not completely negligible, and among future practitioners of constitutional law. Yet the real significance of constitutional theory, or at least of its mushrooming in recent decades, is as a sign of the increased academification of law school professors. They are more inclined than formerly to write for other professors rather than for judges and practitioners. There are so many more law professors than there used to be that they can have a nonnegligible audience for their work even if it is aimed only at other law professors. And as constitutional theory becomes more "theoretical," less tethered to the practice of law, it becomes increasingly transparent to professors in other fields, such as political theory and moral philosophy. This has helped the ranks of the constitutional theorists to grow to the point of self-sufficiency. But the result of that growth is that constitutional theory today circulates in a medium that is largely opaque to the judge and the practicing lawyer.

The problem in political theory to which constitutional theory is offered as a solution is that a judicially enforceable Constitution gives judges an unusual amount of power. This was seen as problematic well before the democratic principle became as central to our concept of government as it now is. Hamilton's solution to the problem, shortly to be echoed by John Marshall, was to claim that it was the *law* that was supreme, not the judges, since judges are (in Blackstone's phrase, but it is also Hamilton's sense) just the oracles, the mouthpieces, of the law, rather than centers of political power in their own, unelected right.[108]

---

108. See William Blackstone, *Commentaries on the Laws of England*, vol. 1, p. 25 (1769); *Federalist* No. 78 (Hamilton); Osborn v. Bank of United States, 22 U.S. (9 Wheat.) 738, 866 (1824) (Marshall, C.J.).

After a century of judicial willfulness, this position was difficult to maintain with a straight face. The Constitution had obviously made the judges a competing power center. James Bradley Thayer argued in the 1890s that this was bad because it shifted the primary lawmaking role from legislatures to courts, contrary to the constitutional design, and (a closely related point, not clearly distinguished by him) sapped legislatures of initiative and responsibility. He said that courts should enforce constitutional rights only when the existence of a right was, as a matter of constitutional interpretation, clear beyond a reasonable doubt.[109] In other words, he thought the erroneous grant of a constitutional right a more serious error than the erroneous denial of such a right, just as the criminal justice system assumes that the erroneous conviction of an innocent person is a more serious error than the erroneous acquittal of a guilty person. He did not attempt to show that it was in fact a more serious error, and relied for his proposed rule primarily on case authority.

Thayer is an ancestor of the "outrage" school of constitutional interpretation, whose most notable practitioner was Holmes. Other illustrious alumni of this school are Cardozo, Frankfurter, and the second Justice Harlan. The school of outrage holds that for a court to be justified in stymieing the elected branches of government, it isn't enough that the litigant claiming a constitutional right has the better argument; it has to be a *lot* better. The violation of the Constitution has to be morally certain (Thayer's position), or stomach-turning (Holmes's "puke" test),[110] or shocking to the conscience (Frankfurter's test),[111] or the sort of thing no reasonable person could defend. As Holmes put it in his dissent in *Lochner,* a statute does not work a deprivation of "liberty" without due process of law within the meaning of the due process clauses of the Fifth and Fourteenth Amendments "unless it can be said that a rational and fair man necessarily would admit that the statute proposed [opposed?] would infringe fundamental principles as they have been understood by the traditions of our people and our law."[112]

These formulations are not interchangeable. A violation of the Constitution can be clear beyond a reasonable doubt without being revolting—

109. James B. Thayer, "The Origin and Scope of the American Doctrine of Constitutional Law," 7 *Harvard Law Review* 129 (1893). He meant this in the same sense as the familiar standard for proving guilt in a criminal trial. See id. at 150.

110. See Richard A. Posner, *Overcoming Law* 192 (1995).

111. See Rochin v. California, 342 U.S. 165 (1952). Can it be an accident that Frankfurter announced his test in a case about pumping the stomach of a suspect for evidence?

112. Lochner v. New York, 198 U.S. 45, 76 (1905) (dissenting opinion).

increasing the number of senators per state from two to three would be an example. And an official act can be revolting without violating the Constitution beyond a reasonable doubt—forbidding families to have more than one child, for example. If Thayer's version is emphasized, the doctrine (if it can be called that) of outrage becomes almost interchangeable with that of judicial self-restraint when the latter doctrine is understood as seeking to minimize the occasions on which the courts annul the actions of other branches of government. The judge who is self-restrained in this sense wishes to take a back seat to the other branches of government, but is stirred to action when another branch does not merely arguably violate, but flouts, the limitations placed upon it by the Constitution.

Even if "outrage" is defined more broadly, to include not only the clear violations but also the really intolerable unclear ones (the concern of Holmes)—and the broader definition is inescapable because the clear violations are largely confined to those areas in which no theory is necessary to guide the judges to a satisfactory resolution—the school of outrage tends to be restrained in the exercise of judicial power. This is especially true when Holmes's qualification of the "fundamental principles" that might warrant a judge in holding a statute unconstitutional—that they be principles "as they have been understood by the traditions of our people and our law"—is emphasized and so the element of a merely personal reaction downplayed. If the outrage approach can thus be given a measure of impersonality as well as tied to the doctrine of judicial self-restraint, a doctrine that is founded on reasons,[113] the approach is no longer so purely visceral as my initial summary may have suggested.

But I cannot pretend that outrage or even self-restraint furnishes much in the way of guidance to courts grappling with difficult issues. And it can be defended convincingly only by showing what may be impossible as a practical matter: that decisions invalidating statutes or other official actions as unconstitutional have, when the decision could not have been justified under Thayer's or Holmes's or Cardozo's or Frankfurter's or Harlan's approach, done more harm than good.[114] I am also mindful that one person's outrage is another's ecstasy or, to put it differently, that emotions of attraction and repulsion can be aroused on either side of any controversial issue. But this is just to say that personal values and political prefer-

113. Which I summarize and elaborate in my book *The Federal Courts: Challenge and Reform,* ch. 10 (1996).

114. I return to the school of outrage briefly in Chapter 4, where I relate it to pragmatic adjudication.

ences are apt to play an important role in courts that have broad discretion,[115] and hence that we want a diverse bench and also that we want our judicial candidates carefully screened not only for temperament and character and intelligence and knowledge of the law but also for their experiences and values. But this is old hat—which shows that, deep down, everyone concedes that the school of outrage has enrolled much of the judiciary.

Hamilton-style formalism now has a defender in Justice Scalia.[116] But he lacks the courage of his convictions. For he takes extreme libertarian positions with respect to such matters as affirmative action and freedom of speech on the ground that these positions are dictated not by the Constitution but by the cases interpreting the Constitution.[117] Take away the adventitious operation of stare decisis and Scalia is left with a body of constitutional law of remarkable meagerness. This is not an objection, but it requires a greater effort at justification than the bromides of democracy that are all that he has yet offered. Complaining that the Supreme Court is undemocratic begs the question, even if one accepts what Dworkin and to a lesser extent Habermas would consider a naive conception of democracy, one that ignores all the obstacles to deliberation. For the Court is part of a Constitution that in its inception was rich in undemocratic features, such as the indirect election of the President and of the Senate (and against the background of a highly restricted franchise), that make it hard to read the Constitution as a simple charter of democracy. Even as amended over the years, the Constitution has a number of undemocratic features. They include the method of apportionment of the Senate, which results in weighting the votes of people in sparsely populated states much more heavily than the votes of people in densely populated ones; the election of the President on the basis of electoral rather than popular votes, which could result in the election of a candidate who had lost the popular vote and does result in candidates' campaigning disproportionately in the

115. Anyone who doubts this should read Richard L. Revesz, "Environmental Regulation, Ideology, and the D.C. Circuit," 83 *Virginia Law Review* 1717 (1997).

116. See Antonin Scalia, "Common-Law Courts in a Civil-Law System: The Role of United States Federal Courts in Interpreting the Constitution and Laws," in Scalia et al., *A Matter of Interpretation: Federal Courts and the Law* 3 (1997).

117. Antonin Scalia, "Response," in id. at 129, 138–139. He says, "Where originalism will make a difference is not in the rolling back of accepted old principles of constitutional law but in the rejection of usurpatious new ones." Id. at 139. But on his understanding of proper constitutional interpretation, most of the "accepted old principles" were themselves "usurpatious" when first announced, and some of them were first announced within the last few decades on the basis of just the kind of nonoriginalist interpretation that he considers usurpative.

sparsely populated states since they are disproportionately represented in the electoral college; the expansion of constitutional rights brought about by the Bill of Rights and the Fourteenth Amendment, which curtails the powers of the elected branches of government; and lifetime appointment of federal judges, who exercise considerable political power by virtue of the expansion of rights to which I just referred and whose power grows yearly with the recession of the constitutional text as a workable limitation on judicial discretion.

The Supreme Court is certainly undemocratic but not in a sense that makes it anomalous in the political system created by the Constitution, given the other undemocratic features that I have mentioned; and anomalous or not, the Court is a part of the Constitution. A further drawback to Scalia's approach is that it requires judges to be political theorists, so that they know what "democracy" is (unless we can accept that Scalia himself has said the last word on that question), and also historians, because it takes a historian to reconstruct the original meaning of centuries-old documents.[118]

But there is this to be said for Scalia's Manichaean vision of a democratic legislature confronting an oligarchic judiciary: it highlights a genuine tension that today's judicial activists (and their academic backers), particularly on the Left, seem intent to obscure. Consider Joshua Cohen's version of "deliberative democracy." It makes of democracy a substantive rather than a procedural doctrine, a shaping rather than an aggregating of citizens' preferences, enabling Cohen to describe a majority's hypothetical desire to suppress some minority group's religious observances as not merely oppressive or illiberal, but undemocratic.[119] On this construal of "democracy," every policy the activist wants can be sought from the Supreme Court in the name of democracy. Dworkin makes a similar point even more brazenly: "The American conception of democracy is whatever form of government the Constitution, according to the best interpretation of that document, establishes."[120] By the "best interpretation" Dworkin

118. The shortcomings of lawyers and judges, and even of law professors, as legal historians has been remarked often. For illustrative discussions, see Alfred H. Kelly, "Clio and the Court: An Illicit Love Affair," 1965 *Supreme Court Review* 119; Martin S. Flaherty, "History 'Lite' in Modern American Constitutionalism," 95 *Columbia Law Review* 523 (1995); Laura Kalman, "Border Patrol: Reflections on the Turn to History in Legal Scholarship," 66 *Fordham Law Review* 87 (1997); Barry Friedman and Scott B. Smith, "The Sedimentary Constitution" (Vanderbilt Law School, Oct. 30, 1997, unpublished).

119. Joshua Cohen, "Procedure and Substance in Deliberative Democracy," in *Deliberative Democracy: Essays on Reason and Politics* 407, 417–419 (James Bohman and William Rehg eds. 1997).

120. Dworkin, *Freedom's Law*, note 2 above, at 75.

means his own richly substantive interpretation—so he is claiming to be the authentic spokesman of the *content* of American democracy. The Constitution contains a democratic principle, but is not a synonym for democracy. Scalia is correct to sense that people who look to the courts for social reform do not take democracy completely seriously. Dworkin is closer in spirit to Plato than to Andrew Jackson.

Most constitutional theorizing in this century has emphasized fidelity to text much less than a Hamilton or a Scalia does, though more than Dworkin does. We may begin with Learned Hand's argument that the Bill of Rights provides so little guidance to judges that most of it ought to be nonjusticiable[121] and move on to Herbert Wechsler's prompt riposte that constitutional law can be stabilized by judicial evenhandedness, what he called "neutral principles," soon recognized as merely principles; since principles can be bad as well as good, Wechsler's riposte failed.[122] Alexander Bickel tried to split the difference between the school of outrage and Wechsler by arguing that judicial devotion to principle should be leavened by prudence.[123]

Eventually the focus shifted to identifying *good* principles to guide constitutional decision making. Among the leading candidates have been John Hart Ely's principle of "representation reinforcement"[124] and Ronald Dworkin's principle of egalitarian natural justice. It is important to distinguish this principle from Dworkin's idea that judges in difficult cases should turn to moral theory for guidance. That is a procedural principle, like the principles proposed by the formalists, by Thayer and his followers, and by Wechsler; it is about how judges should go about finding the substantive principles with which to decide cases. Egalitarian natural justice, Dworkin's conception of what judges find when they do turn to moral theory, is a substantive principle.

Both representation reinforcement and egalitarian natural justice founder as master principles of constitutional law on their arbitrariness (Why *more* democracy? Why *more* equality?) and on their authors' lack of steady interest in and firm grasp of the details of public policy. I have complained

121. Learned Hand, *The Bill of Rights* (1958).

122. Wechsler, note 39 above. The criticisms of the article are summarized in Posner, note 110 above, at 71–75.

123. See Alexander M. Bickel, *The Least Dangerous Branch: The Supreme Court at the Bar of Politics* (1962). On his differences with Wechsler, see id. at 49–65; on his differences with Thayer, see id. at 39–45.

124. Ely, note 22 above.

elsewhere about the egregious underspecialization of constitutional theo-rists[125] (corresponding to the underspecialization of academic moralists). People who devote their careers to the study of political theory and consti-tutional doctrine do not by doing so equip themselves to formulate sub-stantive principles designed to guide decision making across the vast range of difficult issues that spans affirmative action and exclusionary zoning, legislative apportionment and prison administration, telecommunications and euthanasia, the education of alien children and the administration of capital punishment, to name just a few current and recent issues in consti-tutional law.

The formulation of procedural theories has continued. Examples are Bruce Ackerman's "constitutional moments" approach,[126] Lawrence Les-sig's "translation" approach,[127] John Rawls's "public reason"[128] approach, and Cass Sunstein's counter to Rawls, Sunstein's "incompletely theorized" or "judicial minimalism" approach.[129] Ackerman argues that courts should identify political watersheds, such as the New Deal, and accord them the same authority for changing constitutional law as they would accord a formal amendment. This approach requires judges to have the skills of historians, political theorists, and political scientists, so it is open to some of the same objections as Scalia's otherwise quite dissimilar ap-proach. It is also rather too "legal realist," one might even say *realpolitik-isch,* in inviting judges to give constitutional status to powerful currents of public opinion, such as welled up during the New Deal and are now understood to have been to a considerable degree deeply misinformed. The logic of Ackerman's extratextualism is that if a court were confident that some law would be passed by Congress and signed by the President, but for some irrelevant reason (maybe just an oversight by the clerical staff in one of the houses of Congress) it was not enacted, the court could go ahead and enforce it as if it had been enacted. Formalist readers of Acker-man may come away with their faith strengthened.

---

125. Posner, note 110 above, at 207–214. See id. at 198–207 on the shortcomings of Ely's theory. And see McConnell, note 2 above, on the shortcomings of Dworkin's theory.

126. Bruce Ackerman, *We the People,* vol. 1: *Foundations* (1991), vol. 2: *Transformations* (1998).

127. See, for example, Lawrence Lessig, "Fidelity in Translation," 71 *Texas Law Review* 1165 (1993); Lessig, "Fidelity and Constraint," 65 *Fordham Law Review* 1365 (1997).

128. John Rawls, *Political Liberalism* 231–240 (paperback ed. 1996).

129. See, for example, Cass R. Sunstein, *Legal Reasoning and Political Conflict* (1996); Sunstein, "The Supreme Court, 1995 Term: Foreword: Leaving Things Undecided," 110 *Harvard Law Review* 4 (1996); Sunstein, *One Case at a Time: Judicial Minimalism on the Supreme Court* (1999).

Lessig argues that just as a good translation is not necessarily a literal one, so keeping faith with the intended meaning of the Constitution's framers may require rulings that depart from the framers' literal meanings. But whether a literal translation is good depends on the purpose of the translation; for some purposes, literal translations are best. Then, too, fidelity to original meanings need not be the sovereign virtue of constitutional interpretation. The significance of Lessig's approach is that it turns the tables on Scalia by showing that originalism is compatible with what Scalia would think an impermissible flexibility of interpretation.[130]

Rawls does not pretend to be well informed about constitutional law or judicial practice. But his prestige in academic circles is such that his rather offhand suggestion that judges in interpreting the Constitution should confine themselves to what he calls "public reason," defined as the set of considerations that every reasonable person would consider admissible to resolve issues of public policy,[131] has received respectful attention from constitutional theorists. The suggestion if adopted would confine judges to a level of generality so void of operational content as to deny them the tools they need to decide cases.[132]

Sunstein takes almost the opposite tack from Rawls. He points out that people often converge on the resolution of a particular issue though unable to agree on the principles that determine that resolution.[133] This is true of judges, who have after all to agree (a majority of a court's judges have to agree, in any event) on a resolution even if they can't agree on a broad ground that would resolve a host of other issues as well. Sunstein further points out that a "minimalist" approach that eschews broad grounds will reduce the magnitude of the judges' inevitable errors. Sunstein's approach is less a theory than a warning about theory, in the

---

130. For fuller analysis of Ackerman's and Lessig's positions, see Posner, note 110 above, ch. 7; Posner, "This Magic Moment," *New Republic*, April 6, 1998, p. 32; and Posner, *Law and Literature*, ch. 7 (revised and enlarged ed. 1998).

131. "Citizens are to conduct their public political discussions of constitutional essentials and matters of basic justice within the framework of what each sincerely regards as a reasonable political conception of justice, a conception that expresses political values that others as free and equal also might reasonably be expected reasonably to endorse." Rawls, note 128 above, at 1 (footnote omitted); see also Rawls, "The Idea of Public Reason Revisited," 64 *University of Chicago Law Review* 765 (1997).

132. Posner, note 110 above, at 196–197.

133. This point has also been made with reference to moral issues: agreement may be possible on specifics even if there is no agreement about the high-level principles that ought to guide moral inquiry. See, for example, David B. Wong, "Coping with Moral Conflict and Ambiguity," 102 *Ethics* 763 (1992). This is another reason to doubt the fruitfulness of moral philosophy as it is usually pursued.

manner of theoretically oriented constitutional commentators who are not themselves propounders of constitutional theories, such as Jack Balkin and Sanford Levinson.[134] Yet it is close to my own preferred stance, which I call "pragmatic" and elaborate in Chapter 4. And pragmatism may seem just another theory, in which event I am contradicting myself in withholding the name of theory from Sunstein's approach. But while in one sense pragmatism is indeed a theory and a constitutional theory when applied to constitutional law, in another and more illuminating sense it is an avowal of skepticism about various kinds of theorizing, including the kind that I am calling constitutional theorizing.

Although Sunstein's and my approaches are somewhat similar, we frequently disagree at the level of application to particular cases. He commends recent decisions by the Supreme Court, including the *Romer* and *VMI* decisions, as commendably minimalist because they avoid (*Romer* more clearly) announcing principles that might overturn a lot of other laws. To me they are wedge decisions in which the Court takes a first tentative step toward a new abyss, as when the Court moved, and quickly too, and without much thought, from the bare holding in *Baker v. Carr* that legislative malapportionment is justiciable to a rigid rule ("one man, one vote") founded on a naive conception of democracy (where was Dworkin then?). The decisions that Sunstein commends are minimalist when compared to hypothetical decisions holding that all governmental discrimination against homosexuals is unconstitutional and likewise all segregation of the sexes (in public rest rooms, in military units, in college dorms). But they can equally be viewed as uninformed adventures in judicial activism.

The difference between Sunstein and me is similar to the difference between Bickel and Brandeis on the one hand and Holmes and Hand on the other. Bickel had a clear sense of where the nation, and the Supreme Court in the vanguard, should be heading. He had an agenda, like Brandeis, one broadly liberal, like Brandeis's, and also like Brandeis he wanted the Court to display restraint and political sensitivity in the pursuit of his goals, even at some cost in candor and principle. His was like a political scientist's approach to the judicial function.[135] Holmes and Hand assigned

---

134. See, for example, J. M. Balkin, "Agreements with Hell and Other Objects of Our Faith," 65 *Fordham Law Review* 1703 (1997). See also Schlag, note 41 above, ch. 8.

135. For criticisms of such an approach from opposite ends of the legal professoriat's ideological spectrum, see Gerald Gunther, "The Subtle Vices of the 'Passive Virtues'—A Comment on Principle and Expediency in Judicial Review," 64 *Columbia Law Review* 1 (1964); Mark Tushnet, "How to Deny a Constitutional Right: Reflections on the Assisted-Suicide Cases," 1 *Green Bag* (2d ser.) 55 (1997).

a smaller role to the courts, partly because they had a less confident sense of where, as judges, they wanted the nation to be heading; though both were individuals of strong private views on a variety of political, social, and economic issues, their inclination was to leave the political (realistically, the *more* political) branches pretty much alone. But like everyone they had their "can't helps," their sticking points, the points at which they were prepared to use judicial power to check the action of another branch of government, either because the other branch was acting outrageously or because the argument that its action violated the Constitution was irrefutable. It is perhaps, *because* they did not want to make the Supreme Court a political "player" that Holmes and Hand did not formulate ambitious theories of judicial legitimacy. Those theories come almost entirely from the activist side. Bickel and Dworkin and the rest want the courts to be active in the formulation of public policy, so if they are practical minded like Bickel they worry lest the courts overspend their moral capital (that is, lest the courts undermine popular belief that what judges do is law rather than merely politics), while if they are doctrinaire like Dworkin they simply translate their political preferences into justiciable principles and insist that the courts enforce all of them unstintingly. In either case, the fundamental concern is with the tactics of judicial activism; the theorizing is just window dressing.

Sunstein's politics are similar to those of Ackerman, Dworkin, Ely, and Lessig. And he has as much of the crusader as of the detached observer in his makeup. But he recognizes that most judges are put off by constitutional theory. Their background is usually not in any kind of theoretical endeavor even if they are former law professors. For most law professors, still, are analysts of cases and legal doctrines rather than propounders of general theories of political or judicial legitimacy. And even if a judge's background *is* theory, a theoretical perspective is difficult to maintain when one is immersed in deciding cases as part of a committee. The rise of constitutional theory has less to do with its value for judges than with the growing academification of legal scholarship. When Herbert Wechsler was crossing swords with Learned Hand, law professors still thought of themselves as lawyers first and professors second and saw their role in relation to the judiciary as a helping one. Nowadays many law professors, especially the most prestigious ones at the most prestigious schools, think of themselves as members of an academic community engaged in dialogue with the other members of the community, and the judges be damned.

I exaggerate; most constitutional theorists want to influence constitutional practice. One cannot read them without sensing a strong desire to influence judicial decisions or even (in Dworkin's case) the composition of the Supreme Court (I mentioned his polemic against the appointment of Bork). And Scalia is *on* the Supreme Court. But to get the richest rewards available within the modern legal academic community a professor has to do "theory," and this tends to alienate the professors from the judges. Sunstein's anti-theory is more likely to move judges, but he suffers guilt by association. Increasingly judges believe that legal academics are not on the same wavelength with them, that the academics are not interacting with judges and other legal practitioners but instead are chasing their own and each other's tails. Justice Scalia's active participation in the debates over constitutional theory is not inconsistent with my claims. He is plainly unmoved by the academics' criticisms of his position. And most of them plainly regard him as an unsophisticated, because academically superannuated, antagonist, one who among other things tacks between theory and practice, using the constraints of his judicial role (for example, the constraint of stare decisis) to bevel his sharp-edged theoretical stance.

Rights and Consequences: The Case of Criminal Procedure

I would like to see an entirely different kind of constitutional theorizing. It would set itself the difficult, although (from the perspective of today's theorists) intellectually modest, task of exploring the operation and consequences of constitutionalism. It would ask such questions as, What difference has it made for press freedom and police practices in the United States compared to England that we have a judicially enforceable Bill of Rights and England does not (or at least did not, before it became subject to the European Convention on Human Rights and Fundamental Freedoms)? How influenced are judges in constitutional cases by public opinion? How influenced is public opinion by constitutional decisions? Are constitutional issues becoming more complex, and if so what are the courts doing to keep abreast of the complexities? Does intrusive judicial review breed constitutionally dubious statutes because it enables the legislators to shift political hot potatoes to the courts? What is the effect of judicial activism on judicial workloads, and is there a feedback loop— activism producing heavy workloads that in turn cause the judges to pull in their horns in order to reduce the number of cases filed and thus alleviate the workload pressures? Does the Supreme Court try to prevent the formation of interest groups that might obtain constitutional amendments that would curtail the Court's power or abrogate some of its doctrines, or to encourage the formation of interest groups that will defend the Court's prerogatives? And what role do interest groups play in the making and amending of constitutions?—in the appointment of Supreme Court Justices?—in the reception of Supreme Court decisions by the media and, through the media, the public? What have been the actual effects of particular decisions and doctrines? Did *Brown v. Board of Education* produce an improvement in the education of blacks? Did *Roe v. Wade* retard abortion law reform at the state level? What effect have the apportionment cases had on public policy? These questions have not been ignored,[136] but the literature on them is meager in relation to their range and importance. Exploring them in depth would be a more fruitful use of law professors' time and brains than continuing the two-hundred-year-old game of political rhetoricizing that we call constitutional theory. Some of these questions might actually be answerable, and the answers would alter constitutional practice more than theorizing has done or is ever likely to do.

All the questions belong to the realm of positive, not normative, analysis. In contrast to most natural and social scientists, constitutional theorists are inveterate, obsessed normativists. The reason has partly to do with the traditional relation between law professors and judges. Judges have to decide cases whether or not they have a good understanding of the practices out of which the cases arise, or of the economic, psychological, institutional, and systemic circumstances that determine the effect of judicial decisions in the real world. Law professors, looking over the shoulders of the judges as it were, see themselves engaged in critique from the

---

136. See, for example, Gerald N. Rosenberg, *The Hollow Hope: Can Courts Bring about Social Change?* (1991); Rosenberg, "The Implementation of Constitutional Rights: Insights from Law and Economics," 64 *University of Chicago Law Review* 1215 (1997); Rosenberg, "Protecting Fundamental Political Liberties: The Constitution in Context" (University of Chicago, Department of Political Science, 1988, unpublished); William J. Stuntz, "The Uneasy Relationship between Criminal Procedure and Criminal Justice," 107 *Yale Law Journal* 1 (1997); Seth F. Kreimer, "Exploring the Dark Matter of Judicial Review: A Constitutional Census of the 1990s," 5 *William and Mary Bill of Rights Journal* 427 (1997); Stephen J. Schulhofer, "Bashing *Miranda* is Unjustified—and Harmful," 20 *Harvard Journal of Law and Public Policy* 347 (1997) (and studies cited there); Donald J. Boudreaux and A. C. Pritchard, "Rewriting the Constitution: An Economic Analysis of the Constitutional Amendment Process," 62 *Fordham Law Review* 111 (1993); Stewart J. Schwab and Theodore Eisenberg, "Explaining Constitutional Tort Litigation: The Influence of the Attorney Fees Statute and the Government as Defendant," 73 *Cornell Law Review* 719 (1988); Isaac Ehrlich and George D. Brower, "On the Issue of Causality in the Economic Model of Crime and Law Enforcement: Some Theoretical Considerations and Experimental Evidence," 77 *American Economic Review Papers and Proceedings* 99 (May 1987); Geoffrey P. Miller, "The True Story of *Carolene Products*," 1987 *Supreme Court Review* 397.

judges' own perspective—see themselves as a shadow judiciary that differs mainly from the official one in being more specialized, less rushed, less responsible, more intellectual. This is changing, as I have hinted and as I shall explore at greater length in the next two chapters. Academic law is becoming its own profession—and in this development there are grounds for hope for sustained attention to the yawning gaps in our knowledge of constitutionalism.

But this hope will not be fulfilled until the rights fetishism that is so marked a feature of modern constitutional theory is overcome. The religious feelings of secular moderns have been displaced onto various aspects of "civic religion," including the protection and enforcement of rights. Rights, particularly constitutional rights, are treated as Platonic forms, universalized and eternalized, or as trumps that take every trick no questions asked, rather than as tools of government subject to the usual trade-offs and amenable to the usual methods of social scientific inquiry.[137] This approach discourages empirical investigation and cool appraisal. Let me sketch a different, a desacralized, approach, using examples from constitutional criminal procedure as harbingers of a better way of doing constitutional theory.

An effective system of property and personal rights requires an apparatus for keeping crime within tolerable bounds.[138] Immediately we can sense a tension between the rights of the law-abiding and the rights of criminals, and hence the need to make trade-offs between rights and the fatuity of supposing rights an unequivocally good thing. Imagine first how society might minimize the threat of crime and in so doing maximize the protection (one might naively suppose) of the rights of the law-abiding: it would impose savage punishments, deny procedural rights to persons accused of crime, require citizens to carry identification papers, pay informers generously, place judges under the control of prosecutors (or dispense with judges altogether), and allow police a free hand to use brutal methods in investigating crime. Some of these measures might be counterproductive. But as a package—modeled on old-fashioned military discipline culminating in the drumhead court-martial—they would be effective in minimizing the crime rate and thus maximizing the protection of

137. See Ronald Dworkin, *Taking Rights Seriously* 198 (1977), explicitly rejecting the idea that social cost should influence the definition of rights.

138. It would not pay to try to extirpate crime completely, quite apart from the costs to the innocent. Presumably expenditures on criminal law enforcement should not be carried to the point where the last dollar of expenditures buys less than a dollar's worth of benefit (however benefits are computed) in reduced criminal activity.

rights, provided that the judges, the police, and other administrators of the criminal justice system were competent and acted always in good faith. But that is the rub. The criminal justice system would be so powerful that it would endanger the property and personal rights of the law-abiding. Innocent people would find themselves caught in police dragnets, arrested and detained on suspicion of crime, eavesdropped and informed on, "shaken down" for bribes, sometimes beaten, occasionally even convicted and sent to prison, or worse. The system could even, as we shall see, be ineffectual in deterring crime.

To prevent the abuses inherent in a too-powerful system of criminal law enforcement requires altering the incentives of law enforcers, creating countervailing rights, or doing both; but the countervailing rights can be viewed as instruments for altering incentives rather than as trumps. The process is visible in the history of English criminal procedure in the eighteenth century. By the beginning of that century—in fact much earlier—severe punishments for crime were on the books. But there were no organized police forces, and the right of law enforcement officers to enter a person's home was severely limited ("a man's home is his castle"). These two features of the criminal justice system must have greatly undermined the protection of rights yet have seemed justified by the danger of abuse of power if the reins of the law enforcement authorities were loosened. Early in the eighteenth century judges were given secure tenure, emancipating them from control by the prosecutorial authority (the king and his ministers). Yet by the end of the century organized police forces were still few and there was still no general right to search a person's home. At the same time, criminal defendants were prohibited from being represented by counsel, even if they could afford to hire one out of their own pocket.[139] They also had no right to appeal their conviction. So the constraints on law enforcement were offset by constraints on defendants. The state had limited powers but defendants had limited rights. Criminal proceedings were short and cheap.

The evolution of the American criminal justice system in the twentieth century furnishes parallel illustrations. By the beginning of the century there were large police forces, which frequently abused the members of

---

139. The prohibition began to be relaxed in the 1730s, but the permitted role of defense counsel remained extremely limited until the nineteenth century. See John H. Langbein, "The Privilege and Common Law Criminal Procedure: The Sixteenth to the Eighteenth Centuries," in Helmholz et al., note 105 above, at 82, 87–88, 97. On the history of English criminal law, see generally Leon Radzinowicz, *A History of English Criminal Law and Its Administration from 1750* (4 vols., 1948–1968).

socially marginal groups. Prison conditions were brutal. Indigent defendants often had no counsel, even though criminal proceedings were more complex than they had been in the eighteenth century. Beginning in the 1930s but accelerating greatly in the 1960s, the Supreme Court tried to rectify these conditions by creating countervailing rights, including the right to exclude illegally seized evidence from a criminal trial, the right to effective assistance of counsel in all criminal cases, other rights previously possessed only by federal criminal defendants, the right to invoke federal habeas corpus to obtain federal judicial review of state convictions, and the right to bring tort suits (free of artificial rules that had made the tort remedy against official misconduct ineffectual) complaining of police brutality and inhuman prison conditions.

The creation of these countervailing rights made the criminal justice system cumbersome, expensive, and possibly less effective in deterring crime. A great upsurge in crime rates followed on the heels of the "Warren Court's" adventurous rulings in criminal procedure. The upsurge understates the increase in the total cost of crime, since an increased risk of criminal victimization will induce increased effort at self-protection by potential victims, which will dampen the increase in the actual crime rate.[140] There is evidence that the Court's rulings contributed to, rather than merely coinciding with, the increase in crime rates.[141] Federal and state legislators responded to the increase. They authorized greater use of wiretapping and other electronic surveillance, authorized harsher sentences, reduced judicial discretion over sentences, expanded the use of pretrial prevention (thus curtailing the right to bail), curtailed defenses (such as the insanity defense), and appropriated money for greatly expanding prison and jail capacity, for hiring more prosecutors, and for hiring more and better-trained police.[142]

So judicial enlargement of the rights of criminal defendants, while in one respect enhancing rights, may in an equally important respect have

140. See Tomas J. Philipson and Richard A. Posner, "The Economic Epidemiology of Crime," 39 *Journal of Law and Economics* 405 (1996).

141. See Ehrlich and Brower, note 136 above.

142. Consider the increase in the educational level of police in the United States. Between 1960 and 1970—the heyday of the Warren Court—the percentage of police with some college education rose from 20 to 31.8 percent. U.S. Dept. of Justice, National Institute of Law Enforcement and Criminal Justice, *The National Manpower Survey of the Criminal Justice System*, vol. 5: *Criminal Justice Education and Training* 138 (1978) (tab. IV-1). The increased complexity of criminal procedure required better-educated police because they are the frontline administrators of the criminal justice system and their legal mistakes can make successful prosecution of criminals impossible.

impaired them by undermining the protection of property and personal safety, which are endangered by crime, and by stimulating a legislative backlash that resulted in curtailing the rights of those same defendants. In addition, the greater costliness of the criminal justice system entailed heavier taxes, which burden property and hence property rights both directly and indirectly. When all these effects are considered (just the sort of thing that constitutional theorists do *not* do) the possibility emerges that the Warren Court was just running in place, or even retrogressing, from the standpoint of achieving the very goals most plausibly ascribed to it, of making the nation more peaceable, secure, and civilized.

These points are obscured by the origins of the rights of criminal defendants. The people who pressed for, obtained, and asserted the rights that first English law and then the American Bill of Rights conferred on criminal defendants were not poor people, let alone members of the criminal classes. They were businessmen, publishers, writers, merchants, and politicians. The rights they fought for were ones that a society needs in order to make property and political rights secure against abuse by government. In contrast, the rights that the Warren Court derived from the Constitution by flexible interpretation were rights that criminals, and members of an underclass or lumpenproletariat most likely to be mistaken for criminals by overzealous police or prosecutors, want or need. For the most part the enforcement of these rights undermines property rights and personal security by making the punishment of criminals less swift and certain.

The difference is illustrated by the changing interpretation of the Sixth Amendment, one clause of which entitles criminal defendants to the assistance of counsel. The original understanding was that the clause, changing the English practice to which I referred earlier, entitled criminal defendants to hire counsel—if they could afford to.[143] Only in the twentieth century has the amendment been understood to entitle indigent criminal defendants to the assistance of counsel at the government's expense. This interpretive addition dramatizes the shift in the legal system of the United States from protecting rights of the propertied to protecting rights of the unpropertied as well.

The proliferation of constitutional criminal rights may not even have reduced the net costs of *erroneous* convictions. There is a tug-of-war be-

---

143. This at any rate is the conventional understanding of the original meaning of the clause. It is questioned in an interesting but speculative discussion in Akhil Reed Amar, *The Constitution and Criminal Procedure: First Principles* 140 (1997).

tween courts, which are primarily responsible for the creation of new rights, and legislatures. The latter can neutralize the effect of a right that the courts have conferred on criminal defendants by reducing the funding for the defense of indigent defendants, thus making it easier to convict them; by increasing the severity of punishments, with the result that even if fewer innocent people are convicted, those who are will serve longer sentences; and by curtailing criminal defendants' nonconstitutional rights.[144] The total suffering of the innocent will not be reduced unless the courts both invalidate statutes that impose severe punishments and insist on generous funding of criminal defense lawyers. American courts have been unwilling to do either of these things.

The underlying problem, which afflicts most efforts at social engineering by courts, is that the judiciary either does not have, or is unwilling to pull, all the levers that control the legal system, in this case the criminal justice part of that system. Its efforts to expand the rights of a particular class of persons can be offset by executive and legislative countermeasures. The net result may simply be higher costs.

Let us look more closely at the expanded right to counsel. Although most criminal defendants are indigent, the annual expense of providing lawyers for all indigent criminal defendants, state and federal, is only $1.4 billion.[145] This is less than $6 per American per year. Granted, the figure of $1.4 billion is an understatement. Some lawyers are pressured by judges into "volunteering" their services to indigent criminal defendants at below-market rates. (Others truly volunteer their services, but do so either to obtain on-the-job training or as genuine charity; in neither case is there a net cost to the volunteer.) Still, the total costs of defending the indigent are small—but these are only the direct, budgetary costs. A represented

---

144. Let the expected cost of punishment, a measure of deterrence, be denoted by EC. Then $EC = pS$, where p is the probability of apprehension and conviction and S is the sentence. If a court-created right leads to a reduction in p for both innocent and guilty defendants (the likeliest consequence, since a right that makes it more difficult to convict an innocent person will also make it more difficult to convict a guilty one), and the legislature wishes to maintain EC at its previous level, it can do so either by raising S through a law increasing the penalties for crime or by raising p to its previous level by reducing funding for the defense of indigent defendants or by curtailing nonconstitutional procedural rights. All have been legislative responses to perceived judicial excesses in the protection of the rights of criminal defendants and to the increased crime rates that may be the consequence of that protection.

145. U.S. Dept. of Justice, Bureau of Justice Statistics, *Justice Expenditure and Employment in the United States 1988* xix (1991) (tab. F). The figure is for 1990, the latest year for which I have been able to find reliable data. But it is clear that legislatures have not become more generous since. See "The Criminal Law: Too Poor to Be Defended," *Economist* (U.S. ed.), April 11, 1998, p. 21.

defendant is more difficult to convict than an unrepresented one, so the provision of representation to indigent criminal defendants makes the criminal justice system more costly, and possibly less effective in deterring crime.

I say "possibly less effective" because a system of criminal justice in which innocent persons are frequently convicted may actually reduce the expected punishment cost of crime. That cost is net of the expected punishment cost of not engaging in crime. In the limit, if the probability of being convicted were independent of guilt or innocence, the prospect of punishment would not provide any inducement to avoid committing crimes.[146] But it is unclear that the denial of an automatic right to counsel in criminal cases would result in frequent conviction of the innocent. When the crime rate is high in relation to the resources allocated for prosecution, prosecutors will tend to select for prosecution only the strongest cases, and in general these will be the cases in which the defendant is least likely to be innocent. This selection effect will be weaker in a nation that follows the German practice of mandatory prosecution rather than the U.S. practice of discretionary prosecution, or if the nation contains a disliked minority that has a high crime rate. In that case it may be easier to convict an innocent member of the minority group than a guilty member of the majority. This was a serious problem in the southern states of the United States with respect to blacks as late as the 1950s and was an unacknowledged motive for the Supreme Court's expanding the rights of criminal defendants; it is a much less serious problem today.[147]

An extensive literature criticizes as inadequate the current level at which the defense of indigent criminal defendants in the United States is funded, noting the low quality of much of this representation.[148] I can confirm from my own experience as a judge that indigent defendants are generally

---

146. Building on the formula in note 144 above, one can express the expected cost of punishment for committing a crime as the difference between the expected cost of punishment if the accused is guilty and the expected cost of punishment if he is innocent. That is, $EC = EC_g - EC_i$. Equivalently, $EC = p_g S - p_i S$, where p_g is the probability of punishment if the accused is guilty and p_i is the probability of punishment if he is innocent (the sentence is assumed to be the same in either case). This can be simplified to $EC = (p_g - p_i)S$, making it obvious that if the probability of punishment is the same regardless of guilt (that is, if $p_g = p_i$), the expected punishment cost for committing the crime will be zero.

147. See Randall Kennedy, *Race, Crime, and the Law* 94–107 (1997).

148. See Stephen J. Schulhofer and David D. Friedman, "Rethinking Indigent Defense: Promoting Effective Representation through Consumer Sovereignty and Freedom of Choice for All Criminal Defendants," 31 *American Criminal Law Review* 73 (1993), and references cited there; also Stuntz, note 136 above, at 32–35.

rather poorly represented. But if we are to be hardheaded we must recognize that this may not be entirely a bad thing. The lawyers who represent indigent criminal defendants seem to be good enough to reduce the probability of convicting an innocent person to a very low level. If they were much better, either many guilty people would be acquitted or society would have to devote much greater resources to the prosecution of criminal cases. A bare-bones system for the defense of indigent criminal defendants may be optimal. But here is a complicating factor. If constitutional law entitles a defendant to *effective* assistance of counsel, as it is now interpreted to do, then paying lawyers too little to attract competent lawyers to the defense of indigent defendants may cost the system more in the long run by leading to retrials following a determination that the defendant's lawyer at his first trial was incompetent.

These are difficult issues, and I do not pretend to have resolved them by this brief discussion. (I may, for example, be unduly complacent about the unlikelihood of an innocent person's being convicted.)[149] I raise them in order to underscore the shortcomings of constitutional theory, of which the most grievous is blindness to the consequences of constitutional rulings. But let me not leave the impression that the solution is to make litigation a vehicle for gathering social scientific data and testing social scientific hypotheses. The courts' capacity to conduct empirical research is extremely limited, perhaps nil. But their assimilative powers are greater. I would like to see the legal professoriat redirect its research and teaching efforts toward fuller participation in the enterprise of social science (broadly conceived, and certainly not limited to quantitative studies) and by doing so give judges better help in understanding the social problems that get thrust on the courts. It is easy to be cynical about empirical research on the legal system. The legal realists of the 1920s and 1930s talked up empirical research but conducted very little of it, and with deservedly little impact on the understanding or improvement of the law. I think the situation has improved, but I defer discussion of this to the next chapter.

The Military-Academy and Homosexual-Rights Cases

Using the *VMI* and *Romer* cases as my tiny sample, I shall now explore the unfortunate consequences of judicial ignorance of the social realities behind the issues with which the judges grapple.

---

149. See Daniel Givelber, "Meaningless Acquittals, Meaningful Convictions: Do We Reliably Acquit the Innocent?" 49 *Rutgers Law Review* 1317 (1997).

UNITED STATES V. VIRGINIA (THE "VMI" CASE)

The Virginia Military Institute (VMI) is a public college the mission of which is to produce "citizen-soldiers" by bullying methods—the "adversative method," as it is euphemistically called. The model is the well-known brutality of the English public school and the Marine boot camp, institutions designed to forge male solidarity as a condition of effective military action. VMI refused to admit women (who of course had also been excluded from the institutions on which it was modeled), precipitating the suit. VMI lost in the Supreme Court, which begins its opinion by commending "the school's impressive record in producing leaders," but accompanies this polite fluff with the unsubstantiated assertion that "neither the goal of producing citizen-soldiers nor VMI's implementing methodology is inherently unsuitable to women."[150] How does the Court know?[151] And even if the methodology were suitable to women, it would not follow that the school's goal would not be imperiled by admitting women; it would be necessary to consider the effect of mixing the sexes. Both men and women use toilets; it doesn't follow that unisex public rest rooms are just as appropriate as sex-segregated ones. The lower court had found, on the same page from which the Supreme Court quoted with approval the finding about suitability, "that VMI's mission can be accomplished only in a single-gender environment and that changes necessary to accommodate coeducation would tear at the fabric of VMI's unique methodology."[152]

The Court's essential reasoning in nevertheless invalidating VMI's exclusion of women was that in the past men, and many women for that matter, entertained erroneous beliefs about the sexes. (The Court doesn't mention it, but Aristotle for example thought that women had fewer teeth than men.)[153] In ridiculing the mistakes of earlier generations, the Court ignored the possibility that those erroneous beliefs, whatever the motivation, were the best interpretation of the then-existing scientific knowledge (a point that has been made about another of Aristotle's sexist beliefs, that

---

150. 116 S. Ct. at 2269.

151. The court of appeals, in an earlier stage of the case, had based this conclusion on a non sequitur: the success of women's colleges, which are not military, are sex-segregated, and do not employ the adversative method. United States v. Virginia, 976 F.2d 890, 897 (4th Cir. 1992). Nevertheless, the Supreme Court approvingly quoted the court of appeals' conclusion ("nor [is] VMI's implementing methodology inherently unsuitable to women," 116 S. Ct. at 2279, quoting 976 F.2d at 899).

152. 976 F.2d at 897.

153. Aristotle, *History of Animals*, Bk. II, § 3, in *The Complete Works of Aristotle*, vol. 1, p. 797 (Jonathan Barnes ed. 1984) (Bekker reference 501b.20).

a child is, in modern terminology, the clone of its father, the mother being merely an incubator).[154] Moreover, some of the discredited beliefs about women's educational and occupational capacities may once have been reasonable. When a woman must be pregnant throughout her fertile years in order to have a reasonable assurance of producing a few children who will survive to adulthood, and when most jobs in the economy require brawn, equal employment opportunities for women are not going to be in the cards even if a few exceptional women might be able to take advantage of them. Indignation about historical injustice often reflects ignorance of history—of the circumstances that explain and sometimes justify practices that in the modern state of society (comfortable, rich, scientifically advanced, pushbuttony) would be arbitrary and unjust.

It is flattering to think of ourselves as being the moral superiors of our predecessors, but, as I pointed out in Chapter 1, it is false. A related mistake is to attribute insight to Utopian thinkers of the past without considering the issue of their timeliness. The advocacy of "free love" (basically no-fault divorce) by Victoria Woodhull and other radical feminists in the nineteenth century[155] was not progressive or prophetic; given the conditions of life at the time, it was daft, because there was no social safety net to break the fall of women abandoned by their husbands. That conditions have changed, making no-fault divorce feasible, is no greater compliment to its premature advocates than it is a compliment to a broken clock to point out that it is right twice a day.

A worse mistake than failing to make allowances for history is arguing that if in the past the biological differences between the sexes, so far as those differences bear on aptitudes for various jobs, were exaggerated they must be zero; that is to commit the fallacy of naive induction. Not that the Court goes that far in the *VMI* opinion; but the impression it conveys is that it thinks the only significant differences between male and female are physical. The biological differences, so far as relates to a variety of professional activities, were indeed overstated in the past, when biological science was far less advanced than it is today and social conditions far different from what they are today. But it does not follow that there are *no* relevant work-related or education-related biological differences between

154. Johannes Morsink, "Was Aristotle's Biology Sexist?" 12 *Journal of the History of Biology* 83, 110–112 (1979). Yet Judith Jarvis Thomson's abortion analogy in effect treats a mother as an incubator by comparing the relation of a mother to her fetus to a relation between strangers.

155. See David A. J. Richards, *Women, Gays, and the Constitution: The Grounds for Feminism and Gay Rights in Culture and Law,* chs. 3–4 (1998), esp. pp. 157–162.

the sexes. We used not to realize that dolphins communicate with each other by something quite like speech; it doesn't follow that with greater educational opportunities and perhaps a pinch of affirmative action they can learn to speak French. The fact that biology used to be riven with mistake, superstition, and ideology doesn't mean that it's still riven with mistake, superstition, and ideology.

Once the advance of science is conceded, it becomes appropriate to observe that, like many articles of faith, the "no difference" claim is contradicted by modern science. Modern science teaches that along with the obvious physical differences there are inherent *psychological* differences between the average man and the average woman, differences with respect to aggressiveness, competitiveness, the propensity to take risks, and the propensity to resort to violence.[156] These are differences that, along with the acknowledged differences in physical strength, bear on military fitness and performance, especially in combat. When faced with creationists' challenges to the theory of evolution, judges reveal themselves to be resolutely scientific in their outlook. But when faced with evolutionary biologists' challenge to the pieties of political correctness and radical egalitarianism,[157] judges turn pietistic.

It is true that within each sex there is a distribution of characteristics, and the two distributions overlap. Because some women are more aggressive, competitive, and bellicose than some men, the adversarial methods used by VMI may be more suitable for some women than they are for some of the men admitted to VMI. But a concern with the consequences of mixing the sexes in the unusual setting of a military academy is unrelated to whether women are able to function as well in that setting as men are. And the near universality of qualifying examinations and other set requirements for admission to colleges and other institutions of higher learning suggests that a policy of giving everyone a chance to prove himself or herself, in lieu of a preliminary screening for likelihood of success, would be highly inefficient.

And not only inefficient. It is a cruelty to prospective students to admit them to a school without doing any preliminary screening and then to

156. See Kingsley R. Browne, "Sex and Temperament in Modern Society: A Darwinian View of the Glass Ceiling and the Gender Gap," 37 *Arizona Law Review* 971, 1016–1064 (1995).

157. As Browne explains, the psychological differences between male and female that I have mentioned are explicable by reference to biological differences in the male and female roles in reproduction (on which see, for example, Bruce J. Ellis and Donald Symons, "Sex Differences in Sexual Fantasy: An Evolutionary Psychological Approach," 27 *Journal of Sex Research* 527, 546–547 [1990]) and therefore are probably genetic rather than cultural in origin.

flunk out the large number who do not measure up to the school's exacting standards. It is true that whether a large number *would* flunk out in the absence of screening depends on how sensitive the screen is, and gender might not be a sensitive screen. Suppose 10 percent of men were well suited for adversative training and "only" 9 percent of women. Then an absolute exclusion of women would be a blunt instrument for excluding the unqualified. But if instead the percentages were 10 percent and 0.1 percent, and if alternative, more refined screens were infeasible, the exclusion would make compelling sense. For on these assumptions the individualized consideration of women's applications would benefit few. The school would be looking for a needle in a haystack with no apt instruments for finding it.

The Court did not discuss, and probably has no idea, how much overlap there is between the male and female distributions of tastes and aptitudes relevant to VMI's program, or how effective an alternative screen to sex might be. It allowed itself to be deflected into analogizing sex-segregated to race-segregated public educational institutions. Judges have a weakness for analogies, a form of "evidence" (if it can be called that) generated by ingenuity rather than by knowledge. Analogies are typically (and here) inexact and often (and here) misleading. Racial segregation was demonstrably a component of an exploitative social system descended from slavery and seeking to preserve its essential characteristics. Sex segregation has a more complex history, one that is not free from elements of oppression but that is also bound up with a desire to limit sexual contact between young people, to protect women from unwanted attentions from men, and to tailor education to the difference in life roles between men and women—differences reflecting fundamental conditions of society that were not less real yesterday for having largely dissipated today. Even today we don't consider sex-segregated rest rooms or sex-segregated college and professional athletic teams to present the same issue that race-segregated rest rooms or race-segregated athletic teams would.[158]

Even if the history of society's treatment of women is as oppressive and unjust as a majority of today's Supreme Court Justices appear without adequate reflection or inquiry to believe, and is not mainly a function of limited knowledge or different material conditions of social life, it would not follow that a specific "discrimination," for example in military training, was oppressive and unjust. I would be surprised to learn that any

---

158. I am not arguing that because single-sex rest rooms are lawful, VMI should be entitled to exclude women. That would be as illegitimate a use of analogy as the ones that I am criticizing.

Justice of the Supreme Court believes that the maintenance of sex-segre-gated public rest rooms violates the Constitution. This means that public segregation of the sexes has to be evaluated case by case and therefore that the Court can get little mileage from ridiculing, as it did at some length, the former exclusion of women from the practice of law and medicine.

Thousands of words into its opinion the Court finally gets to the issue, but lingers there only briefly, for one short, and evasive, paragraph. The issue, as it might appear to a disinterested student of public policy unbur-dened by commitment to one of the constitutional theories, is whether excluding women from VMI is likely to do more harm to women, whether material, psychological, or even just symbolic (and so perhaps indirectly or eventually material or psychological), than including them would do to the mission of training citizen-soldiers. The Court says noth-ing about the first point, as if it were obvious that the exclusion of women from one obscure though distinguished military academy[159] would be the kind of insult to women that forbidding black people to attend military academies would be to blacks or that the exclusion of male homosexuals from the armed forces is to homosexuals. That the equal status of women depends to even a trivial degree on their gaining admission to the Virginia Military Institute would be a laughable suggestion, which may be why the Court passed over the question in silence. And for the handful of women who might want to attend VMI the state had set up a parallel institu-tion—a "separate but equal" school that was not in fact equal, as the Court pointed out, ignoring however the fact that it *could not* be equal. Too few Virginia women *want* to attend a quasi-military college to justify establishing a women's parallel institution as richly supported and main-tained as the men's.

If a significant number of other public institutions of learning wanted to exclude women and a decision in favor of VMI would be a precedent enabling them to do so, the harm to women would be greater. Few public institutions nowadays want to exclude women, however, and those that do could have used a decision in favor of VMI as a precedent only if they too wanted to use the adversative method. Such a decision would therefore have been a precedent only for the exclusion of women from other mili-tary academies and from the combat branches of the armed forces, the branches most likely to favor the "adversative" style of college education. For those exclusions, however, no precedent would be necessary. If the

159. When one thinks of "military academy," one thinks of the three service academies: the Army's, at West Point; the Navy's, at Annapolis; and the Air Force's, at Colorado Springs.

federal government decided to reduce the percentage of women in the armed forces, it is unthinkable that the Supreme Court would stand in its way. The Court has always and properly been timid about intruding into military and diplomatic affairs. These are areas in which it is either aware of the limitations of its knowledge and the costs of error or convinced that it lacks the political authority to make intervention stick. It is, as it were, the military irrelevance of VMI, its extremely peripheral role in the defense of the nation, that enabled the Court to invalidate a form of military sex discrimination without worrying that VMI's program might be impaired if women participated. All the Court said about that is that "women's successful entry into the federal military academies, and their participation in the Nation's military forces, indicate that Virginia's fears for the future of VMI may not be solidly grounded."[160]

In the word "may" lies a noteworthy concession to reality. No one knows what effect incorporating large numbers of women into the nation's armed forces will have on military effectiveness. It is an experiment the results of which may not be known until the nation is challenged in a major war. It is not as if the armed forces had wanted or welcomed the influx of women. The influx was forced upon them by the civilian leadership of the military, responding to political pressure. This does not make it a bad thing. Military professionals, like other professionals (including lawyers and judges), tend to be narrow, parochial, and reflexively resistant to change. The racial integration of the armed forces was accomplished in 1948 by civil initiative over military objections, and has been a success. The performance of women in the Gulf War of 1991 was by all accounts excellent. But that was a very short war with very light U.S. casualties and therefore with only a very few women killed or injured. Since 1991 the percentage of women in the armed forces has grown, more and more combat slots have been opened to them, new tensions have arisen, and there is increased grumbling in military and national-security circles— much of it focused on sex-integrated training.[161] Maybe this explains that telltale "may." But if simple prudence requires caution about dismantling every vestige of sexual segregation in the military, it becomes difficult to

160. 116 S. Ct. at 2281 (footnotes omitted). The reference is to the service academies. See previous footnote.

161. See, for example, James Kitfield, "Like It or Not, Women Are Rapidly—and Dramatically—Reshaping the U.S. Military," 29 *National Journal* 2124 (1997); Stephanie Gutmann, "Sex and the Soldier," *New Republic*, Feb. 24, 1997, p. 18; "Gender Mending," *New Republic*, Jan. 19, 1998, p. 7; Steven Lee Myers, "To Sex-Segregated Training, Still Semper Fi," *New York Times*, Dec. 26, 1997, p. A1.

understand by what rational process the Court could conclude that Virginia was violating the Constitution by excluding women from VMI. The entire harm to women was the difference between the value of a VMI education and that of the education in the substitute program that the state had created for women, multiplied by the very small number of women who would like to attend VMI. The harm was small, and the Court had no basis either theoretical or empirical for thinking that the admission of women would not impair VMI's educational program disproportionately to the slight harm to women of being excluded from the school.

We live in a period of profound peace—or, rather, that is how it appears to people for whom not only the world wars, but the cold war, are a rapidly fading memory. It is difficult in such a period to take the needs of national defense completely seriously against claims emanating from more contemporary social concerns. In such a period the Virginia Military Institute can only seem a quaint vestige and hence an appropriate subject for social experimentation. It seems to me that this is about the sum and substance of the Court's thinking in the *VMI* case.

It may be objected that in suggesting that the Court should have tried to weigh the harm to women from exclusion against the harm to VMI from their admission, I am propounding my own constitutional theory, one utilitarian in character, and thus inviting the same criticisms that I have made of other theorists, or at least acknowledging that an atheoretical approach to constitutional decision making is impossible. But I never meant to suggest that it is possible to approach constitutional issues free from all predispositions, free, that is, from—an approach, or if you will a theory. I happen to belong to the school of "outrage," and it is natural for the members of that school to ask about the balance of harms; it is when governmental action inflicts severe and seemingly gratuitous injury that the juices of outrage are likely to flow. I would be inconsistent only if I tried to show that the school of outrage had a truer view of the Constitution than its rivals. I have not tried to show that. The intellectual tools necessary to establish which of the competing theories of constitutional decision making is the best have not been forged.

I further acknowledge that the Court could not actually have weighed the harms involved in the *VMI* case. The necessary data were lacking.[162]

---

162. We have a bit of data now: in the first seven months of the first year in which women were admitted to VMI pursuant to the decree of the Supreme Court, seven out of the 30 women admitted dropped out (23 percent) compared to 69 out of the 470 men (16 percent). Wes Allison, "Testing

The fault, in part anyway, lies with constitutional theory, which claims to offer the courts a data-free method of deciding cases, rather than helping in the discovery and analysis of the relevant data. The first thing the courts have to learn is how little they know. What to do in the face of radical uncertainty is a separate issue. A solution that might commend itself to a pragmatist would be to keep options open. Since the service academies are no longer all-male, allowing VMI to exclude women would preserve an alternative approach and facilitate evaluation through comparison.

Justice Scalia's dissent has a different focus from my criticisms of the majority opinion; it is on the implications of the Court's decision for single-sex education in general, apart from the military or quasi-military setting. A court taken with the crude analogy of sexual to racial segregation is unlikely to look with favor on any kind of single-sex education, unless perhaps the sex is female—and it may be willing to sacrifice the benefits of single-sex education for women on the altar of perceived neutrality. But the courts are as poorly equipped to evaluate sex-segregated education in nonmilitary as in military settings. Judges who do not have a military background doubtless think they know more about education than they do about war and are therefore less willing to cut the political branches of government slack when dealing with educational issues. But do they know *enough* more about education to make intelligent decisions? As I implied in my disparaging remarks about educational theory earlier in this chapter, little is known about what makes for effective education. The role of resources, of class size, of curriculum, of racial or other demographic sorting or mixing, of extracurricular activities, of technology, of standardized testing, of tracking, of innovative teaching methods, of family structure, of homework remains largely unknown. Judges can certainly be forgiven for not knowing what people who devote their lives to a specialized field do not know; it is less easy to forgive them for not knowing that they don't know. Part of a sense of reality, of an empirical sense, of just the kind of sense that constitutional theory does *not* cultivate, is knowing which areas of social life are charted and which are not and being willing to follow the chart where there is a chart and to ac-

Their Freedom at VMI," *Richmond Times-Dispatch*, Mar. 22, 1998, p. C1. Whether VMI altered its program to make it easier for women cannot be determined (nor how well the women students are performing relative to the men and how many of the women will stick with the course until graduation—it just is too soon to tell), although school officials deny having done this. What is perhaps more significant than the difference in dropout rates is how few women have been affected by the Court's decision.

knowledge when one is embarking on uncharted seas. If the experts know little about education, and this after two and a half millennia of serious reflection, judges should tolerate continued experimentation and diversity in public eduction.

Even *Brown v. Board of Education* is nowadays (that is, with the benefit of hindsight) considered by many a flop *when regarded as a case about education,* which is how the Court pretended, presumably for political reasons, to regard it. There is no solid evidence that it led to an improvement in the education of blacks, or even to substantial integration of the public schools, which was thwarted by the "white flight" that *Brown* and the cases following it touched off.[163] *Brown* is better viewed as a case about racial subordination, whereas the exclusion of women by the Virginia Military Institute cannot be regarded with a straight face as the warp or woof of a tapestry of sex subordination, given the political and economic power of American women today.

ROMER V. COLORADO

Romer was the second scrape the Supreme Court had with homosexuality, the first being *Bowers v. Hardwick,*[164] which turned back a challenge to the constitutionality of state laws criminalizing homosexual sodomy. The most remarkable thing about both judicial performances is the Court's unwillingness or inability to talk realistically about homosexuality. The majority opinion in *Bowers* and Chief Justice Burger's concurrence treat it as an uncontroversially reprobated horror, like pedophilia, while the dissents in *Bowers* and the majority opinion in *Romer* treat it as a socially irrelevant innate condition, like being left-handed, and Justice Scalia's dissent in *Romer* treats homosexual rights as a sentimental charitable project of the intelligentsia, like the protection of harp seals. The majority opinion in *Romer* finds, sensibly enough, that the state constitutional amendment under challenge, which barred the state's local governments

163. See David J. Armor, *Forced Justice: School Desegregation and the Law* 113 (1995); Rosenberg, *The Hollow Hope,* note 136 above, at 49–57; Martin Patchen, *Black-White Contact in Schools,* ch. 11 (1982); Harold B. Gerard and Norman Miller, *School Desegregation: A Long-Term Study* (1975); James S. Coleman, Sara D. Kelly, and John A. Moore, *Trends in School Segregation, 1968–73* (1975); Charles T. Clotfelter, "Urban School Desegregation and Declines in White Enrollment: A Reexamination," 6 *Journal of Urban Economics* 352 (1979); Sonia R. Jarvis, "*Brown* and the Afrocentric Curriculum," 101 *Yale Law Journal* 1285 (1992); Steven Siegel, "Race, Education, and the Equal Protection Clause in the 1990s: The Meaning of *Brown v. Board of Education* Re-examined in Light of Milwaukee's Schools of African-American Immersion," 74 *Marquette Law Review* 501 (1991).

164. 478 U.S. 186 (1986).

from forbidding discrimination against homosexuals, was motivated by hostility toward homosexuality. The Court then holds that hostility is not an adequate justification for treating one class of people differently from another. And that is about all there is in the opinion. Ignored are the questions that an ordinary person, his mind not fogged by legal casuistry, would think central: why there is hostility to homosexuality and whether the challenged amendment was a rational expression of that hostility.

Many religious people believe that homosexual activity is morally wrong. There is no way to assess the validity of this belief; and what weight if any such a belief should be given in a constitutional case seems to me an equally indeterminate question. The belief in sexual equality that informs the *VMI* opinion is as much an article of faith as the Judeo-Christian antipathy to homosexuality.[165] To suppose that securing equality for homosexuals is part of the meaning of the equal protection clause is equally a leap of faith. In any event, most Americans, whether religious or not, dislike homosexuality and in particular do not want their children to become homosexuals.[166] They are not sure whether homosexuality is acquired or innate, but, unconvinced that it is purely the latter, they worry about their children becoming homosexual through imitation or seduction. They also worry about AIDS spreading from the homosexual to the heterosexual population (although this fear has abated with the peaking of the epidemic in the United States). For these and other reasons, most people dislike the flaunting of homosexual relationships and activities. They don't want government to endorse homosexuality as a way of life entitled to the same respect that we accord to heterosexual relationships, particularly within marriage. An ordinance forbidding discrimination in housing, employment, or public accommodations on the basis of sexual

---

165. Sanford Levinson, "Abstinence and Exclusion: What Does Liberalism Demand of the Religiously Oriented (Would Be) Judge?" in *Religion and Contemporary Liberalism* 76, 79 (Paul J. Weithman ed. 1997), remarks (following Michael Perry) on the double standard that prevails in discussions of the legitimate scope of judicial reasoning: the nonreligious are permitted to make almost any argument they want in support of the positions they take, but the religious are not permitted to make religious arguments in support of their positions. To similar effect, see Stanley Fish, "Mission Impossible: Settling the Just Bounds between Church and State," 97 *Columbia Law Review* 2255 (1997). The double standard is acknowledged but defended in Kent Greenawalt, *Private Consciences and Public Reasons* (1995). For powerful criticisms of Greenawalt's defense, see Fish, above, at 2301–2309. See also Steven D. Smith, "Legal Discourse and the *De Facto* Disestablishment," 81 *Marquette Law Review* 203 (1998).

166. See the summary of polling data in Stephen Zamansky, "Colorado's Amendment 2 and Homosexuals' Right to Equal Protection of the Law," 35 *Boston College Law Review* 221, 245–246 (1993).

orientation is naturally viewed as a form of public endorsement of homosexuality, by treating homosexuality as identical to race, sex, religion, physical disability, ethnicity, and other characteristics that most Americans believe should not, so far as possible, be a basis for differential treatment.

My own view is that there is compelling scientific evidence that homosexual preference is genetic or at least congenital, and not acquired,[167] so that the fear of homosexual "contagion" from flaunting or public endorsement of the homosexual way of life is groundless. The fact that homosexuals are so much more visible today, as a result of the diminution in discrimination against them and in reticence about matters of sex generally, does not mean that they are more numerous. (Jews are more visible today too, and their percentage in the population has been falling.) Increasing the rights of homosexuals would be as likely to discourage the specific sex practices that spread AIDS as to encourage them.[168] No allusion to the scientific and social scientific evidence bearing on the phenomenon of homosexuality was made in the *Romer* opinion, however, so that as it stands the Court seems prepared to forbid discrimination against homosexuals even if Colorado's ban on protective legislation for homosexuals was entirely rational discrimination—the equivalent of "discriminating" against airline pilots who have the misfortune to be old or infirm and as a result are grounded against their will. Granted, this assumes that being homosexual is or at least might rationally be thought a misfortune or disadvantage; otherwise there would be no reason to fear its contagion. But the assumption is reasonable, if only because homosexuals on average find it much more difficult than heterosexuals to form family units, and it is merely an article of left-liberal faith that the difficulties are due entirely or even primarily to discrimination. Parents aren't crazy to want their kids not to be homosexual, though I do think they are mistaken in believing that the repression of homosexuals is an effective way of warding off such a fate. Still, in a repressive environment more homosexuals will marry and have children, if only for the sake of concealment; and this may content the homosexuals' parents, who may be unaware of living in a fool's paradise or may care more about having grandchildren than about their children's happiness.

167. See Posner, note 110 above, at 572; Posner, "The Economic Approach to Homosexuality," in *Sex, Preference, and Family: Essays on Law and Nature* 173, 186, 191 n. 26 (David M. Estlund and Martha C. Nussbaum eds. 1997).
168. See Tomas J. Philipson and Richard A. Posner, *Private Choices and Public Health: The AIDS Epidemic in an Economic Perspective* 179–180 (1993).

The Justices may have been moved by the analogies between hostility to homosexuals and other, now discredited hostilities, notably anti-Semitism. Both homosexuals and Jews are often difficult to spot, are highly urbanized, seem disproportionately successful, first became prominent targets of persecution in the Middle Ages (though both suffered some persecution in antiquity), drew the ire of Hitler, and are traditionally accused of subverting Christian and patriotic values and forming an international "cosmopolitan" network. But analogies, to repeat an earlier point less contentiously, invite inquiry into difference and similarity; they should not elide inquiry. Many people who are not anti-Semitic are hostile to homosexuality. This shows that the grounds of these two antipathies are not identical and therefore that disapproval of anti-Semitism cannot automatically be deemed a sufficient ground for outlawing all forms of discrimination against homosexuals. And the consequences for the family of being Jewish and of being homosexual are different. Some forms of discrimination against homosexuals may be so egregious, hurtful, mean-spirited, even barbarous that the courts should invalidate them without waiting to find out a lot about the phenomenon; that would obviously be true if a state passed a law requiring homosexuals to wear pink triangles in public, and only a little less obviously true if the state banned homosexuals from public employment. But merely barring local governments from making efforts to prevent peaceable private discrimination so as not to be seen as endorsing the homosexual way of life falls far short of savagery.

The most curious feature of the *Romer* decision, in relation to this book, is that it can be, and in fact has been by one of its supporters, read to expel moral considerations from constitutional law. Barbara Flagg writes that, after *Romer,* "a moral position *alone* ought not to constitute a 'legitimate' state interest for the purpose of equal protection review."[169] She thinks that *Romer* stands for the proposition that only functional considerations can support a law that burdens a group; moral disapproval is never enough. No doubt this position could be defended as itself moral; the moral rights and duties of government need not be the same as those of private individuals. But in this realm, anything can be defended; and it is at least a paradox that a moral reading of the Constitution should require rejection of a moral view deeply embedded in the traditions and current beliefs of the American people.

What perhaps can be salvaged from Flagg's argument is the proposition that if judicial authority to declare legislation unconstitutional is to have

169. Barbara J. Flagg, "'Animus' and Moral Disapproval: A Comment on *Romer v. Evans,*" 82 *Minnesota Law Review* 833, 852 (1998) (emphasis in original).

much bite, it cannot be a sufficient defense of a challenged law to say that it has the backing of public opinion, as most laws do. But even this proposition is dubious with reference to as vague a constitutional norm as equal protection. If morality is just the crystallization of public opinion—if moral disapproval of homosexuality (or of the flaunting of homosexuality) has no greater authority than the antipathy of most Americans to mustaches—then the judges cannot appeal to morality as a basis for striking down an anti-homosexuality law; their morality is just the opinion of the tiny public that consists of the Justices of the Supreme Court. In other words, Flagg has a serious self-reference problem; if legislating morality is bad, what's the Court doing legislating morality? She could get around this problem only if she could find some cogent nonmoral basis for making the equal protection clause rule out "morals" legislation. There is no such basis.

As it happens, there was a counterpart in the *Romer* case to the philosophers' brief in the euthanasia cases. Martha Nussbaum testified at the trial to the approving view of homosexuality expressed by Plato in the *Symposium* and by other classical philosophers.[170] Her testimony suffered the same fate as the philosophers' brief: to be ignored (so far as one can tell from the judicial opinions) by the judges. Whether it should have been ignored depends on what role classical learning should play in judicial thinking about homosexuality and homosexual rights in American society today. There is both a sociological and a normative question. The sociological question is how much can Americans (including judges and jurors) be influenced in their view of homosexuality in America by what the Greeks and Romans thought or did. The answer is probably not at all, or not enough to count. And between computer-style modernity and multiculturalism, the role of classical civilization in American lay and judicial thinking, already minute,[171] can only shrink further in the coming years.

The normative question is the extent to which what the Greeks and

170. She has published two academic versions of her testimony. See Martha C. Nussbaum, "Platonic Love and Colorado Law: The Relevance of Ancient Greek Norms to Modern Sexual Controversies," 80 *Virginia Law Review* 1515 (1994), and an abridged version under the same title in *The Greeks and Us: Essays in Honor of Arthur W. H. Adkins* 168 (Robert B. Louden and Paul Schollmeier eds. 1996).

171. Cf. Victor Davis Hanson and John Heath, *Who Killed Homer? The Demise of Classical Education and the Recovery of Greek Wisdom* 4–5 (1998): "Classics is now essentially comatose . . . We Classicists are the dodo birds of academia; when we retire or die, our positions are either eliminated or replaced with temporary and part-time help." See also id. at 2–3. Granted, Hanson and Heath are speaking of the teaching of ancient Greek and Latin and of the study of Greek and Latin literature and philosophy in the original languages. Greek and Latin classics continue to be read in translation, though probably less frequently than in times past.

Romans thought or did about homosexuality *should* influence modern views. Three distinctions are necessary. The first is between critical and constructive analysis. I argued in the first chapter that the proper role of moral philosophers in public debate is limited to knocking down bad philosophical arguments made by other participants in the debate. The same is true concerning experts on the philosophical texts of classical antiquity. If participants in the debate over homosexual rights make arguments based on those texts (as John Finnis did in the *Romer* case—Nussbaum was rebutting his testimony), it is proper for a classicist to point out the mistakes in those arguments. It does not follow that the classicist can extract from those texts pertinent arguments about what rights homosexuals should have in the United States today.

The second distinction is between the reportorial and the analytic or evaluative content of the classical texts. One can mine Plato and Aristotle and the rest of the classical authors, along with vase paintings and statues and every other source of historical or anthropological inference, for information about the *actual* customs, practices, and attitudes of the Greeks and Romans; or one can study the texts for the authors' own views and arguments. Maintaining the distinction is important to avoid confusing an idealized relationship favorably depicted in philosophical texts with an accurate description of typical behavior or attitudes in the society.

The third distinction is a threefold one among ways in which the thinking or practices of antiquity might influence modern opinion. One way might be by enforcing the lesson of relativism: that other civilizations have had different practices and different norms from our own; things we might consider unthinkable and unnatural have seemed otherwise to other cultures. Moral relativism is as likely to undermine efforts to make law track moral theory when the moral theory has a Catholic natural-law cast as when it reflects left-liberal thinking. Second, the classic texts might contain arguments, demonstrations, or data of a logical or scientific character. And third, they might induce sympathy in the reader by presenting an alien practice or norm in a sympathetic light, lit from the inside so to speak.

Discovering that other cultures, especially admired ones or (what is often the same thing) ones that we consider ancestral to or continuous with our own, have done or do things that we unreflectingly consider unnatural or unthinkable may give us at least a momentary jolt and invite us to reexamine our views. But often the jolt is indeed momentary. The Greeks and Romans had a casual or approving attitude not only toward homosexuality (more precisely, male homosexuality, for they disapproved strongly of lesbianism) but also toward infanticide, slavery, censorship, xenophobia and ethnocentrism, torture, cruelty, public nudity, and religious and sexual discrimination. Discovering the ancient Greek views of these matters is not likely to lead to any deep reexamination of our own views on them. This suggests that what is involved in bringing classical works to bear on modern social issues is simply canvassing those works for the views that happen to coincide with our own and ignoring the rest.

Nussbaum urges us to attend to the "valuable concrete arguments" in the Greek texts concerning the morality of homosexuality.[172] But she does not identify any concrete arguments, and I am not aware of any. Aristophanes' charming parable of the separated halves in the *Symposium* is not an argument, but a parable, exemplifying the literary side of the Platonic dialogues. Nussbaum says that Plato shows that homosexual love can serve worthwhile goals apart from procreation. It would be more accurate to say simply that Plato depicts such love approvingly, for he provides no evidence that his description is accurate. Plato may foster a certain empathy for homosexual relations by presenting them as normal and rewarding. But the demonstration is clouded by his evident preference for sublimated over consummated homosexual relations and by the disapproval (which I will come back to) of habitual passivity in sexual relations. Plato seems to have thought that the only unproblematic function of sex was procreation (not that procreation was unproblematic, but that procreation was the only proper function of sex). And although there are examples of fully adult long-term homoerotic relationships in the Greek texts, the standard form of Greek homosexuality seems to have consisted of relations between a man in his middle or late twenties or older and (at least at the onset of the relationship) a teenage boy. We call that, when it has a physical dimension, pederasty (the Greek word, for the Greek practice); and it is about as difficult to get Americans to view pederasty with anything but horror as it would be to get them to approve of infanticide. States that have repealed their sodomy statutes retain a higher age of consent for homosexual than for heterosexual intercourse, even though there is no risk of pregnancy. Pederasty is not pedophilia or child molestation. The boy is pubescent or postpubescent. So it is not as bad. But Americans consider it bad enough. To complicate the picture still further, Greek pederasty was viewed as a transitional stage for both man and boy, who were expected

172. Nussbaum, "Platonic Love and Colorado Law: The Relevance of Ancient Greek Norms to Modern Sexual Controversies," in *The Greeks and Us*, note 170 above, at 168.

eventually to marry women and cease to engage in homosexual activities. This implies that most pederasts were opportunistic homosexuals (like many sailors, monks, and prison inmates) rather than persons with a homosexual orientation.[173]

Then there is the standard problem with examples. We must ask how *representative* are the ideal homosexual relationships depicted in Greek culture. If the question is whether homosexual orientation is conducive to a happy life or a stable relationship, pointing to Achilles and Patroclus, or Socrates and Alcibiades, or Pausanias and Agathon is not going to provide many clues to the answer. For in discussing social problems we are naturally more interested in typical than in exceptional situations.

The Greek and Roman evidence, along with much other evidence both anthropological and biological, does suggest that homosexuality is not "unnatural" in any nonconclusory sense of the word. But I am not sure what more it shows. Nussbaum suggests that it refutes the argument that homosexuality leads to the downfall of civilizations. That argument is ridiculous, but we must remember that the decline and fall of the Roman Empire were long attributed to its toleration of "vice," that the Athenian Empire had a calamitous collapse too, and that Sparta followed shortly. So the people who make the argument will not be assuaged by close study of Plato and Aristotle; they have their "evidence."

The deepest problem with arguing from ancient Greece and Rome to today is the evidence not only from Greece and Rome but also from the entire Mediterranean and Latin world (as far afield as the Philippines) and even from Japan that homosexuality is likely to be relatively unproblematic in a society in which marriage is not companionate. "Companionate marriage" refers to marriage in which husband and wife are expected to be intimates, confidants, and peers, associating continuously, taking meals together, raising their children together, forming in short a partnership. In cultures in which companionate marriage is uncommon we usually find a big age gap between husband and wife, and the wife is cloistered—sometimes literally sequestered—and uneducated. In such cultures, with the most desirable women being unavailable to men before marriage and marriage being late for men, young men may seek unconventional sexual outlets. One such outlet is opportunistic male homosexuality, the homo-

---

173. This discussion of sexual practices is based on my book *Sex and Reason,* ch. 6 (1992). For later, corroborative evidence, see Michael Rocke, *Forbidden Friendships: Homosexuality and Male Culture in Renaissance Florence,* chs. 3–4 (1996). The canonical study of homosexuality in ancient Greece is K. J. Dover, *Greek Homosexuality* (2d ed. 1989).

sexuality of men who prefer heterosexual relations but will settle for homosexual relations in a pinch. It is penetrators' homosexuality; often the receptive partner is either a "real homosexual" or a male prostitute.

By a "real" homosexual I mean a man who prefers homosexual to heterosexual relations, the Kinsey 5 or 6; for Kinsey's scale (which is calibrated 0 to 6) is an index of homosexual preference or orientation, not of activity. When modern Americans speak of homosexuals, these are the people they usually have in mind. The situation of such homosexuals is much easier in a society of noncompanionate marriage. So little is demanded of husbands in such a society that it is easy for even so-called real homosexuals to have stable marriages and pursue erotic satisfaction on the side. So easily do homosexuals blend in that they are socially unproblematic, even invisible (without concealment), so that to this day people in Mediterranean or Latin societies will sometimes deny that there *are* any homosexuals in their society. They are as inconspicuous as left-handers, because like left-handers their "deviance" has little or no social significance. Yet they tend to be looked down on as something less than full men. This echoes the ancient Greeks' disapproval of habitual passivity in sexual relations. Those habitual passives, people who *enjoy* being penetrated (though they may also enjoy penetrating), presumably were what I am calling "real" homosexuals.

It is difficult for homosexuals to have successful companionate marriages.[174] In societies such as ours in which companionate marriage is the dominant and approved form, homosexuals usually marry for disguise or out of self-deception, and the marriages are rarely successful. A society in which companionate marriage is the norm tends therefore to expel homosexuals from a basic social institution, making them for the first time deviant in a socially significant sense, forcing them into their own subculture, making them strange and even threatening, creating the hostility to homosexuals that is a conspicuous feature of our own society as it was for a long time in England, perhaps the earliest European nation to adopt companionate marriage as the norm. One of the factors in the decline of that hostility is the erosion of marriage as an institution. Those who fear and fight that erosion are in the vanguard of contemporary disapproval of homosexuality.

If this analysis of the impact of companionate marriage on the situation of the homosexual is correct, it implies that we can easily be misled by

---

174. I am speaking of course of marriages between male homosexuals and women. Homosexual marriage is now on the policy agenda, and I discuss it briefly in Chapter 4.

taking the ancient descriptions of homosexuality to establish the possibilities for homosexuals in our culture. Even if such legal barriers to full equality for homosexuals as remain are dismantled, as long as our society is dominated by an ideal and a practice of companionate marriage it will be difficult for homosexuals to fit in as easily as they did in the civilizations depicted in the classical texts. Classical learning can no more take the place of an empirical understanding of modern social behavior than moral or constitutional theory can.

The point of all this is not, however, that *Romer,* or for that matter *VMI,* was decided incorrectly. It is that the decisions are so barren of any engagement with reality that the issue of their correctness scarcely arises. The Achilles' heel of constitutional law is the lack of an empirical footing, not the lack of a good constitutional theory. But then what are courts to do when their ignorance is irremediable, though one hopes only temporarily so? Judges who believe in judicial self-restraint in the sense of wanting to minimize the occasions on which the courts annul the actions of other branches of government will consider their ignorance of the consequences of a challenged governmental policy that is not completely outrageous a compelling reason for staying the judicial hand in the absence of sure guidance from constitutional text, history, or precedent. Activists will plow ahead. The poles will not meet until much more is known about the consequences of judicial activism and judicial self-restraint. So one thing that we may hope eventually to get from applying the methods of scientific theory and empirical inquiry to constitutional law is the knowledge that will enable judges to deal sensibly with uncertainty about consequences. Until then the most that can realistically be demanded of judges is that they be mindful of the limitations of their knowledge. And I do not mean their knowledge of constitutional theory.

Part II

THE WAY OUT

Chapter 3

PROFESSIONALISM

The Two Professionalisms

Part One was primarily, although not exclusively, critical rather than constructive. I want now to be more constructive (though still highly critical!). The keys to improving law, I shall argue, are professionalism and pragmatism in senses to be defined. I have traced elsewhere the decline of the law as a profession in the bad sense that relates "profession" to the medieval guild and the modern cartel.[1] In another and virtually opposite sense, however, the law has become more professional by being swept up in a wave of genuine—of substantial rather than formal or atmospheric—professionalization that is one of the big underreported stories of our time. But this wave has not carried the law as far as one might have hoped.

In this chapter I try to untangle these distinct senses of professionalism and relate them to the criticisms of moral and legal theory presented in Part One. In the final chapter I argue for orienting the law in a more pragmatic direction and make proposals for institutional reform. Professionalism and pragmatism are entwined; the "bad" professionalism stands as an obstacle to pragmatic legal reform, while the "good" professionalism is a precondition of that reform.

Professions and Professional Mystique

The terms "profession" and "professionalism" have a wide and vague range of meanings, to the despair of sociology, the discipline that has studied the

---

1. Richard A. Posner, *Overcoming Law,* ch. 1 (1995). See also Jonathan Rose, "The Legal Profession in Medieval England: A History of Regulation," 48 *Syracuse Law Review* 1, 72–73, 79–80, 89–90, 108–109 (1998).

professions the most.[2] At the simplest level, the terms denote a set of occupations conventionally called "professions." They are law, medicine (and related fields such as dentistry, pharmacology, optometry, nursing, physical therapy, and psychology), military officership, engineering, the clergy of organized religions, teaching (plus PhD-level research whether or not conjoined with teaching), certain types of consulting, architecture, actuarial services, social work, and accounting. Occupations that usually are not classified as professions include business management and business generally, advertising and marketing, public relations, farming, politics, fiction writing and other artistic endeavors both creative and performing, investment advising, the civil service, soldiering below the commissioned-officer level, entertainment (including "professional" athletics), construction (other than architecture and engineering), police and detective work, computer programming, clerical work, and most jobs in transportation, as well as blue-collar work. Journalists, clergy of unstructured religions, operators of day-care centers, photographers, and diplomats occupy the boundary area between professionals and nonprofessionals.

The hallmark of a profession is the belief that it is an occupation of considerable public importance the practice of which requires highly specialized, even esoteric, knowledge that can be acquired only by specialized formal education or a carefully supervised apprenticeship. As a consequence of these features a profession is an occupation that cannot responsibly be entered at will but only in conformity with a prescribed and usually exacting protocol and upon proof of competence. Because of the importance of the occupation, and therefore the professional's capacity to harm society, it is often believed that entry should be controlled by government. Not only should the title of "physician," "lawyer," and so forth be reserved for people who satisfy the profession's own criteria for entry into the profession; no one should be allowed to perform professional services without a license from the government. For the same reasons (the profession's importance and its capacity to do harm), but also because the arcane skills of professionals make their performance difficult for outsiders to monitor and therefore facilitates exploitation of the client by the professional, it is usually believed that the norms and working conditions of a profession should be such as to discourage the undiluted pursuit of pecu-

2. See, for example, Andrew Abbott, *The System of Professions: An Essay on the Division of Expert Labor* (1988); Eliot Freidson, *Professionalism Reborn: Theory, Prophecy, and Policy* (1994); Elliott A. Krause, *Death of the Guilds: Professions, States, and the Advance of Capitalism, 1930 to the Present* (1996); *The Authority of Experts: Studies in History and Theory* (Thomas L. Haskell ed. 1984).

niary self-interest. There is a curious joinder here of "professional" and "amateur." The professional is supposed to be a kind of amateur, a lover of his work and not of lucre—but "amateurish" is the very antithesis of "professional."

This description of professionalism, culled from the sociological literature and common observation, fits law and medicine—the most powerful and most studied of contemporary American professions—better than it does the other professions, many of which do not require a license; and some nonprofessional occupations are licensed. But all the professions fit some part or parts of my composite description better than the nonprofessional occupations do, though the line blurs when we consider psychology, social work, and forest management, as well as the borderline occupations mentioned earlier. The rough edges don't matter to my purposes here; it is enough that a family resemblance among the various professions can be discerned despite their heterogeneity.

The key to an occupation's being classified as a profession, it must be emphasized, is not the actual possession of specialized, socially valuable knowledge; it is the *belief* that some group has such knowledge. For it is the belief that enables the group to claim professional status, with the opportunities for obtaining exclusive privileges and the resulting personal advantages that such status confers. The belief need not be true, need not even be positively correlated with the amount of specialized, socially valuable knowledge that the group possesses. We may be more conscious today of the limitations of medical knowledge than people were in the later Middle Ages, even though physicians then had almost no therapeutic resources.[3]

When belief in a profession's knowledge claims is not justified by the profession's actual knowledge, we have a case of "professional mystique."[4] The more impressive and convincing that mystique, the more secure the profession's claim to the privileges of professional status. A profession whose knowledge claims are inherently shaky has a particularly urgent interest in preserving its mystique. Let us consider the techniques by which it can do this.

One is to cultivate an *obscurantist style of discourse* in order to make the

3. Cf. Lawrence I. Conrad et al., *The Western Medical Tradition: 800 B.C. to A.D. 1800* 204–205 (1995).

4. Cf. Berger's definition of professional ideologies—"the official self-interpretations of entire social groups, obligatory for their members on pain of excommunication," Peter L. Berger, *Invitation to Sociology: A Humanistic Perspective* 41 (1963)—and Bourdieu's concept of "symbolic capital": David Swartz, *Culture and Power: The Sociology of Pierre Bourdieu* 43 (1997).

profession's processes of inquiry and inference impenetrable to outsiders. Another (which is really two others, and thus second and third on my list) is to fix demanding educational qualifications for entry into the profession. By raising the educational level of its members, such qualifications make the profession's claim to possess specialized knowledge more plausible because education is a well-accepted route to knowledge and because it makes the professional's thought processes more opaque to outsiders.

One type of educational qualification is insistence on general education or educability, an insistence designed to limit entry into the profession to a stratum of highly intelligent persons. The other is the specialized professional training itself. It is designed not merely to impart essential knowledge but also to establish the uniqueness of that knowledge in relation to the knowledge possessed by outsiders. The two types of qualification correspond to two distinct techniques for preserving professional mystique: screening prospective entrants for *intellectuality*, and maintaining the *impermeability of professional knowledge,* or in other words the profession's autonomy. Although these functions can be separated analytically, they interact. Screening for intelligence increases impermeability because highly intelligent people are comfortable with complexity and special vocabularies. People of average intelligence could not have created something as intellectually complex and challenging as the Internal Revenue Code or the traditional doctrines of property law.

A fourth technique of professional mystification is the cultivation of *charismatic personality*—the selection for membership in the profession of people whose appearance, personality, or personal background creates an impression of deep, perhaps inarticulable, insight and of masterful, unique competence.

Fifth, the profession bent on maximizing its mystique will resist the breaking up of its constituent tasks into subtasks, because that would tend to make the profession's methods transparent. The professional's mysterious mastery might then be seen to consist in an assemblage of routine procedures requiring no specialized education to perform adequately, just as the intricate craft of carriage-making devolved into the assembly-line production of a far more complex vehicle, the automobile, by less skilled workers. A profession concerned with maintaining its mystique will therefore display *underspecialization*.

Sixth is *lack of hierarchy*. When a complex task is broken down into its components, each performed by a different class of worker, a need for supervision and coordination arises, engendering the hierarchical structure, with its tiers of management, that is characteristic of organizations. Traditionally, professionals were not organized hierarchically. Lawyers practiced by themselves or in partnership with other lawyers; likewise doctors. This was indicative of their lack of specialization.

Seventh, a profession is likely to employ *altruistic pretense*. It will try to conceal the extent to which its members are motivated by financial incentives in order to bolster the claim that they have been drawn to the profession by the opportunity to pursue a calling that yields rich intellectual rewards or gratifies a desire to serve. Altruistic pretense reinforces charismatic personality, which is undermined by the appearance of self-seeking.

Eighth, the profession will be *anticompetitive*. It will seek both to repel competition from outside and to limit competition within the profession. It will do these things to advance the pecuniary self-interest of its members directly, but also to reinforce professional mystique. So it will try particularly hard to outlaw competing services whose success might undermine its knowledge claims. If accountants were seen to give just as good tax advice as tax lawyers, the claim of tax lawyers to possess a valuable body of skills that no other group possesses would lose credibility; likewise if pharmacists were permitted to prescribe drugs and not merely dispense them. And competition, especially within a profession, requires "hustling" and self-promotion, which undermine the professional's effort to present himself as a charismatic master, as someone "in control"; in a competitive market it is the customer rather than the supplier who is in control. Altruistic pretense plays a supporting role here by concealing the self-interested character of efforts to limit competition.

Ninth, the profession will resist the systematization of professional knowledge; it will be *antialgorithmic*. As long as "the means of production of a profession's knowledge-based service is contained in their heads," the profession's monopoly is secure.[5] Once the knowledge that is the professional's capital is organized in a form in which people can employ it without having to undergo the rigors of professional training, the professional becomes dispensable. Thus one can imagine computerized diagnostic techniques and artificial intelligence eventually eroding the positions of the physician and of the lawyer, respectively.

That a profession cultivates professional mystique does not prove that it lacks real knowledge. Mystique enhances a profession's status and so is

5. Keith M. McDonald, *The Sociology of the Professions* 185 (1995).

valuable even if the profession does possess a large body of genuinely useful, and unavoidably esoteric, knowledge. Still, the denser the web of mystique-enhancing techniques that the profession spins, the shakier the profession's knowledge claims are likely to be, because the techniques are more valuable, and therefore more likely to be used heavily, the more there is to conceal. Conversely, the more defensible an occupation's knowledge claims are, whether or not it is a profession (and it could be a profession not because of flim-flam but because its members really *do* possess highly specialized, socially valuable knowledge that cannot be accessed by the ordinary person or embodied in algorithms or rote knowledge), the less frequently these techniques will be encountered.

There are two other symptoms of the shakiness of a profession's knowledge claims besides its resorting to some or all of the techniques of creating mystique. The first is defeat when faced by a new challenge. This is conspicuous in the case of the profession of arms, which is uniquely exposed to challenge in an environment that it does not control. Sorcery and prophecy enjoy professional status in many primitive societies, but are overthrown when the practitioners face competition from groups that use rational methods. The status of the clergy has declined markedly with the growth of science.

The second symptom can be called nonrational employment practices—the use of methods of selection into or promotion within the profession that (like selection in favor of charismatic personality) do not further the acquisition of knowledge. These methods include nepotism, credentialism, discrimination, lockstep compensation, and automatic promotion. Anyone familiar with legal education, especially before the 1960s, will recognize this symptom; and anyone familiar with the legal profession in general, especially before the 1960s, will recognize not only this symptom but also every one of the nine techniques by which a profession disguises its epistemological weakness.

The Growing Professionalism of Law . . .

Developments since the 1960s have seemed to make, and to an extent *have* made, the law more professional in the good sense, the sense in which a profession earns its status and attendant privileges by deploying a body of genuine, specialized, socially valuable, knowledge-based skills rather than by cultivating professional mystique. The process by which professional mystique is superseded by fully rational methods is an aspect of what Max Weber called "rationalization" (of which more later). It is visible in the legal profession today, though far from complete. The obscurantist style—legal jargon—is as bad as ever. And the insistence on a heavy dose of formal education, both undergraduate and professional, is unabated. But the professional education itself is more permeable to the claims of other disciplines than it once was. There is less confident assertion of the profession's autonomy, especially in the academic branch of the profession, where new, outside perspectives on law have been most influential. Economists, political theorists, psychologists, and even literary critics are writing about law with sufficient authority to require academic lawyers to take notice and respond.

There is less cultivation of charismatic personality as an important constituent of professional success; a symptom is the much-lamented decline of the "lawyer statesman" model of professional practice.[6] And specialization has grown. This is seen in the emergence of the paralegal as a distinct tier of legal-services provider and in the increasingly standardized division of labor between judge and law clerk. It is seen in the growing division between academic law and practicing law and between academic law and judging; today, almost all worthwhile legal scholarship is the product of the academy, and judges and lawyers, and even the occasional professor, complain about the irrelevance to their concerns of most such scholarship.[7] And it is seen in the increased specialization of legal practice—fewer lawyers hold themselves out as competent in more than one field. Increased specialization has contributed to the decline of the charismatic personality, as clients increasingly demand a specialist's competence rather than a statesman's wisdom. Further contributing to that decline has been the dismantling of many of the impediments to competition in the legal-services industry, a dismantling that has revealed that most lawyers are motivated by the same incentives as the members of nonprofessional occupations. The increase in competition has forced lawyers to serve their clients better and so to rely less on mystique and more on specialized knowledge that has genuine value to the client.

Specialization has been accompanied by an increase in professional

6. See Anthony T. Kronman, *The Lost Lawyer: Failing Ideals of the Legal Profession* (1993), and, for criticism, Posner, note 1 above, at 93–94. See generally Kenneth Anderson, "A New Class of Lawyers: The Therapeutic as Rights Talk," 96 *Columbia Law Review* 1062 (1996).

7. See, for example, Harry T. Edwards, "The Growing Disjunction between Legal Education and the Legal Profession," 91 *Michigan Law Review* 219 (1992); Patrick J. Schiltz, "Legal Ethics in Decline: The Elite Law Firm, the Elite Law School, and the Moral Formation of the Novice Attorney," 82 *Minnesota Law Review* 705 (1998), esp. pp. 763–771.

hierarchies. Take judging. It used to be that judicial work was performed by—judges. In the federal judiciary, there were originally just two tiers of judicial officer: district judges and Supreme Court Justices.[8] Now there are many: interns and externs, staff attorneys and law clerks, magistrate judges, district judges, circuit judges, and Supreme Court Justices. State judiciaries are becoming similarly tiered, and in addition there is a slowly growing number of specialized federal courts. Most large law firms today have paralegals, associates, income partners, equity partners, and managing partners, rather than just partners (or partners plus clerks—that is, apprentices), as was originally the case, or, later, partners and associates. Some firms employ professors of literature to help the lawyers with their writing and are managed by MBA's rather than lawyers.

The impetus to these developments in the legal profession, as it was to parallel developments that I shall discuss shortly in the military sphere, came in part from that tell-tale symptom of a profession's dependence on mystique: defeat. Beginning in the 1960s, the legal profession in all its branches became associated with policies that in time came to be largely discredited. These policies included the judicial activism of the Supreme Court in the heyday of Earl Warren's chief justiceship; a related knee-jerk receptivity to every "liberal" proposal for enlarging legal rights—and incidentally lawyers' incomes; the plain incapacity of legal reasoning, as demonstrated by modern economics, to make sense of the legal regulation of competition and monopoly; a relaxation of the barriers to litigation that contributed to an enormous, unsettling, and unforeseen increase in the amount of litigation; and a host of lawyer-fostered statutory "reforms" in fields ranging from bankruptcy and consumer protection to employment discrimination, safety regulation, and environmental protection that often had perverse, unintended consequences. The traumatic impact of these failures on the legal profession's self-confidence has been much less than the traumatic impact that the Vietnam War had on the military profession. But there has been some impact, which, along with other factors, has spurred the legal profession to become more professional in the good sense. The other factors are a trend toward deregulation that has included the elimination of a number of barriers to competition between lawyers; the destabilizing effect on the legal profession of the enormous growth in the demand for legal services and of the huge increase in the size of the profession in response to that growth; and the increased cost-conscious-

8. Technically three, because there are actually two tiers of Supreme Court Justices: the Chief Justice of the United States and the Associate Justices of the Supreme Court.

ness of the legal profession's business clients, which is due to the increased professionalism and competitiveness of business.

One by-product of increased legal professionalism has been a decline in nonrational employment practices. There is much less discrimination and nepotism in hiring and promotion than there used to be, though a partial offset has been the rise of affirmative action in forms that constitute reverse discrimination (mainly discrimination against white males) rather than mere correction of past discrimination. The decline of nonrational employment practices has particularly affected the gender composition of the legal profession, which until recently was in all its branches completely dominated by men. Harvard Law School did not admit women as students until the 1950s, and the first female U.S. Supreme Court Justice was not appointed until 1981. As a result of the paucity of women in influential positions in the legal profession and the generally subordinate role of women in the society, the law failed to reflect women's perspectives on a wide range of issues, including procedures in trials for rape, the sale and display of pornography, sexual harassment in the workplace, gender discrimination in employment and education, rules governing divorce and child custody, legal restrictions on abortion, and workplace accommodations to pregnancy. All this has now changed.

Automatic promotion has waned both in law firms and in the academy, where the imposition of stiff publication requirements for tenure has enabled the establishment of rational, if sometimes inflexible, criteria for promotion. In the 1960s, law teaching was one of the least professional (most amateurish, least rationalized) branches of the legal profession. The features that had long made university-level research and teaching, despite the absence of licensing, a highly professional occupation[9]—including the requirement of writing a dissertation and of publishing articles in peer-reviewed journals—were largely absent from law. Although doctoral dissertations in law remain uncommon in the United States, law professors increasingly have a doctoral degree in a related discipline; there is a growing number of peer-reviewed journals; heavy emphasis is now placed on publication in respected journals as a criterion of promotion to tenure; and fewer and fewer law professors have a substantial background in legal practice.[10]

9. See Louis Menand, "The Demise of Disciplinary Authority," in *What's Happened to the Humanities?* 201 (Alvin Kernan ed. 1997).

10. See Schiltz, note 7 above, at 748–752. Schiltz points out that only 3 of the 75 members of the Harvard Law School faculty have more than five years' experience in private practice, and of the

The last point—the diminishing number of law professors with significant experience in the practice of law—is particularly important. In the process of becoming more professional, academic law is becoming a separate profession (separate at least from the practice of law, though closer to other academic disciplines, such as economics and political theory). This is the fundamental cause of the growing estrangement between legal academics and other lawyers (including judges). A profession doesn't want to be on the same wavelength as any other occupation. Academic law is not a separate profession if it is totally transparent to judges and practitioners. Against Judge Edwards and the other grumblers (see note 7) it is necessary to observe that a profession can be useful without being transparent to its clientele. The fact that patients don't understand medical science does not disvalue medicine; the growing gap in understanding between the laity and medical professionals reflects nothing more than the growing scientific sophistication of the medical profession. Academic lawyers can be more helpful to the judiciary by developing and analyzing empirical data bearing on the law than by operating as a shadow judiciary of kibitzers and scolds.[11] (Not that these are the only alternatives; doctrinal analysis, especially when embodied in treatises, remains an immensely valuable, yet currently undervalued, form of academic legal scholarship.) And in the process of making itself more opaque to the practical branches of the profession by embracing interdisciplinarity, the legal professoriat has made its scholarship more transparent to other disciplines, such as philosophy and political science, and this has made legal scholarship less provincial.

The changes that I have described in the legal profession are on the whole good, but the qualification ("on the whole") should be kept steadily in view. There is such a thing as too much specialization; this and other drawbacks of even the good professionalism (as distinct from the guild or mystique form) are real dangers for law. But while it is a mistake to overlook these dangers, it is equally a mistake to oppose the increasing professionalization of legal services root and branch, and to pine for the

---

youngest 13 members of the faculty none has that much experience—and 10 of those have none whatsoever. Among the oldest members of the faculty, these figures are dramatically higher. Id. at 761. None of the members of the Yale Law School faculty, old or young, has more than five years' experience in private practice. Id. at 762 n. 221.

11. For properly tart observations on law professors who identify with judges, see Pierre Schlag, *Laying Down the Law: Mysticism, Fetishism, and the American Legal Mind,* ch. 8 (1996).

days of the professional guild and professional mystique, as does Mary Ann Glendon.[12] A traditionalist and something of a nostalgist, she believes that the profession has been going downhill for many years. Casting an admiring eye back over the Anglo-American legal tradition, she finds great value even in such faintly fogeyish figures as Lord Coke, who celebrated the "artificial reason of the law," and in Blackstone, and in the nineteenth-century formalists whom Holmes derided. The best strands in the tradition were, she argues, braided in the 1950s. By 1960—when Glendon herself was a law student—the practicing bar, the judiciary, and the legal professoriat were operating in fruitful harmony. In this, law's heyday, the law's ideal was that of the patient craftsman. Judges, the best of them anyway, "approached the task of judging in fear and trembling" (p. 129).

Since 1960, Glendon argues, the braid has come undone and each of the strands has become frayed. The bar has become flashy, mercenary, and unscrupulous. The "raider" ethic of the litigator has come to dominate the "trader" ethic of the counselor. (Glendon borrows these terms from Jane Jacobs, but they echo distinctions that Nietzsche and Weber had drawn between aristocratic and bourgeois attitudes.) This has occurred because litigation is so much larger a proportion of law practice than it used to be, thanks to the "litigation explosion" that began around 1960. Glendon quotes a lawyers' flyer: "We are pleased to announce that we obtained for our client THE LARGEST VERDICT EVER FOR AN ARM AMPUTATION—$7.8 MILLION" (p. 5). Fierce competition within the profession is not only both cause and consequence of hucksterism; it has made lawyers work harder yet with less job security than in the past.

The bench, too, has, according to Glendon, become an arena of immodesty and self-aggrandizement. Justice Douglas was

> ahead of his time. His contempt for form was regarded as sloppiness; his visionary opinions were seen as evidence he was angling for the presidency; and his solicitude for those he considered underdogs was understood as favoritism. In the 1990s, he would surely have basked in the "Greenhouse Effect"—a term (named after the *New York Times*'s Linda Greenhouse) for the warm reciprocity between activist journalists and judges who meet with their approval. (p. 153)

12. Mary Ann Glendon, *A Nation under Lawyers: How the Crisis in the Legal Profession Is Transforming American Society* (1994).

Glendon quotes with well-deserved derision the pompous self-congratulatory opinion in *Planned Parenthood v. Casey* (reaffirming the core of *Roe v. Wade*) in which three Justices of the Supreme Court declared that Americans' "very belief in themselves" as "people who aspire to live according to the rule of law" is "not readily separable from their understanding of the [Supreme] Court"[13]—this in defense of abortion rights, which, whatever their merit, can hardly be thought securely grounded in the Constitution. The Justices seem to be claiming to be possessed of constitutional ESP. One of the authors of the opinion, Glendon reminds us, just happened to have a journalist in his office the day the opinion was issued, to whom the Justice compared himself to Caesar crossing the Rubicon. He may have forgotten that Caesar crossed the Rubicon to wage civil war and install himself as dictator. Judges have been accused of activism; perhaps a more apt word is Caesarism.

The legal academy, Glendon argues, has been atomized into contending schools of esoteric scholarship that have little to do with the practice of law. Legal treatises are derided by these scholars as "battleships"—useful in their time, but obsolete. Glendon quotes a crusty old Harvard professor as remarking that the Young Turks of legal academia would rather write about the sex life of caterpillars than write treatises that would shape the law (p. 205). As a result of these brats' rejection of traditional norms of legal professionalism, today's law-school graduates are ill prepared to practice law or to serve as judges.

That the legal profession in all its branches has changed greatly since the 1950s, and in approximately the ways described by Glendon, is true. That the changes have brought in their wake many absurdities; that the profession is becoming increasingly an offense to the fastidious; that traditional legal scholarship is stupidly denigrated; that the direct and indirect expenses of law have become enormous, as though the legal system were trying to appropriate as large a share of the Gross National Product as the health-care system—these things are also true. But they do not have the significance that Glendon ascribes to them. The profession was not as wonderful in 1960 as Glendon makes out. Many of the changes since then either are improvements or are inseparable from improvements. And Glendon has no explanation of why or how the changes came about and no program for reversing them.

Competition in the Darwinian jungle is literally genocidal; in the eco-

13. 505 U.S. 833, 868 (1992).

nomic marketplace it is merely painful and vulgar, and its antithesis is not peace, but cartelization. The bar in the 1950s was a regulated cartel. State law limited entry into the profession, forbade competition in the provision of legal services by nonlawyers ("unauthorized practice"), and limited competition among lawyers by forbidding advertising and solicitation, encouraging price fixing, forbidding investment by nonlawyers in law firms, and restricting interstate mobility. (Many of these restrictions remain in force.) "Billing was a fine art," Glendon quotes approvingly (p. 29)—yes, the fine art of price discrimination, whereby monopolists maximize their profits. As for the judiciary, state or federal, it would be extremely difficult to show—Glendon does not show—that it was of higher quality in the 1950s than today. State judges have somewhat more secure tenure today, and there is probably less corruption; aspirants for federal judgeships are screened more carefully; and most judges are harder working and more productive than their predecessors. Although the growth in the number of law clerks and other supporting personnel has its downside, the average judicial opinion is a more professional product than it was in the Golden Age that Glendon celebrates. (Just read and compare.) It is true that most judges today do not approach their task in "fear and trembling," but neither did most judges yesterday. Judges no more quaver at rendering judgments than surgeons quaver at making incisions.

Judges are probably no more aggressive today on balance than they used to be, but I agree with Glendon that they are too aggressive and intrude too deeply into the activities of other branches of government, acting all too often as ignorant policy czars. But as I intimated in Chapter 2 in discussing constitutional criminal procedure, judges may have been too passive in enforcing rights before the Warren Court began its gallop. There was surprisingly little actual enforcement of constitutional rights in the 1950s. A large proportion of criminal defendants who could not afford a lawyer had to defend themselves; the appointment of lawyers to represent indigent criminal defendants was not routine. Many state prisons and state insane asylums were hellholes, and to their inmates' complaints the courts turned a deaf ear. The right of free speech was narrowly interpreted, the better to crush the Communist Party U.S.A. and protect the reading public from Henry Miller. Police brutality was rampant, and the tort remedies against it ineffectual. Criminal sentencing verged on randomness; in some parts of the country, capital punishment was imposed with an approach to casualness. In practice the Bill of Rights mostly protected only the respectable elements of society, who did not need its protection.

And it was not only the Constitution that looked better on paper than in practice. Many private rights were not effectively enforceable. Legal and medical malpractice suits were unwinnable, though we now know that both forms of malpractice were and are common. There were almost no effective legal protections of the environment. Every variety of invidious discrimination was common in employment, and there were virtually no legal remedies for it. Judges were ignorant of economics, and their interpretations of the antitrust laws frequently turned antitrust on its head, discouraging competition and promoting monopoly.

Public policy is a pendulum. If it swings too far in one direction, it will swing too far in the other before it comes to rest (and it may never come to rest, if it keeps getting pushed). If there was too little enforcement of legal rights in the 1950s—but maybe there was not too little; maybe, as I intimated in discussing constitutional criminal procedure, the rule of law should not extend all the way to the margins of society—there is probably too much today.[14] The fallacy is to suppose that if there is now too much enforcement, or too many lawyers, there must have been about the right amount of these things at some time in the past. Glendon is correct that increased competition for legal services makes it less likely that a lawyer will subordinate his client's interests to the lawyer's conception of "higher" social interests; but it also makes it less likely that the lawyer will subordinate his client's interests to his own selfish interests. Women today may, as Glendon remarks, find marriage and children "almost impossible to combine with the fast track in law firms" (p. 88). In the Golden Age they could not get hired by major law firms. A partner at the Cravath firm told Glendon when she interviewed for a job with the firm in the early 1960s: "I couldn't bring a girl in to meet Tom Watson [of IBM] any more than I could bring a Jew" (p. 28).

The law professors of the 1950s were for the most part happily oblivious to the gap between aspiration and achievement in the law. The law's "singing reason" (a phrase of Karl Llewellyn's) was something encountered in the better judicial opinions and law-review articles rather than at the operating level of the legal system. Faith in reason ("reason called law" as Felix Frankfurter and Herbert Wechsler put it) was the complacent faith of academics and judges who either did not know how law was actually being implemented at the operating level or did not think it seemly to let

14. For a powerful polemic against egregious tactics by criminal defense lawyers, which protect the guilty from their just deserts, see Susan Estrich, *Getting Away with Murder: How Politics Is Destroying the Criminal Justice System* (1998).

on. They were intellectually provincial as well, in but not of the university, incurious about what other disciplines might be able to contribute to the understanding and improvement of the legal system. Many of the developments that Glendon deplores, such as the greatly expanded use (and potential for abuse) of pretrial discovery, are the consequence of reforms devised by her academic heroes, who could not predict the impact of those reforms in the real world. She herself acknowledges disappointment that these giants, such as Archibald Cox and Louis Loss (the anticaterpillar man), as senior faculty of the Harvard Law School in the late 1960s and early 1970s, hired nihilistic practitioners of critical legal studies, plunged headlong into affirmative action, genuflected to the "paragons of political correctness" (p. 228), and in these and other ways undermined the edifice of law. She gestures at the possibility that her own paragons lacked the intellectual sophistication and moral courage necessary to take a stand against the antilaw people when she remarks that while "they [her heroes] could 'do' law very well . . . they were tongue-tied when it came to explaining and defending their ingrained habitual doings" (p. 231). Can one really "do" law well without being aware of what one is doing?

Many intellectuals, including legal intellectuals, including Glendon, have a pre-Darwinian outlook. They see the present as a degeneration from a golden past rather than as an evolution from a simpler past. They are thus prone to the fallacy of comparing the best of the old with the average of the new.[15] So James Madison, Abraham Lincoln, Elihu Root, and the cousins Hand are taken to be your typical American lawyers before the Fall and are contrasted with the plaintiff's lawyer in the amputation case.

The clock cannot be turned back, especially to a time that exists only in the imagination. It would be refreshing if leading legal thinkers, rather than pining for a lost yesterday, would think about tomorrow. Glendon is fearful of the "swelling ranks of innovators, iconoclasts, and adversarial advocates" in the profession (p. 102). But it is innovators and iconoclasts, rather than nostalgists and stand-patters, who will adapt the law of today to the challenge of tomorrow. She juxtaposes approving references to Burke's praise of incrementalism and to the American Founders; but the latter were revolutionaries. She quotes with approval Paul Freund's praise of law as the discipline that "teaches us to look through the great antinomies," such as liberty and authority, "in order to discover the precise issue

15. The fallacy is a result of selection bias. The average of the old is forgotten, and the best of the old, which is remembered, is taken as the average.

in controversy, the precise consequences of one decision or another, and the possibility of an accommodation by deflating the isms and narrowing the schisms" (p. 103).[16] This is law conceived pragmatically—and also, one might think, innovatively and even iconoclastically—rather than nostalgically.

. . . And of Everything Else as Well

What has been happening to the legal profession since the 1960s is a bit like what has been happening to the American military profession since the 1970s. The Vietnam War revealed striking deficiencies in the civilian management of national security affairs. But it also revealed the considerable amateurism of the military profession.[17] The officer corps relied heavily on mystique in lieu of serious study of and planning for the exigencies of modern warfare. Nepotism was rife both in routine promotion and in appointments to important commands; charisma frequently substituted for competence; bluff, wishful thinking, and outright misrepresentation were used to conceal failures. A hypertrophy of mystique professionalism developed in the form of lethal interservice rivalries that could be controlled only by the equivalent of noncompete agreements; it was as unthinkable to the navy that the army could direct naval aviation missions as it was unthinkable to lawyers that accountants could conduct tax litigation. The armed services were united only in believing the military a world apart that could neither learn from the civilian sector, for example about the intelligent management of race relations and other personnel problems, nor even communicate with it. A caricature of the warrior as Neanderthal, Curtis LeMay, became emblematic of the U.S. military of the period.

A quarter of a century later, as shown by the performance of the American military in the Persian Gulf campaign, the military profession had been transformed.[18] This was partly in reaction to the disastrous effects of the Vietnam War on the morale, effectiveness, and public esteem of the military, and partly because the end of the draft forced the military

16. Paul Freund, *The Supreme Court of the United States* 75 (1972).

17. For an excellent popular account, see James Kitfield, *Prodigal Soldiers: How the Generation of Officers Born of Vietnam Revolutionized the American Style of War* (1995).

18. See id.; David McCormick, *The Downsized Warrior: America's Army in Transition* 106–111 (1998). McCormick expresses concern about the consequences for military professionalism of the army's precipitate downsizing since 1990. Despite this eddy, the overall trend in military professionalism remains upward since the 1960s.

to design "professional" armed forces. By the end of the period of reform, the system of promotion had been revamped to place emphasis on successful performance in realistic, objectively evaluated military exercises; personnel policies in general had been professionalized. Feedback loops ("after action review") had been created to foster learning from experience. Emphasis on continuing education, both military and civilian, had facilitated the creation of a more intelligent officer corps and one able to make maximum use of modern analytical tools and modern technologies in the waging of war, and also to communicate effectively with civilians, as shown by the military's media relations during the Gulf campaign. Procedures and institutions to assure at least a minimum of interservice cooperation had been created. War remains emotional and unpredictable to a degree not matched by any other professional activity; but American military officership has become legitimately professional to a far greater degree than it once was.

Even more interesting than the increasing professionalization of the traditional professions is the increasing professionalization of all work. The essence of "good" professionalism is the application of a specialized body of knowledge to an activity of importance to society. As knowledge grows—and, as a concomitant of growth, becomes more specialized because of the intellectual limitations of even the ablest human being—we can expect more and more occupations to become professionalized in the good sense. Yet they might never acquire the traditional accoutrements of professionalism, because they would not need to cultivate professional mystique.

The trend toward universal professionalization was first glimpsed by Weber, for whom the hallmark of modernization was the bringing of more and more activities under the governance of rationality. Early and somewhat questionable illustrations were the "rationalization" (actually cartelization or monopolization) of industry through mergers and the control of production by means of time-and-motion studies ("Taylorism").[19] The growth of rational methods would, Weber rightly predicted, foster the disenchantment of the world, as activities became demystified and transparent.[20]

In recent years the process that he foresaw has grown by leaps and

19. See Cecelia Tichi, *Shifting Gears: Technology, Literature, Culture in Modernist America* 76–87 (1987).

20. See, for example, Max Weber, *The Protestant Ethic and the Spirit of Capitalism* 180–183 (Talcott Parsons trans. 1958); Anthony T. Kronman, *Max Weber*, ch. 8 (1983).

bounds.[21] Consider university administration. It was once a bastion of amateurism. The typical university president was a distinguished scholar who had stepped directly from a career of teaching and research into the presidency. He was assisted by a small administrative staff composed primarily of amateurs as well, either former teacher-scholars like him or, at some Ivy League schools, socially well-connected alumni. Today, with the leading universities multi-hundred-million dollar enterprises subject to complex laws and regulations, the typical university president is a professional administrator. He has climbed the lower rungs of an administrative ladder that normally include service as a university provost and earlier as a dean.[22] He is assisted by a large staff of specialists in administration, many of whom do not have substantial academic backgrounds but instead have backgrounds in legal practice, accounting, finance, and business administration. The university's hospital complex will be managed by a professional hospital administrator, hospital administration having become a specialized field in itself.

Business, too, has become rationalized, professionalized, to an extraordinary degree. Although there is still an important role for lone-wolf entrepreneurs in start-up firms and in takeover and turnaround situations, mature firms are increasingly the domain of executives who have a thorough grasp of rational and systematic methods of financial management, personnel ("human resources") administration, inventory control, marketing, production, procurement, government relations, law, and every other dimension of a complex enterprise. As the professions have become increasingly businesslike, business has become increasingly professional, not in the spurious sense in which some of the old-line professions cultivated a professional mystique but in the real sense of deploying specialized knowledge in rational and effective pursuit of clearly defined, socially valued goals.

Law's traditional peer is the medical profession. Its astonishing transfor-

21. Cf. Steven Brint, *In an Age of Experts: The Changing Role of Professionals in Politics and Public Life* 205–207 (1994). The process is deplored by Brint, id., ch. 10, and by another left-wing sociologist, Elliott Krause, in his book *Death of the Guilds*, note 2 above. Brint and Krause regard the rationalization of the professions as a deplorable success of capitalism, bringing all economic activities under the rule of the market. For criticism of Brint, see Anderson, note 6 above, at 1072–1081. The denigration of professionalism is a sign that the left is increasingly reactionary, pining nostalgically for premodern methods of production.

22. Today one hears it said in university circles that no one can be considered for a presidency or provostship who does not have experience in "complex" administration, defined as supervising people who are themselves administrators and who therefore relate to their own supervisors as representatives of their subordinates rather than as individuals.

mation since the 1960s has been powered by an explosion of medical knowledge that has vastly increased the efficacy of medical treatment in prolonging life and alleviating suffering. As one would expect, this explosion has been accompanied by a rapid decline in the mystique elements formerly so conspicuous in this profession—discriminatory selection practices, the concealment of carelessness and incompetence (the "conspiracy of silence" and the often literal "burying of mistakes"), the physician's assumption of omniscience in dealing with patients and refusal to level with them about prognosis, hostility to forms of health maintenance that do not require esoteric medical skills (such as diet and exercise), inadequate specialization that had physicians doing many tasks that nurses could perform as well and nurses doing many tasks that medical orderlies and technicians could perform as well, disdain for outsider methods or disciplines such as statistics and public health, and hostility toward innovations in the pricing and delivery of medical services. The advent of social insurance in the form of Medicare and Medicaid, and of advanced technology, sent the costs of medical services soaring, thus exposing the primitive management techniques of the medical sector. Faced with a defeat potentially of Vietnam proportions, the medical profession together with the other components of the vast medical-services sector discovered and are busy adopting rational methods of medical administration that are designed to prevent doctor and patient from contracting for wasteful treatments paid by hapless third parties—the biggest source of avoidable medical inflation.

Compared to the medical profession, the law's professionalizing has not proceeded far at all. Part of the reason may be the law's entwinement with politics, which, in a democracy anyway, resists professionalization, at least of the sort that might help the law to become more professional. The qualification is important. Politics, too, has become more professional, as a result of improvements in the techniques of public opinion polling, campaign fund-raising and advertising, and identifying, packaging, and promoting political candidates as media stars. But none of this has rubbed off on the law in any useful way. There is no evidence that the televising of trials, appeals, and judicial confirmation hearings enhances the quality of a legal system or that the use of public opinion polling techniques and the insights of social psychology to select and then influence jurors has increased the accuracy of jury trials. Because of the strategic character of litigation, technical improvements can increase the cost to both sides without a commensurate benefit in more accurate determinations; this is a frequent criticism of the heavy use of expert witnesses in many types of litigation. An exactly parallel argument could of course be made against the genuineness of the professionalizing of military officership when viewed in a global perspective (which, however, few Americans are inclined to do). Some medical innovations, too, confer limited or even negative social benefits because of secondary effects—for example, an improvement that saves the patient's life but causes a more expensive, and fatal, illness a short time later, or a treatment that by making a disease less lethal induces people to take less care to avoid it, as in the case of syphilis, and perhaps of AIDS. But the problem of running-in-place improvements seems particularly acute in the case of law (as also of sports, another adversary enterprise).

The law's resistance to genuine improvement is shown, paradoxically, by the rise of moral theory applied to law whether directly or through constitutional theory. The practical side of the profession, as we have seen, resists this type of theorizing, which strikes lawyers and judges as useless; they are content with an untheorized moral vocabulary heavy with undefined terms such as "fairness" and "justice." For the academic lawyer, however, moral theory is an escape from having to think of law as a form of social science or policy science. Law conceived in scientific terms might have an embarrassing transparency, for legal claims might then actually be falsifiable. Moral theory and constitutional theory, in contrast to scientific theory, are at once opaque and spongy. They provide vocabularies in which to make law conform to the theorist's political preferences without seeming to do so. These theories are alternative mystifications to the traditional concept of law as an autonomous and hermetic discipline. A suggestion for using philosophy to guide military strategy, medical treatment, or university administration would be met with open-mouthed incredulity. No greater role for philosophy would be admitted in those fields than that of proposing ethical constraints. The suggestion that law should steer by the light of moral philosophy reflects a conception of law as a preprofessional, unsystematized activity.

In discussing Mary Ann Glendon's jeremiad I mentioned that the Supreme Court's opinions have become more professional over the last forty years. They are more thorough, more accurate, and more methodical. They reflect a greater depth of research, both legal and collateral. They are more carefully written in an effort to avoid misunderstandings and irresponsible dicta. They are more uniform, less idiosyncratic, in style—more "correct," in a grammarian's sense. They are more, one might say, the product of rational methods and rules, less of individual vision. This is not an accident. There have been significant changes in the staffing of the Court. Appointments are scrutinized more carefully, a process that tends to eliminate oddballs. Prior judicial experience has become a de facto qualification; all the Associate Justices have some. The number of Supreme Court law clerks has doubled and the clerks are more carefully selected, with merit playing an even greater role than formerly. And every one of them has already spent a year as a law clerk to another judge, most often a federal appellate judge, whose docket is broadly similar to that of the Supreme Court. The management innovation known as the "cert. pool," whereby one law clerk prepares a recommendation for all the Justices on whether to grant plenary review of a case, has enabled the law clerks to screen applications for review in less time than in the earlier period despite the fact that the number of applications has increased even faster than the number of clerks. Since as a result each law clerk has as much time to work on opinions as in the old days, and the ratio of law clerks to opinions has more than doubled (an additional factor being a decline in the number of cases that the Court accepts for argument), the Justices have much more, as well as more experienced, help in preparing their opinions.[23] Word processing and computerized legal research have further increased the clerks' productivity. All these developments have worked together to generate the improvements in the Supreme Court's opinions of which I spoke.

But the improvements—what are they really worth? The opinions take longer to read, they are duller, and they are harder to use as predictors of the Court's reaction to future cases because of their impersonal cast. Recall how heavily padded the majority opinion in the *VMI* case was. Much of what goes on in the Court's opinions and accounts for their length and their dense texture—such as the ping-pong game between majority and dissenting Justices, the relentless dissection of precedents, and the elaborate statutory histories and exegeses—neither illuminates the Justices' actual thought processes nor instructs the lower-court judges or the practicing bar in analytical techniques that will resolve difficult legal issues. The Court's caseload is dominated by difficult constitutional cases, and only the naive think that the results in such cases owe a lot to disinterested, nonpolitical, "observer-independent" methods of inquiry. No doubt each

23. Screening petitions for certiorari and working on opinions are not all that law clerks do. They also help their Justice prepare for oral argument and review opinions circulated by other Justices. These tasks, too, if done well, should make for better opinions.

Justice *thinks* that his votes owe everything, or at least a great deal, to such methods, while being skeptical about the votes of the other Justices. That is the psychology of judging. It is easy (even for a judge) to be a cynical observer of judges, but it is difficult to *be* a cynical judge. The main result of the measures that have made the Supreme Court a more professional institution has been, at least as far as constitutional decisions are concerned, to thicken the window dressing.[24]

The law is still in the process of building a body of knowledge of the kind that has enabled other professions to move decisively in the direction of genuine professionalism. The strategic and political dimensions of the law may make this project impossible, although I prefer to think that they make it merely difficult. The political dimension is largely responsible for the inroads that affirmative action and political correctness have made in legal education, with retrogressive results from the standpoint of professionalization. Indeed, one prominent component of the political-correctness, affirmative-action beachhead in the law schools is a scholarly movement, critical race theory, that expressly rejects the tenets of rational analysis.[25] Politics may also explain those dreary constitutional law opinions. Efficiency through specialization doesn't mean much if a lack of agreed ends places an activity in the domain not of purposeful, goal-oriented, instrumental rationality but of politics or ideology; what could "specialist in ideology" mean, now that the Soviet Union is defunct? ("Moral specialist" would be an equivalent oxymoron.) But if I am right that a tide of genuine professionalism is sweeping the nation (maybe the world), how likely is it that the law, of all activities, will remain untouched by it?

The Supersession Thesis

The Path away from the Law

The hope for law to become a genuine profession, in the sense in which the developments in other occupations are teaching us to understand professionalism, lies in what I like to call, with deliberate provocation, "overcoming law" or, alternatively, the "supersession thesis." The thesis is

24. Cf. Deborah Hellman, "The Importance of Appearing Principled," 37 *Arizona Law Review* 1107 (1995).

25. See Daniel A. Farber and Suzanna Sherry, *Beyond All Reason: The Radical Assault on Truth in American Law* (1997).

that what we understand as the law is merely a transitional phase in the evolution of social control. Holmes hinted at this in his essay "The Path of the Law."[26] He implied that law as he knew it, and as we largely know it still, is merely a stage in human history. It followed revenge historically and will someday be succeeded by forms of social control that perform the essential functions of law but are not law in a recognizable sense, although they are latent in law, just as law was latent in revenge.

Law in the recognizable sense, the sense that will eventually be superseded, is assumed to be continuous with morality, and it is certainly saturated with moral terms. It is also traditional—today we would say "path dependent." Judges have a duty to enforce political settlements made in the past. A related point is that law is logical, meaning that new doctrines can be created only by derivation, whether by deduction, analogy, or interpretation, from existing doctrines.

This traditional conception of law, which is as orthodox today as it was a century ago, Holmes seems to have regarded as epiphenomenal, obscurantist, and transitory. "The Path of the Law" argues that people care about what their legal duties are because judges have been empowered to decree the use of overwhelming force to enforce those duties. A prudent person wants to know how to avoid getting in the way of that force (or, Holmes should have added, how to get it behind one's claims—for law enforces rights as well as duties). From this standpoint all that matters is being able to predict how judges will rule given a particular set of facts, and this is why people consult lawyers. Statutes and judicial opinions provide the materials for the prediction. Predictions of what the courts will do are really all there is to law. Morality is immaterial. A bad person cares as much about keeping out of the way of state force as a good person; and because law and morality are frequently discrepant, the law's use of moral language is a source of confusion, so it would be good to banish all such language from the law. For example, while both law and morality use the word "duty" a lot, the legal duty to keep a promise is merely a prediction that if you don't keep it you'll have to pay for any harm that breaking your promise imposes on the promisee. It doesn't

---

26. Oliver Wendell Holmes, "The Path of the Law," 10 *Harvard Law Review* 457 (1897). The centennial of this most famous of legal essays produced an outpouring of scholarly commentary. See, for example, Albert W. Alschuler, "The Descending Trail: Holmes' 'Path of the Law' One Hundred Years Later," 49 *Florida Law Review* 353 (1997); Brian Leiter, "Holmes, Economics, and Classical Realism," in *The Jurisprudence of Oliver Wendell Holmes, Jr.* (S. J. Burton ed., forthcoming); David Luban, "The Bad Man and the Good Lawyer: A Centennial Essay on Holmes's 'The Path of the Law,'" 72 *New York University Law Review* 1547 (1997).

matter whether you broke it deliberately or, at the other extreme, for reasons completely beyond your control. As further evidence that the law doesn't really care about intentions or other mental states, it enforces contracts if the parties *signify* assent, whether or not they really assent. In criminal law, words like "intent" or "negligence" denote degrees of dangerousness, nothing more.

The moral and mental baggage of the law is connected with the fact that the basis of most legal principles is tradition, and the tradition, heavily Judeo-Christian, is saturated with moral concepts that emphasize state of mind. (In contrast, the pre-Socratic Greeks placed greater emphasis on consequences.) The backward-looking, tradition- and precedent-ridden cast of legal thinking, which we glimpsed in Glendon's pessimistic assessment of the contemporary legal profession, is to be regretted. The only worthwhile use of history in law is to debunk outmoded doctrines by showing them to be vestigial. Judges have got to understand that the only sound basis for a legal rule is its social advantage, which requires an economic judgment, balancing benefits against costs. If the law submitted to instruction by economics and the other social sciences we might find the tort system replaced by a system of social insurance and the system of criminal law, which is based on a belief in deterrence, replaced by a system in which the methods of scientific criminology are used to identify and isolate, or even kill, dangerous people. And if we were realistic we would realize that what judges do does not conform to the official picture of adjudication. It is sometimes mindless standpatism and sometimes voting their fears, but sometimes, and ideally, it is weighing costs and benefits, though with some concern (much emphasized in Holmes's judicial opinions) for avoiding rapid changes of front that would make it difficult for lawyers to predict the outcomes of new cases. So precedent is important, but for thoroughly practical reasons having nothing to do with any "duty" to the past.

Was Holmes right that "the law" is just a mask or skin that may confuse the wearer but that has no social function in modernity and ought to be stripped away to reveal a policymaking apparatus that could be improved if only it were recognized for what it is? He was half right. There is indeed a lot of needlessly solemn and obfuscatory moralistic and traditionary blather in judicial decision making and legal thought generally. It is immensely useful in dealing with legal issues always to try to strip away the conventional verbiage in which the issues come wrapped and look at the actual interests at stake, the purposes of the participants, the policies behind the precedents, and the consequences of alternative decisions, as Paul Freund suggested in the passage quoted by Glendon. Law can use a big dose of the disenchantment that accompanies real professionalization under the conditions of modernity.

But Holmes overlooked a number of points. One is the tension between a "realistic" conception of judges as policymakers and the idea that the way to predict what the judges will do in the next case is to extrapolate from previous decisions, which implies that the official picture of adjudication, in which judges "reason" from the precedents, is accurate after all. A related point is that the social interest in certainty of legal obligation requires the judge to stick pretty close to statutory text and judicial precedent in most cases and thus to behave, much of the time anyway, as a formalist. Furthermore, the more that law conforms to prevailing moral opinions, including the moral opinions of relevant subcultures such as the commercial community, the easier it is for lay people to understand and comply with law. They can avoid coming into conflict with it just by being well-socialized members of their community.

Another point, one that Holmes could not have understood because it is a lesson of totalitarianism, which did not yet exist in 1897, is that the maintenance of a moral veneer in the law's dealing with the people subject to it, especially the antisocial people subject to it, offers a first line of defense against excesses of official violence. It is not healthy to treat even disgusting criminals as animals, yet Holmes toyed with the idea of doing that when he said, "If the typical criminal is a degenerate, bound to swindle or to murder by as deep seated an organic necessity as that which makes the rattlesnake bite, it is idle to talk of deterring him by the classical method of imprisonment. He must be got rid of."[27] Excluding a class of human beings from the human community can become a habit and spread from criminals to ne'er-do-wells to the sick and the aged and the mentally disturbed or deficient ("Three generations of imbeciles are enough")[28] and finally to nonconformists and to members of unpopular minorities. Do I have to explain, perhaps by reference to moral philosophy, why these would be bad results in the conditions of our society? I don't think so!

Holmes also failed to consider that if through the application of ra-

27. Holmes, note 26 above, at 470.
28. Buck v. Bell, 274 U.S. 200, 207 (1927) (Holmes, J.).

tional methods the practice of law is made as routinized, as cut and dried, as the work now done by paralegals, bookkeepers, inventory clerks, ticket agents, and medical technicians, the legal profession may cease to attract the ablest people and the quality of law may suffer. Of course, a century after Holmes wrote, we are still far from such a pass, yet we shall note in the next chapter the growth of dissatisfaction by American lawyers with their highly remunerated but increasingly corseted professional lives. What Glendon sees as inexplicable moral deterioration may be a symptom of an underlying transformation in the material conditions of practice. Those dull Supreme Court opinions may be another symptom.

The last of Holmes's oversights in "The Path of the Law," and perhaps the most important, is his failure to appreciate the risk of premature enthusiasm for scientific solutions to human problems. There is irony in this oversight, since Holmes was a skeptic, and among the things he was skeptical of were schemes of social betterment based on the latest ideas in economics and other social sciences. Despite his skepticism he could not wholly escape the gravitational pull of the latest and best thinking in his intellectual milieu; hence his enthusiasm for eugenics and his receptivity both to a "therapeutic" model of criminal justice and to replacing the tort system with a scheme of social insurance—another questionable idea, as we have learned from experience with no-fault automobile accident compensation schemes.[29]

The scientific mistakes of the past, so emphasized by the Supreme Court in the *VMI* case, should make us wary about jettisoning the traditional conception of law, barnacled though it is with fusty moralisms, in favor of a wholly scientific conception of law. But the equal and opposite error is to suppose that the present and the future will be just like the past.

29. See Elisabeth M. Landes, "Insurance, Liability, and Accidents: A Theoretical and Empirical Investigation of the Effect of No-Fault Accidents," 25 *Journal of Law and Economics* 49 (1982); Peter L. Swan, "The Economics of Law: Economic Imperialism in Negligence Law, No-Fault Insurance, Occupational Licensing and Criminology," *Australian Economic Review*, Third Quarter 1984, p. 92; Richard A. Derrig, Herbert I. Weisberg, and Xiu Chen, "Behavioral Factors and Lotteries under No-Fault with a Monetary Threshold: A Study of Massachusetts Automobile Claims," 61 *Journal of Risk and Insurance* 245 (1994); Richard A. Posner, *Economic Analysis of Law* § 6.14 (5th ed. 1998). Even viewed purely as a compensation scheme, and ignoring its effect on accident rates, no-fault is not clearly superior to the conventional tort system. Joseph E. Johnson, George B. Flanigan, and Daniel T. Winkler, "Cost Implications of No-Fault Automobile Insurance," 59 *Journal of Risk and Insurance* 116 (1992). For a more favorable assessment of no-fault, however, see J. David Cummins and Mary A. Weiss, "The Stochastic Dominance of No-Fault Automobile Insurance," 60 *Journal of Risk and Insurance* 230 (1993).

To suppose that is to deny, in the face of much contrary evidence, that there has been progress in the understanding of human behavior and social institutions. Economics, psychology both cognitive and abnormal, evolutionary biology, statistics, and historiography have all advanced since Holmes wrote. New methods of apprehending social behavior, such as game theory, have emerged. We know more about the social world than Holmes could have known. We should be able to avoid his mistakes. No doubt we shall make our own. Prudence as well as realism suggests that the entanglement of law with morality, politics, tradition, and rhetoric may well be permanent and the path to complete professionalization therefore permanently blocked. But we should be able to go a long way down that path before reaching the obstruction. We should try, at any rate, which will require more emphasis in the legal academy than at present on economics, statistics, game theory, cognitive psychology, political science, sociology, decision theory, and related disciplines.[30] In trying we shall be joining a great and, on the whole, a beneficent national movement toward the professionalization of all forms of productive work.

The Sociology of Law

Some readers may suspect that when I say "economics . . . and related disciplines" I mean "economics." I do not. I assign large roles, in a mature legal professionalism having a social science orientation, to other disciplines, including sociology—a traditional rival of economics. Sociology plays a large role in this book. Sociologists' skepticism about the knowledge claims of professions and intellectual disciplines, the penetrating analyses of professional behavior that this skepticism has encouraged, and Weber's association of modernization with rationalization and disenchantment have guided my exploration of the relation between theory and practice in moral and legal decision making.

30. See, for example, Douglas G. Baird, Robert H. Gertner, and Randal C. Picker, *Game Theory and the Law* (1994); Frank B. Cross, "Political Science and the New Legal Realism: A Case of Unfortunate Interdisciplinary Ignorance," 92 *Northwestern University Law Review* 251 (1997); Kenneth G. Dau-Schmidt, "Economics and Sociology: The Prospects for an Interdisciplinary Discourse on Law," 1997 *Wisconsin Law Review* 389; Neil K. Komesar, *Imperfect Alternatives: Choosing Institutions in Law, Economics, and Public Policy* (1994); Michael A. Livington, "Reinventing Tax Scholarship: Lawyers, Economists, and the Role of the Legal Academy," 83 *Cornell Law Review* 365 (1998); Lynn M. LoPucki, "The Systems Approach to Law," 82 *Cornell Law Review* 479 (1997).

Yet sociology of law is not at the moment a major "player" in interdisciplinary legal studies.[31] The reasons are various[32] and include an association with discredited ideas, for example in criminology. Criminologists of traditional, which is to say of sociological, bent located the causes of crime in social factors, such as poverty and discrimination, that no longer seem adequately explanatory. Crime rates soared in the United States during the 1960s even though poverty and discrimination were declining. These opposing trends and the correlative changes in public opinion toward crime left criminologists beached. They had long derided deterrence as an objective of criminal law, believing that the threat of punishment does not deter.[33] Instead, they had advocated rehabilitation as the proper objective of punishment. It is now pretty clear that punishment does deter[34] (a fact that criminologists missed not only because of their preconceptions, but also because their empirical methods were primitive) and that rehabilitation is not a feasible objective of a criminal justice system.[35] The emphasis that traditional criminology placed on social factors in crime, its disparagement of deterrence, and its promotion of rehabilitation were related. Rehabilitation tries to change the criminal's social environment; deterrence ignores that environment, viewing the main purpose of criminal punishment as being that of fixing a "price" for crime. Crime rates are now falling, but the fall appears to be due to harsh punishment and aggressive policing rather than to anything that criminologists, with the

31. This is acknowledged by leading practitioners of American sociology of law. Lawrence M. Friedman, in his article "The Law and Society Movement," 38 *Stanford Law Review* 763, 778 (1986), describes the law and society movement—the principal aegis of American sociology of law—as a "wallflower." See also David M. Trubek, "Back to the Future: The Short, Happy Life of the Law and Society Movement," 18 *Florida State University Law Review* 4, 47–49, 55 (1990). Marc Galanter and Mark Alan Edwards, "Introduction: The Path of the Law Ands," 1997 *Wisconsin Law Review* 375, while considerably more upbeat about the law and society movement, do not assign any distinctive role to sociology within it. See id. at 378–379. For a good introduction to the law and society literature, see *The Law and Society Reader* (Richard L. Abel ed. 1995).

32. See Richard A. Posner, "The Sociology of the Sociology of Law: A View from Economics," 2 *European Journal of Law and Economics* 265 (1995).

33. See, for example, Edwin H. Sutherland, *Principles of Criminology* 288–290, 314–315, and ch. 29 (5th ed., revised by Donald R. Cressey, 1955).

34. See, for example, Daryl A. Hellman and Neil O. Alper, *Economics of Crime: Theory and Practice* (2d ed. 1990).

35. See, for example, Robert Martinson, "What Works? Questions and Answers about Prison Reform," *Public Interest,* Spring 1974, 22. "It is discouraging . . . to report that approximately two-thirds of convicted criminals can be expected to commit new crimes within three to five years of their previous offense, regardless of the treatment program or type of incarceration imposed on convicted criminals." Joyce S. Sterling, "The State of American Sociology of Law," in *Developing Sociology of Law: A World-Wide Documentary Enquiry* 805, 811 (Vincenzo Ferrari ed. 1990).

important exception of James Q. Wilson, have been advocating. It is one of many instances in which sociology has lost a round to economics, economists having emphasized the importance of punishment to the control of crime. Yet the most recent wave of economic writing on crime is paying a lot of attention to social factors,[36] one of several signs of the possible convergence of the two disciplines.

The debacle of criminology has contributed to the impression that sociology is a beleaguered discipline. In the United States at least, the eclipse of sociology is undeniable. Student enrollments have fallen; departments have been closed; the field is even said to be "decomposing."[37] But the academic sickness of sociology may be as misleading as the (comparative) academic health of moral philosophy. It would be a big mistake to write off sociology of law on the basis of the failures of criminology, for sociologists of law have made incontestably valuable and important contributions in other areas. One is the study of the legal profession itself. Although the work here is primarily classificatory and descriptive, with emphasis on ethnic and class differences between elite and marginal practitioners, it contains a critical dimension, as in the work of Richard Abel,[38] and important studies of the compensation structure of the modern law firm and of changes in the economic organization of the legal services industry.[39]

Another area in which sociologists of law have made important contributions is the litigation process, with particular emphasis on trial courts,[40]

36. See, for example, Edward L. Glaeser, Bruce Sacerdote, and José A. Scheinkman, "Crime and Social Interactions," 111 *Quarterly Journal of Economics* 508 (1996); Neal Kumar Katyal, "Deterrence's Difficulty," 95 *Michigan Law Review* 2385 (1997); Dan M. Kahan, "Between Economics and Sociology: The New Path of Deterrence," 95 *Michigan Law Review* 2477 (1997).

37. Anthony Giddens, *In Defence of Sociology: Essays, Interpretations and Rejoinders* 2 (1996). The reference is to Irving Louis Horowitz, *The Decomposition of Sociology* (1994).

38. See, for example, Richard L. Abel, *American Lawyers* (1989). The descriptive literature is illustrated by Austin Sarat and William L. F. Felstiner, "Lawyers and Legal Consciousness: Law Talk in the Divorce Lawyer's Office," 98 *Yale Law Journal* 1663 (1989).

39. See, for example, Marc Galanter and Thomas Palay, *Tournament of Lawyers: The Transformation of the Big Law Firm* (1991). See also Robert L. Nelson, *Partners with Power: The Social Transformation of the Large Law Firm* (1988). Some of the most important contributions have been made by sociologists who are not lawyers and do not specialize in law, such as Andrew Abbott, whose study of the professions I cited at the beginning of this chapter (note 2 above), and Edward Laumann. See John P. Heinz and Edward O. Laumann, *Chicago Lawyers: The Social Structure of the Bar* (1982).

40. See, for example, Frank Munger, "Trial Courts and Social Change: The Evolution of a Field of Study," 24 *Law and Society Review* 217 (1990); Lawrence M. Friedman, "Opening the Time Capsule: A Progress Report on Studies of Courts over Time," 24 *Law and Society Review* 229 (1990). Conventional legal theorists, preoccupied as they are with legal doctrine, focus on appellate courts, where that doctrine is fashioned.

the role of the jury,[41] litigiousness,[42] the role of lawyers in the process[43] (and here the two areas of study that I have mentioned merge), and the alleged "litigation explosion." Regarding the last, sociologists have played their traditional debunking role[44] by pointing out that litigation rates were actually higher in eighteenth-century America than they are today and that the sharp growth in federal-court filings in recent decades has probably not been matched by the experience in the state courts, even though about 90 percent of all litigation in this country takes place in state rather than federal courts.[45]

Marc Galanter has pointed to the asymmetry in many areas of law (for example, accident cases against railroads) between plaintiffs and defendants. The former are "one-shot" litigants with no interest in the development of doctrine or the overall success of plaintiffs. The latter are "repeat players" who have a higher stake in winning because they anticipate future such cases if they lose this one. Their higher stake causes them to invest more in winning, and this skews case outcomes in their favor.[46] Sociologists have also conducted a number of useful studies of the settlement process[47] and of alternatives to law for resolving disputes,[48] and a few

41. See, for example, Shari Seidman Diamond and Jonathan D. Casper, "Blindfolding the Jury to Verdict Consequences: Damages, Experts, and the Civil Jury," 26 *Law and Society Review* 513 (1992); Richard O. Lempert, "Uncovering 'Nondiscernible' Differences: Empirical Research and the Jury-Size Cases," 73 *Michigan Law Review* 643 (1975).

42. For an exemplary study, see Sally Engle Merry, *Getting Justice and Getting Even: Legal Consciousness among Working-Class Americans* (1990). Although Merry is a professor of anthropology rather than of sociology and cites (along with much legal sociology) works of legal anthropology by John Comaroff, Sally Humphreys, Laura Nader, and others, it would take a discerning reader indeed to distinguish what she does from sociology of law.

43. See, for example, Herbert M. Kritzker, *The Justice Broker: Lawyers and Ordinary Litigation* (1990).

44. See Peter L. Berger, *Invitation to Sociology: A Humanistic Perspective* 38 (1963).

45. See, for example, Marc Galanter, "The Day after the Litigation Explosion," 46 *Maryland Law Review* 3 (1986); Sterling, note 35 above, at 822. I say "probably" because it is only in recent years that state-court statistics have approached adequacy—and the recent statistics suggest that, at least since the mid-1980s, state-court litigation has been growing faster that federal-court litigation. Compare Richard A. Posner, *The Federal Courts: Challenge and Reform* 60–61 (1996) (tab. 3.2), with Court Statistics Project Staff, *State Court Caseload Statistics: Annual Report 1986* 155, 191–193, 276 (State Justice Institute, 1988) (tabs. 7, 12), and Court Statistics Project Staff, *State Court Caseload Statistics: Annual Report 1996* 138, 171–174 (State Justice Institute, 1997) (tabs. 7, 12).

46. Marc Galanter, "Why the 'Haves' Come Out Ahead: Speculation on the Limits of Legal Change," 9 *Law and Society Review* 95 (1974).

47. See Marc Galanter and Mia Cahill, "'Most Cases Settle': Judicial Promotion and Regulation of Settlements," 46 *Stanford Law Review* 1339 (1994), and studies cited there.

48. An example is *No Access to Law: Alternatives to the American Judicial System* (Laura Nader ed. 1980).

studies of citation patterns in appellate opinions.[49] The sociologist's interest in the legal profession and in the litigation process join in studies of how the outlook and self-interest of the profession influence that process[50] and in studies of the costs of litigation.[51]

Valuable work has been done in other areas of sociology of law as well—including a famous article on the law in action, which finds that businesspeople place relatively little reliance on legal remedies for obtaining compliance with contracts;[52] a study of the settlement practices of liability insurance companies;[53] and a study of the common law of privacy and of other common law doctrines relating to the control of information.[54] What is particularly noteworthy about the sociology of law taken as a whole is its empirical cast and its refusal to take for granted that legal doctrines track legal practices. These are perspectives sorely lacking both in conventional legal analysis and in highfalutin constitutional and jurisprudential theorizing. Sociology of law is refreshingly down to earth.

There is more that sociologists can do to illuminate the legal system. They are experts on social class; and it is doubtful that the savagery with which the United States is attempting to extirpate a seemingly arbitrary subset of mind-altering drugs (cocaine and LSD, but not Prozac; heroin, but not Valium; marijuana, but not cigarettes or alcohol; benzedrine, but not caffeine) can be explained without reference to social class. As I noted in Chapter 2, it is mainly the mind-altering drugs favored by blacks and by members of the "counterculture" that have been criminalized.

Differences in social class—between offender and victim, plaintiff and defendant, judge and litigants, and judge and jurors—may also explain

49. See, for example, Lawrence M. Friedman et al., "State Supreme Courts: A Century of Style and Citation," 33 *Stanford Law Review* 773 (1981); David J. Walsh, "On the Meaning and Pattern of Legal Citations: Evidence from State Wrongful Discharge Precedent Cases," 31 *Law and Society Review* 337 (1997).

50. For example, John Griffiths, "What Do Dutch Lawyers Actually Do in Divorce Cases?" 20 *Law and Society Review* 135 (1986).

51. For example, David M. Trubek et al., "The Costs of Ordinary Litigation," 31 *UCLA Law Review* 72 (1983).

52. Stewart Macaulay, "Non-Contractual Relations in Business: A Preliminary Study," 28 *American Sociological Review* 55 (1963). The subsequent, rather sparse literature is discussed in Peter Vincent-Jones, "Contract and Business Transactions: A Socio-Legal Analysis," 16 *Journal of Law and Society* 166 (1989).

53. H. Laurence Ross, *Settled out of Court: The Social Process of Insurance Claims Adjustments* (2d ed. 1980). For a synthesis of "law in action" research, see Donald Black, *Sociological Justice* (1989). See also Black, *The Behavior of Law* (1976).

54. Kim Lane Scheppele, *Legal Secrets: Equality and Efficiency in the Common Law* (1988).

some of the divergences between the ideals of formal justice and the actual behavior of the American legal system.[55] Blacks who kill whites are more likely to be sentenced to death than blacks who kill blacks or whites who kill blacks; and in general murderers whose victims are above them in the social hierarchy are likely to be punished more severely than murderers whose victims are below them in that hierarchy.[56] The explanation for the pattern may ultimately be economic: wealthier people can hire better lawyers (including lawyers retained by the families of victims to assure a vigorous prosecution of the offender), and juries even in criminal cases may value the lives of victims in part at least by reference to their economic value.[57] The propensity of the drug enforcement authorities to prosecute blacks disproportionately may likewise have an economic explanation. Blacks tend to be concentrated in the street-sale end of the business, and street sellers are easier to catch, so the authorities can maximize their output of convictions by concentrating on them.[58]

These examples bring out the important point that economic theory, and the empirical methods that economists have honed to a high degree of precision, should be regarded as tools available for the use of sociologists of law, just as economists, and economically minded lawyers, are now borrowing topics, concepts, perspectives, insights, data, and even empirical methods (mainly the large-scale survey) from sociologists.[59] This borrowing has produced an important hybrid scholarship illustrated by Robert Ellickson's field study of the difference between legal norms and the norms that actually guide behavior.[60] I shall end this chapter with an

55. See Black, *Sociological Justice*, note 53 above, at 4–19, and studies cited there; also Gary LaFree and Christine Rack, "The Effects of Participants' Ethnicity and Gender on Monetary Outcomes in Mediated and Adjudicated Cases," 30 *Law and Society Review* 767 (1996).

56. Black, *Sociological Justice*, note 53 above, at 9–13.

57. In the calculation of damages for loss of earnings in civil cases, this valuation is explicit.

58. See Eric E. Sterling, "The Sentencing Boomerang: Drug Prohibition Politics and Reform," 40 *Villanova Law Review* 383 (1995).

59. On the growing interaction between sociology of law and law and economics, see Symposium, *Law and Society and Law and Economics: Common Ground, Irreconcilable Differences, New Directions*, 1997 *Wisconsin Law Review* 37. The tensions between the parent disciplines (sociology and economics) are explored in *Economics and Sociology* (Richard Swedberg ed. 1990), a fascinating collection of interviews with economists and sociologists. On the growing though as yet limited influence of economics on sociology, see James N. Baron and Michael T. Hannan, "The Impact of Economics on Contemporary Sociology," 32 *Journal of Economic Literature* 1111 (1994).

60. Robert C. Ellickson, *Order without Law: How Neighbors Settle Disputes* (1991). Similar studies include Lisa Bernstein, "Opting Out of the Legal System: Extralegal Contractual Relations in the Diamond Industry," 21 *Journal of Legal Studies* 115 (1992); Peter H. Huang and Ho-Mou Wu, "More Order without More Law: A Theory of Social Norms and Organizational Cultures," 10 *Journal of*

example of how economic and sociological insights can be combined to improve our understanding of legal phenomena.

But I wish first to counter the cynical reaction that a suggestion to place greater emphasis on empirical work is bound to engender in some quarters of the legal profession. I have heard it said of empirical research on the legal system that there are just two types of empirical questions about law: questions not worth asking and questions impossible to answer. People who say this are probably thinking of the failed manifestos of the legal realists and of the fact that empirical researchers in law occupy a lower rank in the academic pecking order than theorists and even doctrinalists. These cynics are ignorant of the amount of good empirical research being done nowadays, scattered though it is over the vastness that is the modern American legal system, and of the increased pace at which it is being done, in part because of the greater availability and retrievability of data (the Internet is a factor here) and the falling cost of computerized data storage and analysis.[61] I could not, without greatly increasing the length of this book, describe and evaluate the many empirical studies that now exist of major facets of the legal system. But I can describe one of my own studies to give the reader a flavor of the current work.

It is commonly supposed that the United States is an unusually litigious society, especially in comparison to England, even though the legal systems of the two countries are similar in the areas such as tort, contract, and criminal law that generate the most cases. And indeed the per capita number of tort suits filed in the United States is almost three times the number in England.[62] Within the United States, the variance is even greater, ranging from 97.2 suits per 100,000 population in North Dakota to 1,070.5 in Massachusetts, with England coming in at 133.5. These differences are much greater than any differences in accident rates or costs

---

Law, Economics, and Organization 390 (1994); Janet T. Landa, *Trust, Ethnicity, and Identity: Beyond the New Institutional Economics of Ethnic Trading Networks, Contract Law, and Gift-Exchange* (1994); Eric A. Posner, "The Regulation of Groups: The Influence of Legal and Nonlegal Sanctions," 63 *University of Chicago Law Review* 133 (1996).

61. For an example of the sort of empirical study that could not have been conducted before the modern era of computer technology, see William M. Landes, Lawrence Lessig, and Michael E. Solimine, "Judicial Influence: A Citation Analysis of Federal Courts of Appeals Judges," *Journal of Legal Studies* (1998), a study that applies the methodology of statistical inference to hundreds of thousands of citations to judicial opinions.

62. For the sources of the statistics used in this study, see Richard A. Posner, "Explaining the Variance in the Number of Tort Suits across U.S. States and between the United States and England," 26 *Journal of Legal Studies* 477 (1997). Unfortunately I had data for only 34 states (plus the District of

of suit, so it is tempting to ascribe them to cultural factors. If those are the decisive factors, there is probably very little that can be done to reduce the amount of litigation and we might as well stop wringing our hands over our litigiousness. But maybe the conclusion is premature. Maybe, despite appearances, litigation—even tort litigation, an emotional class of cases because most of them arise out of personal injuries—is driven more by incentives than by emotion or character. If so, it may be possible to use quantitative variables to explain the variance in the rate of tort litigation across states and even nations. That is what I shall try to do here: explain variance in tort litigation on the basis of quantifiable variables, both economic and sociological—thus illustrating the complementarity of the economic and sociological approaches and the power of social science to illuminate baffling issues about the legal system.

I begin with a description of the independent variables used in the study. (The dependent variable is the per capita rate of tort filings.)

The rate of accidental deaths in a state. This is a proxy for the figure of real interest, the number of accidents in which the injury was serious (whether or not death resulted) and the injurer is likely to have been at fault. Every such accident is a potential tort suit. But it is very difficult to obtain reliable, comparable data on the number of serious accidents. So in my reduced-form regression[63] I substitute for the rate of accidental deaths variables likely to be correlated with the accident rate: per capita alcohol consumption, the male-female ratio, and the percentages of the population that are under 25 years of age and over 64. Alcohol is a significant factor in many accidents; men are more dangerous drivers than women; and the curve that relates auto accidents to age is U-shaped—both young and old drivers contribute disproportionately to the accident rate.[64]

The degree to which the state is urbanized. Suits are more likely in an urban setting for two reasons. The first is that the parties to accidents are more likely to be strangers, which reduces the likelihood of their being able to resolve their dispute through informal means (substitutes for the

---

Columbia). U.S. data are for 1985–1994, English for 1977–1986, but a comparison of data for the same year (1986) yields the same general picture.

63. A "reduced-form regression" is a regression equation (a statistical method for identifying correlations) in which the only independent (explanatory) variables that are included are those that can be assumed not to have been influenced by the dependent variable, that is, the variable that one is trying to explain—tort litigation rates in this instance.

64. Richard A. Posner, *Aging and Old Age* 122–126 (1995).

courts), without recourse to litigation. The second is that lawyers are disproportionately concentrated in urban areas.[65] This concentration should reduce the search costs and, through greater competition among lawyers, the quality-adjusted price of legal representation.

Population density (number of people per square mile in the state). This is both a proxy for search costs, one that might be important in a relatively nonurbanized but nonetheless densely populated state, and an index to the likelihood of litigation. Most accidental encounters in a densely populated even if not highly urbanized state are between strangers. One's friends and relatives are a more or less fixed number, and hence are a smaller percentage of potential interactors the denser the population of one's locale. A dense population also makes for a higher frequency of interactions, some fraction of which result in injuries.

Average years of education. On the one hand, an increase in this variable could be expected to cause a higher litigation rate because educated people are more likely to be aware of their legal rights and more comfortable dealing with the professionals of the legal system—lawyers and judges. On the other hand, educated people may be more adept at avoiding both injuring and being injured. But because the second effect of education should be picked up by my first variable, the rate of accidental deaths, I would expect the sign of this variable to be positive.

Average household income. A higher average income increases the cost of accidents to accident victims and hence the expected benefits of suits. But by the same token it increases the demand for safety; it also increases the time cost of going to court. So the sign of this variable is indeterminate a priori.

Liability insurance coverage. Injurers who do not have liability insurance are unlikely to be worth suing. And liability insurance has a moral-hazard effect: the marginal cost of causing injury is less for a person who carries liability insurance.

Number of lawyers per capita. As mentioned earlier, the more lawyers there are relative to the population, the lower the cost of search by potential claimants, and also the lower the real price of legal representation, because of greater competition.

65. In 1980 (the most recent year for which the data are available), the ratio of lawyers to population was 1:462 in Standard Metropolitan Statistical Areas and 1:899 in other areas. Barbara A. Curran et al., *The Lawyer Statistical Report: A Statistical Profile of the U.S. Legal Profession in the 1980s* 243–244 (1985).

Cultural factors. Some of the regressions include regional dummy variables[66] to test for cultural differences among states.[67]

There are two problems with the independent variables. First, for three of them—accidental deaths, insurance coverage, and number of lawyers— the likely direction of causation is two-way rather than one-way. A high level of tort litigation might cause a reduction in the number of accidents and accidental deaths, an increase in the amount of insurance coverage (which might however be offset by a reduction in the demand for insurance as a result of the fall in the number of accidents), and, most obviously, an increase in the number of lawyers. Second, a number of the independent variables are highly correlated with each other. The inclusion of highly correlated variables in the same regression equation is likely to obscure any significant correlations.

I make a first stab at solving the first problem—bidirectional causality—by running a reduced-form regression (Table 2) that leaves out the three variables that may be effects as well as causes of the number of tort filings and replaces one of them (the accidental-death rate) with variables that while likely to be correlated with the excluded variable are highly unlikely to be causes of the number of tort filings. (Recall that these are alcohol consumption, male-female ratio, and age distribution.) Table 1 regresses the number of tort filings per capita per state on all the independent variables except those substituted in Table 2 for the accidental-death rate. Table 3 uses a different method of correcting for the problem of bidirectionality of causation.[68]

In Table 1 the sign of the coefficient of the accidental-death variable is significant at the conventional 5 percent level,[69] and in the predicted direction (positive). The sign of the urbanization variable is significant at the 10 percent level (barely missing significance at the 5 percent level),

66. A dummy variable is a variable that takes a value of either 1 or 0. So, for example, a dummy variable for the Northeast would take a value of 1 if the suit was brought in a northeastern state and a value of 0 otherwise.

67. I experimented with using, in lieu of regional dummy variables, ethnic-origin variables (for example, the percentage of a state's population that was of Northern European origin), but they turned out to have no significant effect on the results.

68. Most of the variables vary little over time and those that are based on 1990 census data do not vary at all, so in Tables 1 and 2 I averaged the observations for each variable, producing one observation for each variable for each state. As a result, the regressions in these tables are based on 34 observations.

69. That is, it has a t-statistic the absolute value of which exceeds 1.96. The meaning of significant at the 5 percent level is that there is only a 5 percent probability that the correlation (positive or negative) would have the same sign even if the hypothesis being tested is false.

Table 1 Regression of tort filings (R^2 = .7689)

Independent variable	Coefficient (t-stat in parentheses)
Income	0.392
	(0.484)
Education	−10.212
	(−1.602)
% urban	0.017
	(1.898)
Population density	0.105
	(1.133)
Accidental-death rate	1.385
	(2.335)
Liability insurance coverage	0.467
	(1.160)
Lawyers/100,000	0.228
	(1.238)
West	−0.490
	(−1.730)
South	−0.711
	(−2.806)
Northeast	*
Midwest	−0.386
	(−1.620)
Constant	17.412
	(1.250)

and again in the predicted direction. The southern regional dummy is significant at the 5 percent level and negative, implying that, other things being equal, Southerners are less likely to sue than Northeasterners.[70]

In the reduced-form regression, Table 2, the coefficient of the urbanization variable is significant in the predicted direction, as is the coefficient of the consumption-of-alcohol variable. Two other variables, education and the male-female ratio, also have statistically significant coefficients. The negative sign of the education variable implies that, other things being equal, there are fewer tort filings in states in which the population is highly educated than in states in which it is not. This may mean only that the effect of education in reducing the risk of injury (an effect that may not be wholly captured by the alcohol, male-female, and age-distribution

70. The Northeast regional dummy is the omitted variable in Tables 2 and 3. (Omitting one of the regional dummies was required for statistical reasons; any one of the four could have been omitted.) The other regional dummies thus measure propensity to sue relative to that of Northeasterners.

Table 2 Reduced-form regression of tort filings ($R^2 = .7562$)

Independent variable	Coefficient (t-stat in parentheses)
Income	1.695
	(1.449)
Education	−13.821
	(−2.739)
% urban	0.018
	(2.104)
Population density	−0.115
	(−1.038)
Alcohol consumption	1.031
	(2.143)
Male-female ratio	−10.015
	(−2.125)
Under 25	−0.011
	(1.238)
Over 64	−0.030
	(−0.536)
West	−0.066
	(−0.196)
South	−0.278
	(−1.029)
Northeast	*
Midwest	−0.375
	(−1.634)
Constant	32.348
	(2.924)

variables) more than offsets its effect in increasing tort victims' knowledge of their rights and access to legal remedies. The negative sign on the male-female ratio is intriguing. It implies that when other factors that distinguish men from women are held constant (such as income, education, and alcohol consumption), women are more prone to institute tort litigation.

The regression results presented in these two tables suggest that there is a causal relation running from urbanization and accidents (as proxied by alcohol consumption) to tort filings. Unfortunately, these regressions cannot be used to explain the number of English tort suits and thus to compare England and the United States, a comparison that is important for exploring the impact of culture on the propensity to sue. The regional variables cannot be given a value for England because it is not a region of

Table 3 De-averaged regression of tort filings (R^2 = .7725)

Independent variable	Coefficient (t-stat in parentheses)
Income	2.054
	(4.416)
Education	−13.777
	(−3.997)
% urban	2.336
	(5.623)
Population density	−0.262
	(−3.340)
Alcohol consumption	0.727
	(2.486)
Male-female ratio	−12.268
	(−5.009)
Under 25	−2.574
	(−1.018)
Over 64	−1.555
	(−0.547)
Accidental-death rate	−0.094
	(−0.326)
Liability insurance coverage	0.423
	(2.507)
Lawyers/100,000	0.151
	(1.233)
Constant	28.425
	(3.448)

the United States, yet without them the regressions do not have sufficient power to generate meaningful predictions.

In Table 3 I try to get around this problem by deleting the regional variables, "de-averaging" the observations, and adding back the two-way variables deleted in Table 2. The de-averaging approach not only enables meaningful predictions of English tort rates but also provides at least a partial solution, alternative to the reduced-form approach, to the problem of two-way causation. With averaging over ten years, the number of lawyers, for example, may well be influenced by, as well as influencing, the number of tort suits. But when every observation is limited to one year, the possibility of such influence is much less. It is far less likely that the number of lawyers in, say, 1980 could be the result of the number of tort suits filed that year than the reverse.[71]

71. The problem of two-way causation is not eliminated, because the value of a variable in a particular year may be highly correlated with its value in previous years; it is merely reduced.

Table 3 explains slightly more of the variance in the dependent variable than the previous equations do and yields some interestingly different results. Income and insurance coverage are now positively and significantly related to the number of tort suits, along with urbanization and alcohol consumption; population density and education are negatively and significantly related to that number; and the accidental-death rate, although positively related to the number of suits, is not significant. The significant negative coefficients of the population-density and education variables, like that of the male-female ratio, is unexplained by my analysis. Nevertheless, it is noteworthy that so much of the variance in the data set (a considerable variance, for recall that the per capita tort litigation rate is more than ten times as high in the most litigious state than in the least litigious one) can be explained without recourse to legal or general cultural variables.

Since all the independent variables in Table 3 can be estimated for England, the table can be used to predict the number of tort suits filed annually in England during the period for which I have data. The predicted number is a surprisingly low 29, compared to the actual number of 133.5. The implication is that factors not reflected in Table 3, which could be features of the legal or general culture of England, are *raising* rather than, as one might expect from the different reputations of the United States and England for litigiousness, lowering the number of tort suits. England has one of the lowest per capita tort suit filing rates of any of the jurisdictions in my study (all the other jurisdictions being either U.S. states or the District of Columbia), so it is natural to suppose that this unexpected result may simply reflect the inability of the study to predict the number of tort suits in jurisdictions that have much lower than average numbers. But this is not correct. The predicted values for the five least litigious states in my sample are pretty close to their actual values, or at least much closer than the predicted and average values for England: North Dakota (104.3 predicted, 97.2 actual); Utah (163.2/105.8); Wyoming (158.3/130.7); North Carolina (169.7/136.3); Indiana (247.5/158.8).

Which variables are driving down the predicted number of English suits? Table 4 shows the contribution, in percentages, of each independent variable in Table 3 to the difference between the predicted number of U.S. tort suits (205.5 when Table 3 is used to predict that number) and the predicted number of English tort suits (29).[72] The higher average income

---

72. The figures in the right-hand column of Table 3 sum to 100 percent.

Table 4 Contribution of variables to difference between the U.S. and English
predicted tort filings rates (in natural
logarithms)

Independent variable	Contribution (%)
Income	73.2
Education	−46.8
% urban	25.8
Population density	12.0
Alcohol consumption	10.3
Male-female ratio	−4.5
Under 25	−9.1
Over 64	2.0
Accidental-death rate	−1.8
Liability insurance coverage	29.1
Lawyers/100,000	9.8
Constant	0.0

in the United States is the most important contributor to the higher predicted U.S. litigation rate. But urbanization and insurance coverage are also important contributors, while the higher level of education in the United States tugs the other way because of the negative sign of the education variable.

The prediction for England, with its implication that cultural factors are making the English *more* litigious than Americans, should be taken with a grain of salt, in view of the many limitations of my study and the many reasons to believe that the legal and social traditions of England are far less congenial to litigation as a mode of social control than traditions in the United States.[73] Yet it is at least conceivable that national traditions, rather than having independent causal significance, reflect the material factors that my study suggests make tort litigation a more or less inviting method of resolving legal disputes and controlling the accident rate. The possibility that cultural factors bearing on litigation, like some of the

73. See Richard A. Posner, *Law and Legal Theory in England and America*, lect. 3 (1996).

moral behaviors discussed in Chapter 1, may be epiphenomenal is at least worth exploring. And my findings regarding the role of quantifiable factors in explaining variance in tort filing rates across states of the United States—including the eminently sociological factor of urbanization—seem pretty reliable. Taken as a whole the study suggests the feasibility and fruitfulness of an approach to understanding the legal system that employs the methods of social science. But I do not want to leave the impression that I think that quantitative analysis is the only worthwhile type of empiricism. I do not. It is merely the most distinctive method of social science research—and the one most neglected by legal scholars.

Chapter 4

Pragmatism

The Pragmatic Approach to Law

The key to realizing the promise of the real professionalism sketched in the preceding chapter is pragmatism, but in a distinctly low-key sense of the word—and in particular *not* the sense in which it is used to name a philosophical position.[1] Philosophical pragmatists and their opponents go at each other hammer and tongs over such questions as whether language reflects reality, whether free will is compatible with a scientific outlook, and whether such questions are even meaningful.[2] I am not interested in such issues. I am interested in pragmatism as a disposition to ground policy judgments on facts and consequences rather than on conceptualisms and generalities.

Philosophical pragmatism and pragmatic adjudication are not completely unrelated. The tendency of most philosophical speculation—and it is what makes philosophy, despite its remoteness from quotidian concerns, a proper staple of college education in a liberal society—is to shake up a person's presuppositions. A judge or lawyer who reads philosophy or

---

1. The principal meanings of "pragmatism" are usefully distinguished in Matthew H. Kramer, "The Philosopher-Judge: Some Friendly Criticisms of Richard Posner's Jurisprudence," 59 *Modern Law Review* 465, 475–478 (1996): "Metaphysical or philosophical pragmatism is a relativist position which denies that knowledge can be grounded on absolute foundations. Methodological or intellectual pragmatism is a position that attaches great importance to lively debate and open-mindedness and flexibility in the sciences, the humanities and the arts. Political pragmatism is a position that attaches great importance to civil liberties and to tolerance and to flexible experimentation in the discussions and institutions that shape the arrangements of human intercourse . . . [T]hese three modes of pragmatism do not entail one another."

2. See, for example, *Rorty and Pragmatism: The Philosopher Responds to His Critics* (Herman J. Saatkamp, Jr., ed. 1995).

(more likely) is reminded of the reading he did as a student may feel the presuppositions that define his professional culture shift beneath him. Philosophy, especially the philosophy of pragmatism, incites doubt, and doubt incites inquiry, making a judge less of a dogmatic, more of a pragmatic or at least open-minded, adjudicator.

More important (because the magnitude of the effect just described may well be slight) is the fact that philosophy, theology, and law have parallel conceptual structures. Christian theology was heavily influenced by Greek and Roman philosophy, and Western law by Christianity, and the orthodox versions of the three systems of thought have similar views on scientific and moral realism, objectivity, free will, responsibility, intentionality, interpretation, authority, and mind-body dualism. A challenge to any of the systems is a challenge to all three. Pragmatism in its role as skeptical challenger of orthodox philosophy encourages a skeptical view of the foundations of orthodox law because of the many parallels between orthodox law and orthodox philosophy. That is why Richard Rorty, who rarely discusses legal issues, is cited frequently in law reviews. Philosophical pragmatism does not dictate legal pragmatism or any other jurisprudential stance. But it may play a paternal and enabling role in relation to pragmatic approaches to law. To these I now turn, discussing first the pragmatic approach to administrative law—an approach that has made great strides in the academy but has not yet won over many judges—and then the pragmatic approach to adjudication.

Pragmatic Scholarship: The Case of Administrative Law

I could make life easier for myself by using as my example of the successes of pragmatic legal scholarship antitrust law rather than administrative law. The Sherman Act was enacted in 1890, at a time when economists' understanding of monopoly and competition was limited and communication between economists and lawyers even more so. The early judicial decisions interpreting the Sherman (and later the Clayton) Act exhibited shafts of insight amidst clouds of confusion. The very goal of antitrust policy was obscure and contested—was it to promote economic efficiency or to reduce the power of big business? It is hard to do both. By the 1940s, however, the courts had devised a reasonably successful anticartel policy— the famous "per se" rule of illegality; but they remained deeply confused about mergers, monopolies, and "vertical" restrictions (for example, resale price maintenance and other restrictions on dealers and other distributors). The Warren Court, populist in antitrust matters, deepened the confusion, yet at times displayed receptivity to economic analysis of antitrust issues.[3] Beginning around 1970, increased consensus and sophistication in the economic analysis of antitrust encouraged a more sophisticated judicial approach to antitrust law[4] and, beginning in the 1980s, coincided with a more positive public attitude toward capitalism. The "big business" chimera was largely forgotten. Efficiency became the only generally accepted goal of antitrust.[5] More judges and lawyers learned the rudiments of antitrust economics, and antitrust economists became more effective as consultants and expert witnesses. It is fair to say that at the beginning of its second century antitrust law has become a branch of applied economics, has achieved a high degree of rationality and predictability, and is a success story of which all branches of the law and allied disciplines can be proud.[6]

The evolution of administrative law in the direction of rationality and interdisciplinarity, unlike that of antitrust law, is far from complete. The two systems of law began in this country at about the same time, the end of the nineteenth century. But many of the problems of administrative law have an eighteenth-century origin. The Constitution had established a system of lawmaking that was designed for a small government of circumscribed powers. An essentially three-headed legislature—Senate, House of Representatives, and President—would enact statutes, but not many, because of the transaction costs of tricameralist legislating. A tiny judiciary would make additional law by interpretation and by common law rulemaking. But it would not make much law, hampered as it would be by the informational, remedial, legitimacy, and, again, transaction-cost limitations of courts.

I emphasize transaction costs as impediments to ambitious lawmaking because enlarging a legislature increases the costs of reaching agreement and enlarging a court system increases the costs of maintaining consistency and direction. You cannot have big government—the government that tries to do more than secure the nightwatchman state—with just

3. For example, in United States v. Philadelphia National Bank, 374 U.S. 321 (1963).

4. See, for example, Continental T.V., Inc. v. GTE Sylvania Inc., 433 U.S. 36 (1977).

5. See, for example, Broadcast Music, Inc. v. Columbia Broadcasting System, Inc., 441 U.S. 1, 19–20 (1979); Reiter v. Sonotone Corp., 442 U.S. 330, 343 (1979); Matsushita Electric Industrial Co. v. Zenith Radio Co., 475 U.S. 574 (1986); State Oil Co. v. Khan, 118 S. Ct. 275 (1997).

6. Not all economists would agree with this rosy picture. For a pessimistic view, though one that relies primarily on old studies and on new studies of old cases, see *The Causes and Consequences of Antitrust: The Public-Choice Perspective* (Fred S. McChesney and William F. Shughart II eds. 1995).

courts and legislatures. So when the demand for a larger federal government arose in the late nineteenth and early twentieth century, the constitutional mold had to be broken and the administrative state invented. Opponents of big government, emphasizing the quasi-judicial powers of agencies, pointed to the constitutional illegitimacy and political menace of an administrative state that would grab power from the courts. Supporters of big government sought to allay these concerns by depicting administrative agencies as arenas for the deployment of neutral expertise. Indeed, supporters turned the tables on opponents by noting the ideological character of the judiciary and contrasting it with the scientific neutrality to which the administrative process aspired. They claimed that the administrative process would be less, not more, political than the judicial process. These "Progressives," champions of technocratic public administration, triumphed with the coming of the New Deal.

The struggle that I have just sketched, which defined the first phase of academic thinking about administrative law, ended with the enactment of the Administrative Procedure Act in 1946. The Act signified the acceptance of the administrative state as a legitimate component of the federal lawmaking system, but imposed upon it procedural constraints that have made the administrative process much like the judicial. Even notice-and-comment rulemaking, the most conspicuous departure of administration from adjudication because it enables agencies to make binding rules other than as an incident to deciding cases (to make them, in short, the way legislatures make rules rather than the way common law courts do), is in practice more like litigation than it is like legislation, although the fault (if that is what it can be called) is not entirely that of the Act's draftsmen.

The Administrative Procedure Act was in part a reaction to the politicization of many of the federal administrative agencies, such as the National Labor Relations Board. The Act imparted a measure of political and ideological neutrality to administrative law, just as the Taft-Hartley Act, enacted the following year, imparted a measure of political and ideological neutrality to substantive labor law, correcting to a degree the pro-union bias of the Wagner Act. World War II had created a yearning for normalcy and, incidentally, had crushed the radical right because of its prewar defeatism and isolationism; and the war's aftermath crushed the radical left. The result of these war-induced developments was a temporary suspension of ideological conflict. This allowed administrative law to be assimilated comfortably to a post-formalist, post-realist, consensus era of American law. The focus of academic thinking shifted accordingly from the issues of politics, legitimacy, and economic policy that had dominated the earlier literature of administrative law to issues important to completing the domestication of administration as law—such issues (all closely related to each other) as where to draw the line between questions of fact, as to which judicial review was highly limited, and questions of law; how far to circumscribe agency discretion; how much consistency, care, and reasoning to require of agency decisions; how free agencies should be to consider nontraditional forms of evidence; what types of agency order should be reviewable in what type of court and according to what form of judicial procedure; and how much emphasis should be placed on the use by agencies of rulemaking, as opposed to case-by-case adjudication, to create more definite standards and thus make administrative regulation more objective and predictable.

During this period of consensus, in which Louis Jaffe, Henry Hart, and Kenneth Culp Davis were the dominant voices in administrative law scholarship, and Felix Frankfurter and Henry Friendly in judicial review of agency decisions,[7] few people bothered to ask whether the administrative agencies were accomplishing what they were supposed to accomplish, whether what they were supposed to accomplish was worthwhile, and whether the actual consequences of administrative regulation were good or bad and what the criteria of goodness or badness in regulation should be. As these were not procedural, doctrinal, or even constitutional questions, they were unlikely even to occur to lawyers—or to anyone, the more that agencies were conceived to be, and were in fact, like courts. No serious person asks whether we need courts. If agencies are just another form of judiciary, handling as it were the overload of cases that courts cannot handle either because of the sheer number or because some cases present issues that baffle judges, no one is likely to ask whether we need agencies.

When ideological strife resumed in the 1960s, the administrative state was caught up in it. On the left, Ralph Nader and his followers, building on an earlier but heretofore rather ignored literature on regulatory capture, began asking whether the agencies were the zealous protectors of the public interest that they pretended to be and whether there wasn't a need both to increase citizen involvement in the existing agencies and to expand administrative regulation into new domains, such as automobile safety.[8] On the right and eventually in the center and even the left as well, economists began to question the missions of a number of the most

---

7. The *summa theologica* of this era of administrative law scholarship is Louis L. Jaffe's 792-page treatise, *Judicial Control of Administrative Action* (1965).

8. See Jerry L. Mashaw and David L. Harfst, *The Struggle for Auto Safety*, ch. 3 (1990).

prominent federal administrative agencies.[9] They showed that much of what the agencies did, such as limiting airlines' entry into city pairs, regulating the prices of rail and truck transportation, awarding broadcast licenses in exchange for commitments to provide local programming, putting a ceiling on the price of natural gas, and even fostering unionization and trying to make advertising and labeling more informative, just was not worthwhile; the agencies were performing allocative functions in transportation, labor, advertising, communications, energy, and other important sectors of the economy that the market could perform more effectively and at lower cost. The *real* mission of the agencies, the economists showed, here converging with Nader and his academic allies such as historian Gabriel Kolko, was to cater to powerful interest groups; and no amount of procedural or operational tinkering would change the situation.

The economic critique implied that academic thinking about administrative law had missed the point by failing to understand that administrative agencies were fundamentally different from courts. Agencies belonged to the interest-group state; they were political captives and instruments; they were agents of overregulation. They could no more be improved (whether by better procedures or by better personnel) from the overall social standpoint, the standpoint of the public interest, than a private cartel or a stolen-car ring could be improved. Making them work better would simply increase the drain on society's wealth. The Naderites, in contrast, having little faith in markets, thought that agencies weren't doing enough, or were doing the wrong thing, or that we needed new and different agencies. But they agreed with the economists that the academic lawyers had missed the boat by focusing on the law on the books rather than the law in action—the actual operation and effects of administrative regulation.

The Naderite critique inspired reforms designed to make regulation more public-interested, for example by empowering citizens' groups to obtain judicial review of regulatory actions and inactions. The economic critique helped to power the deregulation movement, which has achieved some remarkable successes—though probably more as a result of fortuitous technological and economic changes than of the power of economic theory and evidence. Some agencies have been abolished, such as the Civil

9. They also produced a vast scholarly literature, which is briefly summarized, with citations to a few of the most notable studies, in Richard A. Posner, *Economic Analysis of Law* §§ 19.2–19.3 (5th ed. 1998).

Aeronautics Board, the Federal Power Commission, and the Interstate Commerce Commission. Others have become spectral, such as the Federal Trade Commission and the National Labor Relations Board. Others, notably the Federal Communications Commission and the banking agencies, have so far relaxed their grip as to become almost deregulatory agencies. Still others, including the Securities and Exchange Commission and the agencies that regulate banks and other financial intermediaries, have been marginalized by the rapid change and growing complexity of the regulated activities.

The trend toward deregulation of the American economy has been masked by the rise of agencies concerned with health and safety, such as the National Highway Transportation Safety Administration, the Department of Labor's Benefits Review Board, and the Occupational Safety and Health Administration; with environmental amenities, such as the Environmental Protection Agency; with discrimination, such as the Equal Employment Opportunity Commission; and with retirement. Less obviously protectionist than the old-line industry-specific agencies that felt the deregulatory axe, these newer programs are legacies of Naderite and other left-liberal movements that arose in the 1960s and 1970s. But at the same time the Immigration and Naturalization Service, whose principal business is deporting people, has become busier because of heavy legal and illegal immigration and the tightening of the immigration laws. As further evidence that the administrative state is not inherently left-wing, the creation of the U.S. Sentencing Commission in the 1980s with bipartisan support marked a notable expansion of administrative at the expense of judicial authority and an overall stiffening in federal criminal penalties.

So there is still plenty of administrative regulation, probably more than ever, though possibly with less aggregate impact (but who knows?). Economists have been critical of the structure and sometimes the goals of much of the new-style regulation, in particular the regulation of pollution and of job safety and health, and the prohibition of discrimination on grounds of age. Much of that regulation appears to be regressive, ineffectual, perverse, needlessly expensive, or all four at once.[10] That is not yet the consensus of legal scholars. But the success of the economic critique in so many of the older areas of regulation has induced administrative law scholars increasingly to address the merits, and not merely the procedures

10. See, for example, id., §§ 11.6–11.8, 26.4; Robert W. Crandall, *Controlling Industrial Pollution: The Economics and Politics of Clean Air* (1983); W. Kip Viscusi, *Risk by Choice: Regulating Health and Safety in the Workplace* (1983); Richard A. Posner, *Aging and Old Age,* ch. 13 (1995).

or other forms, of the new regulation. Administrative law scholarship has acquired in consequence a more substantive, a more economic, a more institutional, a more empirical, in short a more pragmatic cast. There is more interest in what works and less in the forms and formalities of the administrative process except insofar as they have consequences for the regulated activities.

The original form of the economic critique treated regulation largely as a form of cartelizing.[11] This proved a fruitful approach to industry-specific regulatory programs, such as the control of price and entry by public utility and common carrier regulation, programs antedating or created by the New Deal. This kind of regulation confers concentrated benefits on the regulated industry (and sometimes on important customer groups as well, such as the beneficiaries of regulation-mandated cross-subsidies),[12] while diffusing its costs much more broadly; and so is easy to explain by reference to interest-group pressures. Much of the newer regulation, however, exhibits the opposite pattern—diffuse benefits and concentrated costs (most environmental regulation is of this character)—and so cannot easily be assimilated to a model that is derived from cartel and interest-group theory. Instead economists and political scientists have tackled this kind of regulation with public-choice theory.[13] Public-choice theory is the application of the *general* principles of economic theory to the political arena, as distinct from the application of such specific subtheories as cartel theory or interest-group theory. Public-choice theory is nowadays heavily infused with game theory in recognition of the strategic character of the interactions that determine public policy.

The point is that cutting-edge administrative law scholarship today looks very different from what it looked like in the 1950s.[14] Indeed,

11. See, for example, George J. Stigler, "The Theory of Economic Regulation," 2 *Bell Journal of Economics and Management Science* 3 (1971), and studies cited in Posner, note 9 above, § 19.2, p. 569 n. 1.

12. See, for example, Richard A. Posner, "Taxation by Regulation," 2 *Bell Journal of Economics and Management Science* 22 (1971); Sam Peltzman, "Toward a More General Theory of Regulation," 19 *Journal of Law and Economics* 211 (1976).

13. See, for example, *Conference on the Economics and Politics of Administrative Law and Procedures,* 8 *Journal of Law, Economics, and Organization* 1 (1992); also Daniel A. Farber and Philip P. Frickey, *Law and Public Choice: A Critical Introduction* (1991), esp. intro. and ch. 1; *Symposium on the Theory of Public Choice,* 74 *Virginia Law Review* 167 (1988). For a comprehensive analysis of the competing theories of administrative regulation, see Steven P. Croley, "Theories of Regulation: Incorporating the Administrative Process," 98 *Columbia Law Review* 1 (1998).

14. As noted by a number of the contributors to *Symposium on Administrative Law,* 72 *Chicago-Kent Law Review* 951 (1997).

consistent with the supersession thesis and the experience with antitrust law, it looks a good deal less like *legal* scholarship. Consider what are the big issues in administrative law scholarship today. The biggest may be how best to regulate hazards to safety, health, and the environment, a question that has engaged the sustained and imaginative attention of such able economists as Kip Viscusi and such able lawyers as Stephen Breyer and Cass Sunstein. The cardinal findings of this literature are, first, that the law fails to distinguish sufficiently between situations in which transaction costs prevent risks to safety and health from being internalized, as in the case of pollution and other environmental degradation, and situations in which they do not, as in the case of job-related hazards. Administrative regulation is more easily justified in the first class of situations, in which transaction costs are likely to prevent the market from controlling risks to safety and health.

But, second, there may be subtle sources of market failure even where transaction costs appear to be low, as in the case of job-related hazards, which arise out of a contractual relation (employment). The adequacy of normative economics (cost-benefit analysis) to monetize nonmonetary costs such as reduced health or safety or a diminution in the number of animal species has also been questioned. And behavioral economists (really, economic psychologists) have identified quirks in human reasoning that they believe impede the ability of people to think sensibly about low-probability risks to health and safety.[15]

Third, the actual performance of the regulatory agencies in the fields of health, safety, and the environment has often been deplorable. For example, arraying the monetary values (essentially, the cost of compliance with an agency's safety directives divided by the number of lives saved by compliance) that different regulatory programs impute to a human life reveals enormous variance and irrational extremes.[16] Allowing for some differences in antecedent pain and suffering and in the age of death, death

15. See, for example, Christine Jolls, Cass Sunstein, and Richard Thaler, "A Behavioral Approach to Law and Economics," 50 *Stanford Law Review* 1471 (1998); Matthew Rabin, "Psychology and Economics," 36 *Journal of Economic Literature* 11 (1998); Cass R. Sunstein, "Behavioral Analysis of Law," 64 *University of Chicago Law Review* 1175 (1997).

16. See, for example, W. Kip Viscusi, "Regulating the Regulators," 63 *University of Chicago Law Review* 1423, 1432–1435 (1996) (tab. 1). See generally *Risk versus Risk: Tradeoffs in Protecting Health and the Environment* (John D. Graham and Jonathan Baert Wiener eds. 1995). The accuracy of the array, however, and the criticism of administrative regulation of safety and health built on it, are forcefully challenged in Lisa Heinzerling, "Regulatory Costs of Mythic Proportions," 107 *Yale Law Journal* 1981 (1998).

is death whatever the particular causal agent. The agencies that fix the value of a human life at the high end of the scale may actually be impairing human longevity. The heavy compliance costs implied by such valuations have the effect of regressive taxes, disproportionately reducing the real incomes of the poor—and income and longevity are positively correlated.[17] Correlation is not causation, but it is plausible that an increase in disposable income will, up to a point anyway, increase longevity by providing access to better health care and facilitating a healthier style of living.

The current system of environmental regulation has been criticized for inflexibility, heavy-handedness, misplaced priorities, and inefficiency. Economists have pointed out that taxing emissions in lieu of prescribing ceilings on them would obviate the need for regulatory agencies to determine the costs of compliance with environmental standards, as the would-be polluter would have an incentive to optimize the control of emissions by minimizing the sum total of its tax and compliance expenses. Environmental regulation has also been criticized for insisting that all polluting sources reduce their emissions without regard to the differing costs of pollution abatement across different sources. Congress has responded to this criticism by authorizing a system of tradable pollution permits for sulphur dioxide emissions (the cause of acid rain) by electrical utilities.[18] Each permit (called an "allowance") authorizes a utility to emit one ton of sulphur dioxide per year. The total number of allowances has been capped well below the total annual emissions of sulphur dioxide by the nation's electric utilities, so that the program will reduce the total emissions of the pollutant. But utilities are free to sell their allowances to each other, so a utility that can reduce its emissions at low cost can sell some of its allowances to a utility that would incur a high cost to reduce its own emissions, enabling the aggregate costs of sulphur dioxide abatement to be reduced without reducing the abatement—and in fact with more abatement. This example of the use of social science to improve administrative regulation illustrates the primarily institutional rather than doctrinal or even procedural character of the current reform movement. As does Stephen Breyer's proposal of a high-level federal agency to coordinate the

17. See Cass R. Sunstein, "Health-Health Tradeoffs," 63 *University of Chicago Law Review* 1533 (1996); John D. Graham, Bei-Hung Chang, and John S. Evans, "Poorer Is Riskier," 12 *Risk Analysis* 333 (1992).

18. See 42 U.S.C. §§ 7651–7651o; 58 Fed. Reg. 15634 (1993); Madison Gas & Electric Co. v. EPA, 4 F.3d 529 (7th Cir. 1993), 25 F.3d 526 (7th Cir. 1994).

risk-reduction activities of the existing agencies in an effort to iron out some of the discrepancies in their valuations of human lives and other hard-to-monetize goods.[19]

The administrative law scholarship that I have been sketching draws more on economics and political science than on law. But so does much of the best scholarship concerned with the purely procedural aspects of the administrative process, including the scope of judicial review and the distinction between rulemaking and adjudication.[20] This scholarship has exposed a significant lag in judicial thinking relative to academic. The most important administrative law decisions of the Supreme Court during this period of growing sophistication of academic thinking about administrative law include decisions authorizing pre-enforcement review of administrative rules;[21] expanding, curtailing, and then expanding again the right to attack administrative action in federal court;[22] invalidating the one-house veto of agency regulations;[23] insisting that agencies justify their about-faces;[24] squashing intrusive judicial review of agencies' procedures;[25] allowing federal criminal sentencing policies to be consigned to an administrative agency;[26] and curtailing judicial review of agencies' interpretations of the statutes that they administer.[27] The academic response to these decisions has been critical, but what is interesting is that the criticisms owe more to game theory and public choice theory than to conventional legal theory. The most influential administrative law scholars are interested in the impact of these decisions, whether on policy or on the structure of government, rather than in how they fit into a preexisting structure of legal doctrine; and for the study of consequences doctrinal analysis is useless. These scholars have pointed out, for example, that insofar as administrative agencies now exercise a substantial amount of the legisla-

19. Stephen Breyer, *Breaking the Vicious Circle: Toward Effective Risk Regulation*, ch. 3 (1993).

20. See, for example, *Conference on the Economics and Politics of Administrative Law and Procedure*, note 13 above; Emerson H. Tiller, "Controlling Policy by Controlling Process: Judicial Influence on Regulatory Decision Making," 14 *Journal of Law, Economics, and Organization* 114 (1998).

21. Abbott Laboratories v. Gardner, 387 U.S. 136 (1967).

22. Morton v. Ruiz, 415 U.S. 199 (1974); Lujan v. Defenders of Wildlife, 504 U.S. 555 (1992); Northeastern Florida Chapter v. City of Jacksonville, 508 U.S. 656 (1993).

23. Immigration & Naturalization Service v. Chadha, 462 U.S. 919 (1983).

24. Motor Vehicle Manufacturers' Association v. State Farm Mutual Automobile Insurance Co., 463 U.S. 29 (1983).

25. Vermont Yankee Nuclear Power Corp. v. Natural Resources Defense Council, Inc., 435 U.S. 519 (1978).

26. Mistretta v. United States, 488 U.S. 361 (1989).

27. Chevron U.S.A., Inc. v. Natural Resources Defense Council, Inc., 467 U.S. 837 (1984).

tive power of the United States, and insofar as these agencies are more in the control of the President than of Congress, and insofar as federal judges are more likely to enforce original legislative deals than agencies controlled by the President are, the effect of decisions such as *Chadha* and *Chevron,* which curtail federal judicial review of agency determinations, is to displace legislative power into the executive branch. This is a paradoxical result, since the authors of these decisions defend them by reference to the allocation of powers that is prescribed in the Constitution, which endeavored to lodge the legislative and executive powers in different branches except insofar as the President's veto power gives him a legislative role.

It is tempting to suggest that the law that has been most influential in the Supreme Court's administrative-law decisions is the law of unintended consequences. It is unlikely that when the Court authorized pre-enforcement judicial review of administrative rules in the *Abbott Laboratories* case, it realized that it was discouraging the use of notice and comment rulemaking because the agency would have to create an elaborate record in order to withstand that review. If judicial review were deferred until the agency asked a court to impose sanctions for a violation of the rule, a record confined to the issues presented by the enforcement proceeding could be developed on the spot as it were, rather than in advance. It is equally unlikely that the Supreme Court foresaw that its endorsement of the "hard look" doctrine in *Vermont Yankee* would slow down the administrative process with no offsetting gain in greater accuracy.[28] One wonders whether the Court has any clue to the consequences of its administrative law decisions for society. Maybe it doesn't think that consequences are any of its business.

Another concern of modern administrative law scholarship is the management of sheer volume. For example, as more and more federal judges were appointed in the 1960s and 1970s to handle a steeply rising federal judicial caseload, the number of different judges involved in federal criminal sentencing grew (even though the federal criminal caseload itself wasn't growing much). This amplified the variance in sentences, the unavoidable by-product of the traditionally uncanalized discretion of sentencing judges. So we got sentencing guidelines, which alter the relation between the federal district courts and their administrative adjuncts, the

---

28. See Stephen Breyer, "*Vermont Yankee* and the Courts' Role in the Nuclear Energy Controversy," 91 *Harvard Law Review* 1833 (1978).

federal probation service and parole commission; the U.S. Sentencing Commission is the probation service and parole commission writ large. By laying down rules for sentencing, the commission was able to centralize and rationalize the sentencing process to a degree that the courts could not have done by themselves. Sentencing is to an ineliminable degree arbitrary, and courts aren't comfortable making arbitrary determinations.

Earlier the Department of Health and Human Services had done much the same thing in its domain as the Sentencing Commission was to do with sentencing. It curtailed the discretion of the hundreds of administrative law judges who make social security disability determinations by promulgating a detailed set of largely quantitative criteria (emphasizing age and education as well as employment history and the nature and severity of the disabling condition), known as the "grid," to guide the determination of entitlements to disability benefits.[29] I have urged another response to the problem of managing volume, and that is to strengthen the appellate review process within the administrative agencies in order to reduce the burden of appellate review on the federal courts. Specifically I have urged the creation of a court of disability appeals—an interagency appellate tribunal that would review disability determinations by the Social Security Administration, the Department of Labor, and other federal agencies, with further review by the federal courts of appeals limited to determinations of issues of law.[30] The questions that these developments and proposals raise are, it should go without saying, institutional and managerial rather than doctrinal or procedural.

I do not want to leave the impression that antitrust law, and administrative law even when broadly construed to take in the whole area of administrative regulation, are the only promising areas of pragmatic legal scholarship. Most economic analysis of law is pragmatic, in the sense of trying to be usable by the legal profession, rather than doctrinaire or abstract; it has had dramatic effects on legal practice in fields as different as securities law and family law;[31] and lately there have been some efforts explicitly to mix pragmatism and economics in approaching legal issues.[32]

29. See Heckler v. Campbell, 461 U.S. 458 (1983).

30. Richard A. Posner, *The Federal Courts: Challenge and Reform* 266–267 (1996).

31. For textbook-treatise coverage, see Posner, note 9 above.

32. See Thomas F. Cotter, "Pragmatism, Economics, and the Droit Moral," 76 *North Carolina Law Review* 1 (1997); Cotter, "Legal Pragmatism and the Law and Economics Movement," 84 *Georgetown Law Journal* 2071 (1996).

Pragmatic Adjudication Defined, Distinguished from Positivist Adjudication, and Illustrated

WHAT IS PRAGMATIC ADJUDICATION?

The question whether judges should be pragmatists is at once spongy and, for me at least, urgent. It is spongy because "pragmatism" is such a vague term when used to describe a style of adjudication. Among the Supreme Court Justices who have been called pragmatists are Holmes, Brandeis, Cardozo, Frankfurter, Jackson, Douglas, Brennan, Powell, Stevens, White, and Breyer.[33] Others could easily be added to the list. Among theorists of adjudication, the label has been applied not only to self-described pragmatists, of whom there are now quite a number,[34] but also to Ronald Dworkin,[35] who calls pragmatism, at least Richard Rorty's conception of pragmatism, an intellectual meal fit only for a dog[36] (and I take it he does not much like dogs). I will consider the justness of calling Dworkin a pragmatist later. Some might think the inclusion of Frankfurter in my list even more peculiar than that of Dworkin. But it is justified by Frankfurter's rejection of First Amendment absolutism, notably in the flag-salute cases, and to his espousal of a "shocks the conscience" test for substantive due process, a refined version of Holmes's "puke" test. The school of outrage, which I discussed in Chapter 2, is pragmatic in wanting to base decision in difficult constitutional cases on the untheorized "badness" of the governmental act challenged in the case, rather than on a theory that might prove that the act indeed violated the Constitution.

What makes the question whether adjudication is or should be pragmatic an urgent one for me is that my critics do not consider my theory of adjudication pragmatic at all. Jeffrey Rosen, for example, argues that my book *Overcoming Law* endorses a visceral, personalized, rule-less, freewheeling, unstructured conception of judging.[37] And well before I thought of myself as a pragmatist, I was criticized for being "a captive of a thin and unsatisfactory epistemology,"[38] which is just the sort of criticism

33. See, for example, Daniel A. Farber, "Reinventing Brandeis: Legal Pragmatism for the Twenty-First Century," 1995 *University of Illinois Law Review* 163.

34. For a list, see Richard A. Posner, *Overcoming Law* 388–389 (1995).

35. See Richard Rorty, "The Banality of Pragmatism and the Poetry of Justice," in *Pragmatism in Law and Society* 89 (Michael Brint and William Weaver eds. 1991).

36. Ronald Dworkin, "Pragmatism, Right Answers, and True Banality," in id. at 359, 360. For soberer criticism of the pragmatic approach to law, see Michel Rosenfeld, *Just Interpretations: Law between Ethics and Politics*, ch. 6 (1998).

37. Jeffrey Rosen, "Overcoming Posner," 105 *Yale Law Journal* 581, 584–596 (1995).

38. Paul M. Bator, "The Judicial Universe of Judge Richard Posner," 52 *University of Chicago Law Review* 1146, 1161 (1985).

that a purely emotive theory of judging would invite. Am I, then, backsliding? I had better try to make clear what I think pragmatic adjudication is.

I noted earlier that it cannot be equated to pragmatism the philosophical stance. It would be entirely consistent with pragmatism the philosophy *not* to want judges to be pragmatists, just as it would be entirely consistent with utilitarianism not to want judges to conceive their role as being to maximize utility. One might believe that overall utility would be maximized if judges confined themselves to the application of rules, because discretionary justice, with all the uncertainty it would create, might be thought on balance to reduce rather than to increase utility. Similarly, a pragmatist committed to judging a legal system by the results the system produced might think that the best results would be produced if the judges did not make pragmatic judgments but simply applied rules. Such a person might, by analogy to a rule utilitarian, be a "rule pragmatist."

What then is pragmatic adjudication? I do not accept Dworkin's definition: "the pragmatist thinks judges should always do the best they can for the future, in the circumstances, unchecked by any need to respect or secure consistency in principle with what other officials have done or will do."[39] That is Dworkin the polemicist speaking. But if his definition is rewritten as follows—"pragmatist judges always try to do the best they can do for the present and the future, unchecked by any felt *duty* to secure consistency in principle with what other officials have done in the past"— then it will do as a working definition of pragmatic adjudication. On this construal the difference between a pragmatic judge and a judge who is a legal positivist in the strong sense of believing that the law is a system of rules laid down by legislatures and merely applied by judges is that while the latter type of judge is centrally concerned with securing consistency with past enactments, the former is concerned with securing consistency with the past only to the extent that deciding in accordance with precedent may be the best method for producing the best results for the future.

The judicial positivist would begin and usually end with a consideration of cases, statutes, administrative regulations, and constitutional provisions—the "authorities" to which the judge must defer in accordance with the principle that judges are duty-bound to secure consistency in principle with what other officials have done in the past. If the authorities all line up in one direction, the decision of the present case is likely to be foreordained, because to go against the authorities would, unless there are com-

---

39. Ronald Dworkin, *Law's Empire* 161 (1986).

pelling reasons to do so, violate the duty to the past. The most compelling reason would be that some other line of cases had adopted a principle inconsistent with the authorities directly relevant to the present case. It would be the judges' duty, by comparing the two lines and bringing to bear other principles manifest or latent in case law, statute, or constitutional provision, to find the result in the present case that would promote or cohere with the best interpretation of the legal background as a whole.

The judicial pragmatist has different priorities. He wants to come up with the decision that will be best with regard to present and future needs. He is not uninterested in past decisions, in statutes, and so forth. Far from it. For one thing, these are repositories of knowledge, even, sometimes, of wisdom; so it would be folly to ignore them even if they had no authoritative significance. For another, a decision that destabilized the law by departing too abruptly from precedent might on balance have bad consequences. Judges often must choose between rendering substantive justice in the case at hand and maintaining the law's certainty and predictability. The trade-off—posed most starkly in cases in which the statute of limitations is asserted as a defense—will sometimes point to sacrificing substantive justice in the individual case to consistency with previous cases or with statutes or, in short, with well-founded expectations necessary to the orderly management of society's business. Another reason not to ignore the past is that often it is difficult to determine the purpose and scope of a rule without tracing the rule to its origins.

So the pragmatist judge regards precedent, statutes, and constitutional text both as sources of potentially valuable information about the likely best result in the present case and as signposts that he must be careful not to obliterate or obscure gratuitously, because people may be relying upon them. But because he sees these "authorities" merely as sources of information and as limited constraints on his freedom of decision, he does not depend on them to supply the rule of decision for the truly novel case. He looks to sources that bear directly on the wisdom of the rule that he is being asked to adopt or modify. As that is essentially Dworkin's approach despite all his talk about keeping faith with the past,[40] there is indeed a sense (though, as we shall see, only a loose one) in which he too is a pragmatist.

40. That it *is* just talk, doing no real work in Dworkin's jurisprudence, is argued in Michael W. McConnell, "The Importance of Humility in Judicial Review: A Comment on Ronald Dworkin's 'Moral Reading' of the Constitution," 65 *Fordham Law Review* 1269 (1997).

EXAMPLES

1. *Hypothetical Jurisdiction.* The Supreme Court and the lower federal courts used to take the position that if there are two possible grounds for dismissing a suit filed in federal court, one being that it is not within the court's jurisdiction and the other that the suit has no merit, and if the jurisdictional ground is unclear but the lack of merit is clear, the court can dismiss the suit on the merits without deciding whether there is jurisdiction.[41] This approach is illogical. Jurisdiction is the power to decide the merits of a claim; so a decision on the merits presupposes jurisdiction. The pragmatic justification for occasionally putting the merits cart before the jurisdictional horse begins by asking *why* federal courts have a limited jurisdiction and have made rather a fetish of keeping within its bounds. The answer is that these are extraordinarily powerful courts, and the concept of limited jurisdiction enables them both to limit the occasions for the exercise of power and to demonstrate self-restraint. As Isabel said in *Measure for Measure,* "It is excellent to have a giant's strength: but it is tyrannous to use it like a giant."[42] If, however, the lack of merit of a case is clear, a decision so holding will not enlarge federal judicial power but will merely exercise it well within its outer bounds. So in a case in which the question of jurisdiction is less clear than the lack of merit, the prudent and economical course may be to skip over the jurisdictional question and dismiss the case on the merits.

The Supreme Court, however, has now rejected (or at least curtailed) this doctrine of "hypothetical jurisdiction" in a notably unpragmatic opinion by Justice Scalia.[43] The only reason he gives (perhaps having exhausted himself in ingeniously distinguishing, rather than forthrightly overruling, the cases such as *Norton* that had seemed to establish the doctrine) is that "for a court to pronounce upon the meaning or the constitutionality of a state or federal law when it has no jurisdiction to do

41. See, for example, Norton v. Mathews, 427 U.S. 524, 532 (1976); Isby v. Bayh, 75 F.3d 1191, 1196 (7th Cir. 1996); Rekhi v. Wildwood Industries, Inc., 61 F.3d 1313, 1316 (7th Cir. 1995); United States v. Stoller, 78 F.3d 710, 715 (1st Cir. 1996).

42. Act II, scene 2, lines 792–794.

43. Steel Co. v. Citizens for a Better Environment, 118 S. Ct. 1003, 1009–1016 (1998). Actually, a rather enigmatic concurrence by Justices O'Connor and Kennedy (see id. at 1020–1021) leaves it unclear whether the doctrine has been rejected or merely confined to situations in which the reasons for reversing the usual sequence of analysis (first jurisdiction, then, if jurisdiction is confirmed, the merits) are truly compelling.

so is, by very definition, for a court to act ultra vires [beyond its power]."[44] In other words, for a court to act beyond its power is for a court to act beyond its power—a tautology unresponsive to Justice Breyer's question: "Whom does it help to have appellate judges spend their time and energy puzzling over the correct answer to an intractable jurisdictional matter, when (assuming an easy answer on the substantive merits) the same party would win or lose regardless?"[45] Breyer added that in an era of heavy caseloads, rejection of the doctrine would mean "unnecessary delay and consequent added cost"[46]—or, in other words, all costs and no benefits. The difference between these two judges over the doctrine of hypothetical jurisdiction is the difference between formalism and pragmatism.

2. *Prospective Overruling.* Sometimes a court when overruling one of its earlier decisions will announce that the new rule that it is declaring will be applied only to new suits. The implication is that the court is making new law, which could not have been anticipated, rather than rejecting the overruled precedent because the precedent violated (not applied) existing law; that, in short, the court is acting like a legislature. Prospective overruling gives legal positivists fits, because, as Patrick Devlin writes, "it crosses the Rubicon that divides the judicial and the legislative powers. It turns judges into undisguised legislators."[47]

The jurisprudential issue can be bypassed, however, by asking a practical question: Should the community's reliance on a previous decision be a weight in the balance when the court is considering whether to overrule that decision, or should reliance be removed as a factor by authorizing courts to overrule decisions prospectively? The argument for the second position is that otherwise the courts will be unduly hampered in reexamining old decisions. The argument against is that it will make them too quick to overrule previous decisions. Resolution of the debate requires striking a balance between the values of continuity and of creativity in the judicial process, which is a pragmatic task, since the legitimacy of both values is admitted. If we decide that prospective overruling destabilizes the law unduly, we can say that Devlin must be right—when judges overrule precedents, they are creating rather than applying law. But what would be the utility of this further step?

---

44. Id. at 1016.
45. Id. at 1021 (concurring opinion).
46. Id.
47. Patrick Devlin, *The Judge* 12 (1979).

3. *The* Swift *and* Erie *Doctrines.* The issue in *Swift v. Tyson*[48] and *Erie R.R. v. Tompkins*[49] was whether the "laws" of the various states should be understood to include the common law of the states or just their statutes. If the broader understanding was correct, as held in *Erie,* overruling *Swift,* then, under the statute that prescribes the rules of decision in cases that are in federal court solely because the parties are citizens of different states and not because the suit is based on federal law,[50] federal courts in such cases should follow state common law as well as state statutes. If the narrower understanding was correct, as the Supreme Court had thought in *Swift,*[51] federal courts should apply general common law not tethered to the decisional law of any state. The choice between these positions has been thought to be a choice between different concepts of law. Lawrence Lessig argues that when "the notion that the common law is found, not made, . . . changed . . . this [change] *forced* a reallocation of institutional responsibility (from federal courts to state courts). The old view [that of *Swift*] depended upon this earlier understanding of the common law; when this understanding changed, so, too, did institutional allocations *have* to change."[52] Holmes had argued against the narrow understanding on the ground that all law emanates from a sovereign, and so when state courts create common law they are doing it as delegates of the state legislature. They are not taking a stab at discovering the applicable principles of "the" common law in the sense of a body of principles that is not the emanation of any identifiable sovereign, that is instead a composite of the decisional law of many different sovereigns plus principles that federal judges might invent in the very course of deciding a diversity case.[53]

Had the judges in *Swift* and the other cases in its line believed that common law *could not* be thought of as being "law" in the same sense as statute law, their position would indeed have been conceptual rather than either doctrinal or pragmatic and therefore vulnerable to shifting conceptions of law. But if they merely believed that Congress had not intended

48. 48 U.S. (16 Pet.) 1 (1842).

49. 304 U.S. 64 (1938).

50. Rules of Decision Act, now 28 U.S.C. § 1652.

51. The holding in *Swift* was actually merely declaratory of what was already the settled practice of the federal courts.

52. Lawrence Lessig, "The Limits of Lieber," 16 *Cardozo Law Review* 2249, 2266 n. 57 (1995) (emphasis added). But see Jack Goldsmith and Steven Walt, "*Erie* and the Irrelevance of Legal Positivism," 84 *Virginia Law Review* 673 (1998), for an argument similar to mine in the text.

53. See Black & White Taxi Co. v. Brown & Yellow Taxi Co., 276 U.S. 518, 533 (1928) (dissenting opinion).

"laws" to include common law (or that its intentions were inscrutable or irrelevant) and were untroubled by the argument later made by Justice Brandeis in *Erie* that Article III of the U.S. Constitution does not authorize federal judges to create state rules of decision, or if they thought that it would be better on the whole if federal judges tried to create a uniform common law for use in diversity cases, then Holmes's argument would have fallen flat. For the issue would then have been either (or both) the "legalistic" one of the intent behind the Rules of Decision Act (and behind Article III), or the practical one of trading off the additional incentive to forum-shop, and the additional uncertainty of legal obligation, created by *Swift's* approach against the pressure that approach exerted for greater nationwide uniformity and integration of law.

4. *Oil and Gas Law.* When oil and gas first became commercially valuable, the question arose whether they should be treated like other "mobile" resources, such as wild animals, where the rule of the common law was (and is) that you have no property right until you take possession of the animal. The alternative would have been to treat these newly valuable resources like land and other "stable" property,[54] title to which can be obtained by recording a deed in a public registry or by some other paper record without the owner's having to take physical possession of the property.[55] A legal positivist who was asked whether only possessory rights should be recognized in oil and gas would be likely to start with the cases on property rights in wild animals and ask whether oil and gas are enough like wild animals to justify the same legal treatment. If so, property rights in oil and gas would be obtainable only by possession, which would mean that the resource was not owned until it was pumped to the surface. The pragmatic judge would be more inclined to start with the teachings of natural-resources economists and oil and gas engineers, to use the advice of these experts to decide which regime of property rights (possessory or title) would produce the better results when applied to oil and gas, and only then to examine the wild-animal cases and other authorities to see whether they blocked (by operation of the doctrine of stare decisis) the approach that would be best for the exploitation of oil and gas. The wild-animal approach would in fact lead to too rapid exploitation of these

---

54. A chair, for example: it moves only when someone moves it, whereas gravity or air pressure will cause oil and gas to flow into an empty space even if no (other) force is applied. When the rules governing property rights in wild animals were first applied to oil and gas, these resources were erroneously thought to have an internal principle of motion, to "move on their own," like animals.

55. I set to one side property that is not physical at all, i.e., intellectual property.

minerals. Oil and gas fields usually extend under more than one property owner's land. If title to oil and gas requires actual possession of the resource, each landowner will have an incentive to pump as much and as fast as he can, whereas optimal exploitation of the field as a whole might dictate fewer wells and more gradual extraction.

The pragmatic judge may fall on his face. He may not be able to understand what the petroleum engineers and the economists are trying to tell him or to translate it into a workable legal rule. The plodding positivist, his steps wholly predictable, will at least promote stability in law, a genuine public good. The legislature can always step in and prescribe an economically sound scheme of property rights. That is pretty much the history of property rights in oil and gas. Maybe nothing better could realistically have been expected. But American legislatures, in contrast to European parliaments, are so sluggish when it comes to correcting judicial mistakes that a heavy burden of legal creativity falls inescapably on the shoulders of the judges. I do not think they can bear the burden unless they are pragmatists. But they will not be able to bear it comfortably until changes in legal education and practice make law a more richly theoretical and empirical, and less formal and casuistic, field, as I suggested in discussing the shortcomings of the Supreme Court's opinions in the *Romer* and *VMI* cases.

5. *Surrogate Motherhood.* A more recent legal novelty is the contract of surrogate motherhood, which I discussed briefly in Chapter 1. In holding such contracts unenforceable, the Supreme Court of New Jersey in the *Baby M* case[56] engaged in a labored and windy tour of legal sources and concepts, overlooking the two issues, both factual in the broad sense, that would matter most to a pragmatist. The first is whether women who agree to be surrogate mothers typically or at least frequently experience intense regret when the moment comes to surrender the newborn baby to the father and his wife. The second is whether contracts of surrogate motherhood are typically or frequently exploitive in the sense that the surrogate mother is a poor woman who enters into the contract out of desperation. If the answers to both questions are "no," then, given the benefits of the contracts to the signatories, the pragmatist judge would probably enforce such contracts[57] regardless of what moral philosophers have to say about the issue.

These five examples should help us see that although both the positivist

56. In re Baby M, 537 A.2d 1227 (N.J. 1988).
57. See generally Richard A. Posner, *Sex and Reason* 420–428 (1992).

and the pragmatist are interested in the authorities *and* the facts, the positivist starts with and gives more weight to the authorities, while the pragmatist starts with and gives more weight to the facts. This is the most succinct description of pragmatic adjudication that I can come up with, and it helps incidentally to explain two features of Holmes's judicial philosophy that seem at first glance antipathetic to pragmatic adjudication: his lack of interest in economic and other data,[58] of which Brandeis complained, and his reluctance to overrule previous decisions. A pragmatic judge believes that the future should not be the slave of the past. But he need not have faith in any particular bodies of data as guides to making the decision that will best serve the future. If like Holmes you lacked confidence that you or anyone else had a clear idea of what the best resolution of some issue would be, the pragmatic posture would be one of reluctance to overrule past decisions, because the effect of overruling would be to sacrifice certainty and stability for a merely conjectural gain. This point can help us understand Holmes's quintessentially pragmatic insistence that the Fourteenth Amendment not be used to prevent states from experimenting with different solutions to social problems. The less one thinks one knows the answers to difficult questions of policy, the more inclined one will be to encourage learning about them through experimentation and other methods of inquiry.

I have said nothing about the pragmatic judge's exercising a "legislative" function, although the kind of facts that he would need in order to decide the oil and gas case in pragmatic fashion would be the kind that students of administrative law call "legislative" to distinguish them from the sort of facts ("adjudicative") that judge and jury, cabined by the rules of evidence, are called upon to find. Holmes famously said that judges were "interstitial" legislators when deciding a case the outcome of which was not dictated by unquestioned authorities. The many differences between judges and legislators in respect of procedures, training, experience, outlook, knowledge, tools, timing, constraints, and incentives make this a misleading usage; scope is not the only difference, as Holmes's formulation suggests. What he should have said was that judges are rulemakers as well as rule appliers. A judge is a different kind of rulemaker from a legislator. He does not write on a clean slate. An appellate judge has to decide in a particular case whether to apply an old rule unmodified,

---

58. See, for example, letter of Oliver Wendell Holmes to Harold J. Laski, May 18, 1919, in *Holmes-Laski Letters: The Correspondence of Mr. Justice Holmes and Harold J. Laski,* vol. 1, pp. 204–205 (Mark DeWolfe Howe ed. 1953).

modify and apply the old rule, or create and apply a new one. A pragmatist will be guided in this decision-making process by the goal of making the choice that will produce the best results. To do this the judge will have to do more than consult cases, statutes, regulations, constitutions, legal treatises, and other orthodox legal materials, but he *will* have to consult them, and a legislator will not.

6. *Homosexual Marriage.* My final illustration of the pragmatic approach to adjudication will tie the present discussion back to the discussion in Chapter 2 of moral and constitutional adjudication. It is possible to make good lawyers' arguments that there should be a federal constitutional right to homosexual marriage. These arguments, which have been marshaled by William Eskridge, include balancing the benefits of homosexual marriage against the costs to important state interests and finding that the former predominate; distinguishing same-sex marriage from polygamous and incestuous marriage (neither of which, in the current climate of American public opinion, could remotely be thought constitutionally privileged); building bridges from the Supreme Court's decisions striking down state laws against interracial marriage and allowing prisoners to marry—marry, but not have sex (so *Bowers v. Hardwick,* in allowing states to forbid homosexual sex, need not be taken as authority for rejecting a constitutional right to homosexual marriage); and claiming that "as women made gains in politics and the marketplace, middle-class anxiety about gender and the family was displaced onto another object: the homosexual"—so that a refusal to recognize homosexual marriage is a form or product of discrimination against women.[59]

The only thing wrong with these arguments is the tacit assumption that the methods of legal casuistry are an adequate basis for forcing every state in the United States to adopt a social policy that is deeply offensive to the vast majority of its citizens and to do so at the behest of an educated, articulate, and increasingly politically effective minority that is seeking to bypass the normal political process for no better reason than impatience, albeit an understandable impatience. (Americans are an impatient people.) A decision by the Supreme Court holding that the Constitution entitles people to marry others of the same sex would be far more radical than any of the decisions that Eskridge cites. Its moorings in text, precedent, public policy, and public opinion would be too tenuous to rally even minimum public support; it does not even have the full support of the

---

59. See William N. Eskridge, Jr., *The Case for Same-Sex Marriage: From Sexual Liberty to Civilized Commitment* (1996). The quoted passage is from id. at 168.

homosexual community.[60] It would be an almost unprecedented example of judicial immodesty.

I don't want to sound too cynical about legal reasoning. It is not *just* the bag of lawyers' tricks. It employs the methods of argument that since Aristotle have been accepted as useful tools for guiding judgment in areas where exact logical or scientific methods are unusable; and public policy toward homosexuality is one of those areas. But it is a mistake to suppose that legal reasoning alone can underwrite so profound a change in public policy as Eskridge envisages. A complex argument that could not be made airtight would be required in order to derive a right to homosexual marriage from the text of the Constitution and the cases interpreting that text—a tightrope act that without a net constituted by some support in public opinion would be too perilous for the courts to attempt. Public opinion may change, but at present it is too firmly against same-sex marriage for the courts to act.

This is not to say that courts should refuse to recognize a constitutional right merely because to do so would make them unpopular. Constitutional rights are, after all, rights against the democratic majority. But as I suggested in discussing the *Romer* case, public opinion is not irrelevant to the task of deciding whether a constitutional right exists. Judges asked to recognize a new constitutional right must do more than consult the text of the Constitution and the cases dealing with analogous constitutional issues. If it is truly a new right, as a right to same-sex marriage would be, text and precedent are not going to dictate the conclusion. The judges will have to consider political, empirical, prudential, and institutional issues, including the public acceptability of a decision recognizing the new right—and also including, as I suggested might have been the right approach for the Supreme Court to take in the original abortion cases, the feasibility and desirability of allowing the matter to simmer for a while before the heavy artillery of constitutional rights-making is trundled out. Let a state legislature or activist (but elected, and hence democratically responsive) state court adopt homosexual marriage as a policy in one state,[61] and let the rest of the country learn from the results of its experiment.[62]

60. See id., ch. 3.

61. As the Supreme Court of Hawaii is poised to do. See Baehr v. Miike, 910 P.2d 112 (Haw. 1996).

62. I acknowledge the possibility that the full faith and credit clause of the Constitution (Article IV, section 1), which requires states to honor the judgments of each other's courts (the exact language is "public acts, records, and judicial proceedings"), may make it difficult to confine the experiment to one state. Homosexuals from other states may get married in that state and then contend that their

That is the democratic way, and there is no compelling reason to supersede it merely because intellectually sophisticated people of secular inclination find Eskridge's argument for same-sex marriage convincing. Sophisticates aren't always right, and judges in a democratic society must accord considerable respect to the deeply held beliefs and preferences of the democratic majority when making new law. When the Supreme Court moved against public school segregation, it was bucking a regional majority but a national minority (white southerners). When it outlawed the laws forbidding racially mixed marriages,[63] only a few states still had such laws on their books. The constitutional right to abortion was conferred by the Court against the background of a fast-rising and already substantial number of lawful abortions.[64] And only when all but two states had repealed their laws forbidding the use of contraceptives even by married couples did the Court invalidate the remaining laws.[65] Were the Court to recognize a right to same-sex marriage today, it would be taking on almost the whole nation.

Most constitutional theorists would say that the task of the courts should be to do what is right, regardless of the consequences,[66] or at least that the *theorist* should say what is right even if he then advises the judges, in the style of Bickel, to duck the issue because it is too hot. I don't see the sharp line in constitutional law between what is right and what is acceptable. The judiciary is not a debating society. If most parents fear that recognizing same-sex marriage may affect the sexual development of their

---

home state is constitutionally obligated to recognize the marriage "judgment" of the state in which they are married. But the attempt to invoke the clause may well fail. Marriage may not be a judgment (public act, etc.) within the meaning of the clause. And under traditional conflicts of law principles that are available to inform interpretation of the full faith and credit clause as well, states have not been required to recognize marriages that deeply offend their own public policies—polygamous marriages are an example—provided that the state has a significant territorial connection to the parties to the marriage, as in the case in which they are residents of the state. But whatever the difficulty the full faith and credit clause poses for experimenting at the state level with same-sex marriage, it hardly argues for immediate nationalization of the issue by the Supreme Court's recognizing a federal constitutional right to enter into such a marriage. The choice of law issue is discussed in Andrew Koppelman, "Same-Sex Marriage, Choice of Law, and Public Policy," 76 *Texas Law Review* 921 (1998). On the general issue of homosexual marriage, see *Same-Sex Marriage: The Moral and Legal Debate* (Robert M. Baird and Stuart E. Rosenbaum eds. 1996).

63. Loving v. Virginia, 388 U.S. 1 (1967).

64. Gerald N. Rosenberg, *The Hollow Hope: Can Courts Bring About Social Change?* 179 (1991).

65. Griswold v. Connecticut, 381 U.S. 479 (1965).

66. As argued with explicit reference to homosexual marriage in David A. J. Richards, *Women, Gays, and the Constitution: The Grounds for Feminism and Gay Rights in Culture and Law* 453–457 (1998). Richards, unlike Eskridge, bases his argument for a constitutional right to homosexual marriage on moral theory, in particular on a concept of "moral slavery" that he believes describes the traditional position of both women and homosexuals in our society.

children or (otherwise) undermine the family, this is a datum that bears on a judgment whether the Constitution, which can hardly be thought to speak to the issue directly, should be interpreted to override the refusal of the states to authorize same-sex marriage. Similarly, if no other country in the world authorizes such a thing, this is a datum that should give pause to a court minded to legislate in the name of the Constitution. One would have to have more confidence in the power of reason to decide novel issues of constitutional law that lie well removed from the constitutional text and history than I do to be willing to ignore what people directly affected by the issues think about them. The converse of this point is that it is difficult for moral realists to be democrats.

Eskridge does not examine the pragmatic objections to constitutionalizing the issue of same-sex marriage. He wants the Supreme Court to require every state and the federal government immediately to confer all fifteen perquisites of the married state (fringe benefits of various sorts, testimonial privileges, and so forth)[67] on parties to homosexual marriage, including full rights of adoption plus the symbolic crown—the name "marriage." The nation's unreadiness for Eskridge's proposal should give pause to any impulse within an unelected judiciary to impose it on the nation in the name of the Constitution.

Pragmatic Adjudication: Objections and Limitations

DWORKIN'S CRITIQUE

Ronald Dworkin regards the pragmatic approach to adjudication as a rival to his own, yet claims for his approach what I had described in my book *Overcoming Law* as the pragmatic virtues.[68] This approach is only precariously consistent with his view of pragmatism as the dog's dinner, a view incompatible with the idea that pragmatism has any virtues. I had said that "the adjectives that . . . characterize the pragmatic outlook—practical, instrumental, forward-looking, activist, empirical, skeptical, antidogmatic, experimental—are not the ones that leap to mind when one considers [Dworkin's] work."[69] He contends that all but "experimental" describe his work as aptly as that of any pragmatist.

This is a surprise. Dworkin an activist? His critics describe him as one, but his own view is that judges who *refuse* to do law in the elevated

---

67. See Eskridge, note 59 above, at 66–70.

68. See Ronald Dworkin, "In Praise of Theory," 29 *Arizona State Law Journal* 353, 363–367 (1997). Subsequent page references to this article appear in the text.

69. Posner, note 34 above, at 11.

Dworkinian manner are the lawless ones, the activists. Empirical? That is not the impression conveyed by the philosophers' brief or by the discussions in Dworkin's books and articles of abortion, affirmative action, civil disobedience, defamation, pornography,[70] and the environment. Practical? Instrumental? Skeptical? Antidogmatic? Dworkin is a high rationalist with a weak sense of fact.[71] He wants judges to read Kant and Rawls, think hard about moral principles, and try to integrate this reading and thinking into their decision making. None of the pragmaticist adjectives fits him.

He says that if "forward-looking" means "consequentialist," his approach is forward-looking because "it aims at a structure of law and community that is egalitarian" (p. 364); only if "forward-looking" is equated to utilitarian is he not forward-looking. But the term is not used in *Overcoming Law* to denote either consequentialism or utilitarianism. It is used to contrast an approach, the pragmatic, that aspires to make things better for the present and the future, that cares about the past only insofar as the past provides guidance to the present and the future, with an approach that values the past for its own sake—as in "the past must be allowed some special power of its own in court, contrary to the pragmatist's claim that it must not."[72]

Dworkin is not unconcerned with consequences. But he is less concerned with them than I am. Although he denies that pornography contributes to crime or to discrimination against women, he would give less weight than I to any bad consequences of pornography even if they were certain. For he attaches great importance to the nonconsequentialist principle that people ought to be allowed to read what they please (government "insults its citizens, and denies their moral responsibility, when it decrees that they cannot be trusted to hear opinions that might persuade them to dangerous or offensive convictions");[73] to me this is simply one value to be considered.

70. He does glance at the empirical question of whether pornography incites violence against women in Ronald Dworkin, *Freedom's Law: The Moral Reading of the American Constitution* 375 nn. 20–21, 378 n. 4 (1996).

71. See, for example, Richard A. Posner, *The Economics of Justice* 376–377 (1981); also Posner, note 34 above, at 187–188. In the course of defending himself against this characterization, Dworkin has shown that he lacks a clear understanding of what "statistical discrimination" means. Ronald Dworkin, "Reply," 29 *Arizona State Law Journal* 432, 442 n. 33 (1997). Yet it figures prominently in the debate over affirmative action (see, for example, Posner, note 9 above, § 26.5), which he has defended in print.

72. Dworkin, note 39 above, at 167—though in practice, as I have suggested, Dworkin seems not to care about a past any more remote than the Warren Court.

73. Dworkin note 70 above, at 200.

With regard to my suggestion that he is not "experimental," Dworkin says that I must mean that he rejects the idea that "lawyers and judges should try different solutions to the problems they face to see which works, without regard to which is recommended or endorsed by some grand theory," that in other words the judge is "not to worry about what's really true but just to see what works" (p. 366). He calls this advice useless if the question the judge has to decide is whether abortion should be forbidden or whether to hold drug companies in DES cases liable for the harm done by their defective product even if it can't be determined which drug company's DES pills were taken by which plaintiff's mother. Dworkin says the judges would have no standard for what counts as "working" and thus for evaluating the results of the experiment unless they thought through the underlying philosophical issues, such as collective versus individual responsibility for harms or the human status of the fetus.

He is right that judges need rules or standards to guide them. But when I said that the pragmatist "is drawn to the *experimental* scientist, whom [the pragmatist] urges us to emulate by asking, whenever a disagreement arises: What practical, palpable, observable difference does it make to us?"[74] I meant only that judges should avoid becoming entangled in disputes that have no practical significance, such as whether judges "make" or "find" law. This is not advising them to create rules of law by pure trial and error; that is not how experimental scientists proceed. To decide cases without a sense of what the purpose of the applicable law is—and so in the DES cases without asking whether the deterrent and compensatory objectives of tort law would be served by collective responsibility in the circumstances of irremediable uncertainty presented by those cases—is decidedly unpragmatic.

Yet the example of abortion shows that even the trial and error version of experimentalism has a legitimate place in the legal process. As I noted in Chapter 2, a telling criticism of *Roe v. Wade* is that the Supreme Court prematurely nationalized the issue of abortion rights. Had the Court either ducked the issue completely or based its decision on a narrow ground (such as that the Texas law at issue did not contain enough exceptions), the states would have been free to experiment with different approaches to the abortion question. Eventually an answer might have emerged that would have commended itself to the Court and the nation

74. Posner, note 34 above, at 7 (emphasis in original).

as both principled and practical. To such a possibility, with its undoubted element of trial and error, Dworkin is blind.

Causes for Concern

I do not want to seem complacent about pragmatic adjudication. A danger of inviting the judge to step beyond the boundaries of the orthodox legal materials of decision is that judges are not trained to analyze and absorb the theories and data of social science. The example of Brandeis is not reassuring. Although he was a brilliant man of wide intellectual interests, his forays into social science whether as advocate or as judge were far from an unqualified success. His industry in marshaling economic data and viewing them through the lens of economic theory led him to support such since discredited policies as limiting women's employment rights, fostering small business at the expense of large, and subjecting to public utility and common carrier regulation markets such as the sale of ice that are not natural monopolies.[75] Holmes had grave reservations about the reliability of social scientific theories, but his unshakable faith in the eugenics movement, an early twentieth-century product of social and biological theory, undergirds his most criticized opinion (incidentally one joined by Brandeis), *Buck v. Bell.* And recall how the majority opinion in *Roe v. Wade* tries to make the issue of abortion rights seem a medical one and the reason for invalidating state laws forbidding abortion that they interfere with the autonomy of the medical profession—a "practical" angle reflecting Justice Blackmun's long association with the Mayo Clinic. Ignored are the effects of abortion laws on women, children, and the family—the effects that are important to evaluating the laws pragmatically.

A second and related concern about the use of nonlegal materials to decide cases is that it may degenerate into "gut reaction" judging. Cases do not wait upon the accumulation of a critical mass of social scientific knowledge that will enable the properly advised judge to arrive at the decision that will have the best results. The Supreme Court's decisions concerning sexual and reproductive autonomy came in advance of reliable, comprehensive, and accessible scholarship on sexuality, the family, and the status of women. The Court had to decide whether capital punishment is a cruel and unusual punishment at a time when the scientific study of the deterrent effects of capital punishment was just beginning.

75. See Posner, note 9 above, § 24.1, pp. 686–688.

And when the Court decided to redistrict state legislatures according to the "one man, one vote" principle it cannot have had a clear idea about the effects, on which political scientists still do not agree more than thirty years after the Court got into the redistricting business. The examples are not limited to the Supreme Court or to constitutional law. Common law judges had to resolve such issues as whether to extend the domain of strict liability, substitute comparative negligence for contributory negligence, simplify the rules of occupiers' liability, excuse breach of contract because of impossibility of performance, limit consequential damages, enforce waivers of liability, and so forth long before economists and economically minded lawyers got around to studying the economic consequences of these choices. When judges try to make the decision that will produce the "best results" without having any body of organized knowledge to turn to for help, they must rely on their intuitions.

A fancy name for the body of intuitions that guide legal decision making in the most difficult (in the sense of uncertain, not necessarily complex) cases is "natural law." And so the question arises whether the pragmatic approach to adjudication is not just another version of the natural-law approach. I think not. Pragmatists do not look to God or other transcendental sources of moral principle to validate their departures from statute or precedent or other conventional sources of law. They do not have the confidence of secure foundations, and this should make them a little more tentative, cautious, and piecemeal in imposing their vision of the Good on society in the name of legal justice. If Holmes really thought he was applying a "puke" test to statutes challenged as unconstitutional rather than evaluating those statutes for conformity with transcendental criteria, this would help explain his restrained approach to constitutional adjudication. Another pragmatic Justice, however, Robert Jackson, who unlike Holmes had been heavily involved in high-level political matters before becoming a judge, was not bashful about drawing on his extrajudicial experience for guidance to the content of constitutional doctrine.[76] The pragmatic judge is not always a modest judge.

The reason that using the "puke" test or one's "gut reactions" or even

---

76. In his famous concurrence in the steel-seizure case, Jackson said: "That comprehensive and undefined presidential powers hold both practical advantages and grave dangers for the country will impress anyone who has served as legal adviser to a President in time of transition and public anxiety. While an interval of detached reflection may temper teachings of that experience, they probably are a more realistic influence on my views than the conventional materials of judicial decision which seem unduly to accentuate doctrine and legal fiction." *Youngstown Sheet & Tube Co. v. Sawyer,* 343 U.S. 579, 634 (1952) (concurring opinion).

one's government experience before becoming a judge to make judicial decisions sounds scandalous[77] is that the legal profession, and particularly its academic and judicial branches, want the added legitimacy that accrues to the decisions of people whose opinions are grounded in expert knowledge. (This point is related to the discussion in Chapter 3 of professional mystique.) The expert knowledge of another discipline is not what is wanted, although it is better than no expert knowledge at all. Both the law professor and the judge feel naked before society when the positions they take on novel cases, however carefully those positions are dressed up in legal jargon, are seen to reflect intuition based on personal and professional (but nonjudicial) experiences and on character and temperament rather than on disciplined, rigorous, and articulate inquiry.

Things are not quite so bad as that. It is not as if American judges were chosen at random and made political decisions in a vacuum. Judges of the higher American courts are generally picked from the upper tail of the population distribution in terms of age, education, intelligence, disinterest, and sobriety. They are not tops in all these departments but they are well above average, especially in the federal courts because of the elaborate pre-appointment screening of candidates for federal judgeships. Judges are schooled in a profession that sets a high value on listening to both sides of an issue before making up one's mind, on sifting truth from falsehood, and on exercising detached judgment. Their decisions are anchored in the facts of concrete disputes between real people. Members of the legal profession have played a central role in the political history of the United States, and the profession's institutions and usages are reflectors of the fundamental political values that have emerged from that history. Appellate judges in nonroutine cases are expected to express as best they can the reasons for their decision in signed, public, citable documents (the published decisions of these courts), and this practice creates accountability and fosters a certain thoughtfulness and self-discipline. None of these things guarantees wisdom, especially since the reasons given for a decision are not always the real reasons behind it and the factual premises of the decision are often inaccurate or incomplete. But at their best American appellate courts are councils of wise elders meditating on real disputes, and it is not completely insane to entrust them with responsibility for resolving these disputes in a way that will produce the best results in the circumstances rather than resolving them purely on the basis of rules

77. Making the statement by Justice Jackson that I quoted in the preceding footnote remarkable for its candor; but am I mistaken in sensing a faintly apologetic tone?

created by other organs of government or by their own previous decisions, although that is what they will be doing most of the time.

Nor do I flinch from another implication of conceiving American appellate courts in the way that I have suggested. It is that these courts will tend to treat the Constitution and the common law, and to a lesser extent bodies of statute law, as a kind of putty that can be used to fill embarrassing holes in the legal and political framework of society. In the case of property rights in oil and gas, a court could take the position that it had no power to create new rules and must therefore subsume these newly valuable resources under the closest existing rule, the rule governing wild animals. It might even take the position that it had no power to enlarge the boundaries of existing rules. In that event no property rights in oil and gas would be recognized until the legislature created a system of property rights for these resources. Under this approach, if Connecticut has a crazy law (as it did until the Supreme Court struck it down in the *Griswold* case) forbidding married couples to use contraceptives, but no provision of the Constitution limits state regulation of the family, then the crazy law would stand until it was repealed or the Constitution amended to invalidate it. Or if the Eighth Amendment's prohibition against cruel and unusual punishments has reference only to the *method* of punishment or to the propriety of punishing *at all* in particular circumstances (for example, for simply being poor or an addict), then a state can with constitutional impunity sentence a sixteen-year-old to life imprisonment without possibility of parole for the sale of one marijuana cigarette—which in fact seems to be the Supreme Court's current view,[78] one that I find difficult to stomach. I don't think a pragmatic Justice of the Supreme Court *would* stomach it, although he would give due weight to the implications for judicial caseloads of bringing the length of prison sentences under judicial scrutiny and to the difficulty of creating workable nonarbitrary norms of proportionality. The pragmatic judge does not throw up his hands and say "sorry, no law to apply" when confronted with outrageous conduct that the framers of the Constitution neglected to foresee and make specific provision for.

Oddly, this basic principle of pragmatic judging has received at least limited recognition by even the most orthodox judges with respect to statutes. It is accepted that if reading a statute the way it is written produces absurd results, the judges may rewrite it.[79] Judges do not put it

78. See Harmelin v. Michigan, 501 U.S. 957 (1991).

79. See, for example, Burns v. United States, 501 U.S. 129, 137 (1991); Green v. Bock Laundry Machine Co., 490 U.S. 504, 527 (1989) (Scalia, J., concurring).

quite this way—they say that statutory interpretation is a search for meaning and Congress can't have meant the absurd result—but it comes to the same thing. And, at least in this country, common law judges reserve the right to "rewrite" the common law as they go along. A similar approach, prudently employed, could guide constitutional adjudication as well.

The approach, to repeat, is not without dangers. People can feel very strongly about a subject and be quite wrong. Certitude is not the test of certainty. A wise person realizes that even his unshakable convictions may be wrong—but not all of us are wise. In a pluralistic society, moreover, a judge's unshakable convictions may not be shared by enough other people that he can base a decision on those convictions and be reasonably confident that it will be accepted. So the wise judge will try to check his convictions against those of some broader community of opinion, as Holmes suggested in referring in *Lochner* to "fundamental principles *as they have been understood by the traditions of our people and our law.*"[80]

It was not irrelevant, from a pragmatic standpoint, to the outcome of *Brown v. Board of Education* that official racial segregation had been abolished outside the South[81] and bore a disturbing resemblance to Nazi racial laws. It was not irrelevant to the outcome in *Griswold* that, as the Court neglected to mention, only one other state (Massachusetts) had a similar law. If I were writing an opinion invalidating the life sentence in my hypothetical marijuana case I would look at the punishments for this conduct in other states and in the foreign countries, such as England and France, that we consider in some sense our peers. For if a law could be said to be contrary to world public opinion I would consider this a reason, not compelling but not negligible either, for regarding a state law as unconstitutional even if the Constitution's text had to be stretched a bit to cover it. The study of other laws, or of world public opinion as crystallized in foreign law and practices, is a more profitable inquiry than trying to find some bit of eighteenth-century evidence for thinking that the framers of the Constitution may have wanted courts to make sure that punishments prescribed by statute were proportional to the gravity, or difficulty of apprehension, or profitability, or some other relevant characteristic of the crime. If I found such evidence I would think it a valuable bone to toss to a positivist or formalist colleague, but I would not be embarrassed by its absence because I would not think myself duty-bound to maintain consistency with past decisions.

80. Lochner v. New York, 198 U.S. 45, 76 (1905) (dissenting opinion).
81. Which for these purposes, however, included the District of Columbia! See Bolling v. Sharpe, 347 U.S. 497 (1954).

I would even think it pertinent to the pragmatic response to the marijuana case to investigate or perhaps even just to speculate (if factual investigation proved fruitless) about the psychological and social meaning of imprisoning a young person for his entire life for the commission of a minor crime. What happens to a person in such a situation? Does he adjust? Deteriorate? What is the likely impact on his family, and on the larger society? How should one feel as a judge if one allows such a punishment to be imposed? And are these sentences for real, or are preposterously severe sentences soon commuted? Might the deterrent effect of so harsh a sentence be so great that the total number of years of imprisonment for violation of the drug laws would be reduced, making the sacrifice of this young person a utility-maximizing venture after all? Is utility the right criterion here? Is the sale of marijuana perhaps far more destructive than some ivory-tower judge or professor thinks? Do judges become callous if a large proportion of the criminal cases that they review involve very long sentences? If a defendant who received "only" a five-year sentence appealed, would the appellate judges' reaction be, "Why are you complaining about such a trivial punishment?"

The response to the case of the young man sentenced to life for selling marijuana is bound in the end to be an emotional rather than a closely reasoned one because so many imponderables enter into that response, as my questions were intended to indicate. But emotion is not pure glandular secretion. It is influenced by experience,[82] information, and imagination,[83] and can thus be disciplined by fact.[84] Indignation or disgust founded on a responsible appreciation of a situation need not be thought a disreputable motive for action, even for a judge; it is indeed the absence of any emotion in such a situation that would be discreditable. It would be nice, though, if judges and law professors were more knowledgeable practitioners or at least consumers of social science (broadly defined to include history and philosophy), so that their "emotional" judgments were better informed.

---

82. I again refer the reader to the striking quotation from Justice Jackson in note 76 above.

83. On the cognitive dimension of emotion, see, besides the references cited in Chapter 1, John Deigh, "Cognitivism in the Theory of Emotions," 104 *Ethics* 824 (1994); Jon Elster, "Emotions and Economic Theory," 36 *Journal of Economic Literature* 47 (1998); Robert H. Frank, "The Strategic Role of the Emotions: Reconciling Over- and Undersocialized Accounts of Behavior," 5 *Rationality and Society* 160 (1993); Ronald de Sousa, *The Rationality of Emotion* (1987); R. B. Zajonc, "Feeling and Thinking: Preferences Need No Inferences," 35 *American Psychologist* 151 (1980).

84. One wouldn't expect, for example, a person who had become genuinely, disinterestedly convinced that the Holocaust had never occurred to feel the same concern about anti-Semitism that people who believed it had occurred would tend to feel.

My earlier reference to the ages of judges suggests another objection to pragmatic adjudication. Aristotle said, and I agree, that young people tend to be forward-looking. Their life lies ahead of them and they have only a limited stock of experience to draw upon in coping with the future, while old people tend to be backward-looking because they face an opposite balance between past and future.[85] If, therefore, the pragmatic judge is forward-looking, and we want judges to be pragmatic, should we invert the age profile of judges? Should Holmes have been made a judge at thirty and put out to pasture at fifty? Or, on the contrary, is it not the case that judges perform an important balance-wheel function, one that requires them to be backward-looking, one that is peculiarly apt, therefore, for the aged? Have I not myself so argued?[86] Have I not also pointed out that, contrary to the conventional view, the great failing of the German judges in the Nazi period was not their positivism but their willingness to interpret the laws of the New Order flexibly in order to further the aims, the spirit, of those laws?[87]

These criticisms pivot on an ambiguity in the term "forward-looking." If it is meant to carry overtones of disdain for history, origins, and traditions, then the criticisms I have mentioned are just. But I do not understand "forward-looking" in that sense. I understand it to mean that the past is valued not in itself but only in relation to the present and the future. That relation may be a very important one. In many cases the best the judge can do for the present and the future is to insist that breaks with the past be duly considered. In such a case the only difference between the positivist judge and the pragmatic judge is that the latter lacks *reverence* for the past, a felt duty of continuity with the past. That sense of duty would be inconsistent with the forward-looking stance and hence with pragmatism.

Pragmatism is likewise neutral on whether the law should be dominated by rules or by standards. The pragmatist rejects the idea that law is not law unless it consists of rules, because that kind of conceptual analysis is not pragmatic. But he is open to any pragmatic argument in favor of rules, for example that judges cannot be trusted to make intelligent decisions unless they are guided by rules or that decisions based on standards produce uncertainty disproportionate to any gain in flexibility. A prag-

---

85. I elaborate on Aristotle's view in my book *Aging and Old Age,* note 10 above, ch. 5.

86. In id., ch. 8.

87. Posner, note 34 above, at 155; see also Michael Stolleis, *The Law under the Swastika: Studies on Legal History in Nazi Germany* 15 (1998). I would not be inclined to swing to the other extreme and blame Nazi jurisprudence on pragmatism. National Socialism was not a pragmatic doctrine.

matic judge thus need not be recognizable by a distinctive style of judging, and it would be a travesty of pragmatic adjudication to think that a pragmatic judge must be an unprincipled, ad hoc decision maker. What would be distinctive about the pragmatic judge is that his style (of thinking—he might decide to encapsulate his thoughts in positivist or formalist rhetoric) would owe nothing to ideas about the nature of law or the moral duty to abide by past decisions or some other nonpragmatic grounding of judicial attitudes.

I leave open the criteria for the "best results" for which the pragmatic judge is striving, except that, *pace* Dworkin, they are not simply what is best for the particular case without regard for the implications for other cases. Pragmatism will not tell us what is best; but, provided there is a fair degree of value consensus among the judges, as I think there is, it can help judges seek the best results unhampered by philosophical doubts.

The greatest danger of judicial pragmatism is intellectual laziness. It is a lot simpler to react to a case than to analyze it. The pragmatic judge must bear in mind at all times that he is a judge and that this means that he must consider all the legal materials and arguments that can be brought to bear on the case. If legal reasoning is modestly defined as reasoning with reference to distinctive legal materials such as statutes and legal doctrines and to the law's traditional preoccupations, for example with stability and the right to be heard and the other "rule of law" virtues,[88] then it ought to be an ingredient of every legal decision, though not necessarily the be-all and end-all of the decision. Just as some people think that an artist must prove that he is a competent draftsman before he should be taken seriously as an abstract artist, so I believe that a judge must prove—anew in every case—that he is a competent legal reasoner before he should be taken seriously as a pragmatic judge.

To put this differently, the pragmatic judge must not forget that the role of a judge is constraining as well as empowering. Some years ago the Chicago public schools were unable to open at the beginning of the school year because the state refused to approve the school district's budget. An injunction was sought to compel the schools to open, on the ground that their closure violated a judicial decree forbidding de facto racial segregation in the city's public schools. The argument was not that the state's refusal to approve the budget had been motivated by any racial animus—there was no suggestion of that—but that the ultimate goal of the judicial

88. As in Joseph Raz, "On the Autonomy of Legal Reasoning," in Raz, *Ethics in the Public Domain: Essays in the Morality of Law and Politics* 310 (1994).

decree, which was to improve the education and life prospects of black children in Chicago, would be thwarted if the schools were not open to educate them. The trial judge granted the request for an injunction, and did so on an avowedly pragmatic ground: the cost to Chicago's schoolchildren, of whatever race, of being denied an education. My court reversed.[89] We could not find any basis in federal law for the injunction. The desegregation decree had not commanded the city to open the public schools on some particular date, or for that matter to open them at all, or even to *have* public schools, let alone to flout a state law requiring financial responsibility in the administration of the public school system. It seemed to us that what the trial judge had done was not so much pragmatic as lawless. The pragmatic judge may not ignore the good of compliance with settled rules of law. If a federal judge is free to issue an injunction that has no basis in federal law, merely because he thinks the injunction will have good results, then we do not have pragmatic adjudication; we have judicial tyranny, which few Americans consider acceptable even if they are persuaded that the tyrant can be counted on to be generally benign.

The judge in the Chicago school case was guilty of what might be called myopic pragmatism, which is Dworkin's conception of pragmatism. The only consequence that the judge took into consideration in deciding whether to issue the injunction was that children enrolled in the public schools would be deprived of schooling until the schools opened. The consequence that he ignored was the consequence for the political and governmental systems of granting federal judges an uncanalized discretion to intervene in political disputes. Had the power that the judge claimed been upheld, you can be sure that henceforth the financing of Chicago's public schools would be determined by a federal judge rather than by elected officials. The judge thought that unless he ordered the schools to open, the contending parties would never agree on a budget. The reverse was true. Only the fact that the schools were closed (until the injunction was issued) had exerted pressure on the parties to settle their dispute. And indeed as soon as the injunction was lifted the parties came to terms and the schools opened. The consequence that the judge ignored was a consequence for the schoolchildren as well as for other members of society, so that it is possible that even the narrowest group affected by the decree would, in the long run, have been hurt had the decree been allowed to stand.

89. United States v. Board of Education, 11 F.3d 668 (7th Cir. 1993).

But if intellectual laziness is a danger of pragmatic adjudication, it is also a danger of not being pragmatic. The positivist judge is apt not to question his premises. If he either thinks that "hate speech" is deeply harmful, or thinks that banning hate speech would endanger political liberty, he is not likely to take the next step, which is to recognize that he may be wrong and to seek through investigation[90] to determine whether he is wrong. The deeper the belief—the closer it lies to our core values—the less likely we are to be willing to question it. Our disposition will be not to question but to defend. As Peirce and Dewey emphasized, doubt rather than belief is the spur to inquiry; and doubt is a disposition that pragmatism encourages, precisely in order to spur inquiry. One reason that attitudes toward hate speech are held generally as dogmas rather than hypotheses—one reason that so little is known about the actual consequences of hate speech—is that a pragmatic approach has not been taken to the subject.

Does It Travel?

I have been trying to explain and illustrate my conception of pragmatic adjudication and to defend it against its critics. But I would not like to leave the impression that I think pragmatic adjudication is the right way for all courts to go; to think it is would be to fall into the fallacy of jurisprudential universalizing. Although one can find echoes or anticipations of philosophical pragmatism in German philosophy and elsewhere (Hume, Mill, Nietzsche, and Wittgenstein are all examples), it is basically an American philosophy and one that may not travel well to other countries. The same may be true of pragmatic adjudication. The case for it is weaker in a parliamentary democracy than in a U.S.-style checks and balances federal democracy. Many parliamentary systems (notably the English) are effectively unicameral and, what is more, the parliament is controlled by the executive. The legislative branch of so highly centralized a system can pass new laws pretty easily and rapidly and word them clearly. As I noted in Chapter 2, if the courts identify a gap in existing law they can have reasonable (although not complete) confidence that it will be quickly filled by Parliament, so that only a temporary injustice will be done if the judges refrain from filling the gap themselves. The judges can afford to be stodgier, more rule-bound, less pragmatic than our judges; the cost in substantive injustice is lower.

90. The kind of investigation conducted in James R. Jacobs and Kimberly Potter, *Hate Crimes: Criminal Law and Identity Politics* (1998). Hate speech is discussed in id., ch. 8.

Some parliamentary systems have a federal structure; some have constitutional review; some have both. And some, the English for example, have neither. The ones that have neither have clearer law, whereas to determine someone's legal obligation in the United States often requires the consideration of state law (and perhaps the laws of several states), federal statutory law (and sometimes federal common law), and federal constitutional law. Our government is one of the most decentralized in the world. We have effectively a tricameral federal legislature, since the President through his veto power and his role in one of the major political parties is a full participant in the legislative process. This structure makes it extremely difficult to pass laws, let alone clearly worded laws (unclear wording in a contract or a statute facilitates agreement on the contract or statute as a whole by deferring resolution of the most contentious points), and is, moreover, layered on top of similarly three-headed state legislatures. If they want "the best results," American courts cannot leave all rulemaking to legislatures, for that would result in legal gaps and perversities galore. The lateral-entry character of the American judiciary, the absence of uniform criteria for appointment, the moral, intellectual, and political diversity of the nation (and hence, given the previous two points, of the judges), the individualistic and antiauthoritarian character of the population, and the extraordinary complexity and dynamism of the society are further obstacles to American judges' confining themselves to the application of rules laid down by legislatures, regulators, or the framers of the Constitution.

Postmodernism Distinguished

Duncan Kennedy: The Pied Piper

Pragmatism and postmodernism are often confused (understandably, since the differences are subtle—but important), and likewise pragmatic adjudication and the postmodernist approach to adjudication championed by Duncan Kennedy.[91] Kennedy occupies a niche in critical legal studies that he calls "left/mpm" (sometimes just "mpm"), which is short for "left-wing modernism-postmodernism." Perhaps the best-known current occupant of that niche, though he is not a lawyer or identified with

91. See Duncan Kennedy, *A Critique of Adjudication* [*fin de siècle*] (1997). Subsequent page references to this book appear in the text. On the philosophical antecedents of postmodernist thinking in law, see Douglas E. Litowitz, *Postmodern Philosophy and Law* (1997).

critical legal studies, is Richard Rorty. And Rorty is a pragmatist. Is Kennedy? Does that make me a right-wing "crit"? Does our common rejection of constitutional theory à la Dworkin make us soulmates?

The key to understanding Kennedy's approach lies in the sense in which he uses the word "ideology." We usually think of an ideology as a total—coherent and complete—system of thought; examples are communism, national socialism, Fabian socialism, and classical liberalism. Kennedy uses "ideology" more narrowly, to denote "liberalism" and "conservatism" in their modern American senses in which the left wing of the Democratic Party is "liberal" and the center and right of the Republican Party are "conservative." These ideologies begin in material interest and emotional identification (whom do you like to "hang out" with?) but take on an intellectual hue when the contestants begin to articulate their claims in universal terms in order to win over neutrals. Because liberals and conservatives appeal to the same basic values—the rule of law, the importance of rights and limited government, the core moral values of the Judeo-Christian tradition, liberty, prosperity, tolerance, the family, and so forth—these ideologies do not provide adequate tools for resolving specific issues. "Liberals and conservatives share identical major premises and switch back and forth, as they draw lines, between identical intermediate-level arguments" (p. 150). The parallel to the moral arguments discussed in Chapter 1 is apparent.

The indeterminacy of ideological debate is important to Kennedy because so many legal issues cannot be resolved by reasoning from authoritative legal materials. Some can be. He rejects as not "even slightly plausible" the idea that "legal materials and legal reasoning are sufficiently plastic that they can offer an acceptable post hoc rationalization of whatever result the judge favors, and judges are habitual rationalizers" (p. 159). Judges "often, often, often declare and apply rules that they would never vote for if they were legislators" (p. 275). Often, but not always: hence "the simultaneously structured and plastic character of legal reasoning" (p. 285).

He thinks the plasticity bothers judges a lot. They don't want to be seen as reaching decisions on ideological grounds. As a result they "*always* aim to generate a particular rhetorical effect through [their] work: that of the legal necessity of their solutions without regard to ideology" (pp. 1–2, emphasis in original). This aim is shared by law professors and interest-group advocates, who want to help the judge reach the ideologically motivated result that the advocate wants (whether it is abortion on demand, or homosexual rights, or freedom from economic regulation, or religion in the public schools) without tipping his ideological hand.

Kennedy discusses three methods of concealing ideology as neutral legal reasoning. Together they make up "legalism"; when practiced by liberals, it is "liberal legalism." One method, that of Dworkin, is to construct a general theory of legal rights and duties from which the correct outcome of even the most difficult case can be derived objectively. Dworkin claims that his views on the merits of the cases he discusses are generated not by his personal ideology, which is left-liberal, but by impartial reflection on the principles that are seen to be a part of law once positivism is rejected. Kennedy finds this argument laughable; Dworkin's views on such issues as abortion, affirmative action, euthanasia, civil disobedience, and pornography obviously derive from his political beliefs.[92] The only relation between Dworkin's theoretical and applied work is that the rejection of legal positivism, his chief theoretical project, is a precondition to urging judges to do moral theory, which he believes will lead them to decide cases in accordance with his political preferences.

The second way in which judges' academic trainers try to help them conceal ideological argument as neutral legal reasoning is by using notions of public policy, often nowadays informed by economic analysis, to bridge the gap between conventional legal materials and the desired outcome. Kennedy sees this as a legacy of legal realism, which killed formalism and "promoted a hybrid in which policy argument is included as a supplement to deductive reasoning in both liberal and conservative appellate opinions" (p. 94). He believes that policy is every bit as manipulable as Dworkin's coherentist theory; "policy argument is interminably ideological, and like ideological debate, just plain interminable" (p. 177). Kennedy is wrong. Although one can always *argue* both sides of an issue of policy, the arguments for one side may fall completely flat. I would like to see Kennedy argue for raising the minimum wage to $50 an hour. *A Critique of Adjudication* has no sustained discussion of policy issues; it merely asserts, in the face of contradictory evidence to which the author does not so much as allude, the indeterminacy of policy analysis.[93] It

---

92. Recall my quotation in Chapter 1 of Kennedy's description of the happy coincidence between Dworkin's political preferences and judicial philosophy.

93. He used not to think policy analysis indeterminate; he used to *do* it. See Duncan Kennedy, "The Effect of the Warranty of Habitability on Low Income Housing: 'Milking' and Class Violence," 15 *Florida State University Law Review* 485 (1987), and, for criticism, Posner, note 9 above, § 16.6, pp. 517–518.

would be surprising if legal arguments often, often, often achieved closure, as he concedes, and policy arguments never, never, never.

The third way of disguising ideology as law, Kennedy claims, is by recasting ideological issues in the language of rights. Feminist jurists do not just say they want women to be able to obtain abortions on demand, the way a union might just say it wants its members to have a larger share of the employer's profits. They say there's a constitutional right to abortion on demand, thus dressing up an ideological demand in neutral legal language. "Rights reasoning, in short, allows you to be right about your value judgments, rather than just stating 'preferences'" (p. 305). This particular method (early Dworkin, as Kennedy notes) of concealing ideology as legality is so popular that it has led to the "rights-overkill problem" (p. 327). With every interest group agitating for rights, rights pop up on both sides of most legal disputes. We saw this in discussing criminal procedure in Chapter 2. Other examples are the debate over hate speech, which confronts the right to free speech with the right to racial justice; the debate over pornography, where the right of free speech confronts the right of sexual equality; and debates over abortion and custody, where rights of fathers are asserted against rights of mothers. You get no help, as Kennedy points out, from the philosophical concept of rights—the source of what he calls "outside" rights, in contrast to the legal rights ("inside rights") that jurists want to turn the outside rights into. The philosophical discourse of rights is as indeterminate as the legal.

To the extent that it succeeds in fooling people, the disguise of ideological issues as legal issues has three effects, which Kennedy calls empowerment, moderation, and legitimation. The disguise empowers "legal fractions of intelligentsias" (p. 2) to decide ideological issues without reference to majorities. In doing so it also moderates ideological conflict. The legal-judicial community removes ideological issues from the political community, turning what would otherwise be political issues for ideologically organized majorities to decide into technical issues for decision by mandarins. At the same time, by concealing the existence of ideological conflict the reclassification of political issues as legal issues makes the political status quo, whatever it is, seem natural and necessary because ordained by law, not just by power. The "whatever it is" is important. It means that law blocks change in whatever direction, good or bad, the people might want to go. Kennedy believes that both liberals and conservatives fear the people—the "masses" as he calls them. European courts are less ideological than American ones; and, consistent with Kennedy's moderation thesis, European politics are more ideological than American politics. Europeans haven't converted as many of their ideological conflicts into legal disputes for resolution outside the democratic process.

Kennedy believes that the efforts of the judges and their academic seconds and trainers to conceal ideology as legality are beginning to fray badly. Legal liberals, for example, at the same time that they are plumping for social reform through judicial activism feel compelled to defend the idea of adjudication as neutral and objective in order to fend off conservative opponents.[94]

When the duplicity of legal reasoning is exposed through "internal critique" (Kennedy's method, the identification of the internal contradictions in all efforts to bridge the gap between ideology and law), there are two reactions. One is bad faith in approximately Sartre's sense.[95] The judge or law professor senses that his effort to submerge ideology in neutral legal reasoning is phony, but, ostrichlike, he refuses to acknowledge this, pretending instead to be acting under the compulsion of neutral principles. A frank avowal would be too painful because it would take away his self-image as a serious thinker, someone "above" politics. Another reaction, however—Kennedy's own—is loss of faith in legal reasoning. If you see all the way through the pretensions of legal analysis and don't try to conceal your insight from yourself, you lose your enthusiasm for doing coherence theory, or policy analysis, or rights analysis.

For Kennedy, this is a personal experience at once thrilling (the mountaintop thrill of conscious possession of superior insight) and depressing. It is depressing because liberal legalism in general and rights analysis in particular have, he thinks, done a lot of good by "inducing a diffuse but pervasive, unpredictably militant 'rights consciousness' throughout American society that is one of the few effective checks on bureaucratic abuses in both public and private sectors" (p. 114). This makes radical feminists, critical race theorists, homosexual rights activists, and other practitioners of identity politics—Kennedy's natural allies, one might have thought—want to extend the domain of rights to cover the activities that they consider essential to their identity. Kennedy will have none of that.

---

94. "There was something 'weakening' or 'undermining' about the fact that the liberals were using exactly the rhetoric they had denounced before World War II, about the failure to come up with any alternative to balancing as a methodology for protecting rights, about the very facility they began to feel at inventing new rights (privacy being the most striking case), and about the parallel facility of their opponents at inventing counterrights of one kind or another" (p. 325).

95. Well described in Mike W. Martin, *Self-Deception and Morality* 63 (1986).

He rejects "leftist righteousness (whether in the mode of post-Marxist 'systematicity' or of identity politics) and, with equal intensity, . . . the compromises of left liberalism" (p. 339). By "systematicity" he means grand historical causal theories, such as the Marxist theory once propounded by his colleague Morton Horwitz that the American common law assumed the shape it did in the nineteenth century in order to promote capitalism.[96] But he also means efforts to go beyond critique to "reconstruction," that is, to putting something in the place of whatever edifice, such as liberal legalism or capitalist democracy, the critique has just demolished. Kennedy thinks internal critique devastates all systems.

This relentless critiquing places Kennedy at the tip of a thin branch. Since he will have no truck with systems of thought or with totalizing theories, his own leftism is unsystematic, untheorized, and indeed undefended. It is related to anarchism ("we study state power to resist it, not to seize it" [p. 271]), but is informed by a hostility to all large institutions, not just to government; in fact the line beween public and private has no significance for Kennedy. Disliking corporations especially, he is much taken with union militancy and worker ownership. This gives his leftism an archaic cast (like that of Rorty, who is *still* talking about the "oligarchy" and the "bosses"), and is another reason why he doesn't like rights. Emphasis on them has caused the left to abandon the project dear to his heart of representing an oppressed *majority*—the working class.

He is more explicit about the modernism-postmodernism strain in his ideology. "Mpm is the search for intense experience in the interstices of a disrupted rational grid. The characteristic vehicle is a transgressive artifact or performance that 'shatters' the forms of 'proper' expression in order to express something that those forms suppressed." The goal is to induce "the modernist emotions associated with the death of reason—ecstasy, irony, depression, and so forth" (p. 342). This is not to be confused with nihilism or even skepticism. When he says that he is "hostile to rightness in all its forms" (p. 11), he doesn't mean that he thinks there are no right answers to legal questions; such a belief would be inconsistent with his recognition that legal materials do constrain judges. "The experience of core meanings survives the loss of its metaphysical grounding" (p. 32).

The polite word for what Kennedy is talking about is pragmatism, and "pragmatist" is indeed one of his own self-descriptions, though not his favorite (it makes one think of dull sticks like John Dewey). Remember

---

96. Morton J. Horwitz, *The Transformation of American Law, 1780–1860* (1977).

that pragmatism holds that people won't reexamine a deeply held belief unless you shake them hard enough to make them doubt. You do this either by making a relentless intellectual assault on the foundations of their belief or by confronting them with violent or disturbing images that loosen their cultural and emotional moorings sufficiently to "convert" them to a new perspective. Abstract art does not *argue* that representation is inessential to art; it does not proceed rationally at all. Instead it presents a nonrepresentational image which, operating as a "transgressive artifact," may incite us to reconsider our notion of what art is.

Kennedy's mpm is more colorful, certainly, than the usual descriptions of pragmatism. He calls mpm "elitist as well as elite," the "revenge of the nerds" "driven by aggression" (p. 354).

> It aims to *épater les bourgeois* (rather than to nationalize their property), in the modes of aggression and exhibitionism described above. It presupposes the superiority of mpm, the "right" of mpm performers to hurt the audience, as well as to induce ecstasy and depression, in the name of higher values accessible to the artist/performer and "good for" the audience (while commonly denying—defensively and hypocritically—that it cares at all about audience reaction). (p. 354)

This is what used to be called avant-gardism—a kind of intellectual bohemianism—and helps to explain the tension between Kennedy and the practitioners of identity politics. Kennedy supports most of their proposals, but, consistent with the "mode of aggression," he *over*supports them. For example, he argues for rigid racial quotas, while identity politicians avoid the word "quota" like the plague. Those most offended by mpm, he conjectures, are neither liberals nor conservatives; they are the leaders of oppressed groups, who, themselves highly educated and upwardly mobile, embrace anti-elitism as "the price they pay for their roles as leaders" (p. 355). It's a price he's not willing to pay.

He acknowledges that his leftism works at cross-purposes with his mpm to produce what he calls "Pink Theory" (in the lingo of the Russian Revolution, neither Red nor White). Pink is a restful color, and Pink Theory a formula for political quietism (which is fine by me). Kennedy repeatedly and accurately describes "internal critique" as "viral," conjuring up the image of HIV or a computer virus—agents of voracious destruction. It eats up liberal legalism, leading Kennedy to admit that it isn't absurd to argue that "we crits are naively willing to play with fire by questioning a central pillar of humane politics in the modern age of barbarism . . . The securely centrist, first peripheral and then imperial, but continentally isolated American political culture has provided a Galápagos-like enclave for bizarre intellectual mutations" (p. 74). Because viral critique also devours identity politics and leftist righteousness generally, little room remains for leftist "resistance" either.

Kennedy thinks that the law schools induct their students into bad faith by teaching them to submerge awareness of behavior designed to advance an ideological agenda "in a necessitarian discourse that everyone knows is only part of the story" (p. 367). Yet he also believes that a student who keeps his wits about him just may be able when he goes into practice or becomes a judge "to set up a political identity to the left of liberal bad faith, without being or seeming to be a wrecker" (p. 374). There won't be many such, however, if they listen to Kennedy. He not only acknowledges the stability of the American political system and the impotence of academic critique to bring about political change; he also fails to explain how a left liberal who is *not* a wrecker can accomplish anything by boring from within or even how one can *be* a borer from within without being a wrecker. And if policy argument, left or right, is, as Kennedy believes, indeterminate and interminable, there isn't even a vocabulary in which left liberals can defend their principles and proposals.

I have said that I don't think policy analysis is as indeterminate as Kennedy believes. A related point is that I don't think he has the psychology of judges right. No doubt some liberal law professors are in bad faith, that is, half aware that the arguments they make for why some right or other that they or their set likes is "in" the Constitution are grounded in pure political preference. But I have never met a judge who had this kind of queasiness. For a judge, the duty to decide the case is paramount. He wouldn't be doing his duty if he said, "I can't decide this case, because I can't deduce the outcome from the orthodox materials of judicial decision making." He decides as best he can, and in doing this he is doing law. It is true that when he comes to write an opinion in a difficult case he is unlikely to be fully candid about the degree to which he has had to rely on policy or personal values to decide it, although Kennedy exaggerates when he says that judges *always* try to cast their decisions in a rhetoric of necessity or inevitability. But lack of *complete* candor in a judicial opinion, as in any public document, especially an official one, is not hypocrisy or bad faith. There is a role for tact in public life. A judicial opinion is not a confessional document or a *cri de coeur.* The opinion has to be acceptable both to the legal community and to the larger community that is affected by what judges do. And many members of both communities believe in perfectly good faith, though erroneously, that legal materials alone are sufficient to resolve even the most difficult cases. Those are the judges, by the way, who are most likely to be unconstrained activists. Hugo Black was a prime example.

I keep coming back to Kennedy's disbelief in the possibility of cogent policy analysis. It is the error that in the end undoes him. The unsentimental (unironic, unecstatic, and undepressed) legal pragmatist admits that in difficult cases he can't bridge the gap between the formal materials of the law and a sensible outcome without doing policy. So either he rolls up his sleeves and does policy, hoping that the bar or more likely the academy will provide him with the resources for making sensible policy analyses, or he uses his ignorance of policy, as Holmes often did, as a warrant for judicial restraint. The pragmatist like Kennedy who doesn't think that you can do anything with an appeal to sound policy but hide your ideology in it has no resources for deciding a case or advocating a policy change.[97] He is left stranded in the rubble of his transgressive artifacts—which is pretty much where another noted postmodernist latterly interested in law, Stanley Fish, finds himself.

Stanley Fish: Postmodern Thersites

Fish is properly contemptuous of highfalutin legal and political theory. When he says "that there are no different or stronger reasons than policy reasons, and that the announcement of a formula (higher-order impartiality, mutual respect, or the judgment of all mankind) that supposedly outflanks politics, or limits its sphere by establishing a space free from its incursions, will be nothing more or less than politics—here understood not as a pejorative, but as the name of the activity by which you publicly urge what you think to be good and true—by another name, the name, but never the reality, of principle,"[98] I find myself in complete agreement with him. But his contempt for his intellectual opponents and for reasoned argument is insatiable and at times threatens to devour decency, accuracy, and Fish himself.

97. The defeatist, or quietistic, implications of postmodernist social thought have been noted frequently. See, for example, Litowitz, note 91 above, at 80–86.

98. Stanley Fish, "Mission Impossible: Settling the Just Bounds between Church and State," 97 *Columbia Law Review* 2255, 2297 (1997).

He sometimes seems to conceive of intellectual activity, his own included, as a branch of defamation motivated by self-aggrandizement. The implied author of his book nominally on free speech[99] is Homer's Thersites, a trafficker in scurrility and effrontery. Fish's effrontery is illustrated by his remark that *he* "prefer[s] the quieter tones of pragmatic inquiry" (p. 50). His scurrility is illustrated by his treatment of Arthur Schlesinger, Jr. After calling Schlesinger a racist for affirming the worth of Western civilization, because racists have affirmed that worth, Fish remarks that a photograph of Schlesinger reveals features that "are ethnic, Semitic, even a bit negroid," and he criticizes Schlesinger for "nowhere mak[ing] mention of that heritage" (p. 88). Elsewhere Fish remarks: "*Academics like to eat shit, and in a pinch, they don't care whose shit they eat*" (p. 278, emphasis in original). Fish wants to be noticed, not necessarily believed or even taken seriously. Speaking of his debate opponent Dinesh D'Souza, Fish remarks that "our personal interactions were unfailingly cordial. We dined together, traveled together, and played tennis whenever we could . . . In May I danced happily at his wedding" (p. 52). Yet in one of the essays to which these remarks are a preface, Fish describes D'Souza as a racist and a liar. It's like debating Joseph Goebbels over the proper place of the Jew in modern Europe and afterwards dancing at Goebbels' wedding. Either Fish doesn't believe that D'Souza is a racist and a liar or he cares little about either racial justice or truthfulness. Or both. He calls himself a "contemporary sophist" (p. 281) and adds, "I don't have any principles" (p. 298). I believe him. Socrates, thou shouldst be living at this hour.

To those who argue that academic merit rather than race or sex ought to be the exclusive criterion for academic appointments, Fish replies that their opponents simply have a different conception of merit. But race or sex is not anyone's idea of a *meritocratic* criterion of appointment; the disagreement, which Fish wants to recast as a semantic misunderstanding, is over the weight to assign merit. In like sophistic vein he argues that since everything is politics, there can be no such thing as a debate between proponents and opponents of political correctness; there can just be conflicting notions of political correctness. But as he well knows, the term "political correctness" denotes efforts to eliminate terminology and arguments thought to encode hostile or insensitive attitudes toward vulnerable

99. Stanley Fish, *There's No Such Thing as Free Speech, and It's a Good Thing, Too* (1994). Subsequent page references to this book appear in the text. The book is a collection of essays not limited to free speech or, for that matter, to law.

groups. It is those efforts that the opponents of political correctness, many of whom share the politics of the proponents, resist.

Fish quotes with approval, as a telling point against meritocracy in education, someone's remark that the correlation between scores on the Scholastic Aptitude Test and college grades is lower than the correlation between height and weight. But height and weight *are* correlated, and the question is how closely they are correlated and how much weaker the correlation between SAT scores and college grades is. Critical of scholars and publicists who shirk "the hard work of presenting evidence" (p. 20), Fish yet is one of them, content to mouth liberal pieties about the effects of discrimination, refusing to acknowledge that these might be matters for investigation, oblivious to the tension between admitting weak students to a college for the sake of having a diverse student body in which people of different races can learn from each other and allowing them to choose racially segregated living quarters, eating arrangements, and even curricula once they are admitted—both of which positions he holds. He thinks the fact that test scores are correlated with parents' income shows that the scores are arbitrary. He ignores the possibility that the parents' incomes and the children's test scores may be different manifestations of the same values and aptitudes.

He distrusts systematic thought about issues of law or public policy because he believes, in a parody of Wittgenstein, that theory can have no effect on practice. For Fish, every area of human activity is a game that has rigid rules, like chess. You could have a theory about chess—about its origins, people's fascination with it, even how it might be improved by a change in its rules. But you could not use the theory in playing chess. When you play chess you play by its rules, not theory's rules. So no theoretical reflections about law could be expected to alter the way judges decide cases, because judges play the judging game, which has its own rules. The theory game and the practice game never intersect.

Never? The rules of the judicial game are much looser than those of chess, and theoretical insights and perspectives can alter the rules—can make them more like those of economics, say, or of social science generally, or conceivably (though, as I have argued, improbably) of moral reasoning, or (as used to be the legal profession's aspiration) of logic. Fish does not allow for these possibilities because he thinks that judges make decisions *only* on ad hoc political grounds and that they *always* conceal their ad hoc-ery in a phony rhetoric of rule and principle. He thinks

judges equally impervious to interdisciplinary and to formalist conceptions of the judge's role. He thinks they're as cynical as he is, illustrating
the adage that people tend to be highly sensitive to their own weaknesses
when they see them in other people.

His is an odd conception of the judicial "game,"[100] one that is inconsistent with his own previous writings,[101] that disregards what sociologists
have long known about role playing,[102] and that he is unable to substantiate. He offers the following "evidence" of how legal rules are emptied of
meaning so that judges can do justice on a retail basis uncabined by rules.
If a written contract recites that it is the complete agreement between the
parties, the court will not listen to testimony that contradicts the written
agreement. This is the parol evidence rule. It is phony, Fish argues, because
the court *will* hear evidence that the trade to which the contract pertains
attaches a special meaning to words used in the contract, a meaning that
would not be apparent to an outsider. So, says Fish, the parties are allowed
to contradict the written contract after all. He overlooks a vital distinction.[103] Trade usage can be established by disinterested testimony to a
reasonable degree of certainty. To consult trade usage is like consulting a
dictionary. And the use of a dictionary to interpret the words of a contract
does not undermine the parol evidence (and cognate "four corners") rule,
which is founded on concern that written contracts would mean little if a
party could try to persuade a judge or, particularly, a jury that while the
contract said *X*, the parties had actually agreed, without telling anybody or
writing anything down, that the deal was *Y*. Such evidence would be
subjective, unverifiable, unreliable, and self-serving, unlike a dictionary or
trade usage.

It is true that no contract can be made to say anything unless the author
and the readers share a common understanding of the words and of
essential contextual factors such as the purpose of making contracts. But if
contracting parties believe that a judge is likely to be a member of the

100. See Posner, note 34 above, at 132–135.

101. See Stanley Fish, "Still Wrong after All These Years," in Fish, *Doing What Comes Naturally:
Change, Rhetoric, and the Practice of Theory in Literary and Legal Studies* 356 (1989).

102. "Each role has its inner discipline, what Catholic monastics would call its 'formation.' The
role forms, shapes, patterns both action and actor. It is very difficult to pretend in this world.
Normally, one becomes what one plays at." Peter L. Berger, *Invitation to Sociology: A Humanistic
Perspective* 98 (1963).

103. See AM International, Inc. v. Graphic Management Associates, Inc., 44 F.3d 572 (7th Cir.
1995); Joseph D. Becker, "Disambiguating Contracts by Summary Judgment," *New York State Bar
Journal,* Dec. 1997, p. 10.

same interpretive community as they and will thus read the contract as they intend it to be read, then by including an integration clause (a clause saying in effect that the parol evidence rule shall apply if there is a dispute over the meaning of the contract, thus excluding inquiry into the parties' subjective understandings) they can foreclose most disputes over meaning.

Fish is similarly off-base in arguing that the doctrine of consideration— that a promise will not be enforced unless the promisor has received a reciprocal promise or some other benefit—is fake. He points out that promises are sometimes enforced when the promisor had *previously* received a benefit from the promisee.[104] The promisee might have rescued the promisor and been injured in the process. If the rescued person promises for the first time *after* the rescue to compensate the rescuer for his injuries, and thus receives nothing in return *for the promise,* how can the promise be thought supported by consideration? One answer lies in the practical function of the doctrine of consideration. That doctrine, like the parol evidence rule, reduces the likelihood of phony contract claims, because bilateral exchanges are more likely to be intended to give rise to legal duties than purely gratuitous promises. In the rescue case, which is emblematic of the "past" or "moral" consideration cases that Fish considers doctrinally aberrant, the likelihood that the promise was in fact made is high, so a wider mesh for straining out phony claims is appropriate.

Doctrinal aberrance is central to Fish's conception of law, for he believes that "the inconsistency of doctrine is what enables law to work" (p. 169). This is a version of the common misconception, now several centuries out of date, that law is an assemblage of senselessly rigid rules from which unprincipled departures are continually necessary to save the whole clumsy edifice from collapsing. In like vein Fish argues that "'free speech' is just the name we give to verbal behavior that serves the substantive agendas we wish to advance." The judges protect the "speech they want heard" and regulate "the speech they want silenced" (p. 110). At one level this is true. Freedom of speech is not absolute. It is relative to social conditions. It had a narrower scope for Blackstone than it has for us, and it would take careful historical inquiry to substantiate a claim that he had too narrow a conception of it even for his time. Even in today's United States freedom of speech is not absolute. People can still be punished for disseminating obscenity, for revealing military or trade secrets, for defamation, for inciting riots, for copyright and trademark infringement, for

104. See Posner, note 9 above, § 4.2, pp. 108–109.

plagiarism, for threats, for perjury, for false advertising and other misrepresentations, for certain types of verbal abuse, for exchanging information in the hope of facilitating price fixing, for talking back to prison guards, for revealing confidences of various sorts, for certain forms of picketing and aggressive solicitation, for indecorous behavior in courthouses, for publicly criticizing one's employer on matters not deemed to be of public concern, for irresponsible or offensive broadcasting, even for using loudspeakers. Justice Jackson warned against interpretations that would make the Bill of Rights a national suicide pact. But there is a difference between free-speech doctrine shaped and constrained by broadly political considerations and a free-for-all in which judges base decisions on which speech they like and which they don't like. Most of the "speech" that survives legal challenge in the United States—such as neo-Nazi ravings, blasphemous art, pornography that does not cross the line to obscenity, government documents containing diplomatic secrets (the Pentagon Papers, for example), flag-burnings, picketing, and cross-burnings—offends the mostly conservative, mostly middle-aged and elderly persons who, as judges, insist that the government allow such things.

Fish acknowledges this point obliquely in discussing a parody, held constitutionally protected by the Supreme Court, published in *Hustler* magazine in which Jerry Falwell, the fundamentalist religious leader, is represented as having sexual intercourse with his mother in an outhouse.[105] The Court's inability to draw a line that would permit the suppression of so intellectually barren and gratuitously repulsive a personal attack draws a pointed remark from Fish about the judiciary's "self-imposed incapacity to make distinctions that would seem perfectly obvious to any well-informed teenager" (p. 132). That incapacity sounds, however, like the very opposite of the ad hoc political decision making that Fish told us is all that judges do.

The free-speech strategy of civil libertarians and the courts, a strategy to which Fish is oblivious, resembles the U.S. defense strategy during the Cold War. It was a forward defense. Our front line was the Elbe, not the Potomac. The choice between a forward and a close-in defense involves trade-offs. The forward defense is more costly, and the forward-defense line, because it is nearer the enemy forces, is more likely to be overrun. But the forward defense allows a defense in depth, reducing the likelihood that the home front will be penetrated. The analogy to free-speech strategy is

105. Hustler Magazine, Inc. v. Falwell, 485 U.S. 46 (1988).

straightforward. Rather than defending just the right to say and write things that have some plausible social value, the courts defend the right to say and write utterly worthless and deeply offensive things as well. The fight goes on at these outer pickets; it is costly because the claim of free speech is weak because overextended; and sometimes the claim is defeated. But the home front is secure, the enemy having dissipated his strength in penetrating the outer bulwarks. Fish understands the political function of judicial decisions, but not the political function of rules. He does not realize that judges can sometimes strengthen their political hand by binding themselves to rules, as in the case of free speech. He does not understand the possibility of what I earlier called a "rule pragmatist."

For Fish, the judges' pretense that they can detach themselves from their own values and preferences is at one with the liberal pretense that the state can and should be neutral among rival world views. He thinks that liberalism is just another ideology and that every ideology must rest on a fundamental conception of what the world is like—the scientific conception, for example, or the religious conception. Liberalism and religious fundamentalism, the first committed to empirical verification and the second to biblical inerrancy, are simply rival faiths. Fair enough; but what follows? Liberalism is a set of practices and institutions with a long and on the whole a highly successful history when compared with rival systems in point of wealth, power, happiness, social justice, peace, and freedom. The politics of biblical inerrancy has been tried repeatedly as a principle of social ordering and repeatedly found wanting.

I do not think that Fish would disagree with what I have just said about liberalism. He is not a radical or even, despite appearances, a cynic. He actually admires the law. (And why not? He has recast it in his own image.) But for him as for Duncan Kennedy, government and law are constructed out of nothing more solid than rhetoric, politics, and ideology, so that all the "justice" and "fairness" talk in law is an *indispensable* fraud because "the law's job [is] to give us ways of redescribing limited partisan programs so that they can be presented as the natural outcomes of abstract impersonal imperatives" (p. 222). I don't think law is quite so airy as that. Like Kennedy, Fish is blind to the possibility that with the help of social science, professional experience, and common sense, judges and legislators create legal rules, practices, and institutions that have more to commend them than rhetorical hot air and partisan politics. But he is right to emphasize that the judicial game is different from the philosophy game. He is also right that interpretation is something we can do competently without having a theory about it and that theories of interpretation are unlikely to affect the practice of interpretation. He misunderstands, however, the stakes in legal debates over "originalism" and other interpretive theories. As with the parol evidence rule and the doctrine of past consideration, the issue is what kinds of evidence shall be admissible in the resolution of particular types of dispute. Not all debates in legal theory are, as Fish would have it, the product of semantic confusion and stubborn foundationalism. And "pragmatic," in law anyway, need not mean ad hoc.

The hostility of a Kennedy or a Fish to pretentious theorizing is refreshing. But ultimately these and other postmodernist critics of legal theory are as useless as moral theorists. Judges (most of them, most of the time) play the judicial game, not the moral-theory game, but also (albeit with notable exceptions, especially in constitutional decisions of the Supreme Court) not the game of advancing their political preferences behind a fig leaf. Theorists who adjure them to play the theory game, and nontheorists who adjure them to play the willfulness game, are equally out of touch with their audience except insofar as it consists of other, like-thinking academics.

Some Institutional Implications of Legal Pragmatism

I have argued that law should be more pragmatic (but steer clear of postmodernist extravagance) en route to becoming more professional in the best sense of the word. If this is right, it has implications for institutions as well as for attitudes. Moreover, *whether* it is right may depend on whether law's institutional framework can be adapted to the needs of pragmatic professionalism. I conclude this chapter and the book by examining these questions with reference to three institutions. One is legal education. I argue for reforms that while leaving the first year of law school intact would drastically truncate the remainder of a legal education for most students. And I argue that these reforms would come about more or less automatically if legal education were deregulated, that is, if persons wanting to be lawyers were not required, as they are in most states (California is the most important exception), to spend three years studying in an accredited law school.

The second institution that I discuss is the student-edited law review, still the cornerstone of legal publication. I suggest a reorientation of the student-edited law review and a division of responsibilities between it and faculty-edited reviews.

Like legal education and the student-edited law review, the American Law Institute is a bastion of professional tradition. I would like to see it, too, shaken up a bit.

Legal Education

The book by Mary Ann Glendon that I discusssed in Chapter 3 points out that many lawyers, in particular recent law school graduates, are dissatisfied with conditions in the private practice of law.[106] Those conditions include extremely long hours of work, limited job security, unprecedented scrutiny and distrust by clients, a consequent heavy exposure to malpractice suits and other litigation (and therefore a heavy expense of liability insurance), tedious specialization, and the bureaucratization of law-firm management. These lawyers, here joined by judges, are also dissatisfied with the changing character of legal scholarship. This dissatisfaction, symptomatic of the growing estrangement between academic law and the practice of law, is nicely captured in the following statement by a professor at the Yale Law School: "law professors are not paid to train lawyers, but to study the law and teach their students what they happen to discover."[107]

These twin dissatisfactions have different causes (though with some overlap, as I shall point out) and, I suspect, no cure. But they would be ameliorated by the deregulation of legal education and practice. This probably would lead to a two-year JD (or LLB) on the model of the two-year MBA awarded by business schools, and indirectly to a reduction in the pressure on young lawyers to recoup their investment in legal education by working ridiculously long hours, because the investment would be smaller. It would also reduce the element of mystique in law, which we saw is fostered by making entry into the profession contingent on clearing high educational hurdles. I am inclined to favor the complete deregulation of legal services,[108] except that courts should be allowed to

106. See also Patrick J. Schiltz, "Legal Ethics in Decline: The Elite Law Firm, the Elite Law School, and the Moral Formation of the Novice Attorney," 82 *Minnesota Law Review* 704, 722–729, 740–744 (1998), and references cited there.

107. Mary Ann Glendon, *A Nation under Lawyers: How the Crisis in the Legal Profession Is Transforming American Society* 217 (1994), quoting Owen Fiss.

108. Cf. Herbert M. Kritzer, *The Justice Broker: Lawyers and Ordinary Litigation*, ch. 10 (1990).

establish and enforce criteria for the right to appear before them in an advocate's role because incompetent counsel impede and confuse the conduct of litigation to the prejudice of other litigants. But I shall confine my argument to the case for eliminating the requirement of a third year of legal education.[109]

The deterioration in the working conditions of lawyers is a sign of the increased competitiveness of the legal-services industry. That increased competitiveness is, in turn, part of an economywide trend toward greater competitiveness in service industries ranging from medical care to funerals. That trend took off in the 1990s in the wake of the movement in the 1980s to greater competitiveness in manufacturing. In the case of law, as earlier in the case of transportation and communications, the trend toward greater competitiveness has been helped along by a relaxation of regulatory controls, notably over the pricing and advertising of legal services and over the provision of substitute services by accountants, trust officers, paralegals, tax preparers, authors of do-it-yourself probate and divorce manuals, and consultants. Since the tendency of competition is to transform producer surplus into consumer surplus, it is no surprise that one effect of the competitive revolution in legal services has been to make lawyers work harder.

In addition, the computer and communications revolutions have, as air conditioning had earlier, increased lawyers' productivity. There is less down time when courts do not close in the summer, when your letters are answered in minutes by fax or e-mail rather than in hours, and when you can make and receive phone calls from your car or an airplane—or your pocket. Ordinarily an increase in productivity can be expected to increase a worker's income, leading to an increased demand for leisure. But if, at the same time that productivity is increasing, increased competition in the product market is depressing producers' incomes, the increased productivity of the workforce may lead to longer hours of work instead of higher real wages.

I don't want to exaggerate. Lawyers have always worked long hours when they had work. But young lawyers today have heavier family responsibilities than in the past because their spouses are likely to be hardworking professionals too, so that they find long hours of work more costly than earlier generations of lawyers did. As the realities of modern law

109. See also Christopher T. Cunniffe, "The Case for the Alternative Third-Year Program," 61 *Albany Law Review* 85 (1997).

practice sink in, moreover, the mixture of applicants for admission to law school will change in favor of those prepared to cope with those realities. And wages will adjust to compensate for the perceived disamenities of the work, including long hours and lack of job security, though this will depend in part on alternative employment opportunities; if in the conditions of modern capitalism all professionals work long hours and have limited job security, lawyers will not be able to demand a compensating wage differential for themselves.

Longer hours are not the principal cause of dissatisfaction among older lawyers. The principal cause is the competition-induced shift to a buyer's market, which has reduced the job security of partners in law firms and forced them to cut corners, to specialize more (in order to increase their productivity), and to hustle for clients. Young lawyers, looking ahead, can foresee that when they become partners they will have similar complaints; in this way the dissatisfaction of the old becomes an anticipated dissatisfaction of the young.

The MacCrate Report[110] and other complaints by the bar about the training imparted by the law schools are symptomatic of the growing competitiveness of the legal profession. It is difficult in the best of circumstances for a law firm to recoup the full cost of training a new lawyer. The newcomer is likely to leave the firm after a few years, before the firm has had a chance to exploit his enhanced productivity. A firm can try to make a new lawyer pay for his own training by accepting a lower wage, but competition for new lawyers may limit this possibility. The greater the competitive pressure to cut costs, the less firms can afford to confer benefits for which they cannot recover the cost and the more urgently, therefore, they want the law schools to shoulder a larger share of the burden of training lawyers—which is the thrust of the MacCrate Report's recommendations.

I have said that legal work is becoming more tedious. Think once again of those dull Supreme Court opinions that I mentioned in the preceding chapter. The flattening, almost the deskilling, of judicial work (appellate judges, at least, can delegate much of their work to their law clerks, and so don't have to be very able themselves in order to produce a product of acceptable quality) is paralleled as the level of practice by increased spe-

---

110. *Report of the Task Force on Law Schools and the Profession: Narrowing the Gap, Legal Education and Professional Development—An Educational Continuum* (American Bar Association, Section of Legal Education and Admissions to the Bar, July 1992).

cialization of both fields and tasks (so some lawyers just do "rainmaking," and others just do firm management, and others just work in the law library), producing the disenchantment that Weber predicted would accompany the increasing rationalization of work. Increasingly lawyers are "intellectual workers," doing the intellectual equivalent of assembly-line work, working in hierarchically organized teams in large, hierarchically structured organizations (law firms or corporations), turning out a product of acceptable, sometimes of high, professional quality but one deficient in individuality, and thus losing the satisfactions of a sense of craftsmanship.[111]

The changing character of legal scholarship, as distinct from legal practice, is mainly though not entirely the product of developments internal to the scholarly enterprise rather than of the changes in the market for legal services, though the trend toward ever greater rationalization of work is a factor in the change in legal scholarship as well. Beginning in the early 1960s, developments in economics, political theory, history, and even literary criticism enlarged the opportunities for analyzing law by the methods of other disciplines. These methods struck many young legal academics as more exciting than the conventional analysis of legal doctrines (often this was for political as well as purely intellectual reasons) and also more "professional" in a sense that by now should be familiar to the reader. Eventually these people came to occupy positions of influence in academic law and began recasting legal scholarship in their image.

In the academic regime forged by recent generations of legal scholars, fewer lawyers are hired from practice to teach law because a background in practice is valuable mainly as preparation for doing doctrinal analysis. More emphasis is now placed on the scholarly norms that prevail in the external disciplines that the modern academic lawyer wants to draw from, such as economics and philosophy. The most important of these norms is the placing of much heavier emphasis on scholarly output than on teaching ability. And, as in these other disciplines, the primary audience for a law professor's scholarship increasingly is other academics. Academic law is moving away from its traditional function as a supplier of services to the practicing bar and the judiciary, becoming, as we glimpsed in Chapter 3, a separate profession with its own customs and standards. And this is happening just when the bar is increasingly insistent on the academy's service function.

111. This process is sometimes referred to as the "industrialization of service." See Posner, note 34 above, at 64–70. Cf. Kritzer, note 108 above, ch. 10.

As the practice of law becomes less intellectual because of increased emphasis on hustling for business and on narrow specialization, more intellectuals who find themselves in the law want to go into teaching. Another factor in the increased intellectuality of academic law is the continuing decline in good job opportunities in most academic fields, which is pushing people of scholarly bent into the law schools. That decline, which reflects among other things the growing professionalization of university administration and a resulting rationalization (in Weber's sense) of the academic enterprise, has been particularly marked in the humanities. They are financially precarious at best and hence a natural target for cost-cutting university administrators. In fields like philosophy and history, even first-rate graduate students may invest three years in getting a JD to add to their PhD and then seek employment in a law school, where salaries are higher, teaching loads lower, and the prospects for tenure far superior. If the analysis in the previous chapters is sound, this migration is not entirely to be welcomed.

In short, the practice of law is becoming more like a business at the same time that law school is becoming less like a business school and more like a graduate department. The practice and the academy thus are drifting apart. But let me not exaggerate the extent and significance of the drift. Law teaching has changed less than legal scholarship has, and doctrinal scholarship has not so much diminished as shifted from elite to nonelite law schools, where however it is done highly competently because of an overall improvement in the quality of law school faculties. This improvement is due in part to the deterioration in the working conditions at law firms that I remarked earlier, which has made academic law a buyers' market, and in part to laws forbidding employment discrimination. An employer doesn't want to be placed in a position in which a member of a protected group who has been refused employment or promotion can point to less well qualified nonminority employees who have been retained. Antidiscrimination laws are unnecessary in highly competitive markets, because competition exerts heavy pressure on employers to utilize rational employment practices. Nonprofit enterprises (such as universities), governments, monopolies, and competition-limiting professions are all settings in which discriminatory employment practices are likely to emerge in the absence of legal prohibition.[112]

112. See, for example, Armen A. Alchian and Reuben A. Kessel, "Competition, Monopoly, and the Pursuit of Money," in *Aspects of Labor Economics* 157 (National Bureau of Economic Research 1962); Posner, note 9 above, § 26.1, pp. 716–717.

The growing gap between the practical and the academic sides of law has its upside and its downside. The upside is that if law is to be placed on an empirical basis—if, for example, the study of constitutionalism is to be reoriented along the lines suggested in Chapter 2—law schools must become more hospitable to nondoctrinal research. The downside is that the more law schools become a world apart from practice, the less likely they are to produce research of practical value. The application of moral philosophy to law is academic and nondoctrinal—and also useless.

The deregulation of legal education would be a partial answer both to the current dissatisfactions of lawyers and to excesses of the ivory tower in legal education. It would also also foster the right kind of nondoctrinal research and move the entire profession a little closer to the goal of true professionalism. This is the era of deregulation, so one might expect the proposal to get a sympathetic hearing. One's expectations would be dashed. It is difficult to get law professors of any ideological persuasion, and even more difficult to get law school and university administrators, to agree that the market rather than the government can and should determine the length and content of a professional education. Self-interest is one reason for this blindness. Another is an attitude of "we know best." The second may be more important, because many law schools would flourish in a regime in which the third year was optional. They could attract more students to a shorter course of instruction, and many of their students would voluntarily elect a third year though not perhaps until a later point in their career. With the captive-audience character of the third year removed, those students who did stay (or came back) for a third year would be eager and attentive, and this would be a benefit to the professors as well as to the students.

The biggest beneficiaries of deregulating legal education would be students who decided not to take a third year. The shorter the course of instruction, the lower the cost of law school to the student and hence the less intense the pressure to work killing hours in a high-pressure law firm in order to pay off one's student loans. This assumes that lawyers' salaries would not fall as far as the cost of legal education fell, but why should they, unless the third year of law school adds significantly to a young lawyer's productivity? They would fall some, as the reduced cost of becoming a lawyer attracted more people to go to law school and thus increased the supply of lawyers, but perhaps not a great deal; the relation between income and length of postgraduate education is pretty loose. Having invested only two years in legal education, moreover, students would be less committed financially to remaining in law if they didn't like it.

One argument for continuing to require the third year of law school is that we have too much litigation, and therefore too many lawyers already, so anything that cuts down the number, even barriers of entry in education, is to the good. The fewer lawyers there are, the higher the price of legal services will be, so the less demand there will be for those services, resulting in a lower rate of litigation. No one knows, however, whether we have too much litigation or too many lawyers,[113] so I shall set that argument to one side. Another argument is that the value of the third year exceeds its cost but that students, being immature, impatient, and inexperienced, might not realize this. They might not. But their future employers, the law firms, would. Firms which thought that students who had spent another year in law school would be more productive because they would require less on-the-job training would offer a higher salary, and students would balance this benefit of a third year against the cost. This in turn would force law schools to think about what kind of third-year curriculum would actually help students in their careers, as distinct from simply advancing the professors' careers, since law schools would not be able to keep students for a third year unless it conferred a net benefit on them. (The title "JD" could be retained for the degree awarded after three years, and the older "LLB" restored as the title for the two-year professional degree.)

I assume that by the end of the first year of the two-year program most students would know whether they preferred business law or nonbusiness law. Students who preferred the former would in their second year take courses such as corporation law, securities law, commercial law, antitrust, tax, bankruptcy, and pension law. Students who preferred nonbusiness law would take such courses as criminal law, family law, civil rights law, federal courts, constitutional law, jurisprudence, and employment law. (There is overlap between the two categories, especially with regard to employment law.) Common to both areas is administrative law, evidence, conflict of laws, and economic analysis of law. Students who couldn't make up their mind whether they preferred business law or nonbusiness law could take a mixture of courses and still learn enough to practice either type of law. Students who obtained an LLB from an elite law school after completing

113. Posner, note 34 above, at 89–90.

the program that I have outlined would save themselves as much as $100,000—$20,000 or more in tuition for the third year and as much as $80,000 in forgone income in that year (less of course after taxes, but still considerable).

If the third year were not required for a professional degree, it would have to be something special, not just more of the same, for students to elect it. What might that something special be? For students who intended to become law professors, perhaps graduate-style courses in research methodology and in disciplines related to law. Perhaps clinical training for students who intended to become trial lawyers. Perhaps specially designed courses in economics, finance, game theory, statistics, comparative and international law, public health, public administration, taxation, accounting, computer sciences, criminology, ethics, medicine, social work, or engineering for students intending either to specialize in the more esoteric branches of counseling and litigation or to go into academic law. The offerings might be as diverse as they are in business schools, whose faculties include accountants, psychologists, operations researchers, game theorists, marketing specialists, statisticians, finance specialists, economists, and lawyers. The third year would become the foundation for reorienting the law in a pragmatic, truly professional direction.

An incidental benefit would be to curtail the hyperacademification of legal scholarship that now troubles law firms. We have reached the point at which a law professor can specialize in an area of study that holds no interest for a practicing lawyer, and hence for 95 percent of the professor's students (disinterested, career-unrelated intellectual curiosity being uncommon among law students), without causing any raised eyebrows, because the students have to fill up three years with courses. The professor's area might be the use of Wittgenstein or Grice to interpret the Uniform Commercial Code. Or worker-owned cooperatives in Yugoslavia before the death of Tito. Or the law of slavery in the antebellum South. The kinds of legal thinking that I have criticized in this book flourish in the hothouse atmosphere of a required third year of law school. Abolish the required third year and the professor's course enrollments would shrink to the number of students, possibly very small, who were really interested in the subject or the professor's take on it. Even if there turned out to be very few such students—even if there turned out to be none—the law school might decide that the professor's scholarly interest had sufficient importance to the university's mission of advancing human knowledge to be supported. But in making this decision the law school or university would not be under any illusions about student demand for instruction in the professor's area of interest.

A likelier response to the elimination of the third-year captive audience would be a resorting of students and a reduction in the amount of basic research in law. A handful of law schools would cater to students with academic ambitions, and their teachers would be the only law professors who conducted research that had no foreseeable practical payoff. Second- and third-tier law schools would no longer be refuges for moral philosophers manqué. In my opinion this would be all to the good.

Some readers may think me a philistine for saying these things and others, even among those who share my low opinion of normative moral philosophy and constitutional theory, will accuse me of having overlooked the humanizing or civilizing role of an extended legal education—the only hope, they might argue, for restoring the fading ideal of the lawyer-statesman. That would be a wistful hope, greatly exaggerating the moral effect of education, especially when the education is in law school and the morals are those of lawyers.[114] Law is fast becoming a business, and law schools cannot reverse the trend. As business ethics are not clearly inferior to legal ethics, the trend is not greatly to be regretted on moral grounds, and law schools ought therefore to adjust to it rather than fight it. Yet the concern about the trend is not entirely misplaced. Some important tasks in society require the use of highly specialized skills to produce services that are difficult for outsiders to evaluate. This is true of such disparate professions as law, medicine, and military leadership. Because the evaluation of these professionals (given their esoteric skills) is difficult, we want them to be inculcated with values of service and integrity that will give them internal incentives to provide reliable, honest, high-quality service.[115] In short, we want them to have not only the requisite skills but also an esprit de corps, a sense of being different and special. A prolonged period of specialized training is one method of imparting such a spirit. Truncate the period, and the spirit may flag.

This is a legitimate concern. But keeping a restive captive audience for a third year of law school will not allay it. Lawyers didn't have lower

114. Professors and students alike groan over courses in legal ethics, made mandatory by the accrediting authorities. See, for example, Thomas D. Eisele, "From 'Moral Stupidity' to Professional Responsibility," 21 *Legal Studies Forum* 193 (1997).

115. See Daryl Koehn, *The Ground of Professional Ethics*, ch. 4 (1994).

standards of character when legal education was briefer than it is today. And competition is at least a partial substitute for old-fashioned professionalism as a guarantor of the quality of professional services.

A deeper objection to the deregulation of legal education is that it would bring academic research too close to practice. "A dominant value of the scholarly world is a certain disengagement from the contemporary scene and a search for knowledge more fundamental and durable than that required for practical and immediate purposes." This is a genuine value, as is also the scholarly world's emphasis on "the paraphernalia of scholarship . . . Words like rigor and elegance portray this element of academic taste, whereas the world of affairs prefers words such as *effective* and *persuasive*."[116] These values distinguish basic from applied research. It would be a misfortune to destroy basic legal research by reconfiguring legal education to eliminate the demand for it. This is the objection to Adam Smith's proposal that teachers be paid in proportion to the number of students in their courses. Since students have no motivation to finance basic research, the effect of such a per capita wage scheme would be to reduce the financial base of such research. The proposal of a two-year law school would push in the same direction. The compression of the curriculum would deprive students of time to take subjects peripheral to their career objectives.

But this ought not be a source of great concern. Basic research in law would not disappear if the average length of a legal education were shortened. Plenty of basic research in fields such as finance and marketing is conducted in business schools, most of whose students are there for just two years, and in PhD programs whose students are not required by law to be in residence for any period at all. The requirement of three years of law school is giving basic research in law an artificial and, judging from experience in other fields, an unnecessary boost. That it is indeed artificial is the strong implication of this book, which has revealed an imbalance between high theory and practical, useful research. There is too much of the former and not enough of the latter; the deregulation of legal education would cause a shift, to some unknown but perhaps considerable extent, from the former to the latter.

If the third year of law school fades away, the first year will become an even more important component of legal education than it is; and it is already the most important. How should the first year be structured? The

116. George J. Stigler, "The Adoption of the Marginal Utility Theory," in Stigler, *The Economist as Preacher and Other Essays* 72, 77 (1982).

answer may cast further light on the feasibility of eliminating the third year. My answer is severely traditional, but is subject to the qualification that in speaking of "the" first-year curriculum I do not mean to imply that legal education should be uniform across law schools. It should not be, because of the stratification in the quality of students, and to a lesser extent of faculty, among the various tiers of law schools. Students and faculty are not randomly assigned to law schools. Schools compete for the best students and faculty, and students and faculty compete to study or teach (respectively) in the best schools. The consequence is a sorting by quality that results in very different average qualities of student and faculty in different law schools, though with much overlap because there is considerable variance around the mean of the quality distribution at the various schools. It wouldn't make sense for the curriculum of the best law school to be identical to that of the worst, or for that matter to that of the average law school. But I shall be speaking from now on of just the top tier of schools.

To be a first-year student at the Harvard Law School in the late 1950s (as I was) was to spend a year trying to master unfamiliar materials—namely, common law judicial opinions—with little guidance or feedback. It was the heyday of the Socratic method of legal education. This meant that the casebooks consisted of—cases, with only a little explanatory material. The first-year courses other than criminal law and civil procedure were in common law fields—property, contracts, torts, and agency. The teachers disparaged hornbooks, treatises, articles, and other secondary materials; and most of the students, docile me included, dutifully refused to consult any of these materials. Adept at not tipping their hand, and abetted in this by the students' avoidance of secondary materials and the absence of commercial study aids, the teachers orchestrated debates among students who personified the various fallacies to which lay thinking about the law is prone.

These first-year law teachers were intimidating people. They were not sadistic, but they didn't try to put the students at their ease or wait for a student to volunteer in order to call on him (or her, but there weren't many hers).[117] There were no exams until the end of the entire year, so you couldn't tell how well you were doing. This was a big spur to working

---

117. I do not want to leave the impression that I think that the first year of law school should be modeled on the Virginia Military Institute's single-gender adversative-training program! Yet more female than male students complain that the Socratic method of legal instruction, though much gentler than it used to be, is excessively adversative.

hard, as was the knowledge that on the basis of the examination results alone you would be ranked from 1 to 500 and that your rank might have a big effect on your future career. The emphasis of the courses, mirrored by the exams, was not on stuffing students full of rules or case names but on drilling them in fitting factual situations into plausible legal categories, much as medical students learn to fit a set of symptoms into a disease category, and in manipulating the categories in the interest of the client: so the training had both a diagnostic and a treatment aspect. The lesson was the manipulability of the legal categories. Lay people think that the law is something written down in a book. Lawyers learn, in their very first year of law school, that the law is an inference from often ambiguous and even conflicting cases. They learn to be skilled casuists.

The Yale Law School of the period employed a somewhat different model of legal education. There was less emphasis on drilling students in the case system and more emphasis, consistent with the school's legal-realism heritage, on the role of policy in the law and on external critique of the law—on how well the law was serving social needs as distinct from how consistent legal doctrines were with each other and with their premises. This approach tended to impart a more skeptical view of law than the Harvard approach. And because this was fairly widely known it also tended to attract a more skeptical student.

The Yale approach[118] was too radical for the 1950s; the school flinched, and by the end of the period had almost converged with Harvard.[119] But then the 1960s set in; the distinctive Yale approach revived, at Yale and elsewhere; and today the balance in first-year education has swung sharply toward that approach. This is consistent with the changes in academic law that I discussed earlier, but the reasons for the swing go beyond those changes. They include social factors—such as affirmative action and a diminished respect for authority figures, including law professors—that have made the classic Harvard Socratic approach less palatable; and the growth of public law relative to private law. Subjects like administrative law and especially constitutional law are now often found in the first-year curriculum, along with interdisciplinary electives such as economic analysis of law and jurisprudence, compressing the time allotted to common law subjects. And those subjects are now usually taught as mixtures of doctrine and policy, sometimes with emphasis on economic, feminist, or even postmodernist perspectives. Courses that used to be limply taught in

118. Well described in Laura Kalman, *Legal Realism at Yale, 1927–1960* 150–191 (1986).
119. Id. at 204–207.

the second and third years by means of the case method—courses in fields in which cases either are not central (as in tax and corporate law and the law of evidence) or too often don't make any sense or are just more of the same taught less ably because law schools tend to load their best teachers into the first year—have become more interesting because they are now approached from an interdisciplinary perspective.

The best first-year legal education today is probably better than it was in the 1950s. This is true even though some inroads into quality have been made by affirmative action at both the student and faculty levels, by the disappearance of the Socratic bully (who kept the students on their toes), by the rise of commercial study aids, and by the decline in the casuistic brilliance of faculty as the law schools shifted the emphasis in hiring from legal smarts to academic creativity, which are not the same thing. The offsetting factor has been that growth in the number of students and faculty has been slower than the growth in the quality-weighted number of applicants for both admission and teaching. Since there is a limit to how brilliant you can be and want to go to law school, the effect of the improved quality of the applicants for admission has been to compress the distribution of abilities in the student body, or in other words to raise the bottom. But this enables the teaching to move at a brisker pace without losing a significant fraction of the class, with the result that the same amount of knowledge (including the how-to knowledge called "legal reasoning") can be imparted in a shorter period of time. If it took a year to give the first-year students at the Harvard Law School their basic training in the case method in the 1950s, it should take less than a year today, thus making room for additional subjects.

It is true that, despite a mass of new legislation, there is more common law today than there was in 1960. But the common law is not more complex than it was then; in some ways it has been made simpler, less enigmatic and chaotic-seeming, by economics, which provides a framework for understanding and interrelating the doctrines of the common law that was not available back then. So I will stand by my claim that it shouldn't take a year to give the first-year class at an elite law school an adequate education in the case method. This opens up room for other courses, which is an additional reason to think that law school could be compressed to two years without serious loss.

Other than thinking that the policy dimensions of law deserve emphasis, I hold generally conservative views, methodologically speaking, about the teaching of a law course. For example, I consider it a mistake to teach against the grain, as by teaching mainly cases that the teacher thinks wrong or unreasoned—not because it is desirable to indoctrinate the students in the official version of the legal process, in which everything is done on the merits with few mistakes and nary a hint of politics or ideology; but because they will not learn the case-law method if they don't take it seriously, if they think it's just a mask. Legal casuistry is difficult to do well, and students will be less likely to put forth their best efforts if they think it is simply a method of rationalizing results reached on other grounds. "Oppositionist" teachers, the crits and their allies and successors, should park their opposition at the first-year classroom door, reserving it for upper-level courses and seminars. Many of them do.

I also think it a mistake to try hard to find modern substitutes for the nineteenth- and early twentieth-century cases that are the traditional staples of the first-year curriculum. Students need to understand that the law was not created on their twenty-first birthday and that modern law is continuous with the law of the past in a way that modern economics, for example, is not. And now that most judges have given up writing their own opinions, old judicial opinions are usually more colorful than modern ones (and for the additional reason that the judges of earlier generations tended to have a more literary education than modern judges). There is no reason why a legal education should be dull. The old cases also afford a glimpse of history to a generation of students many of whom have studied little history before coming to law school. I hope the cult of political correctness has not reached the point at which the older judges' failures of gender neutrality and ethnic sensitivity require that their opinions be banished or bowdlerized.

One objection to wholesale changes in the first-year curriculum is severely pragmatic. It would be perilous to make such changes in a successful method, especially a successful method of *education*, where success seems so elusive. I have met only a few law students or law school graduates who did not think highly of their first year of law school—more highly, in most instances (as in my own experience), than of any other year of their education.

My defense of the traditional first year may seem inconsistent with the changing character of the legal profession and my own advocacy of a pragmatic approach to law. But it is difficult to imagine, at least in the near term, a transformation of law into policy science so complete that casuistic reasoning, with all its shortcomings, would no longer play an important role in the practice of law. The case-law method has a deep hold on the American legal imagination. Legal thinkers of revolutionary bent might think that the principal goal of legal education should be to loosen that hold, but I don't think so. The purpose of legal education is to equip students to be lawyers. For now and the foreseeable future, that purpose is best served by preserving the first year in essentially its present form.

To stop with this observation, however, would be to leave a misleading impression. I am as critical of the overuse of the case method in upper-class legal education as I am protective of its use in the first year. Reiterated drill in the method encounters sharply diminishing returns and makes the student overly dependent on what is only one way of resolving legal issues, and often not the best way. Subjects like evidence, taxation, corporations, conflict of laws, secured transactions, and pension law are probably best studied without any cases at all, but instead by tackling problems. In the case of evidence, which I believe to be on the whole the worst taught of all law school courses when taught from the rules of evidence and the cases construing those rules, the optimal method of instruction may combine clinical training—drill in presenting evidence at trial and in objecting, and ruling on objections, to evidence—with reflection on the psychological, statistical, and epistemological dimensions of inference, decision making, and the jury system. These dimensions are illuminated by a growing interdisciplinary literature, as yet unknown to most lawyers and judges and even many law professors, in philosophy, statistics, and cognitive psychology.[120]

Legal Publication

The fact that most legal scholarship is published in journals edited by students astonishes academics in other disciplines. But like the Socratic method of instruction it was until relatively recently an unquestioned feature of the landscape of legal education and scholarship. Increasingly, however, there is a sense that all is not right with this venerable institution.[121] And indeed all is not right. In particular what is wrong is the law

120. See, for example, *Probability and Inference in the Law of Evidence: The Uses and Limits of Bayesianism* (Peter Tillers and Eric D. Green eds. 1988); *Bayesianism and Juridical Proof,* 1997 *International Journal of Evidence and Proof* 253 (Special Issue edited by Ron Allen and Mike Redmayne).

121. See, for example, James Lindgren, "An Author's Manifesto," 61 *University of Chicago Law Review* 527 (1994); Kenneth Lasson, "Scholarship Amok: Excesses in the Pursuit of Truth and Tenure," 103 *Harvard Law Review* 926 (1990); Jordan H. Leibman and James P. White, "How the Student-Edited Law Journals Make Their Publication Decisions," 39 *Journal of Legal Education* 387 (1989); Roger C. Cramton, "'The Most Remarkable Institution': The American Law Review," 35 *Journal of Legal Education* 1 (1986). See generally *Law Review Conference,* 47 *Stanford Law Review* 1117 (1995).

reviews' inability to adapt to the changing nature of American law and American legal scholarship.

To determine how the student-edited law reviews are doing, we must first have a clear idea of *what* they are doing. Apart from performing a screening function for employers and providing an educational experience for the review's members, what they are doing is, of course, publishing articles, book reviews, and student notes. But "publication" is not a single thing; it is a composite of tasks. It will promote clarity to distinguish between faculty-written and student-written work. With respect to the former, the law reviews' tasks are selection, improvement, and editing. With respect to the latter, they are selection of topics, writing, improvement, and editing.

In the performance of these tasks the reviews labor under grave handicaps. The gravest is that their staffs are composed of young and inexperienced persons working part time: inexperienced not only as students of the law but also as editors, writers, supervisors, and managers. The next most serious handicap, which is related to the first, is high turnover: members of law review staffs spend less than two years in their part-time job. They do not have time to gain much experience, and their planning horizon is foreshortened. A third handicap is the absence of market forces in law review publishing. Law reviews do not fold if their editors make foolish decisions with respect to what to publish; and the editors receive no financial or, indeed, other rewards if they lower the costs or raise the quality and circulation of their reviews.

Given the considerable handicaps of ignorance, immaturity, inexperience, and inadequate incentives, the wonder is not that the student-edited law reviews leave much to be desired as scholarly journals, but that they aren't much worse than they are.[122] Indeed they used to be quite good by the scholarly standards prevailing at the time. But it was a time when legal scholarship was understood to be doctrinal scholarship, and the more technical and intricate the doctrine, the better.[123] The narrow orbit in

122. A survey of practicing lawyers, law professors, and judges found that the consumers of law reviews are generally pleased with the institution. Max Stier et al., "Law Review Usage and Suggestions for Improvement: A Survey of Attorneys, Professors, and Judges," 44 *Stanford Law Review* 1467 (1992). But the response rate was low—32.7 percent. Id. at 1479 (tab. 1). The displeased are probably underrepresented among responders; those who have no use for law reviews are unlikely to want to bother filling out a detailed (see id. at 1506–1513) questionnaire.

123. Doctrinal scholarship, and the conception of professional autonomy that places it at the center of legal scholarship, are and always have been more deeply entrenched in Europe (including England) than in the United States. Probably what nevertheless prevented the emergence of student-edited law reviews in Europe was that law in Europe was and is an undergraduate subject.

which legal scholarship revolved facilitated the job of law review editors. Inexperienced they might be, but as students who had earned a berth on their school's law review by doing well in their first-year classes they had demonstrated the knack of legal doctrinal analysis that was the very heart of legal scholarship in that era. Adept, albeit apprentice, doctrinalists, they could write, select, improve, and edit doctrinal scholarship. No single field of law mesmerized students, as constitutional law, then a small field, mesmerizes them today, so the scholarship that they wrote and that they chose from the submissions by faculty reflected the diversity of law itself.

This Golden Age—not for law or even for legal scholarship, merely for student-edited law reviews—drew to a gradual close between 1970 and 1990. During this period doctrinal scholarship as a fraction of all published legal scholarship underwent a dramatic decline to make room for a host of new forms of legal scholarship,[124] some of it written by nonlawyers, all of it employing perspectives drawn from other disciplines. The change in the character of legal scholarship has been accompanied by a collapse of political consensus among legal scholars and by a vast expansion in constitutional law—the most political of fields of law as a consequence of the nature of the issues it addresses, the remoteness of the governing text, and the field's domination by a court (the Supreme Court) from which there is no appeal to a still higher court to keep the judges in line. Legal scholarship became more political at the same time that it was becoming centrifugal.

These developments beached not only a number of doctrinal scholars but also most law review editors. They were now dealing with a scholarly enterprise vast reaches of which they could barely comprehend, and they were being tempted by the increasing politicization of the enterprise to employ political criteria in their editorial decisions. How baffling must seem the task of choosing among articles belonging to disparate genres—a doctrinal article on election of remedies, a narrative of slave revolts in the antebellum South, a Bayesian analysis of proof beyond a reasonable doubt, an angry polemic against pornography, a mathematical model of out-of-court settlement, an application of Wittgenstein to Article 2 of the UCC, an essay on normativity, a comparison of me to Kafka, and so on without end. Few student editors—certainly not enough to go around—are competent to evaluate nondoctrinal scholarship. So they do what other consumers do when faced with uncertainty about product quality; they

---

124. This decline is documented in William M. Landes and Richard A. Posner, "The Influence of Economics on Law: A Quantitative Study," 36 *Journal of Law and Economics* 385, 407–423 (1993), and in Landes and Posner, "Heavily Cited Articles in Law," 71 *Chicago-Kent Law Review* 825 (1996).

look for signals of quality or other merit. The reputation of the author, corresponding to a familiar trademark in markets for goods and services, is one such signal, and not the worst.[125] Others—and these dysfunctional—are the congeniality of the author's politics to the editors, the author's commitment to gender-neutral grammatical forms, the prestige of the author's law school, a desire for "equitable" representation of minorities and other protected or favored groups, the sheer length of an article,[126] the number of footnotes in it, and whether the article is a "tenure article" on which the author's career may be riding.

The effects of these dysfunctional features of the law reviews' decisions on what to publish are magnified in the new (for academic law) regime of publish or perish, for these decisions influence the tenure decision, and thus the composition of the legal professoriat. The law review editors have become more powerful at the same time that they have become less able to exercise their power responsibly.

I have been speaking of the selection of articles for publication, and it is here that in the changed climate of legal scholarship law review editors fall down on the job worst. But they don't do all that much better when it comes to making suggestions for substantive improvement in the nondoctrinal pieces that occupy an ever-larger fraction of the space in law reviews. This is an important role of scholarly journals in other fields. Indeed, referees and editors in fields such as economics are far more interested in making suggestions for the substantive improvement of the articles that they review and publish than in trying to improve the author's prose. Law reviews do not use referees to vet articles, so they don't have referees' reports to show the author. And the editors themselves are rarely competent to offer substantive improvements, or catch analytic errors, or notice oversights in research, in nondoctrinal articles.

Law review editors are notoriously erratic in attempting to improve an author's style. (This is not a problem limited to nondoctrinal articles.) Academic presses use professional manuscript editors to edit books, but

125. This will raise hackles; there is a movement to "blind" submissions, in which the author's name is deleted from the manuscript. Extensive scholarly evaluation of the practice has revealed, however, no net advantages. See, for example, Rebecca M. Blank, "The Effects of Double-Blind versus Single-Blind Reviewing: Experimental Evidence from *The American Economic Review*," 81 *American Economic Review* 1041 (1991).

126. See Bennett A. Rafoth and Donald L. Rubin, "The Impact of Content and Mechanics on Judgments of Writing Quality," 1 *Written Communication* 446, 447 (1984). The law reviews fetishize length. They often refuse to label papers that would be articles of normal and even unusual length in any other field as "articles," instead terming them "essays," "comments," or "observations."

law reviews use amateur manuscript editors—the members of the review's staff—to edit law review articles, book reviews, and notes. These inexperienced editors, preoccupied with citation forms and other rule-bound approaches to editing, abet the worst tendencies of legal and academic writing.[127] A partially redeeming factor is that the student editors do check the accuracy of the author's references. This is a useful service rarely offered by faculty-edited journals and never by publishers of books.

Both the good and the bad of student editing—overly intrusive line editing, helpful cite checking—are consequences in part of the sheer size of the reviews' staffs. Because membership in a law review is a valuable educational experience for law students, the tendency has been for the staffs to expand as well as for the number of reviews to mushroom. The expansion in staff activates Parkinson's Law. The editors busy themselves with busywork, including intrusive editing that imposes significant time costs on the authors and sometimes reduces the quality of the final product.

Let me turn to the student-written sections of the reviews. Law review editors, like other law students, are apprentice lawyers, and it is natural for them to imitate their masters—who because of proximity are mainly professors. If the masters do nondoctrinal work, the apprentices will be tempted to try their hand at it. If the masters fulminate against the latest horror of the Rehnquist Court, it is natural for the apprentices to do likewise. If more courses are offered in constitutional law than in any other field, even though only a tiny fraction of the graduates of the law school will ever practice constitutional law, then law review editors will have their heads filled with constitutional law and will want to write their law review notes on constitutional topics[128]—which is almost the equivalent of saying that they want to write their notes on cases decided by the Supreme Court, for the Supreme Court wholly dominates the articulation and application of constitutional law. But constitutional law is only one field of law, and the Supreme Court decides only a tiny fraction of the interesting cases decided every year by American courts. Law review editors' preoccupation with constitutional law and with the Supreme Court has produced an unfortunate warp in the coverage of American law by the student-written sections of the law reviews. This is particularly unfortu-

127. See my article "Goodbye to the Bluebook," 53 *University of Chicago Law Review* 1343 (1986); also the parade of horrors in Lindgren, note 121 above.

128. In recent years, 22 percent of all articles and notes in law reviews have been on constitutional topics. Lindgren, note 121 above, at 533.

nate because of all American judges, Justices of the Supreme Court are the least likely to take their cues from student-written notes. I suspect that student-written notes on constitutional topics have, with the rarest of exceptions, no readership at all. So here is an area where the absence of a market has a painful bite, reducing much law review publication to the level of a vanity press.

What can be done? Not much, because the problems reside in the unchangeable structure of the institution—the inherent inexperience and immaturity of student editors, the absence of the spur of competition, and the absence of continuity, which reduces the incentive to make changes since the fruits are unlikely to ripen in time to be harvested by the editors who planted them. It is easy to suggest reforms, but difficult to find grounds for thinking that any but the most trivial have any chance of being adopted. Fortunately, law reviews have no long-run market power. If other media for the publication of law-related scholarship are superior, the market will supply them. It *is* supplying them. There are more and more faculty-edited journals, there is more and more samizdat publication on the World Wide Web, and more and more legal scholars are publishing books with academic and sometimes trade presses. But the impact of student-edited law reviews on the tenure process is a serious problem, and I am moved by it to offer a few suggestions for improving these reviews.

First, they should concentrate on publishing doctrinal scholarship in both the faculty-written and the student-written sections of the review, leaving to the growing number of faculty-edited journals the principal responsibility for screening, nurturing, improving, and editing nondoctrinal scholarship. Not only do law review editors generally lack the competence to select and improve this scholarship, but the need for heavy editing of it (that specialty of law reviews, enabled by their huge staffs) is reduced by the fact that nondoctrinal papers are usually given at faculty workshops before being submitted for publication. So the authors have already received many of the sorts of criticism that they might expect from a dose of law review editing.

Although doctrinal scholarship has declined relative to nondoctrinal, it remains the largest field of legal scholarship and one of great importance to practitioners and judges—as well as to most law professors, if fewer (relatively) than used to be the case. There would be nothing dishonorable or archaic in the law reviews' rededicating themselves to the production and publication of such scholarship. The educational mission of the law review would be enhanced rather than impaired if members of reviews wrote and edited within the sphere of their competence and the orbit of the professional writing that they will do when they graduate from law school and become (as the vast majority, even at the most exclusive law schools, will) practicing lawyers.

This is not to say that law reviews should refuse to publish any nondoctrinal articles, or refuse to permit students who come to law school from a rich background in another field, as many do nowadays, to write nondoctrinal student pieces. I suggest merely that the law reviews adopt a presumption in favor of the publication of doctrinal scholarship in both the faculty-written and the student-written sections of the reviews.

Second, law reviews should consider having every plausible submission of a nondoctrinal piece refereed anonymously by one or preferably two scholars who specialize in the field to which the submission purports to contribute. They will lose some good submissions by this procedure simply because it will slow down the publication process. One of the competitive advantages that law reviews enjoy over other scholarly journals is that their vast staffs and the huge excess capacity of the law review industry (hundreds of law reviews chasing a small number of worthwhile articles) enable the time between the submission of an article and its publication to be minimized. But since law reviews shouldn't be publishing so much nondoctrinal stuff anyway, the loss of some ground to other types of scholarly journal would not be cause for regret.

Refereed journals do not permit authors to submit their articles simultaneously to other journals, because it would produce a very high ratio of referee reports to articles actually published.[129] Having to submit an article seriatim rather than simultaneously will lengthen the time to publication and further deter authors of nondoctrinal scholarship from submitting their articles to the student-edited law reviews. But that would be no loss. Moreover, concern with publication lags is becoming obsolete as more and more scholarly papers are being posted on the Web before they are even submitted to journals and as more and more journals have electronic editions that appear on the Web long before hard-copy publication. I acknowledge, however, that having different tracks for processing doc-

---

129. Suppose that the average author submits an article to ten journals, each of which commissions reports from two referees. The ratio of referee reports to articles published will be twenty to one (assuming at least one of the journals accepts the article for publication), compared to six to one under a system in which multiple submissions are forbidden, assuming that the average article would be accepted by the third journal to which it was submitted. (Many authors, if their article were turned down by three consecutive journals, would give up.)

trinal and nondoctrinal submissions would give rise to line-drawing problems. The line between doctrinal and nondoctrinal scholarship is often unclear, as more and more doctrinal scholars feel obliged to give some consideration to economic, philosophical, or feminist perspectives.

Third, the reviews should renounce, in their student-written sections, commentary on Supreme Court decisions, and perhaps topics in constitutional law generally. Law reviews should reconceive their central task as being to monitor the performance of other courts dealing with the vast range of technical legal questions to which the Court, preoccupied as it is with the Constitution, pays little attention. My experience as an appellate judge has been that there is a paucity of decent scholarship across the entire range of nonconstitutional issues with which modern courts grapple.

The law reviews should not worry that judges do not "read" them. Scholarly journals are not meant to be read the way the daily newspaper is read. No one has time to read 500, or for that matter 25, law reviews, each published four to eight times a year. The vast majority of articles in scholarly journals are destined to go directly from the subscriber to the library shelf, there to be available for future reference as the need arises. Law students find this difficult to understand, because they find the scholarly enterprise in general difficult to understand. Law review editors are constantly casting about for ways of making their review more "timely" in the sense of being more likely to be read cover to cover upon publication. (I thought that way when I was president of the *Harvard Law Review*.) It is a vain hope, as well as a misguided one. Law reviews are indispensable resources for judges and their clerks, whether or not the judge's opinion actually cites the article or student note that proved helpful in the preparation of the opinion. Law reviews are indispensable resources for practitioners and law professors as well, and again this is true whether or not they are read when they first appear.

When the environment to which a species has become adapted changes, the species must change, or eventually die out. The student-edited law review arose in and became adapted to one environment, that of law conceived as an autonomous discipline centered on the attainment of logical consistency of legal doctrine—what Weber called "formal rationality." The environment has changed. Preoccupation with the formal rationality of legal doctrine has given way, in the upper reaches of the legal academy at any rate, to preoccupation with the relation between those doctrines and the larger society that law is supposed to serve. The change has not been large enough to threaten the survival of the student-edited law review. But it has been large enough to threaten its centrality in the publication of legal scholarship and to require a reconsideration of its role and function.

The American Law Institute

If the first year of law school and the student-edited law review are two of the traditional institutional cornerstones of American law, the American Law Institute is a third. Yet just as the Socratic method was once a revolutionary innovation in legal education, so Natalie Hull's research has revealed that the creation of the Institute in the 1920s was motivated by a genuine zeal for what she calls pragmatic progressive reform—it was not, as many have thought, a rearguard action by traditionalists distressed by the rise of statutes and the first stirrings of the realist movement.[130] But is the Institute today, almost three-quarters of a century after its founding, still such an instrument?

The American Law Institute brings together lawyers, judges, and law professors to formulate, deliberate upon, and adopt proposals for law reform. The Institute's traditional and still preponderant output consists of "restatements" of the law (mainly of bodies of common law such as tort, contract, and property law) that are designed to serve as unofficial quasi-codes for unifying, clarifying, and incrementally improving the law. This model of legal reform—the joint, exhaustive deliberation of lawyers, judges, and law professors meeting as it were on neutral ground—is not unique to the American Law Institute. The advisory committees for the federal rules of civil and criminal procedure, evidence, and appeals have basically the same structure. So do many bar-association committees, as well as ad hoc groups that push for this or that legal reform. But the Institute differs in several important particulars from these other groups. One difference is its scope and permanence, which create a visibility that the other groups lack. Another difference is the meritocratic criteria for elected membership in the Institute—and most members are elected rather than ex officio—and, as a consequence of this selectivity, the elite composition of the membership and the prestige of the Institute. A third important difference is the legislative structure of its deliberations, made bicameral by the requirement of concurrent majorities in the Council (the

130. N. E. H. Hull, "Restatement and Reform: A New Perspective on the Origins of the American Law Institute," 8 *Law and History Review* 55 (1990). On the Institute generally, see *Symposium on the American Law Institute: Process, Partisanship, and the Restatements of Law,* 26 *Hofstra Law Review* 567 (1998).

governing body of the Institute) and at the annual meeting of the membership, where proposals and drafts are discussed and voted on. These distinctive features have contributed to the volume and steadiness of the Institute's output and to the warm reception that courts (which have cited the Institute's restatements and other publications more than 125,000 times), and to a lesser extent state legislatures, have given to its output.

The influence of academics preponderates in the shaping of the Institute's work because they alone have the time to produce the kind of output in which the Institute specializes. But the preponderance of practitioners in the membership, along with a generous sprinkling of state and federal judges, prevents the academic members from losing touch with the practical needs of the profession. On controversial as distinct from technical issues, the influence of practitioners and judges, expressed in voting in both the Council and at the annual meetings, is apt to dominate.

In the 1920s, the structure that I have described was well adapted to the cause of pragmatic law reform. It is less well adapted today. The obvious reasons are first the diminished significance of the common law in the overall landscape of American law, and second the maturing of that law—in part, to be sure, as a result of the restatements themselves—which has reduced the need for doctrinal tidying up. The nonobvious reasons are also two. One concerns the composition of the Institute, which is limited to practicing lawyers, judges, and law professors—that is, to lawyers and only lawyers. The most exciting legal research of the past thirty years has been interdisciplinary. Some of this research, as we know from the previous chapters, is remote from the practical concerns of the profession, but much is not. A great deal of the work that does have practical relevance is done by people with law degrees, of course, but not all—think of the work of Ronald Coase, Gary Becker, William Landes, and Steven Shavell, to name only a handful of the distinguished economists who have worked on legal problems and who ought to be well known to everyone seriously interested in law reform. Even the interdisciplinary *lawyers* are barely represented either on the Council of the Institute, or in the ranks of the reporters and advisors of the Institute's various projects, or in the references in the reporters' notes. The current family-dissolution draft is centrally about the economics of human capital, on which there is a huge literature not cited in the reporters' notes though in fact well known to the reporter (Ira Ellman).[131] The corporate-governance project suffered not

---

131. See American Law Institute, *Principles of the Law of Family Dissolution: Analysis and Recommendations* (Proposed Final Draft, pt. 1, Feb. 14, 1997); Ira Mark Ellman, "The Theory of Alimony," 77 *California Law Review* 1 (1989).

only because of the opposition of business groups but also because the authors did not give due weight to the challenge posed to conventional legal thinking about corporate governance by modern finance theory, as expounded for example by Frank Easterbrook and Daniel Fischel.[132] Indeed, these theorists felt largely excluded from the project. The truncation of the Institute's Enterprise Liability Project, which had engaged contemporary economic thinking on products liability, bespeaks a lack of receptivity on the part of the Institute to modern interdisciplinary scholarship.[133]

The key groups in the work of the Institute—the Council, and the reporters and advisors—lack intellectual diversity, and in the case of the Council generational diversity as well. And in sharp contrast to the experience in the first half century of the Institute, few of the reporters for its projects are drawn any more from the leading law schools. I would not make too much of this, as it is partly a commentary on the hiring policies of those schools; on the growing democratization of the law school world, as a result of which the quality differences between the different tiers of law schools have narrowed; and on the increased goldfish-bowl character of the entire legal process, including the ALI's processes, which have made a reporter's and an advisor's job more time-consuming than in times past. Nevertheless the diminished representation of the most prestigious law schools in the Institute's work has contributed to the sense that the Institute has lost its former centrality in the process of legal modernization.

My second nonobvious point is that the Institute does not seem productively (or in most instances, at all) engaged with many of the *central* issues of law reform. These are institutional rather than doctrinal issues and hence remote from the traditional emphasis of the Institute. They have to do with the structure of the legal profession and the number and behavior of lawyers, the large increase in litigation since about 1960, the explosion of the jail and prison populations, the extraordinary cost and complexity of American law, the burgeoning of legal (especially constitutional) rights, the proliferation of massive class actions and institutional reform litigation, the social as distinct from private costs and benefits of our immense legal profession, the bureaucratization of the judiciary, the large number of frivolous suits, the shifting interface between state and

132. See Frank H. Easterbrook and Daniel R. Fischel, *The Economic Structure of Corporate Law* (1991).

133. This is not to deny the good sense of the new *Third Restatement of Torts: Products Liability* (proposed final draft April 1, 1997, approved May 20, 1997), discussed in James A. Henderson, Jr., and Aaron D. Twerski, "Achieving Consensus on Defective Product Design," 83 *Cornell Law Review* 867 (1998).

federal law, the rampant satellite litigation over attorney's fees and sanctions, the rising doubts about the reliability of juries, the hypertrophy of death-penalty litigation, the critique of administrative regulation, and an alleged pro-plaintiff bias in fields of law ranging from products liability and medical malpractice to securities fraud and insurance litigation. The shift traced earlier in this chapter in the focus of administrative law scholarship from the doctrinal to the institutional responds to a concern that pervades American law.

Occasionally the Institute engages institutional issues, as in its work on complex litigation. But for the most part it has been content to remain in the groove first planed in the 1920s—preparing restatements, now most often subsequent editions of the original restatements, of common law fields. This is valuable work. But with the principal exception of tort law, the doctrines of the common law are on the periphery of contemporary worries about the law—and that seems a strange place in which to concentrate the resources of an organization of the leaders of the profession.

The problem of creeping marginalization is to a considerable extent systemic. The Institute's legislative structure is a source of distinctiveness and strength—it's what makes the restatements more authoritative than treatises. But it causes the Institute to play a diminishing role in the American legal system. The output of a legislative body cannot be expanded by increasing the number of legislators; that would merely increase the transaction costs of securing agreement. This constraint has prevented the ALI from keeping up with the growth of the American legal system in the sense of covering the same percentage of fields of law today as it did in the 1920s through the 1950s.

Additional factors are at work. I mentioned the Institute's heavy dependence on law professors. As the interests of law professors shift away from conventional doctrinal scholarship, the Institute, in part because of its lack of receptivity to interdisciplinary scholarship, finds it increasingly difficult to staff its projects with the most prominent and (not necessarily in a bad sense) most audacious legal thinkers of the day. A related factor is the increasing politicization of American law. Who would have dreamt that special interests would place the Institute under siege, as if it were a real legislature, when it was mulling over reforms in products liability or corporate governance, or that issues as technical-seeming as the payments article of a proposed revision of the Uniform Commercial Code would become embroiled in political controversy? The increasing politicization of American law reflects the increasing heterogeneity of the society in general and of the legal profession in particular, which makes it more and more difficult to achieve consensus on premises for social and legal action—and it is consensus on premises that moves lawmaking from the political to the technical realm. Whatever its causes, the politicization of important areas of American law has made it difficult for the Institute to engage with the most important questions without crossing the line that separates technical law reform from politics. The Institute is to be commended for the provision of the Model Penal Code abolishing criminal punishment of adult consensual homosexual relations. That was in the 1950s. Imagine the uproar were the Institute to take a position on equally controversial issues, ranging from date rape to pornography to lesbian adoption, that pervade the law of sexual regulation today.

Then too there is this growing, gnawing sense, to which certain debacles of legal reform, including the Institute's own *Second Restatement of Conflicts,* have contributed (the corporate-governance project could also be cited here), that lawyers do not have enough of the right answers to issues of legal policy and administration. For example, the problems with products liability law have little to do with details of doctrine but everything to do with the system of enforcement, and in particular the heavy reliance on juries, the expanded use of the class action, and the multistate character of products liability litigation.

I have several suggestions for improvement. The first two are organizational. The first is that the Institute should start electing some nonlawyers as members. Some of the greatest experts on matters under consideration by the Institute at this time, such as trust investment, products liability, the apportionment of tort liability, and family dissolution, happen not to be lawyers, law professors, or judges; they happen to be economists, finance theorists, psychologists, and sociologists. Some of these people actually teach at law schools, some on a full-time basis. Some would be interested in the work of the Institute. They could give that work an empirical dimension that it now lacks and that, if the analysis in this book has any merit, legal research sorely needs more of.

Second, the Institute should consider putting a term limit on membership in the Council. A self-perpetuating board whose members have life tenure is not a structure auspicious for renewal. More rapid turnover of Council members would create room for interdisciplinary scholars and practitioners, who tend to be young. It is not merely prejudice ("ageism") that associates creativity and innovation with the young.[134]

My remaining suggestions concern the allocation of the Institute's re-

---

134. See Posner, note 10 above, ch. 7 ("Age, Creativity, and Output").

search effort. The Institute must acknowledge and embrace the shift in the focus of concern about the performance of the American legal system from doctrine, especially common law doctrine, to administration—including procedure, remedies, bench and bar, and indeed the whole machinery of enforcement of civil and criminal law. What, in the broadest possible sense, are the costs of our legal system and how might they be reduced? Here is a project to challenge the imagination and resources of the American Law Institute. The RAND project on civil justice, the committees of the Judicial Conference of the United States, the American Bar Foundation, and individual scholars have done and are doing much valuable work in these areas, but much more remains to be done. Why shouldn't the ALI play a leading role?

I would also like to see more sensitivity to institutional factors in the Institute's traditional work. Consider the very interesting Tentative Draft Number One on bequests and other donative transfers. With regard to the issues of latent ambiguity and reformation, which are issues involving discrepancies real or alleged between the donative instrument and the donor's intentions, the draftsmen opt for allowing more discretion to judges to depart from the literal interpretation and application of the instrument. Sounds sensible. But any judgment about how much or how little discretion to allow to judges or other fact finders must, if it is to be reliable, draw on an informed and accurate understanding of the honesty and competence of the fact finders. About that the draft is silent. Yet the administration of probate is not an area in which the judiciary has covered itself with glory. It is no answer that one cannot change the whole world at once. If there is little realistic prospect for reform of probate administration, this is a brute fact that must shape intelligent proposals for doctrinal change.

The Institute could magnify its impact by undertaking, in the spirit of a suggestion made by Cardozo many years ago, the task of proposing the correction of the many purely technical, apolitical conflicts that bedevil our law. I am struck as a judge by how often legal disputes arise from errors—not policy choices—in the drafting of statutes or regulations, or in the formulation of judicial doctrine, and how much needless variance there is across states and across federal circuits in points of common law doctrine or statutory interpretation. The simplification of law was one of the Institute's original goals, and it is one that would be well served by the Institute's undertaking to monitor the thousands of appellate decisions, state and federal, handed down every year for conflicts on technical points of law and to propose solutions that I predict would be welcomed by courts and legislatures. The Institute would have to operate through committees in exercising this function—this would be analogous to legislatures' augmenting their output by delegation to administrative agencies.

We do not need a restatement of waiver of arguments on appeal, or a restatement of the defense of laches in suits against the government, or a restatement of promissory fraud, or of self-defamation, or of the standard of appellate review of mixed questions of fact and law, or of judicial estoppel, or of the scope of tort liability of providers of public-utility type services, or of the dozens of other specific doctrinal issues on which the cases are all over the lot. A mechanism is needed for addressing these conflicts, many of which are inadvertent; the ALI could be that mechanism. The growing complexity and politicization of American law and the multiplication of analytical perspectives as a result of the growth of interdisciplinary scholarship have, by promoting confusion and deadlock in efforts at law reform, enhanced the importance of the ALI's mission. The legal system is beset by issues that may not have a technically right answer, yet probably have better answers than the law currently provides—issues such as the numbingly complex rules of habeas corpus and inconsistent standards in discrimination cases and lack of guidance in the award of punitive damages. The Institute's unusual balance of practical lawyerly judgment, legislative-type consensus-generating machinery, and scholarly expertise equips it to provide leadership in these and many other areas.

I end far from where I began. The concerns of and about the American Law Institute are remote from those that foam the waters of moral philosophy and constitutional theory. Pragmatic legal reform occupies the other end of the juridical spectrum from moral and constitutional theory. It is the quiet, to some the dull, and to those in legal academia the unfashionable, end. But it is the end at which the investment of intellectual effort promises the greatest yield in the conditions prevailing in law today.

We have too much theory in law—of the wrong kind; for of course I disagree with William Blake that "to generalize is to be an idiot. To particularize is the alone distinction of merit."[135] Law needs theory—social scientific theory. Even morality needs theory, in the sense that history,

135. William Blake, "Annotations to Sir Joshua Reynold's Discourses," in *The Complete Writings of William Blake* 445, 451 (Geoffrey Keynes ed. 1958). Notice that Blake's pronouncement is itself a generalization.

psychology, biology, economics, anthropology, sociology, and game theory can help us to a better understanding of the origins, scope, determinants, and efficacy of moral norms, which play an important role in the system of social control in our society as in all societies. What no one needs is normative moral philosophy, or the kind of legal theory that is built on or runs parallel to normative moral theory, or postmodern antitheory. We can avoid these dead ends and keep on the path that leads to a true and healthy professionalization of law if we steer by the light of pragmatism.

Index

Abbott, Andrew, 186n, 213n

Abbott Laboratories v. Gardner, 237n, 238

Abel, Richard, 213

Abortion, 23, 25, 28–29, 50, 64, 68, 79n, 28; Gutmann and Thompson's discussion, 57–58; Judith Thomson's discussion, 54–55, 57, 126, 134n, 166n; medical techniques of, 54–55; pro-life versus pro-choice positions, 61; Supreme Court's handling of, 134–136, 250–251, 254–255

Academic law. *See* Legal scholarship

Academic moralism: defined, 5; ineffectuality of, 12–13, 38–42, 68–85, 141, 143–144; versus moral entrepreneurship, 8; versus non-academic moralism, 15; persistence of, 85–90; psychological basis of, 90

Academic research, 290. *See also* Legal scholarship; Theory

Ackerman, Bruce, 144, 152

Adjudication. *See* Judges

Administrative law, 228–239

Administrative Procedure Act, 230

Affirmative action, 118, 139–140, 253, 292–293

Airedale NSH Trust v. Bland, 134n

Alschuler, Albert, 145n, 207n

Altruism, 30–36, 65–66; biology of, 33–34, 37; definition of, 31; dutiful versus natural, 36, 39n; egotism of, 40n; of law students, 72; pretense of, by members of professions, 189; reciprocal, 37; role of, in rescue, 71–72, 126

Amar, Akhil, 161n

American Law Institute, 303–309; politics in, 306–307; possible reforms of, 307–309; problems of, 304–309; structure of, 303–304

Analogy, reasoning by, 53–55, 168. *See also* Casuistry

Anderson, Elizabeth, 5, 86

Anderson, Kenneth, 191n, 202n

Animal rights, 25, 43n, 71, 84. *See also* Zoophilia

Antitrust law, 228–229

Aquinas, Thomas, 77

Arbitrage, moral, 44

Aristotle, 49, 82, 98, 165, 261

Arson, 127

Atheism, 78

Aurelius, Marcus, 84

Baby selling, 87

Bad faith (Sartre), 26n, 269, 272

Baier, Annette, 5, 80n

Baker v. Carr, 154

Balkin, Jack, 154

Bambrough, Renford, 20n, 50n

Barber, Benjamin, 50n

Barnett, Randy, 130n

Bator, Paul, 240n

Becker, Gary, 304

Bentham, Jeremy, 42, 79, 84n, 111. *See also* Utilitarianism

Benthamism, 33

Berger, Peter, 78n, 187n, 214n, 276n

Bestiality, 23

Bickel, Alexander, 151, 154–155, 251

Bill of Rights, 151, 161, 197–198